WORLD

CUP

SOCCER

1994

Group A Colombia, Romania, Switzerland, United States.

Group B Brazil, Cameroon, Russia, Sweden.

Group C Bolivia, Germany, South Korea, Spain.

Group D Argentina, Bulgaria, Greece, Nigeria.

Group E Italy, Ireland, Norway, Mexico.

Group F Belgium, Morocco, Netherlands, Saudi Arabia.

D1294794

WORLD CUP SOCCER

Michael Lewis   Preface by Pele

MOYER BELL   WAKEFIELD, RHODE ISLAND & LONDON

For mom and dad,
who always have been there.

Published by Moyer Bell
Copyright © 1994 by Michael Lewis

First Edition

LIBRARY OF CONGRESS
CATALOGING-IN-PUBLICATION DATA

Lewis, Michael, 1952-
World cup soccer / Michael Lewis.
1st. ed.

p.   cm.
Includes bibliographical references (p. 455) and ap-
pendices (p. 391)
1. World Cup (Soccer) I. Title.

GV943.49.L48   1994
796.334'668-dc20   93-45857
ISBN 1-55921-107-5 CIP

Printed in the United States of America
Distributed in North America by Publishers Group West, P.O. Box
8843, Emeryville CA 94662; (800) 788-3123 (in California 510-
658-3453); and in Europe by Gazelle Book Services Ltd., Falcon
House, Queen Square, Lancaster LA1 1RN, England (524-68765).

Front cover: Clockwise from top left: Diego Maradona (Argentina), Jurgen Klinsmann (Germany), Dino Zoff (Italy),
Pele (Brazil) and Johann Cruyff (Netherlands)

Contents

Foreword

Imust admit. I have been most fortunate. I participated in 4 World Cups and played on 3 championship teams, I also have had the opportunity to witness the world's greatest sporting spectacle in person since my retirement from competitive soccer. So, I feel I have a unique perspective.

The World Cup is the world's grandest sporting event. Every four years, the 24 best teams in the world come to together to celebrate this beautiful game with a spectacular tournament and cultural celebration that cannot be duplicated anywhere.

There had been many, many skeptics who claim the 1994 World Cup would be an absolute failure, We know that is untrue because of the amazing response from the American public to buy tickets a year before the event, even though they did not know who was participating. There is little doubt in my mind that it will be one of the most successful, if not the most successful World Cup, in its long and glorious history.

While there have been a number of books written about the World Cup in other countries, what makes this on special is that it has been authored by a native-born American.

Michael Lewis was born in the United States, grew up in the United States and learned about this beautiful game in the United States. He has been writing about the sport for 20 years.

In a way, Michael's passion for the game is a product of my presence with the New York Cosmos in the North American Soccer League. As it turns out, he was an eye-witness to my first NASL goal in 1975 and to my last competitive game at Soccer Bowl '77 in Portland. Ironically, I have gotten to know Michael better since I retired in 1977, as he has covered some of the events and tournaments with which I have been associated. Moreover, he has been there through thick and thin, especially during the so-called lean years of the 1980s.

What Michael Lewis has authored-a book about the world's greatest game-tells us something about the author and the American public: that the passion of soccer has been growing and has nurtured in the United States.

I hope you find the book as enjoyable and informative as I have, and hope you enjoy USA '94.

Yours in soccer.

Acknowledgements

Now I know how award recipients feel during their acceptance speech. They say they do not want to forget anyone who made their award possible and then ramble off a seemingly endless list of names. The same goes for me, except I don't have any excuses if I forget someone because I have some time to think and write.

The public relations staff at World Cup USA 1994—including senior vice president and press officer Jim Trecker, John Griffin, Jeff Idelson, Eve Hoffman and Gail McEllicott, among others—came through big time for me more often than I can remember, particularly when I needed inside information about the 24 finalists during crunch time (of course, when wasn't it crunch time?).

Deborah Bernstein, a friend for many years, believed in this project and found an agent for me when things looked the bleakest.

The folks at Fifi Oscard Agency, including Nancy Murray, Kevin McShane and Fifi Oscard, took a risk but believed such a project was saleable.

Jennifer Moyer, Britt Bell and the rest of the hard-working staff at Moyer Bell Publishing, who also took a risk and believed this project was marketable. They also had the combined patience and persistence to help me get through this manuscript in a relatively short period of time.

The staff and management of Soccer Week had to put up with my three-month leave-of-absence and gave me permission to reprint several of my works in this publication. At the same time, I had become the editor of *Soccer* magazine, and management and co-workers there also were patient with me juggling so many projects.

A special thank you to Prof. Julio Mazzei, Pele, Lois Emanuelli at the National Soccer Hall of Fame, and Tom Lange, Dean Linke and Paula Martin of U.S. Soccer.

And, I would like to acknowledge and thank a certain Cocker Spaniel named Shannon, who did not always want to sit on my lap every time I went to my word processor, giving me the time to complete the manuscript.

Michael Lewis
Jan. 2, 1994

Introduction

The temperatures hovered in the high seventies and the sun was out, although there appeared to be storm clouds looming far away in Santo Domingo on March 21, 1992.

I stood on the sidelines of Estadio Olympico for the very first match of the 1994 World Cup qualifying competition. I had a camera slung over my left shoulder, a portfolio with World Cup background and files over my right and notepad and pen in hand to chronicle the happenings between the host Dominican Republic and Puerto Rico.

The field was parched, hard and uneven and the inoperable scoreboard looked like it had caught fire at least once. It might have been rather primitive conditions to some sportswriters accustomed to sitting in a state-of-the-art, spartan press box far from the field, but was in my element and in my glory at the same time.

There is nothing like the World Cup. Fans serenading their team, their heroes. Fans waving gigantic flags. Those incredible goal celebrations. That international aura. When did I fall in love with the World Cup? It most likely happened during June and July of 1982, when the World Cup was played in Spain. Where I lived in Brockport in northwestern New York, we were just getting cable television. So, in order to watch the games, I pointed my rotary antenna in from my house toward Toronto to pick up live coverage of the match of the day, usually at noon (5 p.m., Spanish time).

During the final week of the competition, I spent a week's vacation in Toronto to watch more of the competition on TV. After underdog Italy dispatched Poland in the semifinals, I wound up in one of the craziest and joyous traffic jams of all-time—horns were honked for celebration, not for frustration because you were not moving. By the end of the day, I had counted more than 300 cars driving around the downtown area proudly waving the green, white and red of Italy. And this was just after the semifinals. Italy had not won anything yet.

By the time Italy took its victory lap around Bernabeu Stadium in Madrid on July 11, there was no doubt that I was hooked.

At the time, I promised myself I would cover the 1986 World Cup in Colombia. It eventually was switched to Mexico, but I was there, as I was in Italy for the 1990 extravaganza.

Has it been worth it?

Even with sleeping on the floor of a friend's hotel room and standing on a train from Bologna to Florence for more than two hours, I have not been disappointed with the passion, excitement and atmosphere of the event.

There really is no way to truly appreciate the World Cup unless you experience it live. Saying that, the next several hundred or so pages hopefully will whet your appetite and give you an idea of what will occur in the United States from June 17-July 17 and what the World Cup has been and is all about.

WORLD

CUP

SOCCER

Chapter One

The Mystique

Imagine, if you will, the World Series, Super Bowl and the Olympics all rolled into one, and you begin to understand the magnitude of what will occur in the United States this summer. The World Cup—USA '94—is expected to leave scores of countries at a standstill for a month and international soccer fans in a trance watching television, awaiting the latest news from the States.

Beginning June 17, and for 30 days thereafter, 24 teams representing their countries, including the United States, will play a total of 52 games in 9 cities in what is undoubtedly the world's greatest sporting spectacle. These games are expected to be watched in person or on television by nearly 2 billion people—including several million in the United States—and reach a climax when the 2 best soccer teams in the world face off in Pasadena, California on July 17, 1994. The object of desire? The 14-karat gold FIFA World Cup trophy.

Numbers tell only part of the story. The World Cup is about passion, nationalism, beauty, history and controversy. It is about a month-long celebration of soccer that occurs only once every 4 years.

The World Cup has transformed kings into coaches and players into stars and even legends. King Carol of Romania handpicked his squad for the very first World Cup in 1930 and made sure the players did not lose their jobs back home because of the 3 month roundtrip and stay in Uruguay. In 1958, a 17-year-old Brazilian named Edson Arantes do Nascimento, otherwise known as Pele to the rest of the planet, made his international debut, leading his country to the first of 3 unprecedented world championships in 4 tries. In 1982, Paolo Rossi went from pariah to hero in a matter of weeks, wiping away the stigma of a betting scandal by scoring 6 goals to lead Italy to the championship. And in 1986, Argentina's Diego Maradona's Hand of God—he knocked the ball into the net with his hand—and feet of a god—an incredible 60-yard jaunt through the English midfield and defense en route to a goal—forever etched his name into soccer history.

In 1950, the United States staged one of the greatest upsets in sporting annals by stunning heavily favored England, 1–0, as the fans of Belo Horizonte, Brazil, took these unknown warriors onto their shoulders in a post-match victory celebration. In 1966, the Jules Rimet Trophy, the original World Cup trophy, was stolen while it was on exhibit at a stamp show in England. During a massive police and public hunt for the trophy, a dog by the name of Pickles unearthed the trophy

The Hottest Tickets in Town

Incredible as it may sound, tickets for the first and second rounds for U.S. fans—almost one million—were sold out a year in advance in the United States.

"I wish we had more tickets available for everybody that wanted them," said Alan I. Rothenberg, chairman and CEO of World Cup USA 1994. "We have almost a million more tickets available than any prior World Cup. We have the biggest stadiums in the world and we still don't have enough."

With 3.6 million tickets available, the 1994 World Cup is expected to break the event's attendance record of 2,510,686 set at Italia '90.

Where did the tickets go? To the U.S. soccer community, soccer fans, sponsors and marketing partners of the World Cup, the 24 competing teams, the nine venues and FIFA.

Of the nearly 1.8 million available in the U.S., 650,000 were sold to the U.S. soccer community (registered players, coaches, referees and administrators), another 300,000 to soccer fans, 422,000 to commercial affiliates (sponsors and marketing partners) and 414,000 to the nine host communities. A total of 1.3 million tickets were to be distributed internationally.

The process to sell tickets in the U.S., however, left a bad taste in the mouths of many fans and members of the soccer community.

While the prices were higher than any other soccer event in the U.S., that wasn't the main concern The prices for example, ranged from $28 (end zone seats), $45 (corner seats) and $65 (sidelines) for first-round matches and $180, $300, $475 for the championship match at the Rose Bowl on July 17. It was the lack of communication to the media, soccer community and fans that angered and confused potential ticket buyers.

In early February, 1993, more than 1.5 million brochures were sent to the soccer community. Several weeks before the mailing, a reporter asked Rothenberg: What if, by chance, there was a complete sellout of the early-round matches and that some soccer fans would be left out in the cold?

under some shrubs in London. Pickles and his owner collected a $10,000 reward. And as recently as 1990, 38-year-old Roger Milla was coaxed out of retirement, and, as a super-sub, helped a carefree Cameroon side to global fame, thanks to an opening-match upset of the defending champion Argentines and to an amazing, unforgettable, heart-breaking 3-2 loss to England in the quarterfinals.

    The World Cup has all the festivity of Carnival, a joyous event that allows people and fans to put aside everyday cares. In 1978, for instance, Argentines forgot about 300 percent inflation and severe

---

(Hottest Tickets cont.)

"Oversubscribe to a private mailing? I wouldn't even consider thinking about it," said Rothenberg, who added he did not want to jinx the process.

Those words would come back to haunt Rothenberg.

On Feb. 3, those brochures were mailed. Some people received them immediately, some never did.

The ground rules for stadium series packages: Fans had to buy tickets for all first- and second-round matches at a particular venue. They could buy as many as 10 tickets per strip and they had to be purchased on a credit card. For example, a family of four paid $560 for five matches for the most inexpensive tickets before paying for parking, concessions and souvenirs.

Scott LeTellier, World Cup chief operating officer, said there was no advantage in getting orders in early.

"There is no time advantage to the private sale," he said. Anything "received March 30 would have as much possibility of buying tickets as through the early mail," LeTellier added.

Ticket sales, however, proved to be more popular than expected. At the Rose Bowl, for example, a total of 15,046 stadiums series packages were set aside for the soccer community. After the committee freed up more tickets, a total of 22,473 were sold. It was the same story at Giants Stadium, where a total of 22,100 packages were sold, more than double the original amount of 9,256.

So, the organizing committee decided to change the rules to a first-come, first-served basis, but did not bother to tell the media. So, many members of the soccer community took their time, thinking they had until the end of March.

"Unfortunately, we had to change our policy," Rothenberg later said. "We were overwhelmed. We had to do something."

Anyone who missed out on the first sale had an opportunity to purchase tickets on the weekend of June 12-13, 1993 through an 800 number.

Originally, 450,000 tickets were set aside for the second phase, but the allocation was cut

political problems to celebrate their first title. Fans moved en masse out into the streets of Buenos Aires and other major cities for an all-night party. And certainly no World Cup would be complete without Brazil, the only country that has qualified for all 15 editions, and its enthusiastic supporters. Those fans, who can easily be detected by their yellow shirts, put on a show of their own, as they samba before, during and after games—win, lose or draw. But in 1982, nobody could upstage the Italians, who celebrated their country's third title by diving into the Trevi Fountain in Rome, which, no doubt will be duplicated should the again emerge victorious. There is something of a tradition of winners at the World Cup: Only 6 countries—Brazil (3), Italy (3), Germany (3), Argentina (2), Uruguay (2) and England (1)—have won championships.

(Hottest Tickets cont.)
to 300,000 because of extra tickets given to the first sale. That came out to an average of 7,000 per match for the 44 games in the opening two rounds. Not surprisingly, those tickets went quickly.

In October, plans for the quarterfinals, semifinals, third-place and championship matches were announced. Fans had to clip out a coupon in one of several selected newspapers (for example, The New York *Times*, Washington *Post*, Chicago *Tribune*, Los Angeles *Times* and USA *Today*) and pick the games they want. All orders had to be in by Oct. 31, with the "winners" receiving notification by Jan. 31, 1994.

Since there were about only 150,000 tickets available—about 18,750 per match for the eight games, the organizing committee used a random-access selection through a computer.

Asked to explain the process in layman's terms, Rothenberg replied: "Picture an old-fashioned bin and putting all the letters in the bin. Rotate it and Vanna White would pull out the winners, only we would do it with an electronic Vanna White."

If there were any tickets leftover from international sales or returned from the marketing partners and sponsors, they were to go on sale in late April, at the earliest. World Cup officials emphasized that there would not be many available.

Ticket sales were expected to reach $203 million, with an expected surplus of $20 million going to the U.S. Soccer Federation Foundation toward the future of the sport in the U.S. About $100 million will go to FIFA, which would pay for the 24 finalists' preparations and payment commitments.

At Italia '90, a team received $500,000 for each game in participated in. For example, the U.S. received $1.5 million because it played three first-round matches, while world-champion West Germany took home $3.5 million for appearing in seven matches.

Like soccer in general, World Cup does stir passions, only a bit more so. In 1970, Honduras and El Salvador went to war over a qualification match. In 1978, a West Berlin carpenter leapt out of a second-story window shouting, "I don't want to live anymore," after Austria eliminated West Germany, while at a Frankfurt cafe, a nun tried to strangle a man who cheered the Austrians. In 1982, when Brazil was upset by Italy in the quarterfinals, 3 people committed suicide in Rio de Janeiro and a bar customer in Sao Paulo was shot and killed over an argument about the game. And in 1990, 17-year-old Xia Qianli strangled his father in Zhejang, China, because he was not allowed to watch the opening ceremony. What causes such extreme behavior? Soccer is the only organized sport in many countries. National honor is at stake. And sometimes a country's culture and way of life are put on the line.

Perhaps this passion had its seeds at the very first tournament in Montevideo, Uruguay, in 1930. In that final, 2 different balls were used in the championship match between Uruguay-Argentina. With a ball made in Argentina, the visitors grabbed a 2-1 halftime lead. The Uruguayans, using their ball in the second half, rallied for a 4-2 victory. When news of the defeat reached Buenos Aires, an angry mob attacked the Uruguayan Consulate with bricks and stones.

Some 64 years and 14 World Cups later, the tournament is still alive and kicking. In fact, the 1994 World Cup is expected to give soccer in the U.S. a much-needed boost at the professional level. Off the field, the event certainly got off to an impressive start as 650,000 tickets were gobbled up in a matter of weeks by a special sale for the U.S. soccer community in February and March, 1993—without the fans knowing which countries would be playing some 15 months before the tournament was to be staged. Alan I. Rothenberg, World Cup USA 1994 CEO, has predicted that every one of the 52 matches would be a sellout. If he's correct, more than 3.6 million fans, which would break the previous mark by about a million, would watch the games at the 9 stadiums.

Each World Cup has had its own, unique personality, and 1994 will be no different.

The grand experiment will take place at the Pontiac Silverdome in Pontiac, Michigan, where natural grass will be placed over the artificial turf for the 4 opening-round matches. During U.S. Cup '93, which featured the U.S. and such international heavyweights as defending World Cup champion Germany, Brazil and England, natural grass was used at the dome and soccer officials and players gave it a green thumbs up. If successful, a number of Northern European countries might consider using a domed stadium and grass for their soccer seasons during their severe winters.

Grass will also be used over the artificial surface in Giants Stadium in East Rutherford, New Jersey, although that structure doesn't have a roof—at least not yet.

The 7 other stadiums are well known for their football, American football, history. The Rose Bowl in Pasadena, California, will be the site for the most matches, 8, including the July 17 final. There's also Foxboro Stadium (Foxboro, Massachusetts), the Citrus Bowl (Orlando, Florida), Solider Field (Chicago, Illinois), Stanford Stadium (Palo Alto, California), the Cotton Bowl (Dallas, Texas) and RFK Stadium (Washington, D.C.).

The spectacle kicks off at Solider Field on June 17, when an elaborate set of opening ceremonies starts the ball rolling before Germany plays Bolivia. Then, for the next 31 days, the eyes of the world will be on the United States. That's when each of the 24 countries plays 3 games in the first round, which has 4 teams in 6 groups. The top 16 advance to the second round. The top 2 teams from each group automatically qualify, as do the next 4 countries with the highest number of points. The survivors then move onto to the knockout competition: the second round, quarterfinals, semifinals and championship match. But the big question is: Who will play in that final at the Rose Bowl come July 17? There is no clear-cut favorite, but the championship team should come from one of 5 countries: Argentina, Brazil, Italy, the Netherlands and defending champion Germany, although no European team has won a World Cup title in the Americas.

Argentina, the defending South American champion, has blossomed again with a new generation of stars. Diego Maradona who missed 15 months because of a drug suspension, has struggled to regain his former greatness in the Spanish First Division, but don't be surprised if he has a say in one or two key matches. Brazil may be living on borrowed time and a reputation that was forged some 20 years ago. But it will be difficult to ignore a team that has won 3 world titles and produced some of the greatest soccer players. With players like the talented Romario, Brazil might become the first country to take home the cup a fourth time. And besides, the cup is being played virtually in its own backyard.

Germany hasn't played many matches that mean something because it automatically qualified as the defending champion. But it should be in the mix behind a talent-deep team that includes captain

Lothar Matthaeus, who has moved from midfielder to sweeper in a bold move by coach Berti Vogts, workhorse forward Juergen Klinsmann, all-around Karlheinz Riedle and quite possibly defender Andreas Brehme, whose penalty-kick conversion helped the Germans to a 1-0 victory over Argentina in the 1990 finale.

The Netherlands has been considered a contender because of its entertaining, attacking style, led by the modern-day Dutch master, Marco van Basten, who has been sidelined because of an ankle injury, and midfielder Ruud Gullit, who has regained his brilliant form after having his career almost cut short by 4 knee operations. After missing the 1992 European Championship, Italy has struggled to find itself offensively. Despite its ironclad defense, perhaps having all those high-paid foreign forwards in its First Division has taken its toll on Italy developing strikers. Still, players such as Roberto Baggio could play vital roles for the Italians.

Bulgarian scoring-machine Hristo Stoichkov, an outspoken forward who toils for Barcelona (Spain), will have an opportunity to demonstrate that the media was mistaken for selecting him as only the second-best player in Europe in 1992. Van Basten was chosen the best.

Although their teams are not expected to advance past the second round, a number of other players should leave their marks and secure their international reputations. Mexican striker Hugo Sanchez, who began his international career in the 1978 World Cup, is expected to end it in the same event in 1994. The Mexicans, the first team to qualify for USA '94, were among the hottest teams last year. They are led by flamboyant goalkeeper Jorge Campos, who likes to wear a shocking pink shirt with its collar turned up and who likes to wander from the goal. Campos is expected to take the mantle from former Colombian goalkeeper Rene Higuita as the most traveled goalkeeper. Higuita earned the nicknames El Loco and the Merry Wanderer after forging a reputation not as a shot-blocker, but as a keeper who likes to roam the open spaces outside the penalty area. While Colombia, behind the crafty Freddy Rincon and Carlos Valderrama, easily recognizable because his hair looks more like a human fright wig, has qualified, Higuita may or may not play. He has been released from jail for his involvement in a kidnapping case in late 1993.

For Americans, the most interesting part of the Greek team might be the coach Alkis Panagoulias, a naturalized U.S. citizen who directed the U.S. National Team from 1983-85. Panagoulias likes to speak his mind and could make some headlines off the field, win, lose, draw or tie-break. Greece qualified from European Group 5 along with Russia,

West German Defender Franz Beckerbauer (center), who revolutionized the sweeper position, is the only player to have captained a team (1974), and coached one (1990) to a world championship.

which never achieved much success in the Cup as the original Big Red Machine (the Soviet Union). Belgium could be Europe's most under-rated team, but potentially it could be one of the world's most danger-ous. In Mexico, in 1986, the Belgians finished a surprising fourth. In Italy, in 1990, they earned enough respectability to be awarded one of the 6 seeds (in Verona). Romania could very well be Eastern Europe's version of Belgium, not getting enough respect, but having qualified for the final 24 for the second consecutive time. Ireland, coached by an Englishman, Jack Charlton, barely squeezed through and will need more luck than it had in Italy to put forth a decent showing this time around. The Irish reached the quarterfinals without winning a game.

Then there are a number of soccer minnows who will make their debut or a rare appearance. Bolivia, whose only other 2 World Cup appearances have been through invitations, has become a respectacle

South American side, thanks in part to the world-reknowned Taihuichi Youth Soccer Academy, which has produced several of the country's attacking players. Norway will make its first appearance in the Cup since 1938, and Switzerland, another European surprise, qualified for the first time since 1966. Rounding out the European representations is Sweden and Spain.

In the past two World Cups, the Third World started to make an impact. Out of Africa is Cameroon, the team that saved Italia '90; Morocco, the first Third World and African nation to win a World Cup group (Mexico in 1986), and Nigeria, which finally has seen its highly successful international youth program bear some fruit.

Just Another Wednesday Morning at Stephen's Green

The only toast available for breakfast at Stephen's Green (Queens in New York City) on the morning of April 28, 1993, was the one given to the Irish National Team by its fans.

When Ireland's Niall Quinn headed home the equalizer with 15 minutes remaining against Denmark in the World Cup qualifier, the 150 fans who packed the bar erupted. They stood in unison, raised their glasses, cheered, hugged each other and sang, "Ole, Ole, Ole, Ole."

The goal was replayed on one of the televisions and the celebration was repeated with the same energy.

"There is a God," fan Niall Archbold said as his beloved Irish held on for a 1-1 tie against the European champions to remain alive for one of two Group 3 spots in next year's World Cup.

It had been a roller coaster ride for most of the morning as the fans cheered the Irish's near misses, thwarted by the Danes sure-handed goalkeeper, Peter Schmeichel, and verbally groaned at the mistakes, particularly when Kim Vilfort chipped the ball over an out-of-position Packie Bonner in the first half.

It was a time for reveling and singing, including one interesting ditty, "Jackie's Army", named after Irish coach Jack Charlton, that summed up the faithful's feelings:

We're all on the march for
*   Jackie's army*
We're all staying in the U.S.A.
And we really shake them up
When we win the World Cup
'Cause Ireland are the greatest
*   football team.*

On that Wednesday morning, the Irish weren't great, but certainly good enough.

Superfan Paddy Archbold wasn't going to miss this one for the world. He showed up at 7 a.m. to reserve a seat for himself and his friends for the 9:45 match, positioning himself at a table and

The same can be said for Saudi Arabia, which took up soccer only in 1976, but has become an Asian power thanks to its progress at the youth level. Joining the Saudis is South Korea, which qualified for its third consecutive World Cup the first Asian team to accomplish that feat.

The United States? Bora Milutinovic, a Yugoslavian native who has enjoyed success at the last two World Cups, was hired in 1991 to field a competitive team with players scattered all over the world, including several in Europe. The impressive list includes hard-working midfielder John Harkes, who set up the tying goal for Sheffield Wednesday at the prestigious Football Association Cup final at

(Just Another cont.)

about eight feet from a TV. "We sit here often," he said. "We're supersititious."

Eventually, his friends—David Arcbhold, Tony McPhillips and Eamonn Grey—joined him.

At 9:20, the place was hopping. "If I came in now, this table would be gone," Paddy said.

It turned out to be a day of sacrifices for many of the assembled. In fact, most of the viewers did not go to work that day. One fan asked that his name not be mentioned in any story because he called in sick to work to watch the match.

"Many of these guys are giving up a day's wages," Paddy said.

Paddy's sacrifice? His sleep. He went directly from his job as a bartender to Stephen's.

Archbold and his friends aren't just Irish soccer fans: They are soccer fans, rabid soccer fans, at that. "There are very few things important in life. Soccer

is one of them," McPhillips said.

After watching the F.A. Cup final via closed-circuit television at Stephen's in May, 1990, the group decided to journey down to Washington, D.C., to watch the U.S. play Ajax of Amsterdam.

" 'Who's got a car?' and off we went," Paddy said.

Several weeks later, they decided to trek to Italy to watch their favorite national team in the second round and beyond of Italia '90.

"We stayed for a week," Paddy said. "We were supposed to stay for 3 days."

Stephen's, which regularly shows English Premier Division games on Saturday mornings, has become an information center for the latest information on Eire. During one recent Irish World Cup qualifying match, the bar received 300 calls inquiring about the score. It got so hectic that owner Paul Powell put updates on the bar's answering machine.

"The thing that keeps this bar open is soccer," Powell said.

Wembley Stadium (England) in 1993, South African-born striker Roy Wegerle (England), who has enlivened the American attack with his surprising Latin style in his short tenure with the team, offensive-minded midfielder defender Thomas Dooley (Germany) playmaking midfielder Tab Ramos (Spain) and crafty midfielder Hugo Perez (Saudi Arabia), who has struggled to find the form that made him the most dangerous U.S. offensive player in the eighties.

It would be absurd to expect the United States to win, although stranger things have happened. Just reaching the second round would be considered a decent accomplishment in an event that is expected to give the sport a much-needed boost at home. Another lift, no doubt,

(Just Another cont.)

The patrons lived and died with the Irish. They also were brutally honest. Only 41 seconds into the match, an Irish player handled the ball at the top of the box, and the throng waited for a penalty kick call that never came. "We were lucky," someone said.

They certainly had their manners.

When Charlton was interviewed, the bar fell silent. (Asked what he thought of an Englishman coaching an Irish team, Paddy replied: "He adopted a country. That's good enough for me. As long as he's prepared, that's fine with me.").

The fans also did not utter a word during a moment of silence for the Zambian National Team, which was wiped out in a plane accident only hours before the match.

Then came showtime.

By the 9:45 A.M. kickoff, most of the assembled—they had paid $20 apiece to watch the match—had a stout or a beer in their hand.

There were a couple of near-misses and false alarms, especially in the early going as the frustrated Irish had a number of close encounters, until Quinn's late score that saved the day and a point.

"Believe it or not, the European champions are in green," Paddy said, referring to the Irish domination. "I'm relieved to get the draw."

At around 11:45 A.M., the match ended, but few patrons left the bar. Some stayed around to talk, others to drink and some others to get a bite.

So, with Paddy's long night and day, it was time to go home and catch some sleep, or at least a nap, right? Wrong.

He went out to get some lunch, so he could come back and root for the Netherlands against England in a qualifing match that was to be shown later in the afternoon.

But that, is another story.

will come from ABC, which will broadcast 11 live games, mostly on the weekend, and ESPN, which will show the remaining 41 matches live or on a tape-delayed basis the same day, due to several matches being played at the same time.

Whether you watch it live in person or on TV, it should be some show.

Chapter Two

Historical Perspective

How it began

Even before FIFA was formed, there were thoughts of organizing a world championship. FIFA (Federation Internationale de Football Association) was formed in 1904, and several members, including Frenchmen Henri Delaunay and Jules Rimet, the organization's president, pushed for a competition. After several false starts—World War I interrupted the organization's plans, for example—it was voted on in 1919 to establish a world championship. Noticing the success of the 1924 and 1928 soccer championships in the Olympics, FIFA officials, were spurred into organizing a world championship, not just for amateurs, but for professionals as well. After securing its second consecutive Olympic title in 1928, Uruguay was selected as the site for the first world championship—which was to be called the World Cup—in honor of the 100th anniversary of the country's birth. Soccer—international soccer—would never be the same.

The ultimate prize

It has been hidden under a bed, stolen twice and melted down.

The World Cup trophy, the most sought after asard in all of sport, has enjoyed a well-traveled and intriguing existence.

On July 17, 1994 the second incarnation of the trophy will wind up in the hands of the captain of a fortunate national team and paraded around the Rose Bowl in Pasadena, California.

The first, the Jules Rimet Trophy, was retired after the 1970 World Cup by Brazil, which captured its third title. Since then the FIFA World Cup trophy has been the big prize, the object of desire. The original trophy was produced for the 1930 competition in Uruguay. FIFA commissioned French sculptor Abel Lafleur, who created a statuette some 30 centimeters high and weighing 4 kilograms as a winged goddess of victory with her arms raised supporting an octagonal cup. The statue was made of solid gold and at the time cost some 50,000 French francs, which is the equivalent of $35,000 today.

During the final years of World War II, FIFA Vice President

These are two of the most coveted trophies in the world—the Jules Rimet Trophy (*left*), which was retired in 1970 by Brazil after they became the first country to win three World Cups, and the FIFA World Cup (*right*) which will be up for grabs in 1994.

Ottorino Barassi of Italy hid it in a shoe box under his bed to safeguard it against the raids of Germans retreating from his country. FIFA renamed the cup the Jules Rimet Trophy, after the man who made the most significant contribution to the founding of the World Cup.

On March 20, 1966, several months before the next competition in England, the trophy was stolen while on display at a stamp exhibition in the Central Hall of Westminster in England. The authorities, including Scotland Yard, were baffled, fearing the trophy had been melted down. But Pickles, a white-and-black dog of undetermined pedigree, saved the day as the unlikely hero. Pickles found the trophy buried near a tree in a London garden.

Pickles' owner collected an award valued between $15,000 and $20,000. The thief, who demanded a $50,000 ransom for the cup, was given a 2-year jail term. (Pickles, alas, did not meet a fate deserved for a hero. He reportedly strangled himself on his leash while chasing a cat.)

In 1970, the Brazilian Soccer Confederation became the permanent home to the Jules Rimet Trophy, when the Brazilians became the first team to win the cup 3 times—until the night of Dec. 20, 1983. Thieves broke into the confederation offices and stole the gold cup. It was never recovered, and authorities feared it was melted down. Three men were arrested in connection with its theft, but were released the next day because of insufficient evidence (one of those arrested, Antonio Carlos Aranha, was found dead on Dec. 30, 1989, from 7 bullet wounds from a pistol).

"It was terrible," Pedro T. Natal said. "Everybody was sick about this . . . I had a feeling in my skin the robber was not Brazilian. He has no feeling of patriotism."

In stepped Kodak Brazil of Sao Paulo to save the day.

"When we heard about the robbery, we were sick," said Natal, Kodak Brazil Communication Director. "We decided to do something about it. This is the most important display of Brazilian culture. "Certainly there was a tremendous loss in Brazil when the cup was stolen. We wanted to do something that would restore to the Brazilian people the most important symbol of the country's primary sport.

"This is a donation to the people of Brazil. We are not linking this donation to any commerical aspect."

The replacement resides in the confederation office.

Fortunately, the new trophy has not been stolen. In fact, there are so many replicas of the trophy around—including in the U.S.—it is difficult to figure where the actual trophy is. A replica of the trophy was taken on tour to various soccer-related events in the United States in 1991 and 1992 before funding ran out.

FIFA held a special competition for the trophy's design, and 53 models were presented to trophy manufacturers of seven countries. The design of the Italian firm, Bertoni, the work of Milanese sculptor Silvio Gazzaniga was chosen. The cup, 18-karat solid gold, weighs 11 pounds. (4970 grams), stands 14 inches (36 centimeters) high, cost $20,000 to produce. "The lines go from a base rising in a sphere and covering the world," Gazzaniga said. "From the body of the sculpture, two figures stand out—two athletes in a moving celebration of victory."

The trophy's base was banded by two rings of Malachite, which is a green gemstone. It contains enough space for the names of 17 victorious countries to be engraved upon it. With the names of five countries already inscribed on the base—West Germany (1974), Argentina (1978), Italy (1982), Argentina (1986) and West Germany (1990)—there is enough room until the 2038 World Cup.

Then a third trophy will be made.

1930
Uruguay triumphant
at home

The first World Cup was hardly the money-making bonanza of today's tournament. In fact, it was difficult just to get countries to show up at this invitational tournament. Imagine a country giving up an opportunity to play in the cup today.

While organizers would have preferred 16 countries, 13 teams agreed to participate in the first cup. Because of the long voyage across the Atlantic, only 4 European squads—France, Belgium, Romania and Yugoslavia—made the trip, which was expected to take up to 3 months to complete. The rest of the field came from the United States Mexico and South America.

There were other problems. It rained for much of the competition in Montevideo (all games were played in the Uruguayan capital), leaving the playing fields in less than perfect shape. Work on the new, 100,000-capacity Cenentary Stadium fell behind schedule. At the start of the tournament, it was not ready, but with builders working 24 hours a day, it was ready for Uruguay's opening match against Peru on July 18.

The tournament kicked off on July 13, as 1,000 curious souls at Pocitos Stadium watched France defeat Mexico, 4–1. The game included a number of firsts. Frenchman Lucien Laurent scored the first goal of the tournament—the only goal he would score in the competition—19 minutes into the match, and Mexicans Manuel and Felip Rosas became the first brothers to play in the cup. Despite losing its goalkeeper—Alex Thepot had his jaw broken in the 10th minute and there were no substitutes in those days, so midfielder Augustin Chantrel took his place between the posts—the French prevailed as Andre Maschinot scored a goal in each half and Marcel Langiller added another. An interesting footnote to the game: Alex Villaplane, who was the French captain, was executed by a firing squad in 1944 for collaborating with the Germans during World War II.

Argentina, which took the silver medal to Uruguay in the 1928 Olympics and were the winners of the South American championship, was among the favorites to win the title. The Argentines got out of the opening round, defeating France, 1-0, Mexico, 6-3, and Chile, 3-1, but they seemed to be involved in a series of incidents that demonstrated the growing pains of the fledgling tournament. For example, while the Argentines clung to a 1-0 lead against France, referee Almeilda Rego of Brazil signalled the end of the game six minutes prematurely.

Argentine fans ran onto the field to congratulate their team while the French protested. Rego discovered the error of his ways; the crowd on the field was cleared by mounted policemen and the match completed.

Or take, for instance, Argentina's victory over Mexico. Argentine captain Nolo Ferreira could not play because he had to return home to take an important college examination. Guillermo Stabile took his place and recorded the first hat-trick in World Cup history. The Rosas brothers were at it again, each scoring a goal for yet another first.

Group 2 was short and sweet with only 3 nations—Yugoslavia, Brazil and Bolivia. Defying logic and odds, the European team qualified for the semifinals, winning both its matches, 2–1 over Brazil and 4–0 over Bolivia. Ivan Beck led the Slavs, scoring one goal in the first game, two in the second. The Brazilians blanked Bolivia.

Not surprisingly, Uruguay was considered the favorite to win the first trophy, thanks to its Olympic superiority. The hosts got off on the right foot in Group 3 with a 1–0 win over Peru, followed by a 4–0 blanking of Romania, whose team was picked by King Carol. Because of the extended trip, the king promised the players they would still have their jobs when they returned home. While as many as 93,000 fans would watch Uruguay perform at one game, the local population was not as excited about the other matches. A crowd of 300—an all-time World Cup low—turned out to watch Romania defeat Peru, 3-1, at Pocitos Stadium on July 14, three days before 800 witnessed the Yugoslavia-Bolivia encounter at Central Park.

Group 4 produced the most surprising of all results. The U.S. team, nicknamed the shot-putters by the French because of the tremendous bulk of several players, was made up of a number of former professional English players. The Americans, however, emerged victorious with 3–0 wins over Belgium and Paraguay. (To truly appreciate the Americans' accomplishment, they would win only 1 other World Cup match in 8 attempts and would score eight more goals). Bert Patenaude was credited with two goals in the Paraguay match, although U.S. soccer officials claimed that Patenaude had scored the third goal, which would have made him the first player to register a hat-trick in cup history. Depending on your source of information, that third goal was awarded as an own goal Paraguay accidentally knocked the ball into its own net, although U.S. Captain Thomas Florie also took credit for it.

The Americans had their collective heads handed to them by

Argentina in the semifinals, dropping a 6–1 decision as Stabile and Carlos Peucelle finished with two goals apiece. Uruguay prevailed over Yugoslavia by the same score, with Pedro Cea converting a hat-trick.

So, the two best teams in the world qualified for the championship match, which was not without controversy. Each side wanted to use its ball. In a Solomon-esque gesture, referee Jean Langenus allowed Argentina to use its ball in the opening half, the Uruguayans theirs in the second. And guess what happened? The Argentines, with their ball, took a 2–1 halftime lead on goals by Pablo Dorado and Stabile that were sandwiched around a score by Peucelle. Using their ball in the second half, the Uruguayans rallied with 3 unanswered goals—by Cea in the 57th minute—he became the first player to score in an Olympic (1924) and World Cup final; by Santos Iriarte in the 68th and by the one-armed Hector Castro in the 89th.

The Final

The mood of the competing nations' capitals showed varying reactions. There was dancing in the Montevideo streets as the next day was declared a national holiday. In Buenos Aires, angry Argentines vented their anger by throwing bricks and stones at the Uruguayan embassy. The World Cup was born.

Uruguay 4, Argentina 2
Centenary Stadium
Montevideo, Uruguay
July 30,1930
Uruguay: Ballesteros, Nasazzi, Mascheroni, Andrade, Fernandez, Gestido, Dorado, Scarone, Castro, Cea, Iriarte
Argentina: Botasso, Della Torre, Paternoster, J. Evaristo, Monti, Suarez, Peucelle, Varallo, Stabile, Ferreyra, M. Evaristo
Goals: Dorado (U) 12, Peucelle (A) 20, Stabile (A) 37, Cea (U) 57, Iriarte (U) 68, Castro (U) 89.
Referee: Langenus (Belgium)
Attendance: 93,000

Two years before the tournament, Italy, under the reign of terror of Benito Mussolini, was awarded the World Cup, which was seen as a perfect platform to spew his Fascist propaganda. In contrast to the the first cup, which had mostly South American countries, this was European-dominated, as 12 teams came from the continent. The only exceptions

1934
Viva Italia at home

were the U.S., Egypt, Brazil and Argentina. Uruguay was a no-show, becoming the only champion that failed to try to defend its crown.

The first round was an elimination competition. Italy, with 4 Argentine stars on its squad, rolled past the U.S., 7–1, as Angelo Schiavio struck 3 times, only days after the Americans defeated Mexico, 4–2, in a special qualifier in Rome. The Italians should have saved some of those goals, because they scored only 5 goals in their remaining 4 games. Czechoslovakia edged Romania, 2–1 (it was not known whether King Carol picked this team), on a pair of second-half goals. Germany romped past Belgium, 5–2, on Edmund Conen's hat-trick, and Austria ousted France, 3–2, scoring the go-ahead goal by Anton Schall, who was blatantly offside on the play. It was not a good tournament for non-European sides, as Spain beat Brazil, 3–1, Sweden nipped Argentina, 3-2 and Hungary downed Egypt, 4–2. It would be Egypt's last appearance until 1990.

The quarterfinals, which then were called the second round, saw Germany, Austria, Czechoslovakia and Italy emerge victorious, although the Italians needed a replay to get past the Spanish. A day after playing to a 1–1 tie, Italy defeated Spain, 1–0, on Giuseppe Meazza's first-half goal.

Oldrich Nejedly proved to be a one-man show for Czechoslovakia, scoring all the goals in a 3–1 semifinal victory over Germany. The Italians, who suffered a 4–2 loss to Austria in Turin less than 4 months before the cup, avenged the defeat with a 1-0 win during a downpour in Milan. Enrique Guaita scored for the winners in the 19th minute.

The Final   In a rare World Cup occurrence, both teams were captained by their goalkeepers—the Italians by Giampiero Combi, who was playing in his 47th and last international, the Czechs by Frantisek Planicka. Both teams attacked, but it took 70 minutes before anyone found the back of the net. Antonin Puc took a corner kick that bounded back to him and scored from a difficult angle for a 1–0 Czech advantage. But the Italians equalized with 10 minutes remaining in regulation as Raimundo Orsi raced through the defense, faked a shot with his left foot and fired a shot with his right. Five minutes into the first extra period, Schiavio drove a shot barely under the crossbar for a 2–1 lead and eventually the title.

Italy 2, Czechoslovakia 1
PNF Stadium
Rome, Italy
June 10, 1934
Italy: Combi, Monzeglio, Allemandi, Ferraris IV, Monti, Berto-
    lini, Guaita, Meazza, Schiavio, Ferrari, Orsi.
Czechoslovakia: Planicka, Zenisek, Ctyroky, Kostalek, Cambal,
    Krcil, Funek, Svoboda, Sobotka, Nejedly, Puc.
Goals: Puc (C) 70, Orsi (I) 80, Schiavio (I) 95
Referee: Eklind (Sweden)
Attendance: 55,000.

1938
Italy wins again—in France

Believing it would alternate between continents, Argentina ap-
plied to host the 1938 tournament. FIFA, however, remembering the
problems in Uruguay and the travel headaches, decided to keep the cup
in Europe, despite the possibility of war on the horizon. France was
selected as the venue, and an angry Argentina decided not to participate
in the qualifying competition. Brazil and Cuba showed up, and the rest
of field consisted of European teams.

Only 2 years after Hitler's pro-Nazi propaganda of the 1936
Berlin Olympics, the Germans were hoping to use this World Cup to
show how dominant their soccer team could be. Neighboring Switzerland, however, had other ideas, playing Germany to a surprising 1-1 tie
in the tournament opener in the knockout competition. In the subse-
quent replay, the Swiss eliminated the Germans, 4−2, as Andre Abeg-
glen III broke a 2−2 tie late in the match, scoring twice in three
minutes. Cuba, which qualified only because Mexico dropped out, and
Romania played to a 3−3 draw. That forced another playoff, as the
Cubans prevailed, 2−1, despite the benching of goalkeeper Beinto
Carvajeles, who enjoyed a spectacular first game. His replacement,
Juan Ayra, was just as good and Carlos Maquina scored the game-
winner in the 80th minute.

There were more close calls, the Netherlands held the Czechs,
1934 runners-up, to a scoreless tie in regulation, but succumbed in
extra time, 3−0. Defending champion Italy sweated out a 2−1 extra-
time victory over Norway, as Silvio Piola scored. Then there was
Brazil's 6−5 overtime triumph over Poland, the only match in World
Cup history in which players on opposing sides scored four goals.
Leonidas da Silva accomplished that feat for the Brazilians, while
Ernst Willimowski duplicated it for the Poles. Leonadis scored early in
the first extra session and Romeo gave the Brazilians some breathing

room before Willimowski scored his fourth, but it was too late, in one of the most remarkable soccer games of all-time. The rest of the first round fell into place: France 3, Belgium 1 and Hungary 6, Dutch East Indies 0.

In the second round, the defending champs, Italy, prevailed over the hosts, France, 3–1, as Piola struck twice. Sweden had few problems with dispatching Cuba, 8–0, as Gustav Wetterstrom found the back of the next 4 times. Hungary blanked the Swiss, 2–0, as Gyula Zsengeller scored in each half, and Brazil and Czechoslovakia played to a 1–1 tie, forcing another playoff. Of course, it was a minor miracle that either of those 2 teams was standing after that encounter—now called the Battle of Bordeaux—a physical affair that left Oldrich Nejedly with a broken leg and goalkeeper Frantisek Planicka playing part of the game with a broken arm. In the replay 2 days later, Brazil stopped the Czechs, 2–1, as the Brazilians used 6 new players. There were no incidents.

Two days later, Brazil had to face the Italians, who recorded a 2–1 semifinal win behind Luigi Colaussi and Meazza (penalty kick). Hungary had few problems with Sweden in the other semifinal, as Zsengeller connected for a hat-trick in a 5–1 victory.

The Final   The site of the championship match was Colombes Stadium—which had been the venue for the track and field drama of the "Chariots of Fire" Olympics in 1924.

The teams traded early goals—by Italy's Colaussi in the 5th minute and by Hungary's Pal Titkos 2 minutes later. But Piola, who was named player of the tournament, scored in the 16th minute, and the Italians were on their way, extending the margin to 3–1 at half on Colaussi's second goal. Hungary sliced the lead to a goal midway through the second half, but Piola put home an insurance goal 8 minutes from time as Italy became the first country to win the World Cup twice.

Unfortunately, Italy would have to wait some 12 years to defend its title because of World War II, although no one knew it at the time.

Italy 4, Hungary 2
Colombes Stadium
Paris, France
June 19, 1938
Italy: Olivieri, Foni, Rava, Seratoni, Andreolo, Locatelli, Biavati,
    Meazza, Piola, Ferrari, Colaussi
Hungary: Szabo, Polgar, Biro, Szalay, Szucs, Lazar, Sas, Vincze,
    Sarosi, Szengeller, Titkos.
Goals: Colaussi (I) 5, Titkos (H) 7, Piola (I) 16, Colaussi (I) 35,
    Sarosi (H) 70, Piola (I) 82.
Referee: Capdeville (France)
Attendance: 55,000

The 1950 tournament—set for Brazil and a spanking new Maracana Stadium (200,000 capacity)—seemed cursed from the outset.
Only 31 countries entered the qualifying competition. Turkey, for
example, qualified after Austria withdrew, but the Turks decided to
drop out. India followed the same route after its group rival, Burma,
withdrew. Four South American sides had walk-overs in the qualifying
round. Bolivia and Chile made it into the tournament without playing a
match after Argentina withdrew. Likewise for Uruguay and Paraguay,
after Ecuador and Peru decided not to play. Despite that, the World Cup
produced some of the most dramatic wins in the history of the competition.

1950
Uruguay's surprise
in Brazil

Instead of a single-elimination, teams would play 3 matches
apiece in the first round. Maracana Stadium was not completed by the
start of the opener. But 81,649 fans showed up to watch a 21-gun salute,
fireworks, and 5,000 pigeons released and a smashing 4-0 victory by
Brazil over Mexico behind Ademir's 2 goals. It turned out to be an
inauspicious start for Mexican goalkeeper Antonio Carbajal, who
would go on to play in a record 5 World Cups. Brazil won the group,
playing Switzerland to a 2−2 draw and shutting down Yugoslavia,
2−0.

In the second pool, England, playing in its first World Cup, was
considered among the favorites, but could only win one game—2−0
over Chile. The English met their match against an unlikely group of
American amateur players who posted a 1−0 victory in a small mining
town in Belo Horizonte. JoeGaetjens scored the game-winner off a
header in the 37th minute. They held on for one of the most incredible
results in sports history. Stunned, the English dropped a 1-0 decision to
Spain as Zarra scored, and returned home in disgrace. Spain, mean-

while, won the group with a perfect 3−0 mark, rallying from a 1−0 deficit in the final 10 minutes for a 3−1 victoryover the U.S., as Brunet Basora scored twice. The Spanish also stopped Chile, 2−0 as Basora and Zarra had goals.

Sweden barely got past Italy in the 3-team third pool. The Swedes edged the Italians, 3−2, and tied Paraguay, 2−2. Italy downed the South Americans, 2−0, but did not advance because the Swedes had scored more goals (5 to 4) than it did.

Uruguay, meanwhile, could not have had an easier route to the final round, having to play only Bolivia (because France had dropped out after the final pools had been set). The Uruguayans, behind Juan Schiaffino's 4 goals, romped to an 8−0 victory.

The final round was among the most confusing in cup history. Four teams—Brazil, Sweden, Spain and Uruguay-played in a round-robin competition, leaving no true championship game. Fortunately, the success of Brazil and Uruguay ensured there would be an equivalent of one. In front of a crowd of 138,886 at Maracana, the Brazilians, behind Ademir's four goals, leveled Sweden, 7−1. After Spain held Uruguay to a 2−2 tie, the hosts went on the warpath again, rolling over Spain, 6−1, as Ademir and Chico connected twice. Oscar Miguez scored 2 goals as Uruguay squeaked past Sweden, 3−2, and Sweden downed Spain, 3−1, in a rather meaningless affair, to set up the ultimate confrontation—Uruguay *vs.* Brazil.

The Final

As luck would have it, the last game of the final round turned out to be for the championship. Because of the standings, the Brazilians (2-0-0, 4 points) needed but a tie, the Uruguayans (1-1-0; 3) a victory.

A World Cup record crowd of 199,854 (172,772 was paid) showed up at Maracana, anticipating a festive match and post-game celebration. The Brazilians were considered 1−10 favorites to take home the trophy for the first time, with bonuses of $20,000 in the offing (remember, this was 1950). But then again, the Uruguayans had other ideas to spoil the party.

The Brazilians attacked from the outset, but could not score in the opening half. Then, 2 minutes into the second half, Ademir set up Cardosa Friaca for a 1−0 lead. But a miscommunication occurred. Brazilian coach Flavio Costa gave instructions for Jair to drop back to defense, but word never reached him. Uruguay took advantage of the gaps on defense and Schiaffino converted a pass by Alcide Ghiggia in the 66th minute. If the score remained that way, Brazil still would have won the title. Incredibly, Brazil continued to attack instead of defend.

Ghiggia himself scored with 11 minutes left to give the Uruguayans a 2−1 lead before a stunned crowd.

For Uruguay, it would be its last great World Cup glory. For Brazil, it would mean an 8 year wait to take a victory lap with the coveted Jules Rimet Trophy.

Uruguay 2, Brazil 1
Maracana Stadium
Rio de Janeiro, Brazil
July 16, 1950
Uruguay: Maspoli, Gonzales, Tejera, Gambetta, Varela, Andrade, Ghiggia, Perez, Miguez, Schiaffino, Moran
Brazil: Barbosa, Augusto, Juvenal, Bauer, Danilo, Bigode, Friaca, Ziznho, Ademir, Jair, Chico
Goals: Friaca (B) 47, Schiaffino (U) 66, Ghiggia (U) 79
Referee: Reader (England)
Attendance: 199,854

1954
Germans rule
admist Swiss
cheese defense

The 1954 World Cup will forever be remembered for the great comeback by West Germany, which calculated its way to the final in Switzerland. It also will be remembered as the highest-scoring cup in history. The 16 finalists produced 140 goals in 26 games, an average of 5.38 per match (the next best average came in the 1938 competition at 4.66 per match). Victorious teams scored 7 or more goals on 6 occasions, including an amazing 7−5 victory by Austria over the hosts.

The opening match gave very little indication of what was to come as Yugoslavia got past France, 1−0, as a young forward by the name of Milos Milutinovic tallied in the 15th minute. He is the older brother of Bora Milutinovic, who will coach the U.S. in the 1994 World Cup. As it turned out, pool one was a defensive battle, as "only" 13 goals were scored in 4 matches. Brazil and Yugoslavia advanced to the quarterfinals. The Brazilians routed Mexico, 5−0, and tied Yugoslavia, 1−1.

Pool 2 produced some of the most intriguing results in the history of the cup. Favored Hungary, the Magic Magyars who were the dominant national soccer team in the fifties, crushed South Korea, 9−0, as Sandor Kocsis had a hat-trick and Frenec Puskas chipped in with 2 goals. The Hungarians also rolled over the Germans, 8−3, (Kocsis had 4 goals in this one, but Puskas sustained an injury that would sideline him until the final), but scores can be deceiving. German coach Sepp Herberger realized that if his side lost to Hungary it would avoid playing the highly touted Brazilians in the quarterfinals. Instead, the

Germans would have to meet Turkey or South Korea in a special playoff, and the winner of that encounter would play Yugoslavia in the next round. So, Herberger, after a 4–1 win over Turkey, revamped his lineup and lost by 5 goals. Turkey went on to beat South Korea, 7–0, setting up a playoff. Herberger restored his regulars and the West Germans romped past Turkey, 7–3, as Maximillian Morlock led the way with 3 goals and the Walter brothers—Olaf and Fritz—each had a goal.

Every match in the third pool was decided by a shutout with Uruguay and Austria finishing on top.

In the fourth pool, England, still smarting from a 7–1 pasting by Hungary before the tournament, and Italy qualified for the quarterfinals. The English started off slow with a 4–4 overtime draw with Austria, but rebounded with a 2-0 win over the Swiss. Italy struggled with a 2-1 loss to the hosts, but rebounded with a 4-1 victory over Belgium, setting up a special playoff with the Swiss, who beat the Italians for the second time in a week.

The quarterfinals produced some of the highest scoring and most brutal games in cup history. Austria and the Swiss started things off with a World Cup record 12 goals as the Austrians managed to walk away with a 7–5 win. The Swiss bolted to a 3–0 advantage in the opening 23 minutes, but Austria answered back with 5 consecutive goals. The Austrians tied it with 3 goals in as many minutes behind Theodor Wagner, who scored two of his three goals, and Alfred Koerner who scored 1 of his 2 goals during that span. They continued their onslaught as captain Ernst Ocwirk gave the Austrians the lead to stay, 4–3, as Wagner, Koerner and Erich Probst added insurance goals.

The next 2 matches were of the garden variety, as far as this tournament was concerned: Uruguay over England, 4–2, as Schiaffino scored, and Germany—its strategy worked—over Yugoslavia, 2–0, on an own goal and a score by Helmut Rahn. Then there was Hungary's 4–2 victory over Brazil in what turned into the most disgraceful match in World Cup history. It became known as the battle of Berne. The game was chippy from the opening whistle and turned into a physical tussle as Brazilian Nilton Santos and Jozsef Bozsik of Hungary were sent off for fighting; they needed police to escort them off the field. After the final whistle, the battle continued en route to the locker rooms. One version had the Brazilians hiding and attacking the Hungarians in the tunnel.

Even without the injured Puskas, Hungary managed to overcome Uruguay in one semifinal, 4–2, in extra time, as Kocsis scored off a pair of headers in the second extra period. Germany, meanwhile, dispatched Austria, 6–1, as the Walter brothers struck not once, but twice apiece.

The Final

It was a rematch of the first round game, yet it wasn't because the West Germans used completely different players in this encounter at Wankdorf Stadium in Berne on July 4. Puskas, although he was not fully fit, insisted on playing for Hungary. The decision looked good early on as the Hungarians grabbed a 2-0 lead in the opening 8 minutes as Puskas put in a rebound of Kocsis' shot in the 6th minute and Zoltan Czibor made it 2–0 only 2 minutes later.

The Germans, however, refused to give up. Maximillian Morlock cut the lead in half in the 10th minute and Rahn equalized in the 18th minute for a 2–2 tie. The score remained that way until the 84th, when Rahn struck again. He picked up a so-so clearance by Mihaly Lantos, bolted into the penalty area and fired the ball past goalkeeper Gyula Groscis. It appeared that Hungary had tied it on a Puskas goal with only 2 minutes left, but linesman Mervyn Griffiths of Wales ruled it was offside. Two minutes later, the Hungarians had suffered their first loss in 30 internationals, dating back to May, 1950, and the Germans were world champions.

West Germany 3, Hungary 2
Wankdorf Stadium
Berne, Switzerland
July 4, 1954
West Germany: Turek, Posipal, Liebrich, Kohlmeyer, Eckel, Mai, Rahn, Morlock, O. Walter, F. Walter, Schaeffer
Hungary: Grosics, Buzansky, Lorant, Lantos, Bozsik, Zakarias, Czibor, Kocsis, Hidegkuti, Puskas, Toth
Goals: Puskas (H) 4, Czibor (H) 8, Morlock (WG) 10, Rahn (WG) 18, Rahn (WG) 84.
Referee: Ling (England)
Attendance: 60,000

1958
Brazilians storm
Sweden

The 1958 World Cup can be summed up in one word—Pele. The scary thing about it was that he missed the first 2 games and still managed to score 6 goals. And the even scarier thing about it was that he was only 17 years old, with a glorious career in front of him that would make him a household word in virtually every country in the world.

Brazil's triumph in Sweden was noteworthy for several reasons.

Brazil became the only team to win out of its hemisphere, finally establishing itself as one of the great soccer countries, and started an incredible run of 3 world championships in four tries—an accomplishment that will be difficult to equal or surpass.

Using an innovative and attack-minded 4–2–4 lineup, the Brazilians were tough to beat. They started off with a 3–0 triumph over Austria as Altafini Mazzola scored once in each half and Nilton Santos 4 minutes into the second half. England, however, managed to shut down the vaunted attack in a scoreless tie, setting up a must-win situation with the Soviet Union. Brazil made several tactical changes, inserting Zito, Garrincha and Pele into the lineup. While Pele did not score, he and the other two additions opened up the Soviet defense for Vava, who found the back of the net twice in a 2–0 triumph as Brazil reached the quarterfinals along with the English, who played in three ties. As for the other groups:

Defending champion West Germany stumbled to a 1–0–2 mark in the first pool, defeating Argentina, 4–1, but tying Czechoslovakia and Northern Ireland by 2–2 results, and advanced with Northern Ireland. The Irish had to edge the Czechs in a special playoff, 2–1—as Peter McParland scored with 10 minutes remaining in extra time. France, behind the awesome firepower of Just Fontaine, who hit for the hat-trick in a 7–3 thumping of Paraguay, added 2 more in a 3–2 loss to Yugoslavia (also advanced from pool 2) and scored what proved to be the decisive goal in a 2–1 win over Scotland.

The host Swedes, who won the Olympic gold medal 10 years earlier in London, were a pleasant surprise in Group 3. Buoyed by their Italian exports—Nils Liedholm (A.C. Milan), Kurt Hamrin (Padova), Arne Selmonsson (Lazio), Nacka Skoglund (Inter Milan) and Bengt Gustavsson (Atalanta), they went undefeated in pool 3. They blanked Mexico, 3–0, as Ange Simonsson twice beat goalkeeper Antonio Carbajal, playing in his third consecutive tournament; edged Hungary, 2–1, behind Hamrin's 2 scores, and played Wales to a scoreless tie. By then, Sweden had qualified for the quarterfinals, although the Welsh needed a 2–1 comeback win in a special playoff against the Hungarians—as Ivor Allchurch and Terence Medwin scored in the final half—to move on. The Hungarians were a mere shadow of themselves as a team because of the 1956 uprising. Many of their stars had either retired or jumped ship—Puskas to Spain, for example. Only Gyula Groscis, defender Jozsef Bozsik and forward Nandor Hidegkuti returned from that great 1954 team.

Helmut Rahn, who was recalled to the team after falling out of

favor with coach Sepp Herberger, scored in the first half of Germany's 1–0 triumph over Yugoslavia. The Germans were followed into the semifinals by Sweden—Hamrin and Simonsson scored in a 2–0 win over the Soviet Union—and the French, who were led by Fontaine, who connected two more times in a 4–0 victory over Northern Ireland.

In was in the quarterfinals that Pele started to make this a virtual one-man show. He scored his first World Cup goal—he later called it "the most important goal of my career"—in the 73rd minute to lead Brazil to a 1–0 victory over a tough Welsh side. Five days later, the 17-year-old showed his performance against the Welsh was no mistake, scoring 3 times within a 20-minute span in the second half to turn a 2–1 advantage into a 5–2 victory over the French (Fontaine had a goal in that one). The Brazilians' opponents were to be Sweden, which bested West Germany, 3–1, in the other semifinal encounter. After the Germans were reduced to 10 players after Erich Juskowiak was ejected for a retaliation foul, the Swedes scored twice behind Gunnar Gren and Hamrin.

The Final

A day after Fontaine (France) completed one of the finest individual performances in the World Cup—4 goals in a 6–3 triumph over West Germany in the consolation match to give him a record 13 goals that still stands today— Pele and Brazil put the exclamation point on this memorable tournament.

The Swedes took a 1–0 lead 4 minutes into the match as Nils Liedholm scored. Brazil found itself behind for the first time in the tournament, and many soccer observers felt they would self-destruct. If anything, it spurred them on. Only 5 minutes later, Vava equalized off a fine cross from Garrincha. The players duplicated the feat in the 32nd minute as Brazil grabbed a 2–1 halftime lead.

Pele? He owned the second half. In the 55th minute, he scored a goal worthy of highlight films. He trapped the ball with his chest, bolted around his marker and volleyed the ball into the net past goalkeeper Karl-Oskar Svensson. Mario Zagalo was able to follow up his own cross on a corner kick in amidst the defensive chaos in the 68th minute for a 4–1 margin. Simonsson cut the lead in half in the 80th minute. Then, most appropriately, Pele put the finishing touches on the World Cup by heading home the final goal as time was running out.

It was just the start of an amazing run for Brazil.

Brazil 5, Sweden 2
Rasunda Stadium
Stockholm, Sweden
June 29, 1958
Brazil: Gilmar, D. Santos, N. Santos, Zito, Bellini, Orlando,
    Garrincha, Didi, Vava, Pele, Zagalo
Sweden: Svensson, Bergmark, Axbom, Boerjesson, Gustavsson,
    Parling, Hamrin, Gren, Simonsson, Liedholm, Skoglund
Goals: Liedholm (S) 3, Vava (B) 9, Vava (B) 32, Pele (B) 55,
    Zagalo (B) 68, Simonsson (S) 80, Pele (B) 90
Referee: Guigue (France)
Attendance: 49,737

Pele continued to prove his World Cup success was no fluke with
Santos and the Brazilian National Team. But the Brazilians demonstrated how great they really were by winning their second straight
tournament, without the Black Pearl, who suffered a pulled muscle in
their second match. That result was a scoreless tie against Czechoslovakia after Mario Zagalo and Pele scored in a 2–0 Group 3 victory over
Mexico and goalkeeper Antonio Carbajal, playing in his fourth consecutive cup. Like a fairy tale come to life, Pele's replacement,
Amarildo—his full name, Amarildo Tavares de Silveira—stepped to
the forefront. Trailing 1–0 in the second half to Spain, Amarildo took
the match into his own hands—actually, it was his feet—scoring in the
71st and 90th minutes for a 2-1 victory to clinch a spot in the quarterfinals.

1962
Two-in-a-Row for
Brazil in Chile

The rest of the cup seemed like a set-up: Who was going to meet
Brazil in the final?

Group 1's nominations—this was the first time FIFA used the
word "group" to signify opening-round matches—included the Soviet Union (gold medal in 1956) and Yugoslavia (silver medals in 1952
and 1956), who enjoyed great success at the 2 most recent Olympics.

West Germany and Chile emerged as the top 2 countries from
Group 2, but not before the hosts took on Italy in what turned into the
battle of Santiago. Tempers started to boil over before the opening
kickoff as Italian journalists criticized the living and playing conditions in Chile. Referee Ken Aston threw out Italian Giorgio Ferrini for
a retaliation foul, but it was the call Aston did not make that made this
a game to forget. With about 5 minutes before halftime, Leonel
Sanchez, after he was taken down by Humberto Maschio, broke the
Italian's nose with a punch that everyone in the stadium and those

watching on TV had seen—everyone but Aston. Sanchez was not ejected. And oh yes, Chile went on to record a 2−0 victory.

From Group 4 came Hungary and England, which defeated a disappointing Argentina, 3−1, on goals by Ronald Flowers, Bobby Charlton and Jimmy Greaves. Chile should have been a home-field advantage for the Argentines.

Sanchez, who scored 2 goals in Chile's opening victory over Switzerland, proved that he could play some soccer, too, connecting for the first goal in a 2−1 victory over the Soviets in the quarterfinals (Eladio Rojas had the other goal). Yugoslavia avenged a pair of defeats to West Germany in the 2 previous quarterfinals with a 1−0 win behind Peter Radakovic's goal in the 87th minute. The Czechs outlasted Hungary thanks to an early score by Adolf Scherer. Brazil? No problem, as the South Americans bounced the English with a 3−1 win as Garrincha, in the middle of another outstanding tournament, scored twice, and Vava once.

The Brazilians continued their sterling play in the semifinals, disposing of Chile, 4−2, as Garrincha struck twice in the opening half and Vava duplicated the feat in the final 45 minutes. Garrincha was ejected for kicking Rojas, worrying Brazilian officials that the talented winger might have to sit out the final. The Czechs scored 3 times in the second half—Scherer had two and Josef Kadraba 1—in a 3−1 victory over Yugoslavia to set up another confrontration between the Group 3 rivals.

The Final

The Brazilians scored an important victory a couple of days before the match was played, when FIFA officials determined that Garrincha could play. The 6 other players who were sent off during the cup were hit with a one-match ban. Garrincha received but a reprimand. As it turned out, he had a relatively quiet match, but there were others who stepped up to fill the breach.

First, however, the Czechs struck in the 15th minute on a goal by Masopust, who converted a long pass from Schrer. The Brazilians weren't jolted. After all, in 4 of the last 6 final matches, the eventual winner had to rally from a 1-0 deficit. They equalized only 2 minutes later as Amarildo scored from a difficult angle. The score remained that way until the 68th minute, when Zito headed in an Amarildo cross. Vava then took advantage of a mistake by goalkeeper Viliam Schroif, who fumbled a pass from Djalma Santos in the penalty area with 13 minutes left and scored.

In perhaps the ultimate display of teamwork, no Brazilian player

scored more than 4 goals—Garrincha and Vava finished with 4 apiece. Amarildo chipped in with 3, and Zagalo, Pele and Zito had one each.

The Czechs themselves made history by becoming the first European team to play in a World Cup championship game in the Americas. They were followed by Italy (1970), Netherlands (1978) and West Germany (1986).

> Brazil 3, Czechoslovakia 1
> Estadio Nacional
> Santiago, Chile
> June 17, 1962
> Brazil: Gilmar, D. Santos, N. Santos, Zito, Mauro, Zozimo, Garrincha, Didi, Vava, Amarildo, Zagalo
> Czechoslovakia: Schroif, Tichy, Novak, Pluskal, Popluhar, Masopust, Posichal, Scherer, Kvasniak, Kadraba, Jelinek
> Goals: Masopust (C) 15, Amarildo (B) 17, Zito (B) 68, Vava (B) 77
> Referee: Latishev (Soviet Union)
> Attendance: 68,679

1966
Host England overcomes controversial goal

Finally, after 16 years of trying, England ruled the World Cup roost, winning at the crown jewel of soccer—Wembley Stadium.

In contrast to the controversial and exciting eventual final, the cup hardly got off to an auspicious start as England played Uruguay to a scoreless tie in a Group 1 match at Wembley. Still, those 2 teams qualified for the quarterfinals. The English, coached by Alf Ramsey, who was soon to be knighted Sir Alf Ramsey for his World Cup success, had assembled one of their greatest teams. That side included captain and defender Bobby Moore, midfielder and schemer Bobby Charlton, (his brother, Jack Charlton, will coach Ireland in the 1994 World Cup,) a crafty winger in Alan Ball, forward Geoff Hurst and a sure-handed goalkeeper in Gordon Banks.

After the draw, England began to build its momentum, as Bobby Charlton and Roger Hunt scored in a 2–0 triumph over Mexico—no, Mexico's Carbajal was not in the nets for this encounter, Gonzalez Calderon was. (Carbajal played in the 0–0 draw with Uruguay to make it five consecutive World Cups). The hosts added another 2-0 victory as Hunt found the back of the net twice.

The eventual finalists, Germany, sparked by the overall play of sweeper Franz Beckenbauer, won Group 2 by goal differential over Argentina after both sides played to a scoreless tie. In their first match,

the West Germans got off on the right foot with a 5−0 triumph over Switzerland—Beckenbauer and Helmut Haller led the way with 2 goals apiece, and Siegfried Held had 1. Uwe Seeler, performing in his third World Cup, sealed the 2−1 victory over Spain with a goal with only six minutes remaining.

Two-time defending champion Brazil really could never get going in Group 3. The Brazilians defeated Bulgaria, 2−0, in their first Group 3 match, but it was a pyrrhic victory because defender Zhechev put Pele on the sidelines for the next encounter with Hungary with a leg injury. Without Pele, Hungary beat Brazil, 3−1. Pele returned against Portugal, but he was brought down by 2 vicious tackles early on to set the tone of the match. Eusebio, the Portuguese star who had only 1 goal in the first 2 matches, created the first goal and scored the last 2 in a 3−1 win. Portugal booked a spot in the quarterfinals, Brazil, incredibly, did not.

It was in Group 4, however, in which the most intriguing result was produced. The Soviet Union had little trouble advancing, blanking newcomer North Korea, 3−0, and Italy, 1−0, and edging Chile, 2−1. The quest for second place came down to North Korea and the heavily favored Italians. The Korean forwards proved to be too quick for the slow Italian defense. Italy was reduced to 10 players because Giacomo Bulgarelli injured his knee (substitutions were allowed in 1970) in the 34th minute. Only 4 minutes before halftime, the Koreans took advantage of the defensive liabilities as Pak Doo-ik scored. They made the lead hold up for one of the greatest upsets in history.

The North Koreans were ready to make it 2 straight stunners in the quarterfinals, rolling to a 3−0 lead over Portugal 22 minutes into the match. Pak Seung-zin, Dong-woon and Seung-kook scored for the Asians, but Eusebio took charge to slice the margin to 3−2 at the half with goals in the 27th and 42nd minutes, the later a penalty kick (he finished the tournament with 4 penalty kicks). Eusebio equalized from point-blank range in the 55th minute, and the Koreans were never the same. Three minutes later he struck again from the penalty spot for a 4−3 advantage after he was fouled following a brilliant individual run. And as if to show he wasn't selfish, Eusebio's corner kick set up Augusto's goal, an insurance score in the 78th minute in a 5−3 win.

The other quarterfinals were anticlimatic. England got past Argentina on Hurst's goal in the 78th minute in a match that was held up for several minutes because Argentine Antonio Rattin refused to leave the field after he was ejected. Four players—Held, Beckenbauer,

Seeler and Haller—tallied in West Germany's 4–0 win over Uruguay, and the Soviets outlasted Hungary, 2–1.

The West Germans grabbed a 2–0 lead behind Haller and Beckenbauer to reach the finals with a 2-1 victory over the Soviet Union, and England overcame Portugal and Eusebio (he converted yet another penalty kick, and had another penalty in the 2-1 triumph over the Soviets in the consolation match) in a 2–1 win as Bobby Charlton scored in each half before a packed house at Wembley.

It was a match that had everything—lead changes, last-minute heroics and controversial goals. In the end, England had emerged with a 4–2 extra-time victory and its trophy, although the West Germans weren't entirely convinced of that, especially after what transpired in overtime.

The Final

Haller gave the Germans a 1–0 lead in the 13th minute, but Hurst countered 6 minutes later. The score remained tied at 1–1 until Martin Peters lifted the English a 2–1 edge in the 78th minute. As time was running out, Wolfgang Weber put one past goalkeeper Gordon Banks for a 2–2 deadlock.

Eleven minutes into the first extra session, Hurst scored one of the most controversial goals in history, firing a shot that bounded off the crossbar and into the goal. Did the goal cross the line or didn't it? Linesman Tofik Bakhramov of the Soviet Union said yes, much to the chagrin of the Germans. Hurst added an insurance tally in the final minute to become the only player to score 3 goals in a championship game.

England 4, West Germany 2 (OT)
Wembley Stadium
London, England
July 30, 1966
England: Banks, Cohen, Wilson, Stiles, J. Charlton, Moore, Ball,
     Hurst, B. Charlton, Hunt, Peters
West Germany: Tilkowski, Hottges, Schnellinger, Beckenbauer,
     Schulz, Weber, Haller, Seeler, Held, Overath, Emmerich
Goals: Haller (WG) 12, Hurst (E) 18, Peters (E) 78, Weber (WG)
     90, Hurst (E) 101, Hurst (E) 120
Referee: Dienst (Switzerland)
Attendance: 96,924

Returning to their own backyard, the revitalized Brazilians dominated the tournament, winning all six matches while outscoring their opponents, 19–6, to complete their amazing run by becoming the first nation to win three World Cups, retiring the Jules Rimet Trophy.

Pele, allowed to play without the close marking, took center stage once again in the world spotlight. He finished with "only" 4 goals, but his presence in the lineup opened things up for his teammates, particularly Jairzinho, who scored 7 goals.

In what was becoming an unwanted tradition, the opening match of the cup was another boring, scoreless tie. This time Mexico and the Soviet Union were the guilty parties. As it turned out, both teams made it out of Group 1, which was no mean feat for the Mexicans, who entered the tournament having only won World Cup game in 17 tries (1–13–3). The Mexicans' 4–0 triumph over El Salvador was marred by a controversial officiating decision that led to the first goal. As time was running out in the first half, referee Ali Kandil of Egypt whistled a foul on a Mexican player. But Mexico's Gutierrez Padilla took the kick and passed to Huerta Valdiva, who scored. Kandil incredibly allowed the goal to stand. El Salvador goalkeeper Monzon Magana refused to take the ball from the back of the net, and Kandil had to bring it to the center spot.

Italy and Uruguay barely got out of Group 2 in one piece. The Italians (1-0-2) could win only once—a tough Israeli team played them to a 0–0 draw—and Uruguay squeaked past Sweden on goal differential.

Brazil and England had it a lot easier in Group 3. The Brazilians romped past Czechoslovakia, 4–1, on 3 second-half goals, 2 by Jairzinho and one by Pele. The play of the match turned out not to be a goal. Noticing that Czech goalkeeper Ivo Viktor was out of the nets late in the first half, Pele, some 60 yards away, lobbed the ball towards the unattended goal. The ball bounced only inches wide of the post. In a match better-suited for the later rounds, Brazil edged England, 1–0, on Jairzinho's goal in the 59th minute. But like their opening match, this encounter is better remembered for a goal that Pele did not score as goalkeeper Gordon Banks produced one of the greatest saves in soccer history. Standing at the far post, Banks managed to leap toward the opposite corner of the net knock away Pele's head shot. The Brazilians then defeated Romania, 3–2, as Pele struck twice and Jairzinho once to make it 3 games in a row, but the Europeans exposed some weaknesses in the Brazilian defense.

Group 4 was dominated by Gerd Mueller and the West Germans,

who stormed to 3 consecutive victories. Mueller was lethal from the opening match, scoring with 12 minutes left to give the Germans a 2–1 comeback victory over Morocco, which had taken a 1–0 halftime lead on a score by Houmane Jarir. Incidentally, Morocco did not have a full complement of players for the start of the second half and had no one in goal—goalkeeper Allal Ben Kassu was in the locker room—for about a minute. The Moroccan coach complained that referee Laurens Van Ravens of the Netherlands did not notify his players in the locker room that the second half was to begin. The Germans proved they did not need any outside help as Mueller registered a hat-trick in a 5–2 triumph over Bulgaria. Mueller finished off his incredible opening round—a record 7 goals in 3 matches—with yet another 3 goal performance in a 3–1 win over Peru, which had a goal from Nene Cubillas (four first-round goals).

In a rematch of the 1966 championship game, it took Mueller some 108 minutes to connect against England in the quarterfinals, scoring the game-winner in a 3–2 victory. The English were forced to play Peter Bonetti in the nets after Banks woke up with an upset stomach the day of the match. Alan Mullery struck first for the English in the 31st minute, and Martin Peters made it 2–0. But the Germans, who had become adept at comebacks (see the 1954 final), staged another memorable one. Coach Helmut Schoen started the wheels turning by inserting Juergen Grabowski into the match for Reinhard Libuda in the second half against the tiring English. Beckenbauer cut the lead to one with a shot from the edge of the penalty area and Seeler leveled the score at 2–2, heading the ball past Bonetti. Mueller, who had been relatively silent for most of the match, came to life in extra time, volleying in a Johannes Loehr feed from point-blank range for the win.

Uruguay got past the Soviets behind substitute Victor Esparrago's goal with time running out in extra time in a 1–0 win. The Brazilians continued to roll, besting Peru and Cubillas (his fifth goal), 4–2, as Tostao was the hero this time with two goals. Rivellino and Jairzinho also scored.

The match was Brazilians' fifth consecutive at Jaslisco Stadium in Guadalajara, where they were seeded, and they felt right at home. In fact, Uruguay complained to FIFA about an unfair home-field advantage, but the governing body did not take it seriously. They were just following the schedule. The Brazilians had forged a reputation as being a strong second-half team, scoring goals to break close games open, and this match was no exception. After the teams traded goals in the opening 45 minutes, Clodoaldo for Brazil, Luis Cubilla for the visitors, err, Uruguay, the Brazilians took command. Jairzinho scored in the 76th minute and Rivellino added an insurance tally off a Pele pass in the 89th.

The Italians earned a place in the final the hard way; they earned it in a wild, 4–3 victory over the Germans that included 5 goals in 30 minutes of overtime. They struck in the seventh minute as Roberto Boninsegna put home a rebound. Germany tied it as Karl-Heinz Schnellinger knocked in a cross seven minutes from time. Mueller, again silent in regulation took advantage of a defensive error for a 2–1 German lead 5 minutes into overtime. Italy, however, came back as Giovanni Rivera put in a free kick and Riva scored for a 3–2 advantage after the first extra period. With 10 minutes remaining in the second session, Mueller struck again—his 10th goal of the cup—for a 3–3 tie. Barely a minute later, however, Boninsegna set up Rivera, who scored for a 4–3 lead and eventually the win as the Italians had qualified for their first final since 1938.

It was Brazil's first game other than Guadalajara, but nothing could stop the South Americans in Azteca Stadium.

The Final

Predictably, the halftime score was 1–1. Pele, most appropriately, scored Brazil's 100th World Cup goal after 18 minutes, heading in a Rivellino feed. He also became only the second player to score goals in 2 championship matches (he did it in 1958), emulating former teammate Vava's feat in 1958 and 1962. The Italians equalized in the 37th minute as Boninsegna took advantage of a defensive error.

The Brazilians revved things up in the second half as Gerson put Brazil into the lead in the 65th minute. Five minutes later Jairzinho made cup history with a goal and a 3–1 lead as he became the first player to score in every match in every round including the final. Brazilian Captain Carlos Alberto closed out the scoring 4 minutes from time as his teammates retired the Jules Rimet Trophy to their confederation offices as the first country to win the cup 3 times. Brazilian coach Mario Zagalo also made history, becoming the first participant to win as a player (1958) and coach.

No one realized it at the time, but it was the last time Brazil would reach the finals of the World Cup.

Brazil 4, Itally 1
Azteca Stadium
Mexico City, Mexico
June 30, 1970
Brazil: Felix, Alberto, Everaldo, Clodoaldo, Brito, Piazza, Jairz-
    inho, Gerson, Tostao, Pele, Rivellino
Italy: Albertosi, Burgnich, Facchetti, Bertini (Juliano, 73), Ro-
    sato, Cera, Domenghini, Mazzola, Boninsegna (Rivera, 84), De
    Sisti, Riva
Goals: Pele (B) 18, Boninsegna (I) 37, Gerson (B) 65, Jainzinho
    (B) 70, Alberto (B) 86
Referee: Gloeckner (East Germany)
Attendance: 107,412

**1974
West Germans Are
the Best at Home**

After two close calls, West Germany finally had the opportunity to win the cup, even if there was a new trophy. With the Jules Rimet Trophy retired, a new trophy was unveiled—the FIFA World Cup. There were only a handful of players leftover from the 1966 and 1970 teams—Franz Beckenbauer, goalkeeper Sepp Maier, Gerd Mueller and Juergen Grabowski. But the Germans would be a tough side to beat.

They started out slowly, showing very little in a 1–0 victory over Chile as defender Paul Breitner scored. They improved with a 3–0 triumph over Australia behind goals by Wolfgang Overath, Bernhard Cullman and Mueller. But in the most political of battles on the field, the West Germans could not overcome their Eastern counterparts, dropping a 1–0 decision in the first meeting between those two rivals, in Hamburg. Not surprisingly, tight security surrounded the match and only 3,000 East German fans were allowed to cross the border. The West Germans already were assured of a spot in the quarterfinals, but the East Germans needed a point—a draw—to advance. They got more than they bargained for, a 1–0 victory, as Juergen Sparwasser scored the lone goal in the 80th minute.

Defending champion Brazil could never find the magic of its triumph 4 years earlier. Perhaps it was because the great Pele had retired from international soccer. Perhaps it was because a generation of players, including Tostao and Gerson, could not be replaced so quickly. Or perhaps it was because they played a more defensive instead of creative style. In the opening match of the World Cup, the Brazilians wound up with a scoreless draw with Yugoslavia. They added yet another 0–0 tie against Scotland—which has never qualifed

for the second round of a World Cup in seven tries—before securing a place in the quarterfinals with a 3–0 win over Zaire. Brazil, which finished in a second-place tie with Scotland, advanced because it had a better goal differential (3 to 2).

While 2 stalwarts struggled early on, there was a new light—the extremely talented Netherlands. Led by Johan Cruyff, Johan Neeskens, Rudi Krol, Wim Rijsbergen and Robbie Rensenbrink, the Dutch, who were participating in their first cup since 1934, played a style called Total Football, or Total Soccer. That meant any player could become an attacker or a defender. En route to the Group 3 crown, the Dutch showed the world what the style was all about. They stopped a vicious Uruguayan side, 2–0, as Johnny Rep scored a goal in each half. They were held to a scoreless tie by a defensive-minded Swedish team that also would qualify for the quarterfinals And they took Bulgaria apart, 4–1, as Cruyff dominated the match. Neeskens converted 2 penalty kicks and Rep and Theodorus de Jong added goals.

In Group 4, Poland and Argentina qualifed, leaving Italy out in the cold after reaching the finals in 1970. The Poles, in the midst of Olympic domination behind the likes of Grezegorz Lato, Kaz Deyna and Robert Gadocha, won the group, edging Argentina, 3–2, as Lato struck twice, routing Haiti, 7–0, as Andrezej Szarmach netted a hat-trick and Lato added two more, and getting past Italy, 2–1, behind Smarzach and Deyna. The Italians had their problems. In their first match, Haitian forward Manny Sanon, who would go on to play for the San Diego Sockers (North American Soccer League), predicted he would score 2 goals against the slow Italian defense. He connected a minute into the second half to break goalkeeper Dino Zoff'interna-tional goalless streak at 1,142 minutes. Sanon was only half right, not scoring again in a 3–1 Italian victory. Italy, however, could never get it together, playing Argentina to a 1–1 draw and losing to Poland. The Haitians, playing in their first cup, also had their problems. Defender Ernst Jean-Joseph was discovered to have taken illegal drugs and was thrown out of the cup. He returned home in disgrace, although he went on to play for the Chicago Sting (NASL).

Instead of a single-elimination in the quarterfinals, the 8 remaining countries were placed in 2 groups of 4 teams apiece. The winners of each group would advance to the final, changing the strategy of teams from winning outright to accruing points. It all but killed the drama of the knockout rounds. The Netherlands dominated Group A, winning its 3 matches. Cruyff masterminded the 4–0 demolition of Argentina with 2 goals, with Krol and Rep adding 1 apiece. Cruyff was marked out of the East German encounter by Konrad Weise, as the scoring responsibilities fell to Neeskens and Rensenbrink in a 2−0 triumph. Needing but a tie against Brazil, the Dutch recorded a 2−0 victory as Neeskens and Cruyff scored.

West Germany, whose second-place finish to the East Germans, meant an easier group, also won their 3 matches. The Germans shut down Yugoslavia, 2−0, behind Breitner and Mueller. They rallied from a 1−0 deficit against Sweden and registered a 4−2 win as Overath, Rainder Bonhof, Grabowski and Uli Hoeness shared the scoring load. And they stopped the Poles, 1−0, on a muddy field as Mueller tallied, to set up a classic confrontation between 2 European sides in the final.

The game did not get off to a promising start as the game officials   **The Final** noticed that the corner flags were missingso the opening kickoff was delayed as they were placed at their proper spots. With the match barely a minute old, referee Jack Taylor of England awarded the Dutch a penalty kick after Cruyff had been brought down in the penalty area. Neeskens converted for a 1−0 lead. The Germans equalized on a penalty of their own in the 25th minute. Bernd Holzenbein was fouled by Wim Jansen, and Breitner converted. Mueller scored the game-winner with 2 minutes remaining in the first half, putting in a Bonhof pass. It was Mueller's fourth goal of the cup and 14th of his World Cup career, surpassing the total of 13 held by Frenchman Just Fontaine.

It also was the last goal of the match. In the second half, the Germans managed to shut down the great Cruyff, who was given a yellow card in frustration to the close marking. And thanks to injuries to Rensenbrink and Rijsbergen, they held on for their second title. The championship completed a unique hat-trick for Overath. He was on the squad that finished second in 1966 and third in 1970.

West Germany 2, Netherlands 1
Olympic Stadium
Munich, West Germany
July 7, 1974
West Germany: Maier, Beckenbauer, Vogts, Breitner, Schwarzenbeck, Overath, Bonhof, Hoeness, Grabowski, Mueller, Holzenbein
Netherlands: Jongbloed, Suurbier, Rijsbergen (De Jong, 58), Krol, Haan, Jansen, Van Hanegem, Neeskens, Rep, Cruyff, Rensenbrink (R. Van de Kerkhof, 46)
Goals: Neeskens (N) 1, Breitner (WG) 25 PK, Mueller (WG) 43
Referee: Taylor (England)
Attendance: 77,833

Despite political unrest and raging inflation, the 1978 World Cup
With soccer lightweights Tunisia and Mexico in Group 2, Poland
and West Germany had few problems reaching the next round—that
round-robin second round. In fact, the 2 sides played in the tournament
opener. On paper, it looked like a superb matchup between the defending champions and third-place finishers. On the field, it was yet another
dreary scoreless tie. The crowd booed the fourth consecutive scoreless
tie that opened a World Cup. The Germans, who missed Franz Beckenbauer who decided to keep playing with the Cosmos (North American Soccer League), did post a 6−0 victory over Mexico, but played
Tunisia to a 0−0 draw. Poland, with most of its 1974 squad intact,
rebounded with a 1−0 win over Tunisia and a 3-1 triumph over
Mexico.

Brazil, with Rivellino as the only surviving member of the 1970
championship team, did not demonstrate the flair that made it the most
imposing soccer team in the world. The Brazilians reached the next
round on points—a 1−1 tie with Sweden, a scoreless draw with Spain
and a 1−0 win over Austria, which won Group 3—and not by merit.

The Dutch, who did not have Cruyff this time to drive opposing
defenses crazy, still were a formidable bunch. They started out slowly
with a 1−1−1 record, which was good enough to advance behind a
2−0−1 Peruvian side led by Nene Cubillas, who became the first
player to score 5 or more goals in 2 separate cups. Robbie Rensenbrink
converted 2 penalties in the 3−0 win over Iran, which was followed by
a 0−0 draw with Peru and a 3−2 loss to Scotland.

The Netherlands survived Group A (the second round) with a
2−0−1 mark. The Dutch treated themselves to a 5−1 triumph over
Austria as Rep struck twice. They played West Germany to a 2−2 tie
the Germans already had drawn Italy, 0−0 and edged Italy, 2-1, as
Ernie Brandts, making amends for a 19th-minute own goal, and Arend
Haan scored in the second half to rally from a 1-0 halftime deficit.
Haan's goal was considered to be the goal of the tournament as he beat
Dino Zoff from 30 yards. Argentina barely got past Brazil on goal
differential (8 to 5). The hosts blanked Poland, 2−0, and played Brazil
to a scoreless tie. The Brazilians downed Peru, 3−0. Entering the final
day of the competition, both sides were tied in points, but Brazil
enjoyed a better goal differential, 3 to 2. Brazil beat Poland, 3−1, as
Roberto scored twice. Argentina, realizing it needed a big victory,
routed Peru, 6−0, as Kempes and Luque had 2 goals apiece. The 6-goal
margin was enough to boost the Argentines into the final, sparking

speculation that Peru laid down or was paid off. It was never proved, although a number of theories have surfaced through the years.

The Final

The championship game, which was televised in 90 countries, including the United States, pit two countries—Argentina and the Netherlands—which had never won a World Cup crown, the first time since 1958 that situation had occurred.

The Argentines came out and attacked, while the Dutch employed physical tactics. The ploy worked for the hosts as Mario Kempes, scored in the 37th minute. Dick Nanninga, who had boasted to the media before the match that he would score a goal as a substitute in the final, did so. He replaced Rep in the 58th minute, and equalized after Rene van de Kerkhof beat an offside trap with 9 minutes remaining in regulation. Rensenbrink hit the post in the final minutes. Kempes turned out to be the hero. After beating 3 players, he lifted the Argentines into a 2-1 lead with his sixth goal of the tournament in the last minute of the first 15-minute overtime. Bertoni added an insurance tally 6 minutes from time.

> Argentina 3, Netherlands 1 (OT)
> Estadio Antonio Liberti Monumental
> Buenos Aires, Argentina
> June 25, 1978
> Argentina: Fillol, Olguin, Galvan, Passarella, Taratini, Ardiles (Larrosa, 65), Gallego, Kempes, Luque, Bertoni, Ortiz (Houseman, 77)
> Netherlands: Jongbloed, Jansen (Suurbier, 72), Brandts, Krol, Poortvliet, Haan, Neeskeens, W. van de Kerkhof, R. Van de Kerkhof, Rep (Nanninga, 58), Resenbrink
> Goals: Kempes (A) 37, Nanninga (N) 81, Kempes (A) 104, Bertoni (A) 114
> Referee: Gonella (Italy)
> Attendance: 77,260

**1982
Italians reign in
Spain**

There were changes afoot in FIFA and the World Cup. FIFA president Dr. Joao Havelange, who was elected with strong support by Third World countries in 1974, kept his promise by expanding the tournament from 16 to 24 teams. The idea was to open up the cup to the lesser soccer countries of the world. Because of that, a number of countries that might not have gotten to the world stage would have had an opportunity to show what they could do. Cameroon was impressive in the opening round, as was Algeria, which stunned Germany.

The 1982 World Cup, however, belonged to Italy—which started off as 14−1 long shots to win the trophy—although you would have not known the Italians were title contenders due its slow start in Group 1. The Italians wound up playing 3 first-round ties, scoring 2 goals and allowing as many. They showed absolutely nothing in a 0−0 draw with Poland, a 1−1 tie with Peru and a 1-1 result with Cameroon, which missed out on advancing to the second round because Italy had scored one more goal than the Africans.

The West Germans had their problems in Group 2, too, losing to the Algerians, 2−1 as Rabah Madjer and Lakhdar Belloumi, the African Player of the Year, scored for the winners, Karl-Heinz Rummenigge for the losers. The Germans rebounded with a 4−1 triumph over Chile with Rummenigge netting a hat-trick, setting up a disgraceful match with Austria. Germany needed a victory and Austria, at the worst, needed to lose by only a goal. After Horst Hrubesch scored in the 10th minute, both sides were content to hit the ball around midfield. Algeria finished unbeaten with 2 victories, but did not advance because of goal differential (Austria had plus 2, Algeria 0). Defending champion Argentina, playing in Group 3, never found its rhythm to be consistent. Bolstered by the latest superstar pretender to Pele's throne—Diego Maradona—the Argentines stumbled in the World Cup opener as Belgium recorded a 1−0 win on Erwin Vandenbergh's second-half goal. Argentina did rebound in the first round with a 4−1 victory over Hungary and a 2−0 win over El Salvador. It seemed that everyone fed on cup newcomer El Salvador. For example, Hungary rolled to a 10−1 victory as second-half substitute Laszlo Kiss recorded a hat-trick, the best performance by a sub in World Cup history.

England, surprisingly, ruled Group 4, which included France. In fact, the English took care of the French in their first match, 3−1, as Bryan Robson scored the quickest goal in cup history—27 seconds into the match. He added another in the second half, and Paul Mariner also tallied. England finished at 3−0, defeating Czechoslovakia, 2−0, and edging Kuwait, 1−0. France, which took second at 1−1−1, played one of the more unusual matches in cup history against Kuwait, a 4−1 victory. The commotion came with the game all but decided and with the French leading 3−1 with 15 minutes left. Alain Giresse put in a free kick to give his team a 4−1 advantage, or so he thought. The Kuwaitis claimed they had heard a whistle and stopped in their tracks. Prince Fahid, the country's Football Association president, walked from the stands onto the field to protest and argue the decision, which was reserved. France did get an official fourth goal as Maxime Bossis scored in the final minute.

Even though it was host, Spain struggled in Group 5 to reach the next round, tying Honduras, 1–1, edging Yugoslavia, 2–1, and losing to group leader Northern Ireland, 1–0. Criticism was so severe that one Spanish newspaper refused to publish the team's lineup after one match.

In Group 6, it looked like Brazil had rediscovered the magic it had during its 3 world championship run, outscoring the opposition, 10–2, en route to 3 impressive victories. The Brazilians started it off with a 2–1 win over the Soviet Union, with Socrates and Eder scoring. They continued it with a 4–1 thumping of Scotland, as Zico, Oscar, Eder and Falcao found the back of the net. And they completed it with a 4–0 romp past World Cup newcomers New Zealand, 4–0, as Zico tallied twice and Falcao and Serginho once each.

In a new twist to the later rounds, 4 second-round groups were used to determine the 4 semifinalists.

In Group A, Poland prevailed, blanking Belgium 3–0, and playing the Soviets to a scoreless draw after the Soviet Union bested Belgium, 1–0. In Group B, the West Germans emerged on top, playing England to a scoreless draw, but edging Spain, 2–1, on goals by Pierre Littbarski and Klaus Fischer. England and Spain eliminated themselves with a 0–0 tie. Group C brought together Italy, Argentina and Brazil: Italy got past the defending champs, 2–1, as Marco Tardelli and Antonio Cabrini scored in the second half. Maradona, who was closely marked by the Italians, vented his frustration and anger in a 3–1 loss to Brazil several days later. He kicked Batista's groin in the waning minutes and was subsequently ejected by referee Mario Rubio Vazquez of Mexico. Brazil, meanwhile, was brilliant as ever, getting goals from Zico, Serginho and Junior to set up a memorable encounter with Italy. Paolo Rossi, who had recently come back from a 2-year suspension because of his involvement in a game-fixing scandal, was blanked during the opening round. But he could not have picked a better place to break out of scoring slump. He was brilliant, scoring 3 times — in the fifth, 25th and 75th minutes against Brazil, which had goals from Socrates and Falcao. The victory boosted the Italians into the semifinals.

In Group D, France advanced on the basis of its 1–0 win over Austria and 4–1 triumph over Northern Ireland. Austria tied Northern Ireland, 2–2.

Rossi was as hot as the weather — 100 degrees at Nou Camp

Stadium in Barcelona, striking twice in the Italians' 2–0 semifinal win over Poland. And as well as Rossi and his teammates played, their game was anticlimatic compared to the tussle between West Germany and France. The West Germans managed to outlast their rivals, 5–4, in penalty kicks after playing to a 3–3 tie after extra-time in what many observers called the greatest World Cup game ever. The Germans took a 1-0 lead in the 18th minute on Littbarski's goal, but the French tied in on Michel Platini's penalty kick 9 minutes later. In the 57th minute, the game turned on a controversial play. Racing toward the German penalty area, Patrick Battiston was knocked down by goalkeeper Toni Schumacher. Battison was so badly injured, he was replaced. Schumacher, who should have received a yellow card at the very least, and perhaps a red card, did not and remained in the game. So, the Germans were able to play at even strength into extra-time. The French scored twice behind Marius Tresor and Alain Giresse. It appeared the Germans were dead, but they somehow rallied as substitute Karl-Heinz Rummenigge, who had been bothered by a leg injury and Klaus Fischer scored. That set up penalty kicks. With the tie-breaker score at 4–4, Schumacher saved Jean-Luc Bossis' try and Horst Hrubesch converted the game-winner.

The Final

Unless you were a West German fan, the entire world knew what was going to happen at Santiago Bernabeu Stadium in Madrid on July 11—an Italian victory to end a storybook tournament. It appeared the horse-drawn carriage would turn into a pumpkin in the 25th minute, as Antonio Cabrini became the first player to miss a penalty kick in a World Cup final.

The score was 0–0 at the half, and the Germans thought they still had a chance—or so they thought. Rossi found the back of the net one last time with his sixth goal of the tournament, heading the ball past Schumacher in the 57th minute. Marco Tardelli doubled the lead 11 minutes later, scoring from the edge of the penalty area, and Alessandro Altobelli, who came in for Francesco Graziani, made it 3-0 in the 81st minute. Paul Breitner became only the third player to score in 2 finals—Brazil's Vava and Pele also accomplished the feat—2 minutes later, but it was too little and too late to beat this team of destiny.

Italy 3, West Germany 1
Santiago Bernabeu Stadium
Madrid, Spain
July 11, 1982
Italy: Zoff, Scirea, Gentile, Cabrini, Collovati, Bergomi, Tardelli,
   Oriali, Conti, Rossi, Graziani (Altobelli, 8, Causio, 89)
West Germany: Schumacher, Stielike, Katz, Briegel, K.H. Foer-
   ster, B. Foerster, Breitner, Dremmler (Hrubesch, 61), Littbarski,
   Fischer, Rummenigge (Mueller, 69)
Goals: Rossi (I) 57, Tardelli (I) 68, Altobelli (I) 81, Breitner (WG)
   83
Referee: Coehlo (Brazil)
Attendance: 90,080

Diego Maradona dominated this tournament, from start to finish, and although he did not score a goal in the final game, he managed to set up the game-winner with a brilliant, yet simple pass in the waning minutes.

1986
Diego, Argentines dominate in Mexico

The tournament originally was scheduled to be played in Colombia, but with the World Cup expanded from 16 to 24 teams and mounting financial problems at home, Colombia admitted that it did not have enough money or stadiums to organize properly such an enormous event. So, only 3 years before the kickoff—countries usually need 6 years to organize this Herculean effort—Mexico was awarded the cup, becoming the first country to host the World Cup twice.

To complicate matters, only 8 months before the cup, a massive earthquake hit Mexico and Mexico City, killing 25,000 people and destroying or damaging thousands of structures. Despite this horrible disaster, Mexico rebuilt itself and the show went on and what a show Maradona put on.

Even though the cup started with yet another tie—a 1–1 draw between defending champion Italy and Bulgaria—it wasn't a bad game. In fact, the Bulgarian team, which was stuck in a traffic jam on the way to Azteca Stadium, managed to tie the match on a goal by Nasko Sirakov with 5 minutes left after Alessandro Altobelli scored in the 43rd minute. Altobelli, incidentally, scored the final goal for Italy in the 1982 cup.

Maradona showed his brilliance from Argentina's opening match, a 3–1 win over South Korea. He was punished with several fouls by the Asians, but every time he was knocked down within striking distance,

Maradona got even. Maradona's free kick rebounded off the Korean wall to himself, and he passed to Jorge Valdano, who scored. After another foul in the 17th minute, his free kick set up Oscar Ruggeri, who headed it home. And finally, his cross set up Valdano for an easy goal barely a minute into the second half. In Argentina's 1–1 tie with Italy, Maradona set up his team's lone goal on a magnificent long ball to Valdano. As if he realized he wasn't going to be needed in the 2–0 victory over Bulgaria, Maradona had a relatively silent game. He was saving his best for later.

Mexico, which underwent intensive training preparation and several world-wide tours a year before the competition under Yugoslav coach Bora Milutinovic, had some promising results at Azteca. The Mexicans defeated Belgium, destined to be in the Final Four, 2–1, scoring all their goals in the first half—by Fernando Quirarte and Hugo Sanchez. They also got past a tough Iraqi side, 1–0, on Quirarte's goal. Sandwiched between those 2 matches was an intriguing affair with Paraguay, a 1–1 draw, but it was one of the most exciting ties fans had ever seen. The Mexicans, who committed 45 of the game's 77 fouls, had taken a 1–0 halftime lead on a goal by Luis Flores. The Paraguayans equalized with 6 minutes left as former Cosmos forward J.C. Romero—now known as Romerito—headed in a goal. With barely a minute remaining, the hosts were given a chance to win when Sanchez appeared to have been taken down outside the penalty area, but referee George Courtney of England awarded a penalty. Sanchez, who had been appearing in soft drink commercial converting a penalty to the cheers of the crowd, took this one in reality and goalkeeper Roberto Fernandez knocked the ball off the post. Sanchez was jeered by the crowd.

France and the Soviet Union had the best of play and results in Group C. They tied, 1–1. The French, under the midfield leadership of Michel Platini, disposed of Canada, playing in its first World Cup under former Vancouver Whitecaps coach Tony Waiters, 1–0, and Hungary, 3–0. The Soviets, made up of players from mostly Dynamo Kiev, routed Hungary, 6–0, and blanked Canada, 2–0.

Brazil, based in Guadalajara in Group D, the site of its previous success in 1970, scored only 5 goals in 3 matches, but did not allow any. The Brazilians edged Spain, 1–0, on a goal by Socrates, who was a medical doctor when he wasn't playing soccer. The match was not without its controversies. The Brazilian national anthem wasn't played. Instead, *Song of the Flag*, a patriotic tune played at political gatherings, was used. Then, in the 58th minute, it appeared that the

Spanish had scored a goal when Michel's shot that hit the crossbar bounced into the goal, but referee Chris Bambridge of Australia did not signal a goal. Careca provided the only score in the second half, in a 1–0 win over Algeria, one of the Brazilians' most low-key performances. Their offense woke up against Northern Ireland, as Careca struck twice in a 3–0 victory on June 12. It turned out to be an emotional match for Northern Ireland goalkeeper Pat Jennings, who was celebrating his 41st birthday and final international game. After the match ended, both teams allowed Jennings to walk off the field by himself as he disappeared into the tunnel. The Brazilian players signed the game ball and gave it to the veteran keeper.

Group E, with World Cup veterans West Germany, Uruguay and Scotland and promising newcomer Denmark, was rightfully called the Group of Death. After the dust had cleared, the new kids on the block, Denmark won all three of its matches, with Germany finishing second at 1–1–1—a course, incidentally, that would avoid Argentina until the final. The Germans rallied on a late goal by Klaus Allofs to tie Uruguay, 1–1, got past Scotland, 2–1, on another second-half goal by Allofts and dropped a 2–1 decision to Denmark. The free-wheeling Danes—their nickname was Danish Dynamite—might have shot their wad in the opening round. They blanked Scotland, 1–0, rolled over Uruguay, 6–1, as Preben Elkjaer-Larsen recorded a hat-trick and beat Germany. In one of the more forgettable matches of the cup, Scotland and Uruguay played to a scoreless tie after Uruguayan Jose Batista was red-carded 53 seconds into the match after he fouled Gordon Strachan. The South Americans, who needed a tie to advance, had their game reduced to time-wasting tactics and brutal tackling.

Then there was Group F—the Group of Sleep—because the first 4 matches in Monterrey produced a total of 2 goals. For example: Morocco 0, Poland 0; Portugal 1, England 0; England 0, Morocco 0; Poland 1, Portugal 0. It was so bad that one player pleaded with fans to stay away from the stadiums. England, considered one of the world's powers, entered its vital, final match against Poland without 2 key players—injury-prone captain Bryan Robson with a dislocated shoulder and midfielder Ray Wilkins, who was ejected after throwing the ball at referee Gabriel Gonzalez for showing his disgust at a decision. Finally, on the final day of the group competition, at least 2 teams woke up as England posted a 3–0 win over Poland and Morocco defeated Portugal, 3–1, behind two goals by Abdelrazak Khairi to become the first African and Third World country to win a group.

The second round produced some memorable performances.

Manuel Negrete scored on a brilliant volley—newspapers called it the butterfly goal—and set up another in Mexico's 2–0 win over Bulgaria, which managed to advance without winning a match. In one of the great individual performances in a losing effort, Igor Belanov recorded a hat-trick in Belgium's 4–3 victory over the Soviet Union in extra time. Stephane Demol and Nico Claesen scored for the Belgians in OT, while Belanov netted his third. The Brazilians, who finally rediscovered their game, rolled past Poland, 4–0. Platini continued to show his magic, scoring one goal in France's 2–0 victory over a rather listless Italy, which did not use 1982 hero Paolo Rossi for a minute. The claim was that he was out-of-shape. But wasn't that the case 4 years earlier? In the first World Cup meeting between those 2 South American rivals since the 1930 championship game, Argentina edged Uruguay, 1–0, on a goal by Pedro Pasculi in a tight, defensive match that was played during a thunderstorm. Morocco showed that its first-round performance was no fluke, playing the West Germans tough, but the Europeans prevailed, 1–0, on Lothar Matthaeus' free-kick goal in the waning minutes.The Danes, who won over the crowd with their attack-minded performances in the first round, self-destructed against Spain, which scored 4 times in the second half as Emilio Butragueno—nicknamed the Vulture—finished with 4 goals in a 5–1 win. The beginning of the end for the Danes turned out to be an ill-advised pass in the penalty area in the 43rd minute by Jesper Olsen, who had scored earlier. Butragueno intercepted and scored. Gary Lineker scored twice and Peter Beardsley, who once played for the Vancouver Whitecaps (NASL) scored once in England's 3-0 win over Paraguay.

As if to top the previous round's results, 3 of the 4 quarterfinals turned out to be classics. It started with the France-Brazil match, which ended in a 1–1 draw after regulation (the second half was end-to-end action) and extra time. Careca had given the Brazilians the lead, but Platini equalized. It came down to penalty kicks, as Platini and Brazil's Julio Cesar missed theirs, setting up Luis Fernandez to become the hero by converting his. The Mexicans, playing far away from the friendly confines of Azteca and in the heat of Monterrey, managed to play West Germany even through 120 scoreless minutes. But nerves got to the hosts in penalties, as the Germans prevailed, 4–1, with Allofs, Andreas Brehme, Matthaeus and Pierre Littbarski recording their chances. Belgium also outlasted Spain, 5–4, in penalties, after playing to a 1–1 draw.

Back at Azteca, England and Argentina played for the first time since the Falkland Wars in 1982. But Maradona made certain no one would remember the Falklands in a 2−1 victory. Six minutes into the second half, Maradona had tried to play the ball into the penalty area, but English midfielder Steve Hodge outbattled the Argentine for the ball and lifted a backpass to goalkeeper Peter Shilton. Maradona and the keeper arrived at the same time and the Argentine knocked the ball into the net with his left hand. Despite protests by the English, referee Ali Bennaceur of Tunisia pointed to the center spot. Maradona later claimed "The Hand of God" scored that goal. As if to make amends, Maradona embarked on an amazing journey 4 minutes later. He took possession of the ball 10 yards in Argentine territory. He performed an 180-degree turn that left Peter Reid and Peter Beardsley standing in their tracks. He then raced down the right side into English territory past Ray Wilkins. Terry Fenwick tried to pull him down at the top of the penalty area, but Maradona shrugged him off. Shilton came out of the goal, committed himself and fell to the turf, 8 yards out. Terry Butcher tried a last-ditch effort with a sliding tackle under Maradona, who pushed the ball into the unattended net. Total time: 10 seconds. Number of touches: 9. Even his opponents were astonished by the performance. "Today he scored one of the most brilliant goals you'll ever see," England coach Bobby Robson said. "That first goal was dubious, the second goal a miracle. It was a fantastic goal. It's marvelous for football that every now and then the world produces a player like Maradona. I didn't like his second goal, but I did admire it."

It would be difficult to surpass his one-man show in the quarter-finals, but Maradona did his best in the semifinals, scoring twice in a 2−0 victory over Belgium. Though it was only a 30-yard jaunt, his second goal was reminiscent of his goal against England, as he raced around three defenders. In a rematch of the 1982 semifinals, West Germany took on France in Guadalajara, but the result was anticlimatic. It lacked the excitement of the Germans' comeback victory in OT. Brehme scored in the first half and Rudi Voeller tallied off a counterattack in a 2−0 German win that was known for the winners' tenacious defense that shut down Platini and held his teammates in check with tactical precision.

The Final   In front of the second largest crowd for a final, Argentina managed to overcome the Germans, who battled back from a 2-goal deficit with 17 minutes left.

The Argentines struck first, as Jorge Burruchaga's free kick set up Jose Luis Brown with a header goal in the 22nd minute. They doubled their lead on Valdano's goal in the 55th minute. Trailing by 2 goals, the

Germans were forced to open up their attack. It took a while, but they found the back of the net. First, Karl-Heinz Rummenigge headed home a corner kick by Brehme in the 73rd minute; it was the third consecutive tournament in which he had scored. The Germans equalized some 8 minutes later off another Brehme corner as Thomas Berthold headed the ball to second-half substitute Rudi Voeller, who scored.

As the match appeared to be heading for overtime, Maradona, who had been effectively marked out of the match, noticed Burruchaga alone at midfield. He blooped an innocent-looking pass to his teammate, who beat goalkeeper Toni Schumacher with seven minutes remaining. The Argentines held on for a 3−2 triumph, and Maradona was crowned player of the tournament.

Argentina 3, West Germany 2
Azteca Stadium
Mexico City, Mexico
June 29, 1986
Argentina: Pumpido, Cuciuffo,Olarticoechea, Ruggeri, Brown, Batista, Burruchaga (Trobbiani, 89), Giusti, Enrique, Maradona, Valdano
West Germany: Schumacher, Jackos, K.H. Foerster, Bethold, Briegel, Eder, Brehme, Matthaeus, Rummenigge, Magath (Hoeness, 61), Allofs (Voeller, 46)
Goals: Brown (A) 22, Valdano (A) 55, Rummenigge (WG) 73, Voeller (WG) 81, Burruchaga (A) 83
Referee: Filho (Brazil)
Attendance: 114,590

The less said about Italia '90 the better. Except for a handful of golden moments, the tournament brought out, on many occasions, the worst soccer had to offer—brutal defensive plays, gamesmanship and a new philosophy. You've heard of win at all costs? Coaches tried not to lose at all costs, many times content to play for a tie and take a chance with penalty kicks in the elimination rounds. The play was so conservative that the cup turned into the lowest-scoring World Cup ever—averaging 2.21 goals per match. The previous low was 2.53 in Mexico 4 years prior.

Through this mess emerged several encouraging signs, including a Cameroon team that showed the entire world how to play the game, a Cinderella performance by Italy's Salvatore Schillaci and another solid showing by the eventual champions, West Germany. The Germans,

1990
Germans Win a
Cup to Forget in
Italy

who enjoyed a sterling first-round performance, seemed to wear down a bit as the tournament progressed because of the opposition's conservative tactics.

The defending champion Argentines, led by an ailing Diego Maradona, were transformed into anti-heroes and became the masters of the-not lose-at-all-costs school. The fact they were able to reach the championship match without a superb performance—coach Carlos Bilardo masterfully used 20 players in and out of the lineup due to injuries and yellow and red card suspensions—was disturbing indeed, to top soccer officials. One of the most disturbing images that emerged from the cup was a disbelieving Maradona, with his hands extended out from his side, trying to convince the referee that a foul should have been called on an opposing player.

Fans got an inkling of what was to come in the opener in Milan by an aggressive Cameroon side that played open soccer while on attack, but a physical game when on defense. Cameroon players fouled Maradona 13 times in that encounter, as he never could regain the brilliance he had shown in Mexico. Only 5 minutes after Kana Biyik was ejected in the 60th minute in the scoreless game, his brother Francois Omam Biyik headed the ball past goalkeeper Nery Pumpido. With two minutes remaining, Ben Massing was red-carded as Cameroon finished the match with nine players.

It went from bad to worse in Argentina's 2−0 victory over the Soviet Union. Pedro Troglio and Jorge Burruchaga scored, but the real story transpired around the Argentine goal as the defending champions lost Pumpido to a fractured leg after colliding with Julio Olarticoechea. Sergio Goycochea, a relative unknown on the international scene who was destined for glory, replaced him. Several minutes later, it appeared the Soviets were about to score the first goal, but Maradona—the man who gave the world "The Hand of God" goal—knocked a certain goal by Oleg Kuznetsov out of harm's way with his hand. Referee Erik Fredriksson, who stood 10 feet from the incident, did not call anything. Argentina qualified for the second round after it played Romania to a 1−1 draw.

Cameroon, on the other hand, defeated Romania, 2−1, as 38-year-old substitute Roger Milla scored twice in the second half. Milla, who performed in the 1982 World Cup as a spritely 30-year-old, was coaxed out of semi-retirement to play for his country. When he tallied in the 76th minute, Milla became the oldest player to score in the cup. To top off this crazy group, the Soviet Union, which already had been eliminated, romped to a 4−0 win over Cameroon, as the Africans became the

first group winner to finish with a negative goal total (3 goals for, 5 against).

Italy's tough defense gave it a lock on the Group A title. The hosts scored but 4 goals—2 by Schillaci—but, more important, did not allow a goal. Although the Italians played some attractive soccer against Austria, they could not solve the defense, so Schillaci was inserted in place of Andrea Carnevale late in the game. Four minutes later, he scored the lone goal of the match. It looked like the Christians against the Lions when the Italians took on the United States, which suffered a humiliating 5–1 loss to Czechoslovakia in its first World Cup appearance in 40 years. The Americans, however, turned the Roman fans against the home team, playing a conservative match in a 1–0 Italian victory as Giuseppe Giannini scored. The hosts wrapped up a perfect opening round with a 2–0 win over the Czechs as Schillaci made good use of his first start with a goal. Roberto Baggio chipped in a goal.

The Americans' showing against the Czechs was nothing short of a disaster as the Europeans uncovered virtually every weakness of the U.S. team. Tomas Skuhravy, who would have a field day against teams from the Western Hemisphere, led the way with 2 goals. After an encouraging performance against Italy, the U.S. had one more chance to redeem itself, but managed to drop a 2–1 decision to Austria, despite enjoying a one-man advantage for most of the game.

Brazil, which deployed more of a defensive-oriented style, enjoyed similar results as the Italians in Group C, winning all 3 matches, scoring 4 goals and surrendering but one. Careca connected twice in a 2–1 victory over Sweden before the Brazilians recorded 1–0 wins over Costa Rica and Scotland as Muller scored both goals. The surprise team of the group was first-time qualifier Costa Rica, coached by Bora Milutinovic, who was hired some 90 days before the start of the competition. The Costa Ricans managed a 2-1-0 mark, upending cup veterans Sweden, 2–1, and Scotland, 1–0, to reach the next round. The Scots, incredibly, have never advanced to the second round in 7 appearances.

West Germany could have registered a perfect record in Group D had it not been for an 11th-hour lapse in its third match against Colombia. The Germans started off with a 4–1 triumph over Yugoslavia as captain Lothar Matthaeus netted 2 goals and Juergen Klinsmann and Rudi Voeller one apiece, and they continued their overwhelming performance with a 5–1 victory over the United Arab Emirates as Voeller led the way with 2 goals, followed by Klinsmann, Matthaeus and Uwe Bein. They scored in the 89th minute on a Pierre Littbarski goal, but the Colombians countered 2 minutes into injury time as Freddy Rincon scored off a superb pass by Carlos Valderrama, the man with the human fright wig.

Spain prevailed in Group E, as it played Uruguay to a scoreless tie, recorded a 3–1 win over South Korea, thanks to a Michel hat-trick, and then edged Belgium, 2–1 as Michel converted a penalty and Alberto Gorriz scored a goal. Perhaps the most dramatic moment of this group came in the worst match of the first round—Uruguay's 1–0 victory

A Perfect Finish to an Imperfect World Cup

Rome—In many respects, it was a perfect ending to an all-to-imperfect World Cup. West Germany's 1–0 victory over Argentina on July 8, 1990, had many of the elements that made Italia '90 one of the least exciting and the lowest-scoring of the 14 World Cups.

Consider the microcosm of the match:

It was the first World Cup final that saw an ejection—in fact, there were 2—in a tournament that set a record of 14 expulsions, twice more than the previous high.

It was the first World Cup final that so was poorly contested—Argentina took exactly one shot—that it needed a penalty kick by defender Andreas Brehme in the 84th minute to decide the match played before 73,603 spectators at Stadio Olympico and a worldwide television audience estimated at 1.5 billion.

It was a World Cup final that lacked a central figure, a star, until referee Edgardo Codesal of Mexico took center stage in the final 25 minutes, ejecting Pedro Monzon and Gustavo Dezotti and awarding a penalty kick.

And it was a World Cup final that ended the same way the tournament began exactly a month before on June 8—with a 1–0 Argentine loss—that time to Cameroon.

That's how disappointing it was.

Even West Germany coach Franz Beckenbauer admitted, "It wasn't a very good final."

But take nothing away from Germany, which proved it was the best team in the 24-country tournament and in the world by finishing with a 5–0–2 record. The only "blemishes" on its perfect record were a 1–1 first-round tie with Colombia and a 1–1 tie with England in the semi-finals that was decided by a tie-breaker won by the Germans. The Germans, who joined Brazil and Italy as 3-time World Cup winners, outscored their opposition, 15–5, rolling over Yugoslavia, 4–1, and the United Arab Emirates, 5–1, in the opening

over South Korea. Uruguay, which needed a victory to gain the second round, scored on a goal by sub Daniel Fonseca 2 minutes into injury time.

Group F was playfully called the "Hooligans Group" because of the rowdy and rambunctious fans of England and the Netherlands. It was too bad their energy was not transferred to the soccer field as only 7 goals were scored in 6 matches. The only result that was not a tie turned out to be England's 1–0 victory over Egypt, making its first World Cup appearance in more than 2 generations—56 years. The win

(A Perfect cont.)

round, defeated the Netherlands, 2–1, in the second round and shutting down Czechoslovakia, 1–0, in the quarterfinals.

"No team merited the title as much as the Germans," Beckenbauer said. "Today, for 90 minutes, there was no doubt as to who was going to win. There was never a feeling there was a danger to our goal. It was our game all the way."

Argentina? It had several ready-made excuses. The first was that 4 regulars missed the final, one because of a red card—midfielder Ricardo Giusti—and 3 others because of yellow-card accumulations—midfielders Sergio Batista and Julio Olarticochea and forward Claudio Caniggia. The second was that Diego Maradona, arguably the best soccer player in the world, had been hobbling around with a swolen ankle. With defender Gudio Buchwald shadowing him, Maradona was ineffective and a non-factor 4 years after he was the outstanding player of the World Cup in Mexico.

In fact, the Argentines played

for a scoreless tie in regulation and overtime in hope they might get luck in the penalty-kick tiebreaker. It did not get that far. "It was just too bad the Argentines didn't participate in the game," Beckenbauer said. "They wanted to destroy. They were too weak. It is too bad that happened in a final game."

It made for a boring game with only one team trying to score. While Argentine goalkeeper Sergio Goycochea was not severely tested, the Germans continued to pound away. German Rudi Voeller, who eventually was fouled to set up Brehme's penalty kick, started the attack off with a sliding shot 6 yards in front of the net that sailed over the crossbar in the third minute. Twenty minutes later, the hard-working Voeller headed a 12-yard shot wide right. And in the opening minute of the second half, Pierre Littbarski sent a 22-yard shot wide right of the net.

Argentina actually got within striking distance of the goal in the 38th minute when Buchwald tripped midfielder Jose Basualdo 20 yards out on the right side.

broke a logjam. Had England not won, all 4 teams would have been tied. As it was, Ireland, under coach Jack Charlton of England, finished second without winning a match, recording 3 ties—1–1 with the English, 0-0 with Egypt and 1–1 with the Netherlands. The Dutch, picked by many to win the World Cup crown behind the firepower of Marco van Basten, the European Player of the Year, and Ruud Gullit, hardly looked like potential champions, playing a 1–1 tie with Egypt and a scoreless draw with England.

The second round—called the round of 16 by FIFA for some

(A Perfect cont.)

Maradona stepped up to take the free kick, which sailed over the net and goalkeeper Bodo Illgner, who only touched the ball when a teammate passed it back. That was the extent of the Argentine offense.

"It was a very, very difficult match," Argentine Coach Carlos Bilardo said.

Despite the German attempts, it appeared the match was headed for overtime until Codesal red-carded forward Pedro Monzon in the 65th minute. It was a dubious call, at the least. Replays showed Monzon trying to knock Juergen Klinsmann down with hands, not his feet, hardly a capital offense. Despite protests, Monzon, who replaced Oscar Ruggeri at half-time, became the first player to be expelled in 60 years of cup finals.

Limited to 10 players, the Argentines went further into their shell until the Germans found an open door on the right side of the penalty area in the 82nd minute. That's when defender Roberto Sensini tripped Voeller and Codesal called a penalty. Brehme

then barely beat Goycochea to the lower left post for his third goal and a 1–0 German advantage in the 84th minute.

Incredibly, intstead of attacking, the Argentines resorted to even more foul play as Dezotti grabbed German defender Juergen Kohler by the neck 3 minutes later. Dezotti quickly became the second player sent off in a final in what turned into a shameful ending.

The Argentines were bitterly disappointed, so much so that they continued arguing with Codesal after the final whistle. Bilardo had to run onto the field to pull his players away from the referee. "I don't want to say anything about the referees," Bilardo said.

But Maradona, who cried openly afterwards, did. "Football is my work, my life," he said. "I didn't cry because of second place, but because the referee had not the right to blow that penalty against us."

So, the Germans became the second team to qualify for the 1994 World Cup, with the United States as the first as the host. And

reason—produced a couple of surprises or two. Milla magic continued for Cameroon as he came off the bench to score 2 more goals. The game-winner came in overtime as Colombian goalkeeper Rene Higuita, nicknamed the Merry Wanderer because of his forays into the offensive end, was caught some 10 yards out of his goal, and Milla had an easy goal and Cameroon an unlikely 2–1 win. Skuhravy continued to feast off of Western Hemisphere teams as he hit for a hat-trick—all headers—in a 4–1 triumph over Costa Rica. The Brazilians dominated the Argentines, who scored on virtually their only clear scoring chance of the match—Maradona had set up Claudio Caniggia—en route to a 1–0 win. In one of the most intense matches in cup history, West Germany bested the Netherlands 2–1, in an encounter that should have been played in the semifinals or final. Dutch defender Frank Rijkaard was ejected for spitting at Rudi Voeller, who also was given the heave-ho for running into the goalkeeper. Klinsmann and Andreas Brehme scored for the winners, as the Dutch returned home dazed, frustrated and embarrassed. The luck of the Irish continued for Ireland, which played its fourth consecutive tie, a 0–0 result with Romania. But the Irish prevailed in penalties, 5–4. Schillaci's fairy tale continued in Italy's 2–0 victory over Uruguay, which had been whistled for 36 fouls. England edged Belgium, 1–0, on David Platt's goal some 30 seconds from the end of extra time and a penalty-kick tie-breaker, and Yugoslavia squeaked past Spain, 2–1, on Dragan Stojkovic's goal in extra time.

All 4 quarterfinals were decided by a goal or by tie-breakers. The best of the lot was England's 3–2 comeback win over Cameroon, whose lack of subtley on defense caught up with the Africans. Gary Lineker was the man of the match, recording two penalty kicks, the last in overtime. Milla did not score as a substitute this time, but he did set up both of Cameroon's goals.

The others? The Argentines continued to use mirrors as they got past the Yugoslavs on penalties, 3–2, after 120 minutes of scoreless

(*A Perfect cont.*)
with the pending merger of the East and Wes German football leagues and associations, it will be a case of the strong getting stronger.

"We'll have a broader choice of players, more players to choose from the next time around," Beckenbauer said. "The German team will be unbeatable. I'm sorry about that folks, but it will be tough to beat us."

It was tough enough trying to beat the Germans this time around.

soccer. The Yugoslavians had a player ejected, but it was they who played as though they had a man advantage. Schillaci—who else? scored in the first half for Italy in its 1–0 triumph over Ireland, a day after the Irish visited the Pope. Germany shut down Skuhravy, and Matthaeus converted a penalty kick for a 1–0 win.

It looked as if the Italians would play the Germans in the final, but the Argentines had other plans. Italy made a tactical mistake. They scored too early as Schillaci connected for his fifth goal in the 17th minute. That woke up the Argentines, who would have been content to stay in their shell and play for a tie-breaker. Forced to play soccer, Argentina equalized in the 67th minute, with Caniggia heading home a cross from Olarticoechea's. The goal snapped goalkeeper Walter Zenga's goalless streak of 517 minutes, a World Cup record. Goycochea turned out to be the real hero for the Argentines, who prevailed on penalties, 4–3, as he saved attempts by Roberto Donadoni and Aldo Serena. West Germany, meanwhile, outlasted the English, 4–3, on penalty kicks after playing to a 1–1 tie in regulation and extra time after Brehme scored for the winners, Lineker for England.

Andreas Brehme converted a penalty kick in the 84th minute to lead West Germany to its third World Cup title after a 1–0 victory over Argentina at Olympic Stadium in Rome. Oh, you want more? Well, the less said about this game, the better.

The Final

The Argentines, with several players sidelined with injuries and suspensions, were no doubt the less talented side. They had 4 regulars on the sidelines. Midfielder Ricardo Giusti missed the match because of a red card and midfielders Sergio Batista and Olarticoechea and Caniggia due to yellow-card accumulations. So, not surprisingly, they tried to play for a tie-breaker using negative, defensive soccer. "It was just too bad the Argentines didn't participate," German coach Franz Beckenbauer said. "They wanted to destroy. They were too weak. It is too bad that happened in a final game."

The Germans, who tried to play soccer, played down to the level of their opponents and could never get their game going. At least they tried to play. The Argentines got within striking distance of the goal in the 38th minute after Guido Buchwald, who did a masterful job of shadowing Maradona, tripped Jose Basualdo 20 yards out on the right side. Maradona's free kick sailed over the goal and goalkeeper Bodo Illgner, who only touched the ball when a teammate passed it back. That was the extent of the Argentine attack.

Referee Edgardo Codesal of Mexico red-carded Pedro Monson—the first player ejected in a championship match—for tripping Juergen Klinsmann in the 65th minute. The Argentines, down to 10 players, went further into their shell, if that was indeed possible. But the Germans continued to push up and were rewarded in the 84th minute when defender Roberto Sensisi tripped Voeller in the penalty area. Brehme converted the ensuing penalty, beating Goycochea to the lower left post. Before the match was over, Argentine forward Gustavo Dezotti joined Monzon on the sidelines, getting red-carded for grabbing defender Juergen Kohler by the neck in the 87th minute. That set up a disgraceful display by the Argentines, who continued to argue with Codesal after the final whistle. In some respects, the Argentines' exit was an approripriate way to end the most negative of all 14 World Cups.

> West Germany 1, Argentina 0
> Stadio Olympico
> Rome, Italy
> July 8, 1990
> West Germany: Illgner, Berthold (Reuter, 75), Kohler, Augenthaler, Buchwald, Brehme, Haessler, Matthaeus, Littbarski, Klinsmann, Voeller
> Argentina: Goycoechea, Ruggeri (Monzon, 46), Simon, Serrizuela, Lorenzo, Basualdo,Troglio, Burruchaga (Calderon, 53), Sensini, Dezotti, Maradona
> Goal: Brehme (WG) 84 PK
> Referee: Codesal (Mexico)
> Attendance: 73,603

Chapter Three

Qualifying—
Getting there was
Half the fun

It began with a goal from a Fordham University graduate and ended with a goal by Argentina against the team from down under.

In between, there were nearly 500 matches and several thousand goals were scored in pursuit of getting into soccer's promised land—the 1994 World Cup.

The road to the United States was a long and varied one as 141 countries discovered, some the fun way, most others the hard way.

The "paperwork" for the qualifying tournament was prepared at the Paramount Theater at Madison Square Garden in New York City on Dec. 8, 1991, as 141 countries were placed into their respective confederation qualifying groups. The draw was witnessed by a live audience of 4,000 and by more than 300 million people in 60 countries by television.

The draw started with the CONCACAF group, as Guatemala and Honduras were the first 2 countries picked out of a glass, and eventually ended as Austria was the final European side selected, 7 minutes before the end of the satellite feed.

In the Asian part of the draw, FIFA, soccer's world governing body, placed Iraq away from Kuwait and Saudi Arabia in the wake of the Gulf War in 1991, to avoid possible early-round hostilities. The latter two wound up in the same first-round group.

"We have taken into consideration the political situation," FIFA Press Director Guido Tognoni said.

Puerto Rican captain Mark Lugris had finally showed his true colors. Only minutes after Puerto Rico had defeated the Dominican Republic in the very first qualifying match of the World Cup, the Bronx native was draped in the blue-white-and-red flag of Puerto Rico.

Lugris is an American by birth and a Puerto Rican by heritage (his mother). Asked if a person can have two homes, the Fordham Univer-

The qualifying draw

The kickoff

sity graduate replied, "He can have one in his heart and one where he lives."

Lugris' home is New York City, and his heart was with Puerto Rico, for whom he scored the first goal of the competition in its 2–1 victory in Santo Domingo on March 21, 1992.

"This is the world to us," said Lugris, one of 9 players from the metropolitan New York area who started for Puerto Rico. "All the controversy we've gone through, it will shut a lot of mouths back home."

Lugris was referring to the turmoil that had set the Puerto Rican

---

The Final Countdown

Santo Domingo, Dominican Republic—Arnie Ramirez, the special technical adviser to the Puerto Rican National Team, was getting a bit anxious standing in the lobby of the Hotel Commodoro. It was 1:48 P.M. and a tardy defender Martin Alvarez was holding up the squad's departure for 3 minutes for its 1994 World Cup qualifying match against the Dominican Republic at Estadio Olympico on Saturday, March 21, 1992. Finally, the former Long Island University defender walked down the stairs.

"Come on, come on, Martin," Ramirez said as Alvarez carried his bags into the waiting team van.

Carrying his bag? A team van and not a team bus?

World Cup did not always necessarily mean world class as the Puerto Rican National Team rudely discovered for the very first qualifying match.

Ramirez said he had much better accommodations while coaching LIU. "We have a bus every game," he said.

Puerto Rico's stay was a humbling and sometimes bumbling experience. When the team arrived on Wednesday night, a bus supplied by the Dominican Olympic Committee was supposed to transport the team from the airport to its lodgings. The key phrase was *supposed to.*

It never showed. The team chipped in and managed to rent a van.

"Remember the movie, *Romancing The Stone?* defender Milton Espinoza asked. "Well, our bus was like the one in the movie, only without the chickens."

There was no bus for Estadio Olympico this time; a van took the team to the game. It had to make 2 trips—the 16 dressing players on the first run, the non-playing players, team officials and coaching staff on the second.

When they finally arrived at the stadium, Ramirez took one whiff of the locker room—it had backed up toilets—and negotiated quickly for a new home: a

Olympic Committee against its own national soccer team and had the Dominican Republic protesting the match, claiming the New York players were ineligible. The protest was not upheld.

Puerto Rico had 14 mainland Americans on its roster, mostly from the amateur and semi-professional teams in the New York area, 9 of whom had no connection with Puerto Rico by heritage or residency.

Puerto Rican players boycotted training to protest the firing of coach Victor Hugo Barros in December, 1991. Roberto Monroig, president of the Puerto Rico Soccer Federation, asked Arnie Ramirez,

(A Final cont.)

delivery area that was temporarily converted into a make-shift locker room. It had benches and tables.

Life went on as normal, as normal as can be in such primitive conditions, though a dog—a mixed breed who occupied the area—appeared to be terrified of the interlopers. One native man wasn't concerned. He continued delivering bananas as the team quietly prepared for its most important match.

"It's the little things, but they add up," Ramirez said.

Everyone had his own way of getting match-ready. Most of the starters—including Franco Paonessa and Espinoza—laid down on their equipment bags while a couple of players juggled a soccer ball.

At 3 P.M., FIFA representative Richard Ramcharan of Trinidad & Tobago entered the room, asking to see the team's passports. This was an important procedure because there was a dispute over mainland American citizens play-ing for Puerto Rico (because Puerto Rican citizens need only a U.S. passport, American citizens were allowed to perform for the team, although the Dominican Republic claimed it was going to protest the match).

The inspection finished without incident. Before leaving Ramcharan reminded coach Oscar Rosa that dissent from the bench was prohibited, to play fair and that the match would start promptly at 4 P.M..

Instead of using a blackboard to diagram last-minute strategy and assignments, Ramirez was forced to use water bottles, plastic cups and oranges to get his point across.

There was one advantage to having this type of "locker room"—it was large enough that the team was able to do calisthenics and light running.

"If we win today, we make history." Ramirex told his team.

He wasn't blowing smoke. Puerto Rica was winless in 6 qualifying matches entering this encounter.

coach of the Long Island University soccer team, for help, and he came through with 14 players from the New York area.

"Of course we will protest," Dominican Republic Coach Benhard Zgoll said. "The United States has a team in the World Cup. A country cannot participate with two teams in the World Cup."

The Puerto Rican Soccer Federation, whose rules are backed by FIFA, said that a player needed only a U.S. passport to be eligible to play for Puerto Rico. Puerto Ricans are U.S. citizens.

The game went on, and Lugris etched his name into the history books in the 23rd minute when he fired a 15-yard shot from the left side that bounded off the far post and into the net.

(A Final cont.)

He later added: "Be careful in the first 10 minutes. Concentrate a lot so they don't score a stupid goal."

Then it was: "If they spit at you, don't spit back. Don't fight back."

At 3:40 P.M., the rival teams entered the playing field together, much to the delight of the 5,000 or so spectators. "It's showtime," midfielder Stan Koziol said.

Estadio Olympico, an 18-year-old structure that certainly had seen better days, hardly was the ideal site for the opening of a tournament that is supposed to spark interest in the sport in the U.S. The parched field was hard and uneven. The scoreboard, which looked as if it had caught fire (struck by lightning?) at least once, did not work. Neither did the phones at the adjacent soccer federation headquarters. There were no press credentials as the media was allowed to mill around the team benches. Imag-ine that happening at a European or U.S. qualifier.

Just minutes before the starting whistle, a photographer gathered the Puerto Rican side for a team picture. As the players lined up, referee Lancelotte Livingston gestured for the squad to take their positions for the start of the match.

He then stood over the ball in the middle of the field, looking at his watch before he was interrupted by several Dominican soccer officials. They needed both teams back on the sidelines so a local official could shake everyone's hand.

Before going back out, each team sang its national anthem a capella because there was no music to be found in the stadium.

At 4:09 Atlantic Standard Time, Livingston signaled for the game to start. Dominican Republic midfielder Nevis dela Cruz complied as he kicked the ball to teammate Hector Marnol.

Finally, the World Cup had begun.

Lugris was so overcome with emotion, he ran to the sidelines and fell to his knees in front of the Dominican bench to celebrate as his teammates raced over to congratulate him.

"I never scored that many goals," Lugris said. "I'm more of a playmaker than a goalscorer. . . . It was a thrill. It felt great. I wasn't thinking of it being the first goal of qualifying. It was more important, it was the first goal of the game."

Puerto Rico's Mark Lugris celebrates the first goal of qualifying for the 1994 World Cup.

When 28 teams faced off in 14 qualifiers on Wednesday, April 28, 1993 a World Cup record very well could have been set for the most games in one day.

Wonderful Wednesday

The operative phrase is "very well could have been," because there are no official World Cup records kept on how many matches played on a particular day.

Extensive research, however, showed that the closest "busy" day had 11 matches, which had occurred on several occasions.

The biggest winners of April 28 were not Russia, which recorded its fourth successive shutout, or Spain, which solidified its hold of the Group 3 lead, or even France, which held off Sweden, but rather a club team.

Manchester United of the English Premier League had 5 players make headlines on Wednesday, April 28. United's heroes included:

United, they won

- United wing Andrei Kanchelskis, who capped a 40-yard run around 3 defenders with a goal in the 55th minute in Russia's 3−0 victory over Hungary in Moscow.

- Teenage-sensation Ryan Giggs, who set up United teammate Mark Hughes for a goal in the 29th minute for Wales in its 1–1 tie in Czechoslovakia.
- United forward Eric Cantona, who scored his second goal with 9 minutes left for France in its 2–1 victory over Sweden in Paris.
- And United goalkeeper Peter Schmeichel, one of the heroes of the 1992 European Championship, who made a number of key stops for Denmark in its 1–1 tie with Ireland in Dublin.

In all, 9 United players participated for 7 countries in one of the busiest days in World Cup qualifying history. The countries? France, Russia, Denmark, Ireland, Northern Ireland, Wales and England.

While they did not make headlines, several other United players performed Wednesday, including Ireland defender Dennis Irwin, Welsh midfielder Clayton Blackmore, Northern Ireland defender Mal Donaghy and England midfielder Paul Ince, who was fouled by Dutch midfielder Rob Witschge in the 2–2 tie with the Netherlands. The foul set up a free kick on the edge of the penalty area from which John Barnes scored.

United's Premier League game with the Blackburn Rovers, originally scheduled for Saturday, May 1, was moved back to Monday, May 3, because of all the players playing with their national teams.

These butterflies are free

During Cameroon's home African Group match with Guinea in Yaounde on April 18, 1993 millions of black butterflies invaded the stadium. The players appeared unfazed by the butterflies swirling around the stadium, particularly the home side as Cameroon recorded a 3–1 victory.

Africa's fallen heroes

Not everything was fun and games or upbeat. On April 28, 1993 the Zambian National Team, en route to an African qualifier in Senegal, was virtually wiped out when its plane crashed off the Gabon coast. Eighteen members of the team perished, including 5 team officials, 5 crewmen and a journalist. The plane, which had refueled in Gabon, was on its way to a May 2 match. Not all of Zambia's players were killed, as its European contingent, including team captain Kalusha Bwalya of PSV Eindhoven (Netherlands), had not left to join the team.

Africa's fallen heroes rise— then fall again

In its first game back, Zambia started a storybook comeback on the road to USA '94 with an emotional 2–1 victory over Morocco in a Group B match in Lusaka, Zambia on July 4.

The Zambian players wore black arm hands in honor of their fallen comrades. About 50,000 friends, relatives and fans crowded into Independence Football Stadium, where the dead players were buried on May 3. The game began with a minute's silence for the dead, who were buried in a semicircle around the stadium. Johnson Bwalya, who plays for Bulle (Switzerland) broke a 1–1 tie for the hosts in the 77th minute. Rachid Daoudi had put Morocco ahead in the 14th minute, butKalusha Bwalya—no relation to Johnson—equalized in the 70th minute for Zambia, coached by Fred Mwila, who once played in the North American Soccer League.

"Everyone has worked hard and made great sacrifices," said Winston Gumbo, chairman of the Football Association of Zambia. "We're back on the road to the World Cup."

Zambia's lineup consisted of European-based players, plus new players based in Zambia.

Zambia's fairy tale ended with a 1–0 loss in Casablanca on Oct. 10, as Morocco qualified on a goal by Abdeslam Laghrissi in the 50th minute. "We were close, yet so far away," Kalusha Bwalya said.

In February, 1993 Egypt defeated Zimbabwe, 2–1, in Cairo to reach the second round in African qualifying. Or so everyone thought. FIFA ordered a replay of the Group C match after Zimbabwe lodged a protest over stone-throwing by the crowd of 120,000, which injured some of its players.

Zimbabwe's second chance

The match was replayed in neutral Lyon, France, on April 15, as Zimbabwe registered a 0–0 tie to earn a spot in the next round, as Egypt, finalists for the 1990 World Cup in Italy, was eliminated.

Ironically, Liverpool goalkeeper Bruce Grobbelaar, who had a brain scan after he was struck by a lump of concrete during the Cairo match, made several brilliant saves in the second half to secure the draw in the replay before a crowd of 5,000.

Dan Gaspar's short stay in Portugal was an education and eye-opener.

An American in Portugal

"It's soccer, politics and religion over here, and I don't know in what order," he said by telephone during World Cup qualifying. "It's pretty close."

Then again, he did some educating himself, in the unlikely role of teaching the Portuguese National Team goalkeepers the finer points of the game as they made their final run for a World Cup berth.

It was unlikely because Gaspar's an American-born coach teaching Europeans. The U.S. traditionally imports foreign coaches to direct its National Team, such as current coach Bora Milutinovic (Yugoslavia).

"Quite frankly, being American is an obstacle you have to overcome when you're overseas," Gaspar said. "That's unfortunate because we have quality coaches. The American coach has to structure the team, teach the game in many cases and promote the game . . . I consider myself to be very fortunate to be recognized and respected. I hope this opens the door for other American coaches to be recognized."

Despite Gaspar's help, Portugal fell short in its final qualifying match, losing to Italy, 1–0 on Nov. 17, 1993, although goalkeeper Vitor Baia was outstanding.

Gaspar, a professional goalkeeping coach who operates camps—Star Goalkeeping Academy and clinics-admits he was fortunate to latch onto his latest role. While he was directing the Portuguese U-17 keepers in Algrave, the National Team wanted to sequester itself from the media and other distractions near the beach area where the younger squad was training. The National Team heard about Gaspar's successful methods and offered him a job—in the country of his mother's and father's birth. "Destiny has a lot of do with it," he said.

Just being there was an experience. "Victories and losses are emotional," Gaspar said. "If you win, nobody works, everyone celebrates. If you lose, it's a state of depression. There's no inbetween."

Gaspar had the time of his professional life. "How can I not have fun when I am fulfilling a dream," he said. "It has always been my dream to reach the highest level. I am in my element. This is drastic: Things can end tomorrow and I will be the happiest man on the face of the earth."

Welcome back

Lebanon returned to World Cup qualifying after a 15-year absence on May 7, 1993 although India spoiled its return by scoring two late goals in a 2–2 tie in the Asian Group D match in Beirut..

Hundreds of Lebanese troops guarded Bourj Hammoud Stadium but no trouble was reported. Local officials understood the significance of the game as entertainers led a motorcade of 200 flag-bearing cars from the ruins of the city's Sports City stadium, once the biggest in the Middle East, to Bourj Hammoud Stadium.

The youngest player?

Farooq Aziz, a 15-year-old Pakistani schoolboy, made his World Cup debut at 15 on May 22, 1993 and may very well be the youngest player to have participated in the competition. Because official qualifying records were few and far between through the years, Aziz has to be at least *among* the youngest, making his World Cup debut as he did at the age of 15 years, 4 months and 28 days in an Asian qualifier against China in Irbid, Jordan.

Aziz, a forward, played in 3 matches for Pakistan.

"I spotted him playing in a school match in Lahore. He's got stamina and skill and he is a bright prospect for the future," Pakistan

Coach Muhammad Aslam told Reuters about Aziz, who missed 2 weeks from Lahore's Pakistan Railways High School.

Aziz will not break the record of Northern Ireland's Norman Whiteside as the youngest player to compete in the finals because Pakistan failed to reach USA '94. Whiteside, incidentally, was 17 years, 42 days old when he played against Yugoslavia in the 1982 World Cup in Spain, besting the record set by Pele in the 1958 championship in Sweden.

It was a tough qualifying run for financially beleaguered Albania, which failed to reach the finals. Albania did not have a coach or bus to transport its players, and several days before its Sept. 22, 1993 match with Spain, the country discovered it was 3 shirts short of having a full complement. So, Coach Bekjush Birce asked his players not to trade jerseys after the game.

Shirts vs. skins?

"It is the players' right to swap shirts after playing famous national sides, but they have to realize that we are too poor," Birce said.

There was Bolivia's 2–0 stunner of Brazil in La Paz, Brazil, on July 25, 1993 handing the Brazilians their first World Cup qualifying loss—ever—in 26 matches. Afterwards, several Brazilian players complained that the thin air of La Paz, the capital of Bolivia, did them in. Perhaps. But why did we not hear of complaints in the past 44 years when Bolivia was failing to reach the final round?

Upset city

And there was Colombia's improbable 5–0 triumph over Italia '90 runner-up Argentina in Buenos Aires as Freddy Rincon and Faustino Asprilla scored 2 goals apiece for the winners on Sept. 5. It might not have been surprising that Colombia defeated the Argentines, but the way it was accomplished—a runaway in the host country!

So, you want to coach a national soccer team someday? A few words to the wise: Don't quit your day job. Translated, the mortality rate of coaches during qualifying was quite high.

Coaching carousel

- Paraguay used five coaches. Alicio Solalinde, the final coach, took over the day of its scoreless tie with Argentina on Aug. 29, a day after Valdir Espinoza walked out on Saturday night and took a flight to Brazil.
- African champions Ivory Coast axed its coach Philippe Troussier after only 4 months on the job on Aug. 5, several days before an important match against Nigeria while it still had an excellent opportunity to qualify. Troussier's crime? Two weeks prior, Troussier had said that it would take a miracle for the team to reach the final. Perhaps he was trying to use psychological war-

fare to pump up the players, but soccer federation officials did not see any psychological ploy in the statement. "He has insulted the Ivory Coast, the national team and the federation," an official said.

- Controversial Cornel Dinu was fired by Romania after a 5–2 loss to Czechoslovakia, even though the country was still within striking distance in European Group 4. In fact, only days after Romania had qualified on Nov. 17, its federation found itself in court over the sacking of Dinu, who claimed his contract should have lasted through the final match. He was replaced by Anghel Iordanescu.

- Mexico lost Cesar Menotti not once, but twice. Menotti quit over political problems in the Mexican Federation. The second time was permanent. Menotti left the team, and Miguel Mejia Baron, a qualified dentist, took over. Mexico became the first country outside of the 2 countries that qualified automatically—the host U.S. and world-champion Germany—to reach USA '94 by defeating Canada on May 9, 1993.

- Iraqi coach Adrian Dirjal dreamed how much he wanted to go before President Saddam Hussein with U.S. visas for the World Cup, but he was nowhere to be found when Asian qualifying ended in Qatar. Dirjal was fired on Oct. 18, 1993 after only one game after Iraq lost a two-goal lead and eventually the game to North Korea, 3–2. Dirjal, was already under fire for poor tactical decisions was warned by FIFA after he broke a chair in the team dugout and failed to attend the post-match press conference. The decision to fire Dirjal and his staff was made by Odai Hussein, the oldest son of Saddam Hussein, who personally supervised the team's qualifying efforts. Ahmed Baba was named the new coach.

- Although Saudi Arabia was undefeated at 1–0–3 and on the verge of qualifying, Brazilian Jose Candido was sacked and replaced by Mohammed Al-Khrashe, coach of the Under-16 national team. Candido's sin? The royal family demanded he replace the goalkeeper during a 1–1 draw with Iraq after the player allowed a goal. Candido did not comply, and subsequently was axed.

- Graham Taylor resigned as coach 6 days after England failed to qualify after he endured severe criticism and heavy pressure to resign during most of his 3 year reign. It was the first time England did not qualify for the cup since 1978. "No one can grasp the depths of my personal disappointment at not qualifying," Taylor said. "If we did not qualify for the World Cup finals, it was always my intention to offer my resignation from the job as England manager."

- Only 8 days after the French were eliminated, coach Gerard Houllier stepped down.

When the subject is the World Cup, temperatures run high and passions are intense. There is a lot at stake in qualifying. There is the material end, as each qualifying county receives $1.5 million ($500,000 for each first-round match, and the same amount for every game thereafter) from FIFA. And, the honor and pride of a country is on the line.

Costly celebrations

- After Mexico defeated Honduras, 4–1 in Tegucigalpa in May, 1993, several thousand angry fans rioted, destroying vehicles, including 2 mobile broadcast vans used by Honduran radio stations to transmit the match, and setting fire to banners. They also threw stones at the players as they left the field and refused to allow either team to leave the stadium until riot police intervened.
- After Colombia defeated Argentina, 5–0, on Sept. 5, to qualify for the World Cup, a number of Colombian took the ensuing celebrations seriously. A total of 20 fans died and another 100 were injured.
- And after Bolivia won a crucial match, fans celebrated so ferociously that they did not notice their village had caught on fire. It burned down.

Only days before the Nov. 17, 1993 clash between Argentina and Australia in Buenos Aires, impatient and irate fans showed their displeasure—The reason: several youths cut in front of them in line—after ticket sales were stopped, by wrecking cars and smashing shop windows outside the Argentine federation. The solution? Police announced tickets were being sold at River Plate Stadium, which was the case.

The great ticket rush

Looking at the participants and potential political ramifications, it was indeed the mother of all tournaments—Iraq, Iran, North Korea, South Korea, Saudi Arabia and Japan—playing for 2 spots at USA '94 in the final Asian round in Doha, Qatar.

The mother of all tournaments

World Cup officials in the United States, although they did not publicly admit it, wanted Japan, Saudi Arabia and South Korea over

Iraq, Iran and North Korea. These last 3 countries would have provided headaches in the obtaining or visas for them, although the Reagan administration had agreed to grant visas to any team that had qualified. And there would have been more problems with security.

After the dust had settled, Saudi Arabia and South Korea had qualified.

On paper, the most intriguing matches involved Iraq and Iran and Iraq and Saudi Arabia. In the first encounter, on Oct. 22, between 2 countries embroiled in a 9 year war in the 1980s and 1990s, Iraq prevailed, 2–1, as its supporters went wild, waving pictures of Iraqi president Saddam Hussein. The fans of the rival teams were separated by barriers, and there were no major incidents.

In a classic encounter with political overtones on Oct. 24, Iraq and Saudi Arabia played to a 1–1 tie. Remember that the United States used Saudi Arabia as a major base during the Gulf War with Iraq in early 1991. Iraq struck 4 minutes into the match as captain Ahmed Radhi put home a cross from Selim Hussain. In support of their team, Iraqi fans switched photographs of Saddam, praying to one of him smiling, after the goal. The Saudis equalized in the 34th minute as Saeed Owarian scored. They could have taken the lead in the 56th minute, but midfielder Khalid al-Muwallid missed a penalty kick, sending a shot over the crossbar. Incidents were kept to a minimum.

While Saudi fans did not jump onto the field as they did after a 1–1 tie with South Korea on Oct. 22, a fight broke out in their part of the stadium on Oct. 24. It apparently was provoked by an Iraqi fan. The Saudis threw shoes, water bottles and trash at local riot police.

The great collapse

France twice was within minutes of securing a berth. Enjoying a 2–1 lead against lowly Israel in Paris on Oct. 13, the French allowed 2 goals in the final 7 minutes in a 3–2 loss. Needing a draw against Bulgaria at home on Nov. 17, the French and their visitors were locked in a 1–1 tie in the final minute. With 10 seconds left to qualify for the World Cup Emil Kostadinov scored his second goal of the match for Bulgaria to leave France as stunned outsiders.

"It's truly terrible. I have no words," said David Ginola, who with 21 minutes left replaced star striker Jean-Pierre Papin.

Added French coach Gerard Houllier: "It was the worst possible scenario."

Japan, whose soccer interest was revived big-time with a professional league—the J-League—suffered a similar fate in its final match. Needing only a draw to qualify for its first World Cup, the

Japanese surrendered a goal with 10 seconds left in its 2–2 tie with Iraq. Jaffar Omran scored the equalizer.

And while on the subject of 10 seconds, San Marino, which entered the match with just 1 goal in nine qualifying games, scored only 10 seconds into its match with England on Nov. 17, 1993 after a player intercepted a backpass by England captain Stuart Pearce. It was the quickest goal England had allowed in 702 internationals, even though the English rebounded with a 7–1 victory. Still, the English were eliminated because the Netherlands defeated Poland, 3–1.

"Of course it's the worst moment I've known," England Coach Graham Taylor said. "You're talking about World Cup football and England is not going to the finals. It has to be the worst."

The final day of qualifying had 12 matches with 9 berths still up for grabs and 16 countries still alive and kicking.

The biggest winners of the day were Italy, Switzerland, the Netherlands, Ireland, Spain, Belgium, Romania, Bulgaria and Argentina.

Among some of the more interesting highlights:

- Switzerland recorded a 4–0 victory over Estonia in Zurich, to reach the finals for the first time since 1966. "When it was scoreless after 20 minutes and we had burned up several good scoring chances, one might have thought it wouldn't work," coach Roy Hodgson said. "But the players had different ideas."

  Local police allowed bars to stay open 2 extra hours to 2 p.m. in celebration. Swiss president Adolf Ogi congratulated Hodgson on television and unveiled a postage stamp that commemorated the victory.

- Spain overcame the ejection of its goalkeeper and playing with only 10 men for 80 minutes to outlast Denmark in Seville, Spain, 1–0. Andoni Zubizarreta was red-carded for tripping Michael Laudrup in the 10th minute. Defensive midfielder Francisco Camarasa was replaced by back-up goalkeeper Santiago Canizares who made several key saves to preserve the win, as Fernando Hierro scored in the 63rd minute. "I can only say thanks to my teammates," Zubizarreta said. "They turned my failure into nothing more than a small detail . . . It was horrible being on the bench and when Hierro scored, I don't think I ever screamed louder."

- Wales found itself looking in again, losing to Romania, 2–1, in Cardiff. The Welsh last qualified in 1958. "It has all dealt Welsh

The final whistle

football a cruel blow again," coach Terry Yorath said. "We will be stuck with that nearly tag again. The players were crying at the end out on the pitch and there were tears, too, in the dressing room afterwards."

A Welsh fan was killed during the match, when a missile hit him while sitting in the stands.

There was a contrasting mood in Bucharest as 10,000 young fans put aside the cold and worries of the 300 percent inflation their country had been experiencing to march through the streets after the game. Romania's flag was entwined with that of the United States.

- The final match of the competition—Argentina vs. Australia-kicked off after the European matches on Nov. 17. The Argentines won, 1–0, as Gabriel Batistuta scored the lone goal.

How They Got There In The 13 Other World Cups

Expect the unusual to happen when the subject is World Cup qualifying. There's never a dull moment in the preliminary competition, whether it's a ruse to fool FIFA or the opposition, a real, honest-for-goodness war, coaches dying or a player playing 2 matches in a day. Through the years, lightly and darkly:

The great hoax

Chile tried to pull a fast one on Brazil in the return leg of its South American qualifier on Sept. 3, 1989. With Brazil enjoying a 1–0 advantage with 21 minutes left, fireworks launched by Brazilian fan Rosemary de Mello landed near Chilean goalkeeper Roberto Rojas. Rojas crumpled to the ground and eventually was carried off the field by teammates as he had some sort of red stain on his face. The entire Chilean team left the field, refusing to play.

Brazil was awarded a 2–0 forfeit victory because Chile did not consult game officials. As for Rojas' injuries, they turned out to be a hoax.

The Chilean trainer and several top soccer officials resigned or were fired. Rojas was banned for life by FIFA, and Chile from the 1994 World Cup. Brazil was fined $31,000 because of the fireworks.

As for the culprit in the affair—de Mello, a 24-year-old secretary wound up posing nude in the Brazilian edition of Playboy, although the Brazilian confederation tried to make her pay the fine.

The soccer war

A soccer war? Yes, a soccer war between El Salvador and Honduras on the road to the 1970 World Cup in Mexico.

The groundwork for the violence in Tegucigalpa, Honduras, with a 1–0 Honduran victory on June 7, 1969 as Amelia Bolanios, 18, shot herself to death after watching the game on TV.

Before the June 15 return leg in San Salvador, which El Salvador won, 3–0, several home fans burned the Honduran flag. A soiled rag was hoisted on the flagpole instead.

Two people were killed and countless others injured while Honduran fans left the country. Honduras expelled all Salvadorans.

A tie-breaker was played in Mexico City July 27, with El Salvador recording a 3–2 win eventually returning to Mexico for the World Cup a year later.

War eventually broke out between the 2 countries as more than 3,000 people died, another 12,000 were wounded or injured and yet another 150,000 lost their homes over 4 days of fighting.

Sudden death

Scotland Coach Jock Stein suffered a heart attack and died in the runway to the locker rooms after his side played Wales to a 1–1 tie at Nianian Park on Sept. 10, 1985. Alex Ferguson, who now directs Manchester United in the English Premier League, replaced Stein on Dec. 4, 1985, as the Scots qualified for Mexico.

Sudden death—again

The Nigeria-Angola match in Lagos on Aug. 12, 1989, saw the death of 13 fans and 1 player. The fans died from an overcapacity crowd of 80,000 (20,000 more than the limit) and stifling heat. Sam Okwaraji, a 24-year-old Nigerian, collapsed and died on the field.

Some of those 13 fans could have been saved, but the key to the locker containing resuscitation equipment could not be found.

The longest road

New Zealand played an all-time qualifying record 15 games to reach the 1982 finals in Spain, recording an 11–1–3 mark along the way, scoring 44 goals and allowing 10. Goalkeeper Richard Wilson registered 9 consecutive shutouts, a streak of 15 hours and 20 minutes without allowing a goal.

The shortest road

The easiest trips to soccer's promised land were taken by Bolivia, Chile, Uruguay and Paraguay in 1950. They could have mailed their results in. Because of its differences with host Brazil, Argentina withdrew, giving Bolivia and Chile a free ride to the finals. Ecuador and Peru dropped out of Group 8, allowing Uruguay and Paraguay to reach the final without playing a match.

FIFA has since changed the rules, which stipulate that a country must play at least one match to qualify. Fair enough.

You're in, you're out ...

Then there's the case of France, which could not make up its mind for 1950. The French originally were eliminated, losing to Yugoslavia in a special Group 3 playoff, 3–2. But because Scotland and Turkey had withdrawn, they were invited back. They accepted, but pulled out of the final Pool 4 when they saw how much traveling was involved to play Uruguay and Bolivia. No country would do that today with so much money on the line.

Piling it on

New Zealand rolled to a 13–0 victory over Fiji on Aug. 16, 1981. Fiji goalkeeper Akuila Nataro Rovono allowed 7 goals in the first half. His replacement, Semi Bai, did not fare much better, surrendering 6 in the final half. Fiji lost to Australia, 10–0, just 2 days later.

Against all odds

That Iraq made it to the 1986 finals in Mexico was a miracle in itself. Not that it had a bad side. Iraq was forced to play its home qualifying matches at neutral sites because it had been declared a war zone. Iran was required to do the same, but withdrew from qualifying.

Goal machine

West German forward Gerd Mueller, who had played for the Fort Lauderdale Strikers (North American Soccer League) near the end of his career, scored 19 goals in 1970 qualifying and the final competition. That includes 9 in the qualifiers and 10 in 6 World Cup games, a feat that has not been matched or approached since.

Marathon man

Danish midfielder Soren Lerby pulled off one of the most unique feats in soccer history, playing more than 2 hours of soccer for 2 different teams in 2 different countries on Nov. 13, 1985. Lerby's incredible and exhausting day began in Dublin, Ireland, helping Denmark to a 4−1 European qualifying victory over Ireland. He left in the 58th minute with Denmark enjoying a 3−1 advantage.

Lerby then took a private jet, furnished by his club, Bayern Munich, and he was flown back to West Germany for a third-round cup game in Bochum. There, he came on as a halftime substitute in a 1-1 tie.

"My legs feel pretty tired," Lerby said. "The pitch in Dublin was really heavy."

The pot of gold

Just for reaching the World Cup in 1982, Crown Prince Sheik Saad Abdullah Al Sabah of Kuwait gave each of the 24 players a Cadillac, a villa, a plot of land, a gold watch and a speedboat.

Famous firsts—Part I

For the first time, West Germany (now Germany) dropped a qualifier—on the road to Mexico. It happened in Stuttgart on Oct. 16, 1985, a 1−0 loss to Portugal. Until then, Germany had an incredible record of 32−0−4. Germany, which did not have to qualify for the 1994 World Cup as defending champions, is 35−1−8 lifetime.

Famous firsts—Part II

Ireland's Paddy Moore became the first player to score 4 goals in a qualifier. He accomplished that feat in Ireland's 4−4 tie with Belgium in Dublin on Feb. 25, 1934.

Famous firsts—Part III

Although a World Cup final match never been has played in a domed stadium on artificial turf (that will change in 1994), the U.S. and Canada pulled off a pair of firsts within a month in 1976. Their 1−1 tie in Vancouver on Sept. 24 was the first qualifier played on an artificial surface and the Americans' 2-0 triumph in Seattle on Oct. 20 was the first match played under a dome.

Because the U.S. and Canada were tied for second place in their group with 1–1–2 records, they played off at a neutral site—on grass in Port au Prince, Haiti on Dec. 22. The Canadians won, 3–0.

Chile's free lunch

Chile received an easy ride to the 1974 finals in West Germany when the Soviet Union refused to play the South Americans in the second leg of a special qualifying playoff. After playing to a scoreless tie in Moscow, the Soviets refused to play at Estadio Nacional in Santiago, claiming left-wing prisoners had been shot there. So, FIFA booted the Soviets out of the tournament.

To make the accomplishment official, the Chilean National Team lined up in Estadio Nacional at midfield against a phantom Soviet team, dribbled down field and scored. In a friendly match that took the place of the qualifier, Santos of Brazil drubbed Chile, 5–0.

Wales' free lunch

Wales thought it was going to watch the 1958 World Cup from the stands in Sweden after it had been eliminated by Czechoslovakia in its qualifying group. However, the Welsh were given a second chance at life when it was asked to play Israel in a special playoff. The Israelis had reached the playoff without kicking the ball because its Arab opponents—Egypt, the Sudan, Turkey and Indonesia—had refused to play them.

Wales won both legs and advanced all the way to the quarterfinals in Sweden before it was eliminated by eventual-champion Brazil.

Closest call

Referee Tom Reynolds and linesmen Gerald Morgan and John Davies were locked in the game officials' room for their safety for more than an hour after Austria's 1–1 tie with East Germany in 1978 qualifying in Vienna on Sept. 24, 1977. Reynolds needed a police escort after disallowing an Austrian goal with 4 minutes left. Rioting fans tried to burn down the stadium. By the way, Austria eventually qualified.

If at first you don't . . .

If you thought the United States had a difficult time reaching the World Cup—a 40-year drought until Italia '90—consider poor, poor Luxembourg, which has failed in 14 tries since qualifying began in

1934. Luxembourg's record is 2−70−2, including 25 losses in a row. Luxembourg has scored 40 goals and surrendered 258.

It's only victories? A 4−2 win over Portugal at home for the 1962 finals and a 2−0 win over Turkey at home for the 1974 World Cup.

Winners, but losers

Then there's the story of Belgium, which did not allow a goal in the 1974 competition, but was eliminated from European Group 3. Both the Netherlands and Belgium finished with 4−0−2 records, but the Dutch got the nod to play in West Germany through goal differential (24 goals for, 2 against, compared to the Belgians' 10 for and none against).

Losers, but winners

The United States qualified for the 1950 World Cup despite finishing with a 1−2−1 record scoring 8 goals and allowing 15 in a round-robin competition with Mexico and Cuba. The Americans finished second to Mexico.

Don't count your chickens

For the 1954 World Cup, Spain had been seeded for the final round in Switzerland, but there was one slight problem: It still had to qualify. Which it didn't. Spain tied Turkey, 2-2 in a special Group 6 playoff and was eliminated after drawing lots.

A neutral site

How would you like to travel several thousand miles to play one game and discover you're out of the World Cup? Well, the U.S. and Mexico took that gamble in 1934. The Americans managed to defeat the Mexicans, 4−2, in Rome, one of 7 times they have beaten their archrivals. The Americans' prize? Italy in the opening round, which turned into a 7−1 loss.

Ineligible player

The Switzerland-Romania 1934 Group 10 qualifying match ended in a 2−2 tie, but the game was awarded to Switzerland because Romania had used an ineligible player, Gyulal Baratki. It was feared that Romania, which had reached the final 16 as the second-place team, was going to be disqualified, but it was allowed to play.

Stupid, stupid, stupid

Had Italy not been so short-sighted in its game against Northern Ireland in Belfast, it would have played in the 1958 World Cup. FIFA referee Istvan Zsolt of Hungary could not get out of Heathrow Airport in London because of fog. The Italians refused to use a local game official, so the game became a friendly an exhibition, turned into an unfriendly (vicious tackling in a match that eventually was called "The Battle of Belfast") ending eventually in a 2–2 tie.

The match was replayed a month later on Jan. 15, 1958, with Northern Ireland securing a berth in the finals, with a 2–1 upset victory.

Close call—Part I

England, which needed a tie over Ireland to win Europe Group 1 in 1958 qualifying, almost did not get one in Dublin. John Atyeo's last-minute goal lifted the English to a 1–1 draw.

Close call—Part II

To reach a special playoff against Spain for the 1974 World Cup finals, Yugoslavia needed to win its final European Group 7 match over Greece by at least 2 goals. The Slavs scored the winning goal in a 4–2 triumph in the final minute, although there were rumors (subsequently unfounded) that some bribery was involved. Yugoslavia defeated Spain in the playoff in Frankfurt, 1–0.

Coaching carousel

Fact of life No. 1 in international soccer: Just because you guide a team into the World Cup, doesn't necessarily mean you will coach it there. Translated, don't quit your day job if you are the coach of a national team.

A few of the more interesting cases:

- Ecuador had five coaches before its qualifying run for the 1982 competition began. Ecuadorian Hector Morales resigned, followed by Argentine Miguel Ignominielo, who also quit. Brazilian Otto Vieira then took over, but complained that the team was playing in too many matches in a short period of time. He was replaced by Ecuadorian Juan Araujo, the country's national youth coach. Then, three weeks before the opening game, Eduaro Hohberg, an Argentine-born former Uruguayan international forward, assumed control. Not surprisingly, Ecuador did not qualify.

- Costa Rica employed 4 coaches over 13 months and still qualified for the 1990 World Cup. The Costa Ricans eventually wound up with Yugoslavian Bora Milutinovic, now the U.S. coach. He replaced Marvin Rodriguez, who directed the team into the cup. Rodriguez had replaced Antonio Moyana of Spain, who took over for Uruguayan Gustavo de Simone, who had been given a $125,000 buyout.

- Cameroon went through 3 coaches within 4 months before the 1982 World Cup. Yugoslav Branko Zutic, who directed the team through qualifiers, had a disagreement with national association officials during the African Cup. He was replaced by West German Rudi Gutendorf, who had guided Australia in the 1974 World Cup. But Cameroon tied all three games in the African Cup, scoring only once. Gutendorf was replaced by Jean Vincent, a former French international forward who played in the 1958 World Cup, who directed the team in Spain.

- The United Arab Emirates used 3 coaches during its run for Italia '90. Brazilian Mario Zagalo, one of only 2 men—Franz Beckenbauer is the other—to play for (1958 and 1962) and coach (1970) a world champion, was sacked by the UAE, which claimed his preparation had major problems. Federation officials also were unhappy over remarks he made about the country's chances in Italy. He was replaced by Poland's Bernard Blaunt, who resigned (the federation asked for it) because it was upset over his handling of the national team in the wake of the UAE's poor showing in the Gulf Cup. He was replaced by Brazilian Carlos Alberto Parreira—not the Carlos Alberto of World Cup and New York Cosmo fame, but another Brazilian-who will direct his native country at USA '94.

- Midway through qualifying for the 1974 World Cup, Tommy Docherty left Scotland to coach with Manchester United. Scotland still qualified under Willie Ormond.

- Like Docherty, Don Revie left England midway through qualifying for the 1978 World Cup. He decided to take the money from the United Arab Emirates, which was just starting the sport. Revie did a fine job planting the seeds because the UAE eventually qualified for Italia '90.

- Thijs Libregts was fired as coach of the Netherlands, one of the favorites at the 1990 World Cup in Italy, after the team voted against him as coach. The Dutch Soccer Federation backed the players, who were led by star midfielder Ruud Gullit. Libregts went to court to obtain an injunction to force the federation to honor his contract. He lost.

Did you know . . .

- That the host team in 1934—Italy—had to qualify for the competition. Italy defeated Greece, 4–0 (the second leg never was played). As of the 1938 Cup, however, the host country and defending champions were was given automatic bids.
- That the largest crowd to watch a World Cup qualifying match was 183,341 at Maracana Stadium in Rio de Janeiro, Brazil, to witness Brazil's 1–0 victory over Paraguay on Aug. 31, 1969 . . . Some other interesting crowds: 120,000 fans watched Cameroon clinch a spot in the 1982 finals, with a 2–1 victory over Morocco in Yaounde, Nov. 29, 1981.
- That Real Madrid star Alfredo di Stefano scored his only World Cup goal in Spain's 2–1 win over Wales in a Group 4 match of the Africa-Europe Group on April 19, 1961. It was the Africa-Europe group for the 1962 World Cup, which included Morocco, Tunisia, Ghana, Nigeria, Spain and Wales. That's not to be confused with the Asia-Europe Group, which included South Korea, Japan, Yugoslavia and Poland.
- That Yugoslavia, Ireland, Portugal and Luxembourg are the only countries to participate in all of the 13 previous World Cup qualifying tournaments.
- That South Korea was the first Asian country to appear in 2 finals—1954 and 1986—and again in 1990.

Chapter Four

The United States Challenge

In many soccer circles, Bora Milutinovic is considered a miracle worker, turning Third World soccer countries into World Cup overachievers.

In 1986, he took a Mexican team that had achieved nothing but disastrous results in 8 previous World Cups and directed it into the quarterfinals.

In 1990, only 90 days before the start of the Italia '90, he was named the fourth coach in 13 months for Costa Rica, which had qualified for the Cup for the first time. He guided the Central Americans into the second round past such international veterans as Scotland and Sweden.

In 1994, Bora, as he prefers to be called, faces perhaps his greatest challenge. He must transform the U.S. from a mediocre team into a competitive and respectable one as World Cup hosts. No host country has failed to reach the second round, and Bora and the U.S. do not want to be the team to start that negative precedent.

Of course, that might be easier said than done, but since Bora took over the coaching reigns on March 27, 1991, the U.S. has made some significant progress. Under the man with the outdated Beatles' haircut, the Americans have scored some impressive triumphs, including a 2–0 victory over archrival Mexico in the CONCACAF Gold Cup in 1991, an upset that caused such a furor south of the Rio Grande that the Mexican coach quit in embarrassment the next day; a sparkling 3–1 victory over 1990 World Cup quarterfinalist Ireland en route to the U.S. Cup '92 championship; a 1–1 draw with World Cup-bound Italy that secured the tournament title; a 2–0 victory in Romania, a 1–1 tie with European Club Cup champion A.C. Milan; and a 2–0 upset over England in U.S. Cup '93.

Still, there's much work to be done as Bora has tried to build a team that is dispersed throughout the world—players from the American Professional Soccer League, promising players who perform at the local club level, college graduates, several native-born stars who perform in Europe and a few naturalized citizens.

"The problem is we have players who don't touch the ball for one month," Bora said about the lack of serious competition for the U.S. players back home. "You don't play, you lose your sensitivity for the game. You lose your conditioning. You lose everything."

Bora then rattled off the names of the key players performing in Europe: John Harkes (England), Roy Wegerle (England), Dooley, Tab Ramos (Spain), Frank Klopas (Greece) and Ernie Stewart (the Netherlands).

"With one player, you change many things," he said. "It's another story."

But Bora said he was not downcast. "I'm not frustrated," he said. "I knew when I came over here that it wasn't going to be easy. America is a big country. For soccer it isn't easy. We don't have promotions. We don't have TV [televised soccer games]. Those are big things."

If there is pressure on the engaging coach, he hasn't shown any.

When he was introduced to the media on that March day, U.S. Soccer Federation president Alan I. Rothenberg placed a heavy burden on his new coach.

"Our goal is to win the 1994 World Cup," Rothenberg said matter-of-factly. "I subscribe to what Robert Browning said, 'Ah, but a man's reach should exceed his grasp or what's a heaven for.'"

Bora? He just gave one of his well-known infectious smiles. "The Yugoslavians and Mexicans have a saying," he said through an interpreter. "The third time is victory."

Something must have been lost in the translation because what Bora probably meant was the word charm, instead of victory.

Bora's English is halting, but that didn't stop Rothenberg from hiring the 49-year-old coach. "His English isn't perfect, but his communication level is excellent," Rothenberg said. "In a perfect world, we would have a native [born] American take the job. But this isn't a perfect world. If I had a choice between someone whose English isn't very good and someone who has international coaching experience, I'd pick the experience. I'll let his record on and off the field speak for itself."

Most important, the message has reached his players.

"It's great for American soccer," veteran forward Peter Vermes said. "Before you start out, you have a very high respect for the man. He

understands the game tremen-
dously, especially the mental part
of the game."

He has been a player's
coach. If a player is a couple of
minutes late for a 4:30 practice,
Bora doesn't mind. "Make it
4:45," he said.

His coaching methods are
also not too traditional. Forget
about whistles and playbooks.
He likes to play head tennis, as
the players knock the ball across
a string 3 or 4 feet above the
ground. When he first joined the

Bora Milutinovic

team, Bora got so carried away during video sessions at the team hotel
that he scribbled on the television screen with a Magic Marker to make
his point. "We can be in a restaurant, and next thing you know he has
the salt and pepper shakers and the ketchup bottle and a wine glass and
he's positioning them like players on the field," said Renato Capobianco, the U.S. National Team's administrator told Newsday. "Or he'll
be walking down the street and he'll ask somebody passing by for a
piece of paper to write down something to make a point about soccer.
He's what, in basketball terms, you'd call a gym rat."

The players seem to like the method behind the madness. "Every-
day we're learning more from Bora and we can only get better,"
midfielder Hugo Perez said.

Mexico got better, too, as Bora transformed them from an also-ran
into a force to be reckoned with before they succumbed to eventual
runner-up West Germany via penalty kicks in the quarterfinals. Bora
prepared Mexico, host of the 1986 World Cup, through a grueling,
62-game exhibition schedule over 3 years that included performing on
5 continents and winding up with a 38−7−17 record.

The Mexicans were ready for the 1986 World Cup. In the first
round, they defeated Belgium, which went on to finish fourth, in its
opener, 1−0; tied Paraguay, 1−1, and then defeated Iraq, 1−0, to reach
the second round. There, they recorded a 2−0 win over Bulgaria before
Germany busted their bubble. Still, it was one incredible ride for a
country that had a 3−17−4 record in World Cup competition before
Bora took over.

In fact, the easygoing and outgoing Bora was so successful that he earned the Aztec Eagle, Mexico's highest award given to foreigners. Then Mexican President Miguel de la Madrid presented the honor to Bora for "the positive achievements of the national soccer team under his direction."

As it turned out, Bora also won over the hearts of the Mexicans even before the team stepped onto the field at Azteca Stadium in Mexico City. He became a media darling. Bora, who is fluent in several languages—Spanish, French, Serbo-Croatian and Italian (his English is always improving)—is always available for interviews, even after unsettling defeats.

After losing that heart-breaker to Germany, Bora tried to put it all in perspective. "We began our preparations for the World Cup in Monterrey and so our campaign has ended here as well," he said. "My players have done their best, but sometimes it is difficult to give the fans what they want.

"I must congratulate the West German team on the way they have achieved in reaching the semifinals, but we are sad to go out on penalties. It is unfortunate to lose in such a way, but several very fine players have missed penalties today.

"I am going to go home now and I will spend some time with my baby and relax."

Another time, a sportswriter from the United States approached him for a tape-recorded interview at the 1986 World Cup draw in Mexico City. Bora said he did not know enough English for an interview. But instead of walking away, he offered to answer the questions in Spanish. He did—into a tape recorder—and the interview was later translated into English.

He also can get away with being a little absent-minded. At the 1992 NCAA Division I soccer championships in Davidson, NC, Bora had to make a telephone call. Noticing a sportswriter had two press passes—one as a writer, the other as a photographer—Bora asked if he could borrow one to get into the media center to make his call. The writer said no problem, although the pass never was returned because the two could not hook up. Now every time the writer sees Bora, he playfully demands to have his press pass returned.

His personality and international travels have made him recognizable the world over. "If I tell you I am a citizen of the world, it's very pretentious," he said. "But you know the world is one world."

Capobianco understood what Bora meant. "We can go to any city, anywhere and whether we're passing a flea market or walking a little side street toward a restaurant, Bora will run into someone who recognizes him and calls him by name," he said. "He could get on the wrong plane and land in Ogden, Utah, and he'll find his way back because he always will bump into two Hispanic guys or a guy from Yugoslavia who will take care of him."

That personality, coupled with his coaching ability, impressed Costa Rican Football Federation President Dr. Isaac Sasso in 1990. Sasso said he picked the Slav as coach because "we are confident of Bora's experience."

The Costa Rican circumstances were slightly different from the Mexican venture. Instead of having 4 years to prepare a team, Bora had all of 90 days. He took over under controversial circumstances, becoming the fourth coach to direct the Central American side. He worked on a 90-day contract for $12,000 a month. "Not for the money," he said, "but to be involved in the World Cup. I am a soccer gypsy."

He made 6 bold, dramatic moves, including the benching of well-known forwards Leonel Flores and Evaristo Coronado for such no names as defender Ronald Gonzalez.

"Everyone told me I was mad," Bora said. "I would have liked to play, open, attacking soccer, but Costa Rica is condemned to defense—absorb the opposition's play and counterattack. I was lucky to find players capable of putting my ideas into practice. It worked."

It worked well beyond Costa Rica's or Bora's fondest dreams. In its very first try in the World Cup, Costa Rica reached the second round, which was a pretty impressive accomplishment considering Scotland has been to the tournament 7 times and never has gotten out of the opening round.

And in the most ironic of results, in the first round in Italy, Costa Rica stunned Scotland, 1–0, dropped a 1–0 decision to Brazil and defeated Sweden, 2–1. Costa Rica came back down to earth, losing to a more physical Czechoslovakian team, 4–1, but Bora's reputation had been solidified.

In this melting pot of a nation, Bora might have been a perfect choice to guide the U.S. National Team. He was born into a soccer family and has either coached or played in 8 countries. Early on, his home life was unsettling as he and his 4 brothers and sister lost their parents (Bora named his 6-year-old daughter Darinka after his late mother) when he was a 1-year-old living in the Serbian town of Bajina Basta during World War II. "The Yugoslavian thing," Bora said. "I don't like to talk about it."

They wound up living with an aunt and uncle, a baker, in Bor for 10 years before moving to Belgrade.

Bora would tag along with his 2 older brothers, Milos and Milorad, picking up soccer when he was 4-years-old. "You would kill a porker [a pig], dry out the bladder and blow it up, and you play," he said. "Me and my brothers would get one team and play, three-on-three in the street."

Remember, this was Yugoslavia in the fifties and early sixties. There was no televised soccer, so Bora and his brothers relied on radio and newspaper accounts and their imaginations to follow their favorite teams and favorite players. Bora's favorite was Stjepan Bobek, a former Partizan Belgrade star who performed in the 1950 and 1954 World Cups. Once in a while, he and his brothers would take a 16-hour train ride to Belgrade to watch a first-class match.

"You would take a little bread and cheese and go with friends," he said. "I remember the first time I see Bobek, the most important player in my country. And, years later, I'm on the national team, and there is Bobek, coaching. Ohhhhh."

He was hooked. In the big city, Bora watched his brothers, Milos and Milorad, play for Partizan Belgrade of the Yugoslavian First Division. Milos, who now coaches his former team, was a dangerous forward who was "the best player I ever saw," Bora said.

Milos, who made 33 international appearances for Yugoslavia, performed in 2 World Cups (1954 and 1958), including scoring the very first goal in the 1954 competition in Switzerland. Milos almost coached against Bora in the 1986 World Cup but Yugoslavia lost out to France in qualifying. Milorad, a central defender, also was a member of that World Cup squad.

So, it's not surprising Bora followed in their footsteps, even if he has taken several more steps off the field since then, living up to his reputation as an international soccer gypsy.

He started his career as a 17-year-old with Partizan Belgrade of the Yugoslavian First Division. He went on to play for Yugoslavia's National B Team and was a member of the Olympic team that reached the quarterfinals of the 1964 Summer Games in Tokyo before performing for Monaco, Nice and Rouen in the French First Division and FC Winterthur in Switzerland.

Bora eventually surfaced in the Mexican First Division with Universidad Autonoma de Mexico, now known as Pumas, for which he played 5 years.

In 1977, he was named Pumas coach, starting a successful run, finishing second his first two seasons, winning the Mexican championship his third and capturing the CONCACAF (Confederation of

North, Central American and Caribbean Federations) Cup of Champions his fourth.

1994 U.S. Men's National Team

After his success at the 1986 World Cup—he became the first non-Mexican to coach the national team—Bora coached San Lorenzo de Almagro of Argentina and Udinese of Italy, both First Division clubs.

Then he latched on with Costa Rica, and the rest is history, something Bora hopes to duplicate in June and July, 1994.

If you want to get technical, the U.S. National Team has a split personality and is really two teams in one.

There's team Mission Viejo, where the less-talented players are based in this country at the squad's state-of-the-art training complex in Southern California.

Then there's team Brigadoon, the squad of European-based pay-ers that gets together for just a handful of games during the year.

The dichotomy never was more apparent that at U.S. Cup '93. Without several of its European players—the U.S. did have John Harkes and Roy Wegerle after their teams completed their English season—the Americans, at times, looked lost and certainly were outclassed by the more skillful Brazilians, losing, 2–0, at the Yale Bowl on June 6.

Thanks to the infusion into the starting lineup of Tab Ramos (Spain), Thomas Dooley (Germany) and Eric Wynalda (Germany), the U.S. looked like an entirely different team just 3 days later in Foxboro, MA. That "other" team stunned England, 2–0, and the world, for that matter. And then in their final game showed a lot of resiliency, rallying from a big deficit to make the score respectable in a 4–3 loss to world champion Germany in Chicago on June 13.

The main problem lies with the fact that the inferior Team Mission Viejo plays most of the home matches, which are televised, and that has not painted a particularly pretty picture to promote to the U.S. National Team, which needs all the promotion it can get as a viable entity to the American public.

Through the beginning of November, 1993, the U.S. was 6–3 when most of the Team Brigadoon players were in the lineup and only 1–9–11 at other times.

What's a coach to do? Live with it.

"My biggest problem is you need to play with the best team," U.S. Coach Bora Milutinovic said. "You need the best players. I don't have the best. "I don't cry."

Bora figured that he will begin forging a final team for the World Cup in May, 1994.

Until then, Bora was forced to use lineups like the one he fielded in a 2–1 loss to the Ukraine in High Point, NC on Oct. 17. That included veterans Tony Meola, Fernando Clavijo, Dooley, Hugo Perez, relative newcomers Mike Lapper and Mark Chung and retreads like Peter Vermes and Janusz Michallik. And until then, Bora will have to rely on hearing about the exploits of the U.S. players overseas. He'll hear about how Wegerle scores goals for Coventry City of the English Premier League, about how Harkes helps settle the midfield for Derby County of the First Division, about how goalkeeper Kasey Keller has pulled off one of his miraculous saves to keep Millwall in a First Division match, about how Bruce Murray scores a game-winning goal to make Keller a winner. He'll hear about the scoring feats of Wynalda for Saarbruecken in the German Bundesliga. Or how Ernie Stewart has filled the net for Willem in a Dutch First Division match. Or how Ramos is coping with Real Betis in the Spanish Second Division. Or how defender Cle Kooiman has marked another scoring threat out of the game for Cruz Azul in the Mexican First Division.

If Bora can field his optimum lineup in every game—that is, stay away from injuries and yellow and red cards—the Americans can reach the second round and perhaps the quarterfinals.

As alarming as some of the results have been, the organization and performance of the National Team improved markedly over the past. Here's why:

- In 1989, the U.S. won at Trinidad & Tobago, 1–0, to qualify for its first World Cup since 1950. "This game will have a tremendous impact on the sport in the United States," said U.S. midfielder Paul Caligiuri, who scored the game-winning goal.

- In 1990, the U.S. played in the World Cup. The results were not sterling—a 5–1 opening loss to Czechoslovakia; a 1–0 defeat to heavily favored Italy in which the Americans turned the Roman fans against their hosts, and setback a 2–1 decision to Austria. "The main thing was that we played against the best in the world," U.S. Coach Bob Gansler said.

- In 1991, the U.S. defeated Mexico, 2–0, in the semifinals of the CONCACAF Gold Cup, causing the Mexican coach to resign a day later. "I think we showed Mexico that they're going to have to show us some respect in the region," Vermes said.

- In 1992, the U.S. captured U.S. Cup '92, going undefeated in the process (2–0–1). The U.S. surprised Ireland, 3–1, with 3 second-half goals in Washington, D.C., edged Portugal, 1–0, and beat the defensive-minded Italians at their own game, frustrating their foes in a 1–1 tie. "We showed around the world that we can play world-class football," said U.S. midfielder John Harkes, who scored the lone goal against Italy and walked away with MVP honors.

- And in 1993, the U.S. pulled off one of the great upsets of alltime with a stunning 2–0 triumph over England in U.S. Cup '93 in Foxboro, MA. "Are we surprised?" said U.S. midfielder Tab Ramos, who set up both goals. "Sure, we're surprised. This will be headline news in Europe."

The reasons for the improvement? It's revolution and evolution.

The revolution comes from the fact the U.S. is hosting the World Cup. After the U.S. was awarded the World Cup in 1988, U.S. Soccer Federation officials realized that qualifying for Italia '90 was a No. 1 priority or face world-wide embarrassment for getting the planet's most prestigious soccer tournament without being able to qualify for it. Also, the U.S. needs a decent showing at home, and it's no secret that the host team has never failed to reach the second round. So the National Team program became a top priority.

Because there was no true First Division professional league in the U.S., the National Team has been forced to play as many as 20–25 games a year, a tremendous amount. They needed a proper training facility for the team, signed players to annual, fulltime contracts and moved them out to Mission Viejo, CA in 1992.

When USSF officials realized the 1990 U.S. World Cup squad did not measure up to the standards of a host team, they went "recruiting," finding players around the world with American citizenship or backgrounds. They found Stewart, whose father was a U.S. Air Force veteran stationed in the Netherlands. They found Dooley, whose late father was a U.S. Army veteran who married in Germany. And they benefitted by a decision by Wegerle, who had several citizenship options to consider. Wegerle, a native South African who attended college and played professionally in the U.S., could have played for 5 countries. He was eligible to play for Germany, the birthplace of his father; Scotland, the birthplace of his mother; England, where his residency made him eligible for a British passport; and for the U.S., because his wife Marie is a native of Miami; and, of course, South Africa.

While critics claim that the U.S. team isn't a true American side, meaning born and bred here, federation officials state that they are not doing anything wrong, and they are correct, thanks to FIFA's version of the grandfather clause. The Irish National Team, for example, is made up of players from the British Isles and from all over the world, players who might not have been born in Ireland but who have Irish ancestry.

Living up to the tradition of the United States, the U.S. National Team indeed is a melting pot. For the record, the U.S. player pool represents 13 nationalities as the place of a players' birth—Switzerland, Canada, Uruguay, Germany, Nigeria, Scotland, Greece, Poland, El Salvador, Northern Ireland, the Netherlands, South Africa and of course, the U.S.

Then there's the evolution. More than 2.2 million children play soccer in affiliated leagues in the U.S., and another 2 million could very well be playing in police, church, neighborhood and ethnic leagues. The great soccer boom that began in the late seventies has begun to make an impact and the quantity, slowly but surely, has been translated into quality. Harkes, a former Cosmos ball boy, and Ramos, a team-mate of Harkes in youth soccer, are two excellent examples of how well the system can work, because they matured into viable players, given the opportunity to play against the best in the world.

The U.S.'s progress in several international youth tournaments—the U-17 and U-20, both sponsored by FIFA—has been encouraging. The Americans are only a handful of countries that regularly qualify for World Cups, a pair of bi-annual international competitions that bring together the teen-age soccer stars of tomorrow. For example, they have reached the quarterfinals of the last two U-17 championships in 1991 and 1993, respectively. And the U.S. raised eyebrows throughout the international soccer community when it finished fourth in the U-20 championship in Saudi Arabia in 1989.

When those 17- to 20-year-olds "graduate" into the first teams in Europe and South America, the U.S. starts falling behind the rest of the world.

"We must have a professional league," said Bob Contiguglia, chairman of the U.S. Youth Soccer Association. "You are faced with a dilemma. Do you tell 16- and 17-year-olds to go to Europe and play with a professional club and give up their education or to go to college and compromise a soccer career?"

Besides the local club soccer scene, the next highest level of play is college. But there are 2 major roadblocks at the collegiate level—a two-month season and restricting Division I players (the highest level at which a player can perform) from playing with their local club teams until the end of the academic year or after their senior season.

So, the next stage of development is a professional league, and that is another story, or in this case, another chapter.

Unites States Team

(Statistics through Jan. 15, 1994)

JEFF AGOOS
Defender
5-foot-10, 168 pounds
Born: May 2, 1968
International appearances: 32
Goals: 2

Jeff Agoos is the answer to a trivia question: Who was the player who set up the U.S's first goal against England in that 2–0 upset in U.S. Cup '93? He started the scoring sequence in the 43rd minute as he brought the ball down the left wing and crossed into the penalty area. Tab Ramos got to the ball before it bounded over the touchline and he sent an air ball into the middle of the box that Thomas Dooley headed home from 6 yards.

Agoos, who appeared to have found a home at left fullback, realizes he will never be one of the team's big stars. The Dallas native is more of a blue-collar worker who brings his lunch pail to work every game and every practice. "Any time Jeff steps on the field, he feels that he has to prove his worth," said Gordon Jago, coach of the Dallas Sidekicks (Continental Indoor Soccer League), for whom Agoos played.

"Sometimes the media doesn't understand my role on the team," Agoos said. "It's hard making headlines when you are one of the blue-collar players. It's very difficult being recognized when your name is not in the stat column as a goal scorer or assist maker. No one recognizes the grunt worker. I am not upset at them. I just wish they would take the time to see the whole picture."

The whole picture for Agoos has been performing for the Under-16, 17 and 20 National Teams, the World University Games team and on the five-a-side National Team, which took home a silver medal at the FIFA championship in Hong Kong in 1992.

Agoos, who finished second to former University of Virginia teammate and present National Team goalkeeper Tony Meola for the 1989 Hermann Trophy, college soccer's version of the Heisman Trophy, is single.

DESMOND ARMSTRONG
Defender
6-foot, 175 pounds
Born: Nov. 2, 1964
International appearances: 74
Goals: 0

Like it or not, Armstrong was thrust into the national, and sometimes international, spotlight after regular sweeper Marcelo Balboa went down with his knee injury in March, 1993. Armstrong, who usually has played on the right flank on defense, was switched into the middle because of his experience.

He has not performed as well as expected, sometimes being overaggressive and sometimes not being quick enough to stay up with the speedy and skillful forwards of Brazil and Germany. Armstrong was expected to return to right fullback when Balboa recovered in December, although there were rumors that Armstrong's position there was in jeopardy.

Regardless, Armstrong has enjoyed a full career, starting all 3 matches at Italia '90 and distinguishing himself in the 1–0 loss to Italy. He has also represented the U.S. in the UNICEF world all-star game in Munich, Germany, in 1991, performed in the 1988 Olympics in Seoul, and played for the Baltimore Blast (Major Indoor Soccer League).

Armstrong, who calls Columbia, MD, home, is one of the most likable players on the team. In fact, he is an accomplished illustrator and has done several drawings of his teammates.

Armstrong, who has one semester left in his pursuit of an English degree at the University of Maryland, is married to Qena and has a daughter, Arielle, born March 17, 1992.

MARCELO BALBOA
Defender
6-foot-1, 170 pounds
Born: Aug. 8, 1967
International appearances: 76
Goals: 7

Marcelo Balboa will be happy just to play in USA '94, after suffering a severe knee injury in 1993. He tore the anterior cruciate ligament in his right knee in a game against Iceland on April 17 of that year. Supposed to be sidelined from 9 to 12 months, he returned to the U.S. lineup as a substitute in the 7−0 victory over El Salvador on Dec. 5, 1993, climaxing an 8-month recovery.

"His comeback has been exceptional for the type of activity he's going to be getting into," physical therapist Randy Bauer said. "I've seen other athletes come back sooner and be active, but never like this. The demands he will be putting on his knee are much, much greater. I mean he's not going back to an office job. It will be demanding on his knee every step of the way."

Even though he is only 26, Balboa epitomizes the U.S. National Team with 76 international appearances, which ranks him second only to forward Bruce Murray. Balboa only started playing with the National Team in 1988, but has shown so much grit and determination that he has been nicknamed the "Iron Man" by several sportswriters.

He had played every minute of every game since Italia '90, except for a match in the CONCACAF Gold Cup in 1991 when he sat out a game because of an ejection. Balboa led the team in minutes played (2,149). So, it was not surprising Balboa was named U.S. Soccer Federation Player of the Year for 1992.

His success is not an accident, because Balboa has performed internationally at several levels, including captaining the Under-20 World Cup in Chile in 1987 and in the 1990 World Cup in Italy. Balboa, who played 2 years at San Diego State before turning pro, has performed with the San Diego Nomads, San Francisco Bay Blackhawks and most recently with the Colorado Foxes (American Professional Soccer League), helping them to the regular-season title and the playoff championship. He also played in 3 games, starting twice, at the 1990 World Cup in Italy.

Balboa, who is single, coached the junior varsity in Cerritos, CA and assisted the varsity the last 2 years at Cerritos High.

His father, Luis, played professional soccer in Argentina and for the Chicago Mustangs (North American Soccer League).

BRIAN BLISS

Defender
5-foot-8, 168 lbs.
Born: Sept. 28, 1965
International appearances: 37
Goals: 2

If there was an award given to the USSF comeback player of the year, Brian Bliss would have to be the leading candidate. Bliss, who has played with Carl Zeiss Jena in the German Second Division the last two seasons, returned to the National Team against Germany on Dec. 18, 1993, after a three-year absence. He replaced Jeff Agoos in the second half of a 3–0 loss. The Rochester, N.Y. native's last international appearance had been on Nov. 21, 1990, in an international friendly against the Soviet Union in Trinidad & Tobago.

Bliss, who made his international debut against Ecuador on Dec. 2, 1984, was a regular in the national program from 1987–90. He played in three games in the 1988 Summer Olympics in Seoul, nine games in qualifying for the 1990 World Cup and once at Italia '90. He replaced Paul Caligiuri in the Americans' final match, a 2–1 loss to Austria. He has scored twice internationally in the 5–1 World Cup qualifying victory over Jamaica in 1988 and against Peru in the Marlboro Cup in 1989.

He starred at NCAA Division II power Southern Connecticut State before he became the top choice in the 1987 Major Indoor Soccer League draft (by the Cleveland Force). Bliss has also played for the Albany Capitals and Boston Bolts in the American Professional Soccer League.

Through the beginning of 1994, Bliss had played in 22 games for Carl Zeiss Jena, who had reached the quarterfinals of the German Cup, losing to Rot-Weis Essen on penalty kicks.

DARIO BROSE
Midfielder
5-foot-6, 150 lbs.
Born: Jan. 27, 1970
International appearances: 1
Goals: 0

Brose, a creative midfielder, seemed to be destined to play for the U.S. A native of Hughsonville, N.Y., Brose played his entire senior season at Kaiserslautern American H.S. in West Germany. He scored a goal for the Americans in their fourth-place finish in the Under-20 World Cup in Saudi Arabia in 1989 and a world-class goal in a 3–1 triumph over Kuwait at the 1992 Summer Olympics. In-between, Brose twice earned All-American honors at North Carolina State before joining St. Brieuc for the 1992–93 season.

But success can be a double-edged sword. Brose was an important part of St. Brieuc climb into the French First Division, which helped him get proper recognition to be invited to join the National Team. But when he had an opportunity to make his international debut against Germany on Dec. 18, 1993, he could not because St. Brieuc had an important game back home. Brose was patient, and a month later, he played for the U.S. for the first time, coming on as a substitute for Chris Henderson at halftime in the 2–1 win over Norway on Jan. 15, 1994.

Through Dec. 4. Brose scored 6 goals in 21 appearances for St. Brieuc during the 1993–94 season.

MIKE BURNS
    Midfielder
    5-foot-9, 165 pounds
    Born: May 14, 1970
    International appearances: 2
    Goals: 0

Mike Burns has completed U.S. soccer's version of
the grand slam. The Hartwick College graduate
performed for the Under-16 squad that performed
in the World Youth Championships in Canada in
1987, the Under-20 squad that finished a surprising
fourth in that age group's World Championship in
Saudi Arabia in 1989, the Under-23 side that participated in the Summer Olympics in Barcelona in
1992 and for the National Team. He made his full
international debut in a 2–2 draw against Canada on Sept. 3, 1992.
Burns, who has forged a reputation as a good two-way player, also was
a member of the gold-medal winning team at the Pan-Am Games in
1991.

Burns, who started 73 of 79 games at Hartwick College, captained
the team his senior year. He is single.

PAUL CALIGIURI
Defender/midfielder
5-foot-10, 175 pounds
Born: March 9, 1964
International appearances: 73
Goals: 4

Regardless what happens the rest of his career, Paul Caligiuri forever will be remembered as the man who saved U.S. soccer. He scored the winning goal, a twisting, 25-yard shot, that gave the U.S. a 1–0 victory over Trinidad & Tobago on Nov. 19, 1989 and secured a spot in the 1990 World Cup. He also became the first American to score in the World Cup since 1950, connecting in the 5–1 loss to Czechoslovakia.

The Diamond Bar, CA, native also represented the U.S. at the FIFA All-Star game in 1987.

One of the U.S.'s first players to pursue a career in Europe, Caligiuri has played with several teams in Germany, primarily in the Second Division. He started out with M.V. Meppen (1986) and SV Hamburg (1987, First Division), SC Freiburg (1991) and Hansa Rostock (1992), helping the club gain promotion to the First Division, also known as the Bundesliga.

But life—at least in soccer—has not been as kind to Caligiuri since then. He has been beset by injuries and has found himself falling down on the depth chart at left fullback. Whether he will make the final cut remains to be seen.

Caligiuri, who was named National Team Player of the Year in 1986, is married to Dawn and has a daughter, Ashley.

MARK CHUNG
Midfielder
5-foot-7, 140 pounds
Born: June 18, 1970
International appearances: 18
Goals: 0

Unlike many of the domestic-based players, Chung did not come up through the system by playing with any of the youth national teams. Instead, he was "discovered" by coach Bora Milutinovic during the 1991 Olympic Festival in Los Angeles. Bora liked what he saw and Chung joined the team late that year and made his international debut against Costa Rica in 1992.

The Pembroke Pines, FL, native became the third University of South Florida player to finish his careerwith at least 25 goals and assists, collecting 26 goals and 25 assists, including 13 goals and 9 assists in his senior year. He is a longshot to make the final cut, unless Bora sees him as a role player.

FERNANDO CLAVIJO
Defender/midfielder
5-foot-10, 160 pounds
Born: Jan. 23, 1957
International appearances: 54
Goals: 0

At 37, Clavijo is the oldest member of the National Team, and while he is not as sprite as he once was, he still can keep up with the fastest forwards and midfielders around. A naturalized citizen from Uruguay, Clavijo probably became one of the oldest players in international history to make his debut with a National Team. He was 33 when he stepped onto the field to play the Soviet Union in 1990.

During his heyday with the New York United (American Soccer League), New York Arrows, San Diego Sockers and St. Louis Storm (Major Indoor Soccer League), he was one of the fastest players in the country. Clavijo is considered one of the top indoor players around, having performed for 6 MISL championship teams, having been named to the league's 10th anniversary all-star team and having been a member of the U.S.'s silver-medal winning team at the FIFA five-a-side championship in Hong Kong in 1992.

After Clavijo earned his first cap, there was talk of him trying the sweeper role, but there were fears he was not big enough to take the pounding in the middle on the backline.

Clavijo is married to Martha and has 2 sons, Jonathan and Fernando.

CHAD DEERING
Midfielder
6-foot-1, 165 pounds
Born: Sept. 2, 1970
International appearances: 2
Goals: 0

No one will ever consider Chad Deering as unpatriotic. When the U.S. qualified for the Under-17 World Cup in 1987, an emotional Deering, the team captain, wrapped himself up in the American flag to celebrate.

He had further reason to celebrate on Oct. 13, 1993, as he made his American debut as a substitute in the 1−1 tie with Mexico at RFK Stadium in Washington, D.C.

After earning consecutive all-American honors in his 2 years at NCAA Division I power Indiana (21 goals, 22 assists), Deering opted to go overseas and sign with Werder Bremen in Germany, for whom he played on the reserve squad for 3 years. He is currently on loan to Schalke 04, having made five appearances through the end of 1993.

He attended Plano High School in Texas, earning honors as a two-time high school player of the year.

THOMAS DOOLEY
Defender/midfielder
6-foot-1, 168 pounds
Born: May 12, 1961
International appearances: 23
Goals: 4

Thomas Dooley made one big sacrifice for the U.S. National Team. Instead of returning to 1991 German First Division champion Kaiserslatern and a salary in the neighborhood of $300,000, he decided to become a fulltime member of the U.S. National Team at about $80,000 per year.

Regardless of his salary, he has been a bargain. In the U.S. 2–0 upset of England in U.S. Cup '93, Dooley, usually a defender, was deployed as a defensive midfielder, so, not suprisingly, he took to the offensive, scoring his U.S. goal and first goal of the match, and had several other dangerous opportunities.

Back 4 days later as defensive midfielder against Germany, Dooley was the man of the match for the Americans, scoring twice as their late rally fell short in a 4–3 defeat. Some observers felt Dooley had something to prove against players he had faced in Germany. Dooley has continued that high level of play, even though his supporting cast now is nowhere near the caliber of player he is. There was little argument Dooley was the U.S. Soccer Federation's Male Player of the Year in 1993.

Dooley—no, he has no relationship to the Kingston Trio's song of the same name—was born in Bechhofen, Germany. His father, now deceased, was a U.S. Army veteran from Albany, OR, who married a German woman. Dooley also has performed for Homburg, a club in Germany.

He joined the U.S. in time for U.S. Cup '92, and quickly became a defensive force, causing havoc to opposing offenses.

Dooley is married to Elke and they have 2 sons, Marko and Dennis.

JOHN DOYLE
    Defender
    6-foot-3, 185 pounds
    Born: April 16, 1966
    International appearances: 56
    Goals: 4

After the U.S. dropped all 3 of its games in the 1990 World Cup, few American players earned praise for their performances. Doyle was the exception. His poise and solid play against Italy and Austria—he replaced Steve Trittschuh—turned heads in the international media and with several coaches. Eventually, Doyle was offered and accepted a contract with Orgryte IS of Sweden.

Because of his height, he sometimes has trouble covering smaller and quicker players, but he is excellent in the air.

He comes from an athletic family. His father played golf on scholarship at Western Michigan University. His mother was a star high-school basketball player in Jessup, GA. And his wife Kaarin, who gave birth to a girl on Feb. 25, 1992, was named most athletic in her high school class.

BRAD FRIEDEL
Goalkeeper
6-foot-4, 202 pounds
Born: May 18, 1971
International appearances: 17
Goals: 0

Brad Friedel is giving incumbent Tony Meola a run for his money. Although he does not have the international experience Meola has, Friedel has acquitted himself well just about every time he has worked the nets. Take, for instance, the U.S.'s 1–1 draw with Mexico on Oct. 13, 1993. He made several important saves to keep the Americans in the match. In fact, Friedel just might have the Mexicans' number. Friedel is 3–0–1 against the Mexicans, an excellent mark considering the U.S. is 7–29–8 lifetime. Friedel's trophies include a pair of victories in 1992 Olympic qualifying—one in Mexico City, where it is difficult for any visiting team to come away with a win, and another in the Pan-Am gold-medal match in 1991.

His ascension to the National Team is not by mistake. The Bay Village, OH, resident helped UCLA to the NCAA Division I crown as a freshman in 1990, stopping Rutgers' third shot in the penalty kick tie-breaker in the final, after saving a penalty kick by North Carolina in the semifinals. Friedel, who unsuccessfully tried for an English work permit in his bid to play with Nottingham Forest in 1993, went on to capture the Hermann Trophy as the best college player for the 1992 season.

Friedel was also in the nets for every Olympic qualifier and every match in the Barcelona Summer Games.

JOHN HARKES
Midfielder
5-foot-11, 165 pounds
Born: March 8, 1967
International appearances: 52
Goals: 4

John Harkes is a player who has a history of making things happen. The human dynamo was the U.S.'s most consistent player during World Cup qualifying in 1990 and in the tournament itself. The Kearny, NJ, native has continued that work ethic for Sheffield Wednesday of the English Premier League and Derby County of the First Division, to which he transferred during the summer of 1993. During his Wednesday career, he scored a goal at hallowed Wembley Stadium in the 1993 English League Cup and set up the tying goal in the prestigious F.A. Cup final in May, 1993.

He certainly is not a token American. The British press has claimed that Aston Villa of the English Premier League—its coach, Ron Atkinson, brought Harkes to Sheffield in 1991—was interested in obtaining the former all-American for $1.5 million, an unheard of sum for an American soccer player.

Among his accomplishments:

His 30-yard goal against Derby's international keeper Peter Shilton in the English League Cup was spectacular enough to be picked as the 1991 Goal of the Year. He became the first American to play at Wembley as Wednesday captured the English League Cup that year. And he was a regular on Wednesday's fifth-place finish in 1992, which was good enough to play in the UEFA Cup, one of 3 annual major European club competitions.

Perhaps one match demonstrated Harkes' value to Wednesday. On the short end of a 2−1 score to Luton Town late in the second half in February, 1992, Harkes headed a left-side cross from Trevor Francis to Paul Williams, who headed it into the net in the 79th minute. Seven minutes later, Harkes had his chance, heading in a short David Hirst pass for the game-winner in a 3−2 victory.

On this front, Harkes has been just as impressive. He scored the lone U.S. goal in a 1−1 tie with Italy, to give the Americans the U.S. Cup '92 championship.

Harkes married his college sweetheart, Cindy Kunihiro, a soccer player herself at the University of Virginia, where he starred and earned All-American honors. As a youth player in his native New Jersey, Harkes was a teammate of fellow U.S. National Team member Tab Ramos.

CHRIS HENDERSON
Midfielder
5-foot-10, 150 pounds
Born: Dec. 11, 1970
International appearances: 59
Goals: 2

You name it, Chris Henderson by the age of 23 has just about accomplished it in the national program. He was named Gatorade's national high school player of the year in 1988. He was named newcomer of the year by the Western Soccer League as a player with the Seattle Storm. He scored a goal against Iraq in the quarterfinals of the Under-20 World Championships in Saudi Arabia in 1989 (the U.S. finished fourth). He became the youngest player on any of the 24 teams at the 1990 World Cup in Italy, although Henderson did not play a minute. As a sophomore, he helped UCLA to the NCAA Division I title in 1990. And then he decided to forgo the final 2 years of college to sign a contract with the National Team.

The federation certainly got their money's worth out of Henderson, a fast man on the wing, with an excellent work ethic. So, it was not that surprising when he pulled double duty between the Olympic and National Teams in 1992, helping the former to qualify for the Barcelona Games. But fate pulled a cruel trick on Henderson. Only a week before the Olympic opener, he suffered a knee injury that sidelined him. He most likely won't start in the World Cup, but could very well come off the bench.

ERIK IMLER
Defender
5-foot-9, 160 pounds
Born: June 1, 1971
International appearances: 1
Goals: 0

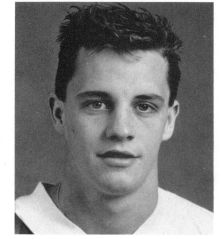

Talk about bad luck. Only 43 minutes into his National Team debut against El Salvador on March 23, 1993, Erik Imler suffered torn ligaments in his right knee. Subsequently, he missed a good portion of the year.

That was too bad, because Bora wanted to get a decent look at Imler, who was a vital defensive cog on the University of Virginia's NCAA Division I champions in 1989, 1991 and 1992. Until the injury, Imler did just about everything right for a soccer player. He was a 2-time *Parade Magazine* all-American in high school, a 2-time all-American at Virginia, as he captained the Cavaliers in 1992, a member of the U.S. Under-16 and 20 youth teams, and a member of the squad that captured the Pan-Am gold medal in 1991. He also started the 3 matches at the 1992 Olympics in Barcelona.

Imler will be heard from again.

COBI JONES
Midfielder
5-foot-7, 145 pounds
Born: June 16, 1970
International appearances: 34
Goals: 4

Since joining the National Team in 1992, the speedy Jones has opened up eyes with his end-to-end runs and endless enthusiasm. In fact, some soccer observers felt that he has been wasted playing with the national side and should be playing overseas somewhere. He was just about the only American who did anything offensively in the 2–0 loss to host Ecuador in the opening match of Copa America, the South American championship, in June, 1993. He also scored the winning goal with only seconds left in the U.S.'s 2–1 victory over Norway on Jan. 15, 1994.

The Westlake Village, CA, native made a positive impression early in only his third international match as he connected on a brilliant goal and set up 2 others in the 5–2 victory over Ivory Coast in the consolation match at the Intercontinental Championship in Saudi Arabia on Oct. 19, 1992.

Jones knows what it means to work hard. He earned a spot on the UCLA soccer team as a non-scholarship player and wound up as one of its leading scorers in his senior year in 1991, the same year he was a member of the Pan-Am championship team.

KASEY KELLER
Goalkeeper
6-foot-2, 180 pounds
Born: Nov. 29, 1960
International appearances: 8
Goals: 0

The big question is: Will Kasey Keller get a chance to show what he has learned as one of the top goalkeepers in the English First Division. The Lacey, WA, native took a chance in 1992, when he decided to forgo a backup role at the 1992 Olympic Games for a chance to play with Millwall.

It has paid off more than anyone could imagine. In 45 matches in the 1992–93 season, Keller allowed about a goal a game and keeping the sheets clean—the English phrase for shutouts—on 16 occasions. He was named Millwall's Player of the Year by the club's fans and a number of Premier League teams have inquired about his availability.

"He's done a brilliant job," said Millwall Coach Mick McCarthy, who captained Ireland in the 1990 World Cup in Italy "He's just doing very well. He's kept us in games under pressure."

Keller, who was the backup to Tony Meola at the FIFA Under-20 World Championship in Chile in 1987, came into his own at the international level two years later in Saudi Arabia, helping the U.S. to a surprising fourth-place finish while earning the Silver Ball Award as the second best player of the tournament.

A 2-time All-American at the University of Portland, Keller was named the Western Soccer League Player of the Year in 1990 as a member of the Portland Timbers.

DOMINIC KINNEAR
Midfielder
5-foot-11, 150 pounds
Born: July 26, 1967
International appearances: 48
Goals: 9

Dominic Kinnear's career has been on an upward curve for the past 6 years. Kinnear had just been named an all-American as a freshman at Hartwick College in 1988, when he decided to turn pro with the San Francisco Bay Blackhawks (American Professional Soccer League). He spent 2 seasons with the Blackhawks, earning all-star honors while getting an opportunity to train with the National Team in January, 1989.

Kinnear, known for his skill and touch on the ball, eventually made his international debut against Trinidad & Tobago in November, 1990, collected his first goal in a 1–1 tie with Costa Rica on Nov. 24, 1991 and converted an important penalty kick during the tie-breaker in the CONCACAF Gold Cup championship match with Honduras in 1991.

FRANK KLOPAS
Forward
5-foot-9, 155 pounds
Born: Sept. 1, 1966
International appearances: 23
Goals: 5

If Frank Klopas had been able to stay away from injuries, he could have made more of an impact with the team. Because of a knee injury in 1992 and commitments to his club in Greece, AEK Athens, Klopas' playing time has been limited. That's too bad, because he always has had a nose for the goal, connecting twice in a 5–1 World Cup qualifying victory over Jamaica in 1988. Not many present day National Team players can say they scored twice in a full international.

Klopas, a native of Athens, Greece, has made but 2 appearances since 1989, but he still is part of the pool of players available to coach Bora Milutinovic.

CLE KOOIMAN
Defender
6-foot-1, 190 pounds
Born July 3, 1963
International appearances: 10
Goals: 1

One of the great "finds" of 1993, Kooiman, a rugged, tenacious defender, is the captain of Cruz Azul of the Mexican First Division. Bora, who played and coached in Mexico, scouted Kooiman and liked what he saw, bringing him on for 10 matches in 1993. Kooiman, who will turn 31 during the World Cup, started his international career rather late, after earning all-American honors at San Diego State (1982), playing 5 years with the Los Angeles Lazers of the Major Indoor Soccer League, starting in 1983, before joining the Juarez Cobras in Mexico.

He was a teammate of fellow U.S. international Paul Caligiuri with the Diamond Bar Kickers (CA) and once kicked a school-record 59-yard field goal at Chaffey High (CA). Kooiman's status for the World Cup was put in doubt after he suffered a severe knee injury for Cruz Azul in late October, 1993.

ALEXI LALAS
   Midfielder/defender
   6-foot-3, 195 pounds
   Born: June 1, 1970
   International appearances: 30
   Goals: 4

Everything this man touches seemingly turns to gold. Alexi Lalas could not have picked a better time to have scored his first international goal. Only 2 minutes after he entered the match as a substitute for the injured Thomas Dooley, Lalas connected on a header off a Tab Ramos corner kick to help secure the 2–0 upset over England on June 9 in Foxboro, MA. In fact, his first several goals were scored off of set plays. There are more skilled and talented players on the team, but Lalas always seems to get the job done.

A 3-time captain at Rutgers University, Lalas hit the jackpot in 1991, as he took home the 2 most important awards in college soccer—the Hermann Trophy and the Missouri Athletic Club Award.

Lalas' scraggly red hair, goatee and height make him look like a wild man and this could be intimidating to an uninformed opponent. But the Birmingham, MI, native happens to be one of the friendliest players on the team. When he isn't playing soccer, he's playing with a band called "The Gypsies" in the New York City area.

MIKE LAPPER
Defender
6-foot, 172 pounds
Born: Sept. 28, 1970
International appearances: 31
Goals: 0

Mike Lapper holds the rare distinction of being the lone U.S. player who has scored a winning goal in Mexico. It happened during the 2–1 Olympic qualifying victory on March 25, 1992, the first time an American team emerged victorious in Mexico City.

Lapper, however, is better known for his tight marking on defense, which was brought out in the fact he played every minute for the U.S. at the 1992 Summer Games in Barcelona. He also is yet another member from UCLA's NCAA Division I championship team in 1990.

His National Team career, which is just beginning, is not as distinguished, but the Huntington Beach, CA, native has plenty of time left.

TONY MEOLA
> Goalkeeper
> 6-foot-1, 205 pounds
> Born: Feb. 21, 1969
> International appearances: 76
> Goals: 0

Regardless what he accomplishes the rest of his career, Tony Meola will always have Foxboro—as in Foxboro, MA—the site of the U.S.'s stunning 2–0 victory over heavily favored England. Meola played the game of his life that June 9 night, making several key saves throughout the match, including 2 on English-scoring terror Ian Wright in the final minutes to preserve the win.

Since Bora Milutinovic took over as coach of the U.S. National Team in March, 1991, there have been rumors he was unhappy with and going to replace Meola. Meola, however, was named captain and has tended goal in the vast majority of games the past 3 years.

Even though he is only 24, Meola has seen more international matches than most goalkeepers see in a lifetime.

Meola began to make a name for himself internationally in 1987, starring for the U.S. at the Under-20 World Cup in Chile. In 1989, he dropped out of a successful college career at powerhouse University of Virginia to pursue a pro career and a spot on the 1990 World Cup team. Only days before he was in goal for the U.S.'s 1–0 victory in Trinidad & Tobago, which qualified the Americans for their first World Cup in 40 years, Meola was named winner of the Hermann Trophy, which is given to the top college player in the States.

JANUSZ MICHALLIK
Defender
5-foot-11, 170 pounds
Born: April 22, 1966
International appearances: 29
Goals: 1

Once a regular for the nationals, making 15 appearances in 1992, Michallik appears to have fallen out of favor with Bora.

While the Polish native is a hard-worker, he has experienced a number of defensive lapses. In the U.S.'s scoreless tie with Italian powerhouse Juventus in 1991, his back pass to the goalkeeper almost went over Tony Meola's head and into the goal. His first international goal came against Saudi Arabia on April 9, 1993.

Michallik, who now calls New Britain, CT, home, started playing with the Gwardia Warsaw as a youth and turned pro when he was 16, before moving to the U.S. in 1983.

Soccer is in his blood. Kris, his father, made 50 appearances with the Polish Olympic and National Teams and played with the Hartford Bicentennials (North American Soccer League) in 1976. Janusz is married to Marzena.

JOE-MAX MOORE
Midfielder
5-foot-9, 150 pounds
Born: Feb. 23, 1971
International appearances: 25
Goals: 8

Joe-Max Moore feels right at home in Mission Viejo, CA, site of the U.S. training center. After all, he went to school at Mission Viejo High and then went on to college at UCLA, where he earned All-American honors.

His specialty is the free kick, which he aptly demonstrated in the 2–1 loss to Italy, bending the ball around the wall in the 1992 Olympic opener. A year before, Moore scored the game-winning goal in overtime in the Pan-Am Games semifinal win over Mexico. And in only his second full international start, Moore scored first goal in the 2–2 tie with European Champion Denmark on Jan. 30, 1993. His most impressive performance was 4 goals in the 7–0 victory over El Salvador on Dec. 5, 1993.

BRUCE MURRAY
Midfielder/forward
6-foot-1, 170 pounds
Born: Jan. 22, 1966
International appearances: 93
Goals: 21

Whether Bruce Murray resurfaces again with the National Team, it remains to be seen. It sounds funny to talk that way about the man who has made more appearances and scored more goals than any other U.S. player in history, but when the overseas players returned for the big games, Murray saw himself sitting more and more on the bench.

So, he and the National Team went a mutual parting of the ways over the summer of 1993. Murray joined Millwall of the English First Division, joining fellow Americans Kasey Keller, a goalkeeper, and John Kerr, a forward. Murray made himself felt in his very first match, scoring the game-winner in the waning minutes of Millwall's 2–1 victory over Stoke.

Murray was used primarily as a forward on the 1990 World Cup team—he was one of two Americans who scored a goal—but he seems more comfortable and makes a greater impact in the midfield, where can can score and create goals.

He played his college ball at Clemson, scoring 48 goals and setting up 46 others, and leading his school to the NCAA Division I championship in 1987. His career was capped by being named winner of the 1987 Hermann Trophy, which goes to the college's top player. Murray also played in 2 games at the 1988 Olympics in South Korea.

HUGO PEREZ
Midfielder/forward
5-foot-8, 155 pounds
Born: Nov. 8, 1963
International appearances: 62
Goals: 13

Once the mainstay of the U.S. attack, Hugo Perez sometimes appears out of it, especially when the European-based players return. Perhaps he is used to being ithe main man taking on many responsibilties, rather than just another cog in the wheel.

In the 1 – 1 draw with Mexico on Oct. 13, 1993 Perez was not a factor at all. Several days later in a 2 – 1 loss to the Ukraine, Perez appeared to be his usual self, moving forward and attacking.

One of the most creative players in U.S. soccer, the El Salvadoran native became one of the first U.S. players to perform in Europe—with Red Star of Paris (French Second Division). After a knee injury kept him out of the 1990 World Cup, Perez was the main offensive force with the National Team in 1991 and 1992 before he played the 1992–93 season with Ittihad Club in Saudi Arabia.

It seems that Perez has been playing forever because he began his pro career at such a tender age. He came to the U.S. at the age of 11 and signed as a 16-year-old with the Los Angeles Aztecs (North American Soccer League).

How important has Perez been to the U.S. attack? He has 12 full international goals, but it seems he has at least twice that many because he has always been in the thick of things. A return to his former form is needed if the Americans are to make an impact at USA '94.

BRIAN QUINN
Midfielder
5-foot-9, 155 pounds
Born: May 24, 1960
International appearances: 40
Goals: 1

Consider Brian Quinn a gift to the U.S. National Team. A native of Belfast, he and his wife Sharon became U.S. citizens during a special halftime ceremony at a San Diego Sockers game (Major Indoor Soccer League) on April 20, 1991.

Since then, he has made 36 international appearances. He made his international debut against Ireland on June 1, 1991. The Belfast, Northern Ireland, native's never-say-die attitude, grittiness and steadying force has made him a perfect complement to his younger teammates. His most memorable goal wasn't even scored in a full international. He connected on a 35-yard blast against Sheffield Wednesday in 1991.

Quinn, who now lives in Poway, CA, has been around the block and then some. He started out at Larne (Ireland) in 1978–79, moved to Everton (English First Division) in 1979–81, then joined the Los Angeles Aztecs (North American Soccer League) in 1981, and finally signed with the Sockers in 1984. He wound up playing for 7 indoor championship teams as a member of the Sockers and earned MISL playoff MVP honors twice.

Brian and Sharon have 6 children.

TAB RAMOS
Midfielder
5-foot-7, 140 pounds
Born: Sept. 21, 1966
International appearances: 50
Goals: 3

Tab Ramos came into his own during Italia '90. With No. 1 offensive midfielder Hugo Perez sidelined with a leg injury for the World Cup, Ramos was forced to grow up in a hurry and became one of the few bright spots for the U.S. in the tournament.

His consistent performances opened the eyes of many European clubs before he signed with Figueras of the Spanish Second Division. He transferred to Real Betis (Second Division) for the 1992–93 season, although Ramos has let it be known he wants to play in the First Division.

The Hillside, NJ, native has enjoyed much success at every level. While playing for St. Benedict's Prep in 1983, he was High School Player of the Year. Ramos, who is single, also was a first-team All-American at North Carolina State and was the Atlantic Coast Conference's top scorer in his senior year. He was an all-star in his 2-year stint in the American Soccer League (1988–89). He also was a member of the 1988 Olympic team and of U.S.'s bronze-medal winning team at the first FIFA world five-a-side championship in the Netherlands in 1989.

His father, Julian, played professionally in Uruguay.

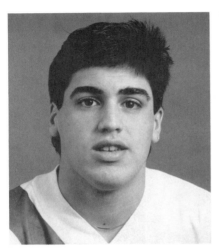

CLAUDIO REYNA
Midfielder
5-foot-10, 150 pounds
Born: July 20, 1973
International appearances: 1
Goals: 0

Claudio Reyna could wind up being Ramos' understudy or play alongside him in the World Cup, he is that talented. Reyna, who calls Springfield, NJ, home, led the University of Virginia three consecutive NCAA Division I titles, winning the offensive MVP award twice. Not bad for someone who completed his junior season in 1993. He earned the Hermann Trophy as the top college player in 1993.

At the 1992 Final Four in Davidson, NC, Reyna was so on target on every one of his passes that he was never intercepted. Former U.S. Olympic coach Lothar Osiander has said that Reyna was slow—Reyna still was the playmaker for the Olympic team—but the National Team can use a dynamic presence in the midfield who is noted for pin-point passes.

Reyna was offered a multi-year contract by Barcelona of the Spanish First Division because of his impressive performance at the 1992 Games, but he opted to return to college. It is only a matter of time before Reyna goes overseas to play professionally.

Reyna made his international debut in the 2–1 victory over Norway on Jan. 15, 1994, setting up Cobi Jones' winning goal on a rebound shot in the final seconds.

MARK SANTEL
　　Midfielder/defender
　　5-foot-10, 165 pounds
　　Born: July 5, 1968
　　International appearances: 10
　　Goals: 1

After a 2½-year absence, Santel rejoined the National Team for a match against the Ukraine on Oct. 23, 1993. Several weeks after, he helped the Colorado Foxes capture their second American Professional Soccer League title and earned all-star honors in the process. Santel, who had made six appearances for the U.S. from 1988-91, then scored his first international goal against the Cayman Islands on Nov. 14. Impressed with his performance, the National Team signed Santel in December.

　　Santel has spent most of his life in the Midwest. A Parade All-American from Christian Brothers H.S. in St. Louis, the versatile Santel went on to become a three-time All-American at St. Louis University. He was drafted first overall in the 1991 Major Indoor Soccer League draft by the Wichita Wings, but wound up playing for the St. Louis Storm in 1991-92, before joining the Foxes.

　　He is married to Lori.

MIKE SORBER
  Midfielder
  5-foot-10, 175 pounds
  Born: May 14, 1971
  International appearances: 28
  Goals: 1

For someone just out of college, Mike Sorber certainly has seen a lot of action at the international level. He appeared 12 times in 1992, and another 7 times in 1993. He made his debut against the Commonwealth of Independent States, now Russia, on Jan. 25, 1992, and his first start against Costa Rica on Feb. 12, 1992. He tallied his first goal against Canada on Oct. 3, 1992.

At St. Louis University, he was better known for his creative ability (17 assists in his senior year) than scoring prowess (4 goals).

ERNIE STEWART

Forward
5-foot-9, 145 pounds
Born: March 28, 1969
International appearances: 14
Goals: 2

Even though Ernie Stewart did not score in his first 11 international appearances, no one was about to give up on him. One, he was one of the fastest U.S. players on the field. And two, it looked as if he knew what he was doing. He finally connected against world champion Germany in the U.S. Cup on June 13, 1993, and added his second in his next appearance, against Iceland on Aug. 31, 1993.

He should look as if he knows what he's doing, because he plays in the Dutch First Division. With V.V. Venlo of the Second Division in 1989–90, he scored 14 goals. After transferring to Willem II in the First Division, Stewart struck for 17 goals, good for third in the league in 1990–91, and then 8 in 1991–92. Because of a knee injury, Stewart's production fell in 1992–93 to 3 goals in 16 starts and 20 games.

Used on many occasions as a substitute by Bora, it would be intriguing to see how he would perform on a regular basis as a twin striker with Roy Wegerle.

Stewart, named after his father, a retired U.S. Air Force veteran, was born in Veghel, the Netherlands. He lived in the U.S. from age 2 to 7, but did not play soccer.

PETER VERMES
Forward
6-foot, 175 pounds
Born: Nov. 21, 1966
International appearances: 67
Goals: 11

Don't expect Peter Vermes to start or even play at USA '94, despite his many appearances. While he is one of the "good guys" on the team and talkative to the media, his goal production has fallen short of expectations. He plays when the Euro-based players are overseas. In fact, some observers have been surprised that the Delran, NJ, resident is still with the team. Vermes' best attibute is shielding the ball, but he has needed to develop his game more to make a bigger contribution and impact on the team. His attitude and work ethic has set an example for the younger players to follow. Sometimes players like Vermes are more important than a regular.

The experience he brings to the team off the field is invaluable, because the Rutgers graduate has been around the world and then some, playing for Raba Eto (Hungary) in 1989, F.C. Volendam (Netherlands) in 1990, Figueras (Spain) in 1991, before returning home to become a fulltime player with the U.S. National Team.

ROY WEGERLE

Forward
5-foot-11, 170 pounds
Born: March 19, 1964
International appearances: 14
Goals: 1

Roy Wegerle may be the missing link to the U.S. National Team's puzzle.

For years the Americans have been searching for someone who can consistently put the ball into the back of the net. In just a handful of appearances with the squad, Wegerle already has demonstrated he just might be that man, with a few more tricks up his sleeve.

Take, for instance, his performance in the U.S. Cup '92, which was won by the Americans. He was the second-half spark behind the U.S.'s 3–1 victory over Ireland, creating one goal; he then scored the lone goal for the U.S. in its 1–0 triumph over Portugal.

Ironically, that goal was the only one Wegerle has tallied for the U.S., but his presence in the lineup has raised the team's level of play.

Even though the South African-born Wegerle has played in England professionally in the past several years, he has demonstrated a Latin influence and flair, as he likes to back-pass the ball to a teammate while on the run.

Wegerle is no stranger to U.S. soccer as his brother Steve starred for the Tampa Bay Rowdies in the North American Soccer League in the seventies and eighties. In 1984, Roy followed in his footsteps after 2 superb seasons at the University of South Florida. He was selected first in the draft by the Rowdies and then lived up to that promise by becoming NASL Rookie of the Year. He also played for the Tacoma Stars of the defunct Major Indoor Soccer League, scoring 36 goals from 1984–86.

In England, he went on to perform for Chelsea for 2 seasons in the First Division before moving onto Luton Town, collecting 23 goals in 1½ seasons. He was honored as player of the year in 1989. Wegerle transferred to Queens Park Rangers, scoring 47 goals in 2½ years. He enjoyed his finest season in 1991, finishing seventh in league goalscoring (18 in 35 matches), while capturing team player of the year honors.

After a short stint with the Blackburn Rovers, Wegerle finished up the 1992–93 with Coventry City of the English Premier League, scoring 10 goals in 39 games.

Wegerle is married to Marie, a native of Miami whom he met while attending South Florida in the early eighties.

PETER WOODRING
Midfielder
5-foot-11, 170 pounds
Born: Feb. 5, 1968
International appearances: 3
Goals: 0

He is one of the newest members of the National Team as Bora noticed him after he earned a spot in the starting lineup of Hamburg SV (German Bundesliga). Woodring is capable of scoring or setting up teammates. During his 4-year career at the University of California-Berkeley, the Kent, CA, native collected 20 goals and 30 assists.

ERIC WYNALDA

Midfielder/forward
6-foot-1, 172 pounds
Born: June 9, 1969
International appearances: 50
Goals: 14

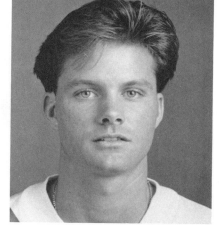

Wynalda dropped out of San Diego State to pursue his dream of playing in the World Cup, and while things always haven't gone perfectly, he has been one of the most productive American-born players.

Take, for example, his debut with Saar-bruecken in the German Bundesliga. He scored 9 goals in his first 10 games in the 1992–93 season, before tailing off in the second half of the season. Despite a 7-game scoring drought, the Westlake Village, CA, native had 5 goals through the beginning of November, 1993.

His production—14 goals in 50 matches (one goal per 2.8 matches)—is among the best goals-per-game of any U.S. player.

Wynalda's problem has been his temper. Like it or not, Wynalda wrote his name into soccer history by becoming the first American player to be ejected from a World Cup match. It happened in the 53rd minute against Czechoslovakia in the opener as he retaliated against midfielder Lubomir Moravcik; the referee had not seen the Czech's original foul. The former San Diego State forward was like a fish out of water at Italia '90, anyway. Wynalda, an attacking player, was asked to play a defensive midfielder's role.

Chapter Five

Twenty Four Nations:
How They Stack Up

Group **A** (Pasadena/Los Angeles, Palo Alto/San Francisco, Pontiac/Detroit): United States, Colombia, Switzerland, Romania

Group **B** (Pasadena/Los Angeles, Palo Alto/San Francisco, Pontiac/Detroit): Brazil, Russia, Cameroon, Sweden

Group **C** (Chicago, Foxboro/Boston, Dallas): Germany, Bolivia, Spain, South Korea

Group **D** (Chicago, Foxboro/Boston, Dallas): Argentina, Greece, Nigeria, Bulgaria

Group **E** (New York/New Jersey, Washington, D.C., Orlando): Italy, Ireland, Norway, Mexico

Group **F** (New York/New Jersey, Washington, D.C., Orlando): Belgium, Morocco, Netherlands, Saudi Arabia

The World Cup draw, which was held in Las Vegas on Dec. 19, 1993, was supposed to be a sorting-out process. In some respects, it did sort things out. In other respects, it seemed to make things only more confusing.

There were 6 seeded teams—the host U.S., defending champion Germany, Brazil, Argentina, Italy and Belgium. Only that U.S. (Los Angeles) and Germany (Chicago) knew where they would play 2 of their 3 opening-round matches. World Cup organizers had stated before the draw they had hoped to place countries in cities represented by their respective ethnic groups. In such an ethnically diverse country as the U.S., it was a logical way of doing things.

For example, in a perfect world, Ireland would be placed in Foxboro/Boston because of the huge Irish population in that region. The United States, being a relatively weak soccer country, and a nation that FIFA wanted to reach the second round, was rumored about getting an easy first round. Mexico supposedly was headed to Dallas. Not surprisingly, this increased speculation from the media and interested soccer observers that the draw was going to be fixed, as supposedly it has been in the past. It has never been proven, but there has been talk and speculation that magnetic rings, hot balls and cold balls have been used to put teams in their so-called proper places.

It didn't work out this time.

If the draw had been fixed, then the U.S. would not have gotten Colombia, considered the darkhorse to win the title, and solid European teams, Switzerland and Romania, in Group A.

If the draw had been fixed, Mexico would have been in Dallas, and not Washington, D.C. and Orlando.

Each World Cup has a Group of Death and USA '94 is no exception, with Group E—Italy, Ireland, Norway and Mexico.

The next most difficult group is Group B (Brazil, Russia, Cameroon and Sweden. And then there is the aforementioned Group A.

Germany should have an easy first round in Group C, with Spain, and longshots Bolivia and South Korea. So should Belgium and the Netherlands, with Morocco and Saudi Arabia in Group F.

Somewhere in the middle is Argentina, Bulgaria, Greece and Nigeria.

How The World Cup Works

The top 2 teams in each of the 6 groups will qualify automatically for the second round. The 4 third-place teams with the next best records will be given wild-card berths into the second round. The rest of the tournament, from second round, to quarterfinals to semifinals to the championship match will be a single-elimination tournament.

In an attempt to liven up the first round, 3 points, instead of the traditional 2, will be awarded for a victory. A tie will still be worth one point. FIFA wants to avoid a situation like the one in 1986 when Bulgaria advanced to the second round without winning a match, finishing with 2 ties and 1 loss.

As for the favorites, Germany, Brazil, Italy, Netherlands and Argentina were considered to be the top 5 teams as of Dec. 19, 1993.

Colombia was picked as the unofficial dark horse to win it. The host U.S. would be happy just to reach the second round.

Almost immediately after the draw, British bookmaker Ladbrokes came out with the odds of winning for the 24 finalists:

4–1—Germany, Brazil.

The Odds

9–2—Italy.

7–1—Netherlands.

8–1—Argentina.

10–1—Colombia.

16–1—Spain.

20–1—Belgium.

25–1—Russia.

33–1—Bolivia, Switzerland.

40–1—Ireland, Mexico, Norway, Sweden.

50–1—Bulgaria, Romania, United States.

80–1—Nigeria.

100–1—Cameroon, Greece.

150–1—Morocco.

250–1—Saudi Arabia, South Korea.

GROUP A

UNITED STATES

COLOMBIA

ROMANIA

SWITZERLAND

UNITED STATES

POPULATION: 250,000,000

COLORS: Blue shirt, red shorts, blue socks

WORLD CUP APPEARANCES: Fifth. 3–7–0, 14 goals for, 29 against. 1930 (semifinals), 1934 (first round), 1950 (first round), 1990 (first round)

World Cup History

For a country that has played in only 4 World Cups and waited 40 years between appearances, the U.S. has a surprisingly rich history. In the very first tournament in 1930, the Americans, nicknamed the shotputters by the French because of the size of their players, reached the semifinals before Argentina rolled to a 6–1 victory. In 1950, the U.S. lost 2 of its opening-round matches, but pulled off the upset of the ages, a 1–0 stunner over England.

How They Qualified

The U.S. was an automatic qualifier as hosts of the World Cup. The Americans were awarded the cup on July 4, 1988, beating out Brazil and Morocco.

Players To Watch

Defender-turned-midfielder Thomas Dooley has emerged as the team's most important all-around player. Midfielders John Harkes and Tab Ramos, who grew up together in New Jersey, have returned from Europe as improved and more confident players. Midfielder-forward Roy Wegerle was born in South Africa and plays in England, but displays cleverness and craftiness that usually is found in Latin players.

Goalkeepers: Tony Meola (U.S. National Team). **Defenders**: Jeff Agoos (U.S.), Marcelo Balboa (U.S.), John Doyle (U.S.), Cle Kooiman (Cruz Azul, Mexico). **Midfielders**: Thomas Dooley (U.S.), John Harkes (Derby County, England), Tab Ramos (Real Betis, Spain), Eric Wynalda (F.C. Saarbruecken). **Forwards**: Roy Wegerle (Coventry City, England), Ernie Stewart (Willem II, Netherlands).

Probable Lineup

Goalkeeper: Brad Friedel (U.S. National Team), Kasey Keller (Millwall, England), Tony Meola (U.S.). **Defenders**: Jeff Agoos (U.S.), Yari Allnutt (U.S.), Desmond Armstrong (U.S.), Marcelo Balboa (U.S.), Brian Bliss (Carl Zeiss Jena, Germany), Paul Caligiuri (U.S.), Fernando Clavijo (U.S.), John Doyle (U.S.), Erik Imler (U.S.), Cle Kooiman (Cruz Azul, Mexico), Mike Lapper (U.S.), Janusz Michallik (U.S.). **Midfielders**: Dario Brose (St. Brieuc, France), Mike Burns (U.S.), Mark Chung (U.S.), Chad Deering (Schalke 04, Germany), Thomas Dooley (U.S.), Eric Eichmann (Fort Lauderdale Strikers), John Harkes (Derby County, England), Chris Henderson (U.S.), Cobi Jones (U.S.), Dominic Kinnear (U.S.), Alexi Lalas (U.S.), Joe-Max Moore (U.S.), Bruce Murray (Millwall, England), Hugo Perez (U.S.), Brian Quinn (U.S.), Tab Ramos (Real Betis, Spain), Claudio Reyna (University of Virginia), Mark Santel (U.S.), Mike Sorber (U.S.), Peter Woodring (SV Hamburg, Germany), Eric Wynalda (F.C. Saarbruecken, Germany). **Forwards**: Jean Harbor (Tampa Bay Rowdies), Frank Klopas (AEK Athens, Greece), Ernie Stewart (Willem II, Netherlands), Peter Vermes (U.S.), Roy Wegerle (Coventry City, England).

Player Pool

An indepth look at the U.S. players can be found in Chapter Four.

PLAYER PROFILES

For the third consecutive World Cup, Bora Milutinovic will coach a team that already had qualified before he was hired. He was brought in as Mexican coach in 1983, leading Mexico to the quarterfinals in 1986 before losing to West Germany, which went on to finish second. He was brought in as Costa Rican coach only 3 months before Italia '90, and guided the World Cup first-timers to the second round, while Scotland failed to get out of the first round for the seventh consecutive time. USA '94, however, will be his most challenging assignment.

Coach

    The conversation took place in the back of a bus as it rolled through the streets of Zurich, Switzerland, on the night of July 4, 1988, hours after FIFA awarded the United States the 1994 World Cup. A number of American sportswriters, returning from an affair hosted by

1994

the U.S. embassy after the historic announcement, talked about the U.S.'s chances 6 years hence.

"Come on," said one writer who thought he understood how FIFA—soccer's world governing body—operated. "The U.S. will get an easy draw. FIFA wants the U.S. to do well. We'll get an African team, an Asian team and a so-so team from Europe. You just wait and see."

On Dec. 19, 1993, the entire world saw what happened at the World Cup draw in Las Vegas. There were no African or Asian teams in the U.S. group—Group A. Instead there loomed Colombia, Romania and Switzerland.

Translated: It won't be easy for the U.S. this June and July.

Switzerland and Romania might not be Italy and Belgium, but they are formidable sides. Colombia, off 2 big victories over Argentina, very well could be the hottest national team in the world.

Switzerland, playing in its first World Cup since 1966, defeated Italy, 1–0, at home and enjoyed a 2–0 lead in Cagliari before the Italians rallied for a 2–2 tie.

Romania? The team reached the second round at Italia '90 and beat Belgium, one of the 6 seeded teams, in a qualifier, 1–0.

Then there's Colombia, which was picked as the darkhorse in a survey of international journalists.

The U.S., at best, is expected to finish third in the group, which may or may not be enough to reach the second round. The top 2 countries in each of the six-team groups will qualify for the second round, plus the 4 third-place teams with the best records.

To reach the next round, the U.S. will probably need 4 points—3 points for a victory (teams will receive 3 points, instead of 2, for a victory under the new system) and 1 point still for a tie.

So, where will those points come from?

The best possibility for a victory could come in the Americans' very first match against the Swiss at the Pontiac Silverdome on June 18, the first World Cup match ever to be played under a dome. They are not given much of a chance against Colombia at the Rose Bowl on June 22 before completing the opening round against the Romanians at the Rose Bowl on June 26.

No, it won't be easy, although the U.S. team put on an optimistic face in Vegas.

"Colombia has beaten the United States twice, 1–0 and 2–1," U.S. Coach Bora Milutinovic said. "It's time for the United States to beat Colombia."

Midfielder Alexi Lalas wasn't fazed. "I'm psyched," he said. "Colombia is tough, but I'm raring to play."

Added team captain and goalkeeper Tony Meola: "I'll be very disappointed if we don't move on. We'll have to fight but we would have to fight in any group."

Probably the most interesting fight inside the U.S. camp will be for the No. 1 goalkeeper. Meola, the incumbent who started all 3 opening-round matches at Italia '90, had the inside track through early winter. But he had a pair of challengers who have some impressive credentials of their own—Brad Friedel, the 1992 Hermann Trophy winner as the best player in college soccer, who has stood out when he has started, and Kasey Keller, the only one of the 3 in a daily soccer environment. Keller stars for Millwall, which has been competing for the league lead (and possible promotion to the Premier League) in the English First Division.

As for the rest of the lineup, the starting 11 is solid and competitive. As it turned out, the defense, once the cornerstone of the U.S. squad, is the weak link. It was particularly weakened when sweeper Marcelo Balboa, strongly criticized for his play, went down with a knee injury. Sometimes you are not appreciated until you are gone; Balboa's replacements did not do the job. The midfield, led by European-based John Harkes and Tab Ramos and German-born Thomas Dooley, the U.S. Soccer Federation's Player of the Year in 1993, is expected to do a bulk of the offensive work. Depending on whether Bora wants to use one or two forwards, Roy Wegerle could wind up as an attacking midfielder or as a subdued center forward, with either Eric Wynalda or Ernie Stewart as the targetman up front. Missing from this mixture is midfielder-forward Hugo Perez, who was instrumental in helping the U.S. qualify for Italia '90, but has not regained his form after returning home from a club team in Saudi Arabia in 1993. If Perez can return to form, the U.S. could be dangerous.

For the U.S. to be competitive and consistent, the starting 11 must avoid serious injuries or red cards. When Bora has been forced to go to his bench, there has been a tremendous drop off in quality. There is little depth to be consistently successful at the World Cup level.

In late 1993, Bora added 3 players to the national team pool—defender Brian Bliss, a member of the Italia '90 team, midfielder-defender Mark Santel, who played with the team from 1988–91, and midfielder Dario Brose, who scored a goal in the 1992 Olympics and who now performs for St. Brieuc in France. Those players, however, are not expected to break into the starting lineup and make an impact.

A bit of interesting information for World Cup history buffs: No host team has ever failed to reach the second round of the World Cup, so the U.S. will try to avoid making history.

COLOMBIA
POPULATION: 34,000,000
COLORS: Yellow shirts, blue shorts, red
   socks
WORLD CUP APPEARANCES: Third.
   1–4–2 record, 9 goals for, 15 against
   1962 (first round), 1990 (second
   round)

World Cup History

There isn't much success here. Colombia has won only 1 game—a 2–0 victory over the United Arab Emirates in 1990, but managed to play eventual champion West Germany to a 1–1 tie on a last-minute goal by Freddy Rincon. The Colombians were eliminated by Cameroon in the second round.

How They Qualified

Colombia finished first in South American Group A with a 4–0–2 record and 10 points scoring 13 goals and allowing 2. The results (home team listed first)—Colombia 0, Paraguay 0 (Aug. 1, 1993), Peru 0, Colombia 1 (Aug. 8), Colombia 2, Argentina 1 (Aug. 15), Colombia 1, Paraguay 1 (Aug. 22), Colombia 4, Peru 0 (Aug. 29), Argentina 0, Colombia 5 (Sept. 5). The clincher: Colombia stunned South American champion Argentina, 5–0, in Buenos Aires, as Freddy Rincon and Faustino Asprilla scored 2 goals apiece and Adolfo Valencia 1.

Players To Watch

Freddy Rincon, who is a quiet man, prefers to let his talented feet do the talking for him as an attacking midfielder. Faustino Asprilla, on the other hand, isn't afraid to express his opinions—he is controversial—and can put the ball in the back of the end. So can Adolfo Valencia, who is one of the hottest players on the Colombian market. He did not score any goals in qualifying, but Carlos Valderrama—who cannot notice his hair—is an excellent set-up man.

Probalbe Lineup

Goalkeepers: Oscar Cordoba (One Philips) **Defenders:** Luis Fernando Herrera (Atletico Nacional), Luis Carlos Perea (Independiente Medellin), Alexis Antonio Mendoza (Atletico Junior), Wilson Perez (America Cali) **Midfielders:** Leonel Alvarez (America Cali), Gabriel Gomez (Atletico Nacional), Carlos Valderrama (Atletico Junior), Freddy Rincon (America Cali) **Forwards:** Jose Adolfo Valencia (Bayern Munich, Germany), Faustino Asprilla (Parma, Italy).

Player Pool

Goalkeepers: Oscar Cordoba (Once Philips), Farid Mondragon (Deportivo Cali), Jose Maria Pazo (Atletico Junior). **Defenders:** Geovannis Cassiani (America Cali), Luis Fernando Herrera (Atletico Nacional), Alexis Antonio Mendoza (Atletico Junior), Diego Leon Osorio (Atletico Nacional), Luis Carlos Perea (Independente Medellin), Wilson Perez (America Cali), Wilmer Cabrera (America Cali). **Midfielders:** Leonel Alvarez (America Cali), Oscar Cortes (Millonarios), Alexis Garcia (Atletico Nacional), Herman Gaviria (Atletico Nacional), Gabriel Gomez (Atletico Nacional), Victor Danilo Pacheco (Atletico Junior), Ricardo Perez (Millonarios), Freddy Rincon (America Cali), Mauricio Serna (Nacional Medellin), Carlos Valderrama (Atletico Junior). **Forwards:** Victor Aristizabazal (Atletico Nacional), Faustino Asprilla (Parma, Italy), Jorge Cruz (Huracan, Argentina), Harold Lozano (America Cali), Orlando Maturana (America Cali), John Trellez (Atletico Nacional), Jose Adolfo Valencia (Bayern Munich, Germany), Ivan Valenciano (Atletico Junior), Anthony De Avila (America Cali).

Leonel Alvarez, Midfielder (America Cali): Born: July 29, 1965 5-foot-10, 154 pounds., 12 caps, no goals—When Alvarez was young, his father abandoned his mother and three sisters, and she wound up working at all hours in a clothing factory. Alvarez promised that he would become successful and she would live like a queen. After becoming a star with America, he brought his mother a house. But the road to stardom was a long one—literally. As a 14-year-old on Antioquia's junior team, Alvarez had no money for bus fare. So, he would wake up early in the morning, missed breakfast and ran for more than an hour to reach practice on time. His coach discovered what was transpiring and provided the budding star with money and meals. He eventually was traded to Deportivo Independiene Medellin, Atletico Nacional and America. His younger sister is married to a soccer player—Marcos Velasquez. "That's why one should not bring friends at home," Alvarez said. "They end up marrying your sister."

Faustino Asprilla Forward (Parma, Italy) Born Nov. 10, 1969, 5-foot-6 161 pounds 9 caps, 3 goals—He has emerged as a legitimate star in Europe, helping Parma reach the championship game of the European Cup Winners Cup in May, 1993, although he sat out the final with a leg injury. Asprilla's weakness is his temper, which seemingly can snap at any minute. He found himself in coach Francisco Maturana's doghouse during Colombia's qualifying run. He claimed he was embarrassed by being a reserve and promised to quit international soccer. He didn't and scored 2 goals in the clinching win over Argen-

PLAYER PROFILES
(Caps and goals
through Oct. 6,
1993)

tina. "Faustino was a little upset because he was not finding his best form," Maturana said. Asprilla was transferred from Atletico Nacional to Parma, where he had seven goals in 26 matches in 1992-93, plus 3 in the cup competition.

Oscar Cordoba, Goalkeeper (America de Cali), Born: Feb. 3, 1970, 6-foot-1, 176 lbs, 16 caps, no goals—With Rene Higuita embroiled in his legal problems, Cordoba stepped to the forefront and took over the No. 1 keeper's position. Cordoba, who had only two international appearances before 1993, starrted 14 of the the team's 15 matches that year, including every World Cup qualifier. He allowed only eight goals, never surrendering more than one a game. Cordoba, who performed at the Under-20 World Cup in Saudi Arabia in 1989, has played for Nacional, Quindio, Millonarios and Once Phillips.

Gabriel Gomez, Forward (Atletico Nacional), Born Dec. 8, 1959, 5-foot-6, 150 lbs, 36 caps, 1 goal—Gomez learned the facts of life early when his father sent him to the tough neighborhood of Medellin called Guayaquil. Noticing how he defied danger in that part of the city, his grandfather called Gomez "barrabas"—demon. He had been kicked out of school 3 times—once for placing a dead lizard on the desk of a teacher—and frequently skipped school to watch Atletico Nacional players train. In other words, he was soccer crazy. He transformed that passion into the skills of a superb player, first performing for Atletico, then for Millonarios before returning to Atletico in 1988.

Luis Herrera, Defender (Atletico Nacional), Born June 12, 1962, 5-foot-6, 136 lbs., 13 caps, 0 goals—Herrera returned from a career-threatening knee injury that he suffered in December, 1988. He came back after 3 knee operations (a piece of plastic replaced a broken tendon) and 9 intense months of recuperation before returning in September, 1989. He has performed for 4 teams—Independiente Medellin, Atletico Bucaramanga, America Cali and Atletico Nacional.

Rene Higuita, Goalkeeper (Atletico Nacional), Born Aug. 27, 1966 Actually, Higuita is not in the Colombian player pool because as of late 1993, he had been released from prison after serving time on charges of breaking the country's anti-kidnap laws. If he does play, Higuita is able to put on quite a one-man show, sometimes dribbling as far as midfield. In fact, he has revolutionized goalkeeping, as more and more keepers are coming out of the nets to become another sweeper. That style does have its drawbacks, as Higuita and his teammates learned the hard way in their second-round defeat to Cameroon at Italia '90, as the wandering goalkeeper was caught way out of the nets by Roger Milla, who scored the game-winning goal in extra time.

Alexis Mendoza, Defender (Atletico Junior), Born Nov. 8, 1961, 5-foot-11, 152 lbs., 14 caps, 1 goal—Mendoza never had any delusions of grandeur of playing professional soccer while growing up. He felt it was an unrealistic dream. At the age of 16, he went to work in a plastic factory to help his family financially as he attended evening classes before graduating from the National Institute of Commerce in 1982. His passion for soccer, meanwhile, had grown as he wound up training by himself at 10 P.M. in the evenings. He joined Atantico team and eventually was transferred to Atletico.

Luis Carlos Perea, Defender (Independiente Medellin), Born Dec. 29, 1963, 5-foot-10, 191 lbs., 5 caps, 0 goals— Like Alvarez, Perea's father abandoned his family. When he was a teen-ager, Perea legally changed his name to bear only his mother's last name, not both his parents, as is the custom in Colombia. When he was asked by a journalist what his father's name was, Perez responded, "I've forgotten it. It's not worthwhile remembering." He started playing with the Antioquia junior team and eventually signed with Independiente Medellin in 1983.

Wilson Perez, Defender (America Cali), Born Aug. 9, 1967, 5-foot-6, 145 lbs., 12 caps, 0 goals—Greatness was predicted for him as a teen-ager. When he was 17, he made his debut for Atletico Junior in 1985. "Wilson will soon be the best No. 10 in Colombia," Atletico Coach Roberto Saporiti said. A year later, a similar prediction was made by Atletico goalkeeper Carlos Mario Goyen. "Take note and remember me: In Atletico Junior there is someone who will soon be the best winger of Colombian soccer." The rest is history. His performance was so overwhelming at Copa America in Brazil in 1989 that there were rumors he would wind up with a Brazilian club. He signed with America Cali. Perez scored once in qualifying, in the 4–0 win over Peru.

Freddy Rincon, Midfielder (America Cali), Born Aug. 14, 1966, 6-foot-1, 176 lbs., 12 caps, 5 goals—Rincon, whose full name is

Freddy Eusebio Rincon Valencia, led Colombia in scoring with 5 goals in its qualifying run. He connected for the lone goal in the 1−0 triumph at Peru, in the 1−1 draw vs. Paraguay, the second victory over Peru and twice in the clinching win at Argentina. A timid soul who does not talk very much, Rincon first raised eyebrows by scoring twice in a 3−1 Santa Fe victory over Atletico Junior. Rincon, who moved to America Cali in 1989, has one sister and 6 brothers—all of whom played soccer.

Carlos Valderrama, Midfielder (Atletico Junior), Born Sept. 2, 1961, 5-foot-9, 161 lbs., 10 caps, 2 goals—Valderrama who was sidelined for at least a month after he tore knee ligaments in a game against Sweden on Feb. 18, 1994, has never had a problem with expressing himself. He is perhaps the most recognizable Colombian player because of the human fright wig he wears atop his head. He also has made an impact on the field, controlling the midfield with deft touches, yet seemingly spending most of the match walking around the field. Valderrama began his professional career with Union Magdalena in 1981, and transferred to Millonarios in 1984 and then Deportivo Cali soon thereafter. He had spent a year with Montpellier (France), but Valderrama returned to his homeland to play for Independiente Medellin, which transferred him to Atletico Junior for $900,000 in January, 1993, due to the club's financial problems. Two of his brothers play soccer—Alan with America Cali and Ronald with Union Magdalena.

Adolfo Valencia, Forward (Bayern Munich, Germany), Born Feb. 6, 1968, 5-foot-11, 163 lbs., 2 caps, 2 goals—Valencia, nicknamed El Tren (The Train), became the hottest soccer property in Colombia. A great individual player, he scored a goal in the 2−1 qualifying victory that snapped Argentina's 31-game unbeaten streak. Bayern purchased Valencia's contract from Sante Fe for $2.5 million in 1993.

Coach   Francisco (Pacho) Maturana, is one of two coaches from Italia '90 who are still with the same team; Ireland's Jack Charlton is the other. Maturana, who has a degree in odontology, started his coaching career in 1983 after he joined the University of Antioquia as a professor. But Atletico Nacional coach Luis Cubilla asked him to return as a player. He refused, but after much begging by Cubilla he wound up as a youth coach. He became the head coach of Cristal Caldas in 1986 before leading Atletico Nacional to the Copa Libertadores title in 1989. Maturana, born Feb. 2, 1949, coaches America Cali when not directing the fortunes of the National Team, with which he has been associated since 1987. As a player, he was named Colombian Player of the Year in 1973, also playing with Atletico Nacional, Atletico Bucaramanga and Tolima. He is married to Margarita Agudelo and has 3 children.

Colombia played an entertaining style en route to qualifying for the World Cup, and coach Francisco Maturana expects his side not to skip a beat at USA '94. "We are going to the World Cup to enjoy ourselves," he said. "If we win, that will be a bonus. I would rather we play well and make a good impression than win the competition playing badly."

1994

Few coaches, if any, will take that tact. Most will do anything to win, including playing negative soccer (see Argentina in 1990).

The Colombians, however, might have enough talent to accomplish both. Unless Rene Higuita, recently released from prison, finds his form, Oscar Cordoba is expected to man the nets. He isn't as flashy as Higuita, but he was a solid addition to the squad. The defense usually gets lost in the offensive shuffle of the $4-4-2$ formation. (4 defenders, 4 midfielders, 2 forwards). Carlos Valderrama sets the tempo with his pin-point passing to either fellow midfielder Freddy Rincon and forwards Adolfo Valencia and the temperamental Faustino Asprilla, who all are dangerous.

They played attacking soccer while stunning Copa America champion Argentina not once, but twice. The first victory—a a $2-1$ triumph—snapped a 31-game unbeaten streak that went all the way back to the final match of Italia '90. The second—a $5-0$ rout in Buenos Aires—qualified Colombia for the World Cup and embarrassed the Argentines in the process. Only weeks after the victory, the match already was legendary. Appliance stores repeatedly have shown tapes of the second game in their windows. A song titled "Cinco a zero" (Five to nothing) was released by a leading band.

"It was very exciting," Rincon said. "The Argentines were talking too much before the game. They said that they had history in football, that we didn't and that we weren't going to change history. But we didn't get involved. We just went out and did our thing."

The team also hopes to use the World Cup to show the world that there is more to Colombia than the image of a nation overcome by drug traffickers. "We have a mission to change this unfortunate situation through our football," Rincon said. "Every game will be important for us in this respect."

A bit of interesting information for World Cup history buffs: Colombia could not prepare for the 1990 World Cup as most of the other participating teams because the season was suspended in November, 1989. A referee, Daniel Ortega, was shot outside a stadium after a game in which he officiated cost a local drug gang a large sum of money.

ROMANIA

POPULATION: 23,400,000

COLORS: Yellow shirts, yellow shorts, yellow socks

World Cup Appearances: Sixth. 3–6–3 record, 6 goals for, 16 against. 1930 (first round), 1934 (first round), 1938 (first round), 1970 (first round), 1990 (second round)

While Romanian soccer has made some great strides in the past decade or so, its World Cup history is not one to write home about. Only once in 5 appearances has Romania reached the second round—in 1990—and the team was eliminated by Ireland via penalty kicks, finishing at 1–1–2. Romania participated in the first 3 World Cups, winning its first game against Peru, 3–1.

World Cup History

Romania finished first in European Group with a 7–2–1 record, scoring 29 goals and allowing 12. The results (home team listed first)—Romania 7, Faroe Islands 0 (May 6, 1992), Romania 5, Wales 1 (May 20, 1992), Belgium 1, Romania 0 (Oct. 14, 1992), Romania 1, Representation of Czechs and Slovaks 1 (Nov. 14, 1992), Cyprus 1, Romania 4 (Nov. 29, 1992), Romania 2, Cyrpus 1 (April 14, 1993), Representation of Czechs and Slovaks 5, Romania 2 (June 2), Faroe Islands 0, Romania 4 (Sept. 8), Romania 2, Belgium 1 (Oct. 13), Wales 1, Romania 2 (Nov. 17). The clincher: Romania managed to record a 2–1 victory over Wales in Cardiff on Nov. 17, 1993, as Gheorge Hagi and Ilie Dumitrescu scored goals.

How They Qualified

Midfielder Gheorge Hagi, a superb dribbler, is considered the best player of his generation in Romania, and is called "The Maradona of the Carpathians." Florin Raducioiu, a forward who has played for 4 First Division clubs in Italy since the 1990 World Cup, isn't too far behind. Forward Ilie Dumitrescu is a budding star.

Players To Watch

Goalkeeper: Florian Prunea (Dinamo Bucharest). **Defenders:** Gheorge Popescu (PSV Eindhoven), Miodrag Belodedici (Valencia, Spain), Dan Petrescu (Genoa, Italy), Daniel Prodan (Steaua Bucharest). **Midfielders:** Angelo Lupescu (Bayer Leverkusen, Germany), Ioan Ovidiu Sabau (Brescia, Italy), Gheorge Hagi (Brescia, Italy), Dorinel Munteanu (Cercle Bruges, Belgium). **Forwards:** Florin Raducioiu (A.C. Milan, Italy), Ilie Dumitrescu (Steaua Bucharest).

Probable Lineup

Goalkeepers: Adrian Constanin (Progresul Bucharest), Florian Prunea (Dinamo Bucharest), Bogdan Stelea (Mallorca, Spain), Alexandru Tene (Otelui Galati). Miodrag Belodedci (Valencia, Spain), Vasile Bratianu (Dacia-Unirea Bralla), Anton Dobos (Steaua Bucharest), Gheorge Mihali (Dinamo Bucharest), Dan Petrescu (Genoa, Italy), Ionel Antonei Pirvu (Steaua Bucharest), Gheorghe Popescu (PSV Eindhoven, Netherlands), Daniel Claudiu Prodan (Steaua Bucharest), Tibor Selymes (Cercle Bruges, Belgium). **Midfielders:** Pavel Badea (Lausanne, Switzerland), Ilie Dumitrescu (Steaua Bucharest), Constantin Galca (Steaua Bucharest), Gheorge Hagi (Brescia, Italy), Ion Lupescu (Bayer Leverkusen, Germany), Dorinel Munteanu (Cercle Bruges, Belgium), Constantin Pana (Dinamo Bucharest), Nica Panduru (Steaua Bucharest), Ioan Ovidiu Sabau (Brescia, Italy), Ilie Stan (Steaua Bucharest), Ovidiu Stinga (Univ. Craiova), Ion Timofte (F.C. Porto, Portugal). **Forwards:** Gheorge Ceausila (Sportul Studentsec Bucharest), Gheorge Craioveanu (Univ. Craiova), Florin Raducioiu (A.C. Milan, Italy), Constantin Varga (Politehnica Timisoara), Ion Vladoiu (Steau Bucharest).

PLAYER PROFILES
(appearances and
goals through Dec.
6, 1993)

Miodrag Belodedici, Defender (Valencia, Spain), Born: May 20, 1964, 6-foot-1, 165 lbs., 28 caps, 4 goals—Considered to be one of the best sweepers in the world—he also can play midfield—Belodedici became the first player to win the European Cup with 2 clubs: Steaua Bucharest in 1986 and Red Star Belgrade in 1991. Belodedici, who comes from a Serbian family, sought political asylum in Yugoslavia in 1988. He transferred from Red Star to Valencia at the beginning of the 1992–93 season.

Ilie Dumitrescu, Midfielder-forward (Steaua Bucharest), Born: Jan. 6, 1968, 5-foot-9, 158 lbs., 35 caps, 9 goals—Dumitrescu, who has excelled in counterattacks, made his international debut against Greece in 1989. He scored both goals in the 2–1 qualifying victory over Cyprus, and finished with 5 overall. He has scored 54 league goals in 138 matches for Steaua from 1988–93.

Gheorge Hagi, Midfielder (Brescia, Italy), Born: Feb. 5, 1965, 5-foot-8, 156 lbs., 81 caps, 21 goals-Hagi, closing in on the all-time Romania record of 30 goals, is excellent dribbling in close quarters, which has been the key to his success internationally. A member of the Romania national youth team at 15, Hagi signed with Sportul Studentsec of Bucharest of 1983. He led the First Division in scoring for 2

consecutive years, with 20 in 1984–85 and 31 in 1985–86. He signed
with Real Madrid after Italia '90, scoring only 3 times in 1990–91 and
12 goals in 1991–92. Hagi was sold to Brescia before the 1992–93
season, connecting 6 times in 31 matches. He led Romania in scoring
during qualifying with 7 goals, including 2 in a 5–1 victory over
Wales.

Ion Lupescu, Midfielder (Bayer Leverkusen, Germany), Born: Dec.
9, 1968, 5-foot-10, 154 lbs., 26 caps, 3 goals—Lupescu, a member of
Romania's 1990 World Cup squad, starred for Dimano Bucharest until
he transferred to Bayer for $1 million in 1990.

Dorinel Munteanu, Defender (Cercle Bruges, Belgium), Born: June
25, 1968, 5-foot-7, 145 lbs., 28 caps, 2 goals—-Taking advantage of
fewer traveling restrictions, Munteanu signed a 2-year deal worth
$500,000 with Bruges before the 1993–94 season. He also played with
FC Olt, Inter Sibiu and Dinamo Bucharest in 1991. He finished with 12
goals in 33 matches for Dinamo in 1991–92

Gheorghe Popescu, Midfielder (PSV Eindhoven, Netherlands), Born:
Oct. 9, 1967, 6-foot-1, 187 lbs., 8 caps, 1 goal—Considered an efficient player, Popescu was the best Romanian player in 1989. He made
his international debut vs. Albania in 1988 and was a member of the
World Cup team that reached the second round in 1990.

Florin Raducioiu, Forward (A.C. Milan, Italy), Born: March 17,
1970, 5-foot-8, 150 lbs., 22 caps, 19 goals—Raducioiu, who finished
with 6 qualifying goals, scored his most important one against Wales,
the game-winner that clinched a berth at USA '94. He also scored all 4
of Romania's goals in its win over the Faroe Islands. Raducioiu began
his career with Dinamo Bucharest. Since the 1990 World Cup, he has
performed in Italy, signing with Bari in 1990, joining Verona in 1991,
moving to Brescia in 1992 (13 goals in 29 matches) and finally to Milan
before the 1993–94 season. Where he goes next season is anyone's
guess.

Ioan Ovidiu Sabau, Midfielder (Brescia, Italy), Born: Feb. 12, 1968,
5-foot-9, 154 lbs., 43 caps, 7 goals—Sabau, who is considered in
excellent shape, joined Dinamo Bucharest in 1988–89, quickly earning a spot on the National Team. Before joining Brescia, he performed
for Universitatea Cluj, Tirgu Mures and Dinamo Bucharest in his

native country and Feyenoord Rotterdam (Netherlands), collecting 11 goals in 39 matches over 2 seasons.

Coach   Anghel Iordanescu took over Romania under fire. Some 3 weeks after a disastrous 5–2 loss to the Representation of Czechs and Slovaks, he was named coach on June 24, 1993, replacing Cornel Dinu, who was fired. The international level was not new to Iordanescu, who scored 26 goals in 64 appearances for Romania. That doesn't include more than 150 goals in 300 matches for powerhouse Steaua Bucharest. He led the Romanian First Division in scoring in 1981–82 (20 goals). His coaching career began in Greece as a player-coach with OFI Iraklion in Crete. He returned home as an assistant coach to Emeric Jenei at Steaua, eventually directing the team's fortunes from 1986–90. Steaua reached the final of the European Cup in 1989. After a 2-year stint with Anorthosis Famagusta (Cyprus), he came back to Steaua in 1992, guiding the side to the Premier Division championship.

1994   Romania reached the World Cup the hard way. The team earned it. After sacking their coach and needing 3 victories in their final 3 games—two on the road—the Romanians won all 3. While they are far from the flashiest team around, the Romanians get the job done.

The U.S. will have its hands—or in this case, feet— full with Romania, perhaps the most underrated team in Europe. Perhaps it was because the Romanian played behind the iron-curtain for so long that the rest of the world did not hear of or appreciate the talents of Gheorge Hagi or Florin Raducioiu. Now, it will be difficult to hide emerging star Ilie Dumitrescu. Those 3 attacking players are expected to be the Romanian's force offensively, or the team could be in trouble.

Drawn into Group A with favored Colombia, Switzerland and the United States, Romania is expected to finish second, although coach Anghel Iordanescu is not taking anything for granted.

"It's difficult because we have to travel a lot," said Iordanescu, who added that Los Angeles "is our first game, Detroit is our second game, and L.A. is our third game. And L.A. is the place where the U.S. does all its preparation."

An bit of interesting information for World Cup history buffs: King Carol selected the Romanian National Team that participated in the first World Cup in 1930. He also ensured the job of each of the players because the team would be away for 3 months.

SWITZERLAND
> POPULATION: 7,000,000
> COLORS: Red shirts, white shorts, red
>   socks
> WORLD CUP APPEARANCES: Sev-
>   enth. 5–11–2 record, 28 goals for, 44
>   against. 1934 (quarterfinals), 1938
>   (quarterfinals), 1950 (first round),
>   1954 (second round), 1962 (first
>   round), 1966 (first round)

World Cup History

The Swiss had some glorious moments in the early years of the cup, participating in 4 of the first 5 tournaments, hosting the 1954 tournament and reaching the quarterfinals twice. But as the rest of the world caught up to them, they found it more difficult to reach the finals. In their most recent performance (1966), the Swiss were ousted in the first round, losing to West Germany, Spain and Argentina.

How They Qualified

Switzerland finished second in European Group 2 with a 6–1–3 record, scoring 23 goals and allowing 6. The results (home team listed first)—Estonia 0, Switzerland 6 (Aug. 16, 1992), Switzerland 3, Scotland 0 (Sept. 9, 1992), Italy 2, Switzerland 2 (Oct. 14, 1992), Switzerland 3, Malta 0 (Nov. 18, 1992), Switzerland 1, Portugal 1 (March 31, 1993), Malta 0, Switzerland 2 (April 17), Switzerland 1, Italy 0 (May 1), Scotland 1, Switzerland 1 (Sept. 8), Portugal 1, Switzerland 0 (Oct. 13), Switzerland 4, Estonia 0 (Nov. 17). The clincher: 4 players—Adrian Knup, Georges Bregy, Christophe Ohrel and Stephane Chapuisat—scored in the final win over Estonia.

Players To Watch

Crafty and skillful, striker Stephane Chapuisat is considered the best Swiss forward to play the game. Adrian Knup might not have the same reputation, but his ability to fill the nets (21 goals in 31 appearances) makes him a difficult man to cover.

Probable Lineup

Goalkeeper: Marco Pascolo (Servette FC). **Defenders:** Marc Hottiger (FC Sion), Dominique Herr (FC Sion), Alain Geiger (FC Sion), Yvan Quentin (FC Sion). **Midfielders:** Georges Bregy (BSC Young Boys), Alain Sutter (FC Nuremberg, Germany), Christophe Ohrel (Servette FC), Ciriaco Sforza (FC Kaiserslautern, Germany). **Forwards:** Adrian Knup (VfB Stuttgart, Germany), Stephane Chapuisat (Borussia Dortmund, Germany).

Player Pool

Goalkeepers: Stefan Lehmann (FC Sion), Marco Pascolo (Servette FC). **Defenders:** Andy Egli (Servette FC), Alain Geiger (FC Sion), Stephane Henchoz (Neuchatel Xamax), Dominique Herr (FC Sion), Marc Hottiger (FC Sion), Yvan Quentin (FC Sion), Regis Rothenbuhler (Servette FC), Ramon Vega (Grasshoppers Zurich). **Midfielders:** Thomas Bickel (Grasshoppers Zurich), Georges Bregy (BSC Young Boys), Christophe Ohrel (Servette FC), Blaise Piffaretti (FC Sion), Ciriaco Sforza (FC Kaiserslautern, Germany), Alain Sutter (FC Nuremberg, Germany), Patrick Sylvestre (Lausanne-Sports). **Forwards:** Stephane Chapuisat (Borussia Dortmund, Germany), Marco Grassi (FC Zurich), Adrian Knup (VfB Stuttgart, Germany), Beat Sutter (FC Nuremberg, Germany), Kubilay Turkyilmaz (Galatasaray, Turkey).

PLAYER PROFILES
(Appearances and goals through Nov. 24, 1993)

Georges Bregy: Midfielder (Young Boys), 5-foot-9, 155 pounds, Born: Jan. 17, 1958, Caps: 44, Goals: 14-After a 5-year absence, Bregy returned to the National Team in the spring of 1992. He presence was felt, scoring 4 times in World Cup qualifying. He scored in the first win over Estonia, in each of the Scotland matches and finally in the clinching victory over Estonia. At 36, he is considered to be the old man of the team, giving it some steady leadership.

Stephane Chapuisat, forward (Borussia Dortmund), 5-foot-11, 164 pounds, Born: June 28, 1969, Caps: 32, Goals: 9-Unquestionably the best player on the team, having made his mark in Germany the past 4 years, Chapuisat joined Bayer Uerdingen in 1991, but he played in only 10 games because of an injury suffered in indoor soccer. He was loaned to Borussia 6 months later and eventually was acquired permanently. He scored 20 goals in 1991–92 and added 15 more the next season. "Although the competition for places is formidable, I couldn't be happier," said Chapuisat, who was named Player of the Year by the Bundesliga team captains in 1991. He receives about 50 fan letters a week.

Alain Geiger, Defender (FC Sion), 5-foot-11, 175 pounds, Born: Nov. 5, 1960, Caps: 87, Goals: 8-Considered to be one of the best defenders in Switzerland, Geiger is the team captain and one four Sion defenders who start. He has performed for Sion in 2 stints, and with Neuchatel Xamax, Servette and St. Etienne (France). Geiger played for 2 Swiss Cup champions—for Servette in 1983 and Sion in 1991—scoring the game-winner in extra time. He is a connoisseur of Japanese and Italian cooking.

Dominique Herr, Defender (FC Sion), 6-foot , 172 pounds, Born: Oct. 25, 1965, Caps: 33, Goals: 2-He has performed with 3 clubs, beginning his career with Basel in 1983, moving to Lausanne in 1988 and Sion in 1992.

Marc Hottiger, Defender (FC Sion), 5-foot-9, 148 pounds, Born: Nov. 7, 1967, Caps: 33, Goals: 3-Hottiger could not have timed his only goal of qualifying any better, connecting for the lone score in the 1−0 victory over Italy on May 1, 1993. He scored 7 times for Sion in the 1992−93 season, after spending six years with Lausanne Sports.

Adrian Knup, Forward (VfB Stuttgart), 6-foot, 174 pounds, Born: July 2, 1968, Caps: 31, Goals: 21-Knup forged his reputation as a deadly scorer during the 1990−91 international season, connecting 11 times in as many matches, the best performance by any European player. Subsequently, he was voted Swiss Player of the Season by players and coaches. He then scored twice to lead Lucerne to the 1992 Swiss Cup. Slowed down some after fracturing his cheekbone during the 1−1 qualifying tie with Portugal, Knup bounced back to finish tied for second in scoring with 4 goals. He scored at Estonia, twice in the first Scotland game and once in the clinching victory over Estonia.

Marco Pascolo, Goalkeeper (Servette), 6-foot-2, 188 pounds, Born May 9, 1966, Caps: 14, Goals: 0-A steadying influence on defense, Pascolo played in all 10 qualifying games. He joined Servette in 1991 from Neuchatel Xamax, playing for coach Roy Hodgson.

Yvan Quentin, Defender (Sion), 5-foot-9, 159 pounds, Born: May 2, 1970, Caps: 7, Goals: 0-He won a spot during the 1991-92 season and has been a regular since.

Ciriaco Sforza, Midfielder (FC Kaiserslautern), 5-foot-11, 166 pounds, Born: March 2, 1970, Caps: 18, Goals: 3-He has made the rounds and then some. He started his pro career with Wohlen in 1985, joined Grasshoppers in 1986, moved to Aarau in 1989, returned to Grasshopper in 1990 and signed with Kaiserslautern in April, 1993.

Alain Sutter, Midfielder (FC Nuremburg), 6-foot-1, 175 pounds, Born: Jan. 22, 1968, Caps: 38, Goals: 3-He also has been around, as the long, blond-haired midfielder has spent time with Bumpliz (1984), Grasshoppers (1985−86), Young Boys (1987−88), Grasshoppers

(1988–90), before moving to Germany. He is not related to midfielder Beat Sutter.

Coach   Roy Hodgson, who will be among a few English present at the World Cup, took over the coaching reins, replacing German Uli Stielike in January, 1992. Born on Aug. 9, 1947, Hodgson had a rather undistinguished career in England, playing with Crystal Palace, Gravesend and Maidstone and then for Berea Park and Carshalton in South Africa. His coaching career includes stints at Bristol City (England), Halmstads BK, Oerebro SK and Malmo (Sweden) and Neuchatel Xamax (Switzerland), whom he guided from 1990–1992.

1994   That Switzerland managed to qualify for the World Cup was a miracle in itself because the Swiss had not reached the finals since 1966—7 cups ago. Give a lot of credit to coach Roy Hodgson, who molded a formidable side despite criticism from the media. Under Hodgson, the Swiss enjoyed a 14-game unbeaten streak, broken by Portugal in a 1–0 loss on Oct. 13, 1993.

He built his back 4 from the FC Sion defense of Alain Geiger, Dominique Herr, Marc Hottiger and Yvan Quinn. It worked extremely well during qualifying, as the Swiss allowed but 6 goals in 10 matches and surrendered only 2 goals once—in the 2–2 draw with Italy, which rallied in the final minutes to salvage a point in Cagliari. In fact, 7 Sion players are in the player pool.

Though the Swiss, who usually play in a 4–4–2 formation, are not expected to do much at USA '94. One man who bears watching is striker Stephane Chapuisat, whose shifty moves and talented left foot has made him a scoring terror in the German Bundesliga. If opponents concentrate too much on Chapuisat, then Adrian Knup could become the main man.

The rest of the team is a hard-working side, although not spectacular. Still, the Swiss managed to tie the powerhouse Italians on the road, 2–2, and beat them at home, 1–0.

If qualifying for the World Cup has helped Swiss soccer, it has not been felt at the turnstiles back home.

Young Boys of Zurich, an 11-time Swiss champion, was in third place in the First Division in November, 1993, yet was 2 months behind in paying its players. For its 3–1 victory over Lucerne, for example, a sparse crowd of 1,279 showed up. "I could cry," club finance chief Roland Schoenenberg said. "After deductions for taxes and other match-related expenses, there was just . . . ($75) left."

A bit of interesting information for World Cup history buffs: The Swiss own one of the longest losing streaks in World Cup history, having dropped their last 7 matches. Their last victory came in the 1954 cup, a 4−1 triumph over Italy.

GROUP B

BRAZIL

RUSSIA

CAMEROON

SWEDEN

BRAZIL

POPULATION: 144,400,000

Colors: Yellow shirts, blue shorts, white socks

WORLD CUP APPEARANCES: 15th. 48−12−13 record, 148 goals for, 65 against. 1930 (first round), 1934 (first round), 1938 (third place), 1950 (second place), 1954 (quarterfinals), 1958 (champion), 1962 (champion), 1966 (first round), 1970 (champion), 1974 (fourth place), 1978 (third place), 1982 (second round), 1986 (quarterfinals), 1990 (second round)

World Cup History

Brazil is synonymous with World Cup success, having participated in every tournament and having captured an unprecedented 3 World Cups in 4 attempts from 1958−1970. Pele led 3 marvelously talented teams dripping with flair and artistry that won in 1958, 1962 and 1970. Since then, however, the Brazilians have struggled as a hard luck team. They have compiled a solid 17−5−5 record, but have managed to advance past the quarterfinals only once in 5 competitions.

How They Qualified

Brazil won South American Group B with a 5−1−2 mark and 12 points, scoring 20 goals and surrendering 4. The results (home team listed first)—Ecuador 0, Brazil 0 (July 18), Bolivia 2, Brazil 0 (July 25), Venezuela 1, Brazil 5 (Aug. 1), Uruguay 1, Brazil 1 (Aug. 15), Brazil 2, Ecuador 0 (Aug. 22), Brazil 6, Bolivia 0 (Aug. 29), Brazil 4,

Venezuela 0 (Sept. 5), Brazil 2, Uruguay 0 (Sept. 19). The clincher: Romario scored 2 goals as the Brazilians continued their streak of qualifying for every World Cup.

Romario—most Brazilian players use only one name because their names are so long—was recalled to the national team after a 10-month exile because of his outspokeness. He is the top striker of Spanish champion Barcelona and can score at will—when he puts his mind to it. Bebeto, who led the Spanish First Division in scoring in 1992–93 (29 goals), could make a lethal combination up front with Romario. Rai, the younger brother of former Brazilian World Cupper Socrates, performs for Paris St. Germain after playing for Sao Paulo, the 1992–93 world club champions. Brazil is better known for its offensive flair rather than for its defense, but Claudio Taffarel, who performs for Reggiana, (Italy) is considered the country's best international goalkeeper in almost 2 decades. Right backs Jorginho, who plays with Bayern Munich (Germany), and Cafu, who performs for Sao Paulo (Brazil), are among the squad's superb attackers from defense.

Players to Watch

Goalkeeper: Claudio Taffarel (Reggiana, Italy). **Defenders**: Jorginho (Bayern Munich, Germany), Ricardo Gomes (Paris St. Germain, France), Ricardo Rocha (Real Madrid, Spain), Branco (Genoa, Italy). **Midfielders**: Dunga (Stuttgart, Germany), Mauro Silva (Deportivo Coruna, Spain), Rai (Paris St. Germain, France), Zinho (Palmeiras, Brazil). **Forwards**: Bebeto (Deportivo Coruna, Spain), Romario (Barcelona, Spain).

Probable Lineup

Goalkeepers: Carlos (Portuguesa, Brazil), Claudio Taffarel (Reggiana, Italy) and Zetti (Sao Paulo, Brazil). **Defenders**: Branco (Genoa, Italy), Cafu (Sao Paulo, Brazil), Julio Cesar (Juventus, Italy), Jorginho (Bayern Munich, Germany), Ricardo Gomes (Paris St. Germain, France), Jose Mozer (Benfica, Portugal), Nonato (Cruzeiro, Brazil), Ricardo Rocha (Santos), Celio Silva (Internacional, Brazil), Marcio Santos (Gironds Bordeaux, France). **Midfielders**: Boiadeiro (Cruzeiro, Brazil), Dunga (Stuttgart, Germany), Luis Henrique (Monaco, France), Luisinho (Vasco da Gama, Brazil), Rai (Paris St. Germain, France), Marquinhos (Flamengo, Brazil), Mauro Silva (Deportivo Coruna, Spain), Valdo (Paris St. Germain, France), Zinho (Palmeiras, Brazil). **Forwards**: Almir (Santos, Brazil), Bebeto (Deportivo Coruna, Spain), Careca (Kashiwa, Japan), Elivelton (Sao Paulo, Brazil), Muller (Sao Paulo, Brazil), Palhinha (Sao Paulo, Brazil),

Player Pool

Renato (Cruzeiro, Brazil), Romario (Barcelona, Spain), Valber (Corinthians, Brazil), Valdeir (Gironds Bordeaux, France).

PLAYER PROFILES   **Claudio Taffarel,** Goalkeeper (Reggiana, Italy), 5-foot-11, 176 pounds, Born: May 8, 1966, Caps: 75, Goals: 0-He emerged internationally at the Seoul Olympics in 1988, as he saved 3 penalty kicks in the semifinal against West Germany—1 during the match and 2 in the tie-breaker. Taffarel took over as Brazil's top keeper in Copa America in 1989 and played in Italia '90. He excels at catching high crosses and positioning. Other goalkeepers to watch: Zetti, who stood out for world club champion Sao Paulo, Carlos and Gilmar.

Cafu, Defender (Sao Paulo), 5-foot-9, 163 pounds, Born: June 7, 1970, Caps: 35, Goals: 0-Cafu, whose full name is Marcos Evangelista de Moraes, is one of Brazil's rising stars. He and veteran Jorginho give the South Americans depth at right fullback, although Cafu has demonstrated his versatility when Sao Paulo coach Tele Santana brought him into a match at halftime as a left wing.

Jorginho, Defender (Bayern Munich, Germany), 5-foot-9, 152 pounds, Born: Aug. 16, 1964, Caps: 63, Goals: 5-Another one of those great Brazilian attacking fullbacks, Jorginho also is a class act off the field. Jorginho, whose full name is Jorge de Amorim Campos, is a practicing Christian and has described God as his "playmaker." Jorginho, who performed at the 1990 World Cup, was awarded FIFA's Fair Play Prize in 1991 for serving as a model and inspiration to others on and off the field.

Ricardo Gomes, Defender (Paris St. Germain, France), 6-foot-2, 183 pounds, Born: Dec. 13, 1964, Caps: 47, Goals: 4-The captain of the 1990 World Cup team, Gomes has established a reputation as an elegant player and for keeping his cool under pressure as a central defender. He has spent most of his career overseas, first playing at Benfica (Portugal).

Ricardo Rocha, Defender (Santos), 6-foot, 167 pounds, Born: Sept. 11, 1962, Caps: 37, Goals: 4-As one of Brazil's most versatile players, Rocha can play several positions well in the back. For example, he took over for Jose Mozer at central defender for his country's final 2 games at Italia '90 and played an important role at Copa America in 1991.

Branco, Defender (Genoa, Italy), 5-foot-11, 167 pounds, Born: April 4, 1964, Caps: 70, Goals: 8-Branco, whose full name is Claudio Ibraim Vaz Leal, is lethal in free-kick situations as he has scored from seemingly safe distances outside the penalty area. He usually gives himself a 10-yard head start and fires away with his left foot. Branco, who played 5 games for Brazil at Mexico '86, was a member of the 1990 World Cup squad.

Dunga, Midfielder (Stuttgart, Germany), 5-foot-10, 164 pounds, Born: Oct. 31, 1963, Caps: 45, Goals: 4 In Portuguese, his name means Dopey, as in *Snow White and the Seven Dwarfs.* Throughout Europe, however, he is known as "Dunga the Destroyer," because of his vision and quick thinking that brings about a counterattack. Dunga, whose full name is Carlos Caetano Bledorn Verri, is a superb midfield general who sometimes can be overzealous when tackling. Another veteran of Italia '90.

Mauro Silva, Midfielder (Deportivo Coruna, Spain), 5-foot-11, 176 pounds, Born: Jan. 12, 1968, Caps: 35, Goals: 0-How good is Silva? Pele himself predicted that the midfielder will emerge as a star at USA '94. Silva, who can attack and defend well, plays with national teammate Bebeto in the Spanish First Division.

Rai, Midfielder (Paris St. Germain, France), 6-foot-2, 191 pounds, Born: May 15, 1965, Caps: 47, Goals: 12-Even before he joined the National Team, Rai—whose full name is Rai Souza Vieira de Oliveira—had a reputation to live up to. He is the younger brother of former Brazilian star Socrates. So far, he has not disappointed. He was named the No. 1 South American player in 1992 and scored both goals for Sao Paulo in its 2–1 upset of European champion Barcelona in the Intercontinental Club Championship. He impressed so much that he transferred to Paris St. Germain for $3.1 million in 1993.

Zinho, Midfielder (Palmeiras), 5-foot-7, 158 pounds, Born: June 17, 1967, Caps: 30, Goals: 1-Brazil seemingly has loads of players who can fit into several positions, and Zinho is one of them, having acquitted himself well at forward or in the midfield.

Romario, Forward (Barcelona, Spain), 5-foot-6, 154 pounds, Born: Jan. 29, 1966, Caps: 46, Goals: 20-Romario isn't afraid to speak his mind and therein lies his true weakness. He was exiled from the

National Team for almost a year before his recall in that vital qualifier against Uruguay, in which he connected twice. Romario, whose full name is Romario di Souza Faria, started to raise eyebrows with a stellar performance during the 1988 Olympics. He also performed at the 1990 World Cup. He has a sense of flair off the field, too. When Romario married his 17-year-old girlfriend, the ceremony took place on the penalty spot of a local stadium in front of a live TV audience. He transferred from PSV Eindhoven (Netherlands), where he earned $500,000 every 6 months, to Spanish defending champions Barcelona over the summer of 1993. He still led the Spanish First Division in scoring after the new year.

Bebeto, Forward (Deportivo Coruna, Spain), 5-foot-10, 145 pounds, Born: Feb. 16, 1964, Caps: 75, Goals: 27-He led the Spanish First Division in scoring in 1992–93 with 29 goals, following an excellent performance with the Brazilian National Team with 7 goals in 10 matches in 1992. For some reason, Bebeto has not been used to his full potential. After collecting 6 of Brazil's 11 goals, sparking it to the 1989 Copa America crown, Bebeto played just 7 minutes in the 1990 World Cup. Bebeto, whose full name is Jose Roberto Gama de Oliveira, has superb ball control around the penalty area.

Careca, Forward (Kashiwa, Japan), 5-foot-10, 172 pounds, Born: Oct. 5, 1960, Caps: 69, Goals: 30-Careca, whose full name is Antonio de Oliveira Filho, was given that nickname because he enjoyed a well-known clown named Careghina. But no one laughs when this veteran of 2 World Cups steps onto the field. Even though he is starting to get on a bit in years for a striker, Careca has managed to score almost a goal every other game at the international level. Careca, Brazil's Sportsman of the Year in 1986, missed the 1982 World Cup due to an injury sustained right before the tournament. But he led Brazil in scoring with 5 goals in 1986. He also formed a lethal one-two punch with Diego Maradona at Napoli (Italy) before the Argentine left the club in 1991.

Coach   Carlos Alberto Parreira—no relation to former Brazilian captain and New York Cosmos defender Carlos Alberto—is in his second tenure with the team, having directed the National Team's fortunes in 1983, when the squad reached the Copa America final, losing to Uruguay. Born on March 25, 1943, Parreira will become one of two coaches who has guided 3 countries in the World Cup (U.S. coach Bora Milutinovic is the other), having coached Kuwait in the 1982 World Cup and the

United Arab Emirates in 1990. Parreira, who had a brief career in the Brazilian Second Division, turned to coaching in his early 20s. His first international coaching position was with Ghana at the 1968 African Nations Cup. He went on to coach Saudi Arabia at the 1984 Olympics in the U.S. and then the United Arab Emirates. Fluent in English, Parreira is expected to be a hit with the American media at the 1994 World Cup. Due to Brazil's sub-par performance in the early qualifying matches, Parreira was severely criticized by media and fans, who called for his head. Parreira has been Brazilian coach since October, 1991.

Perhaps Alan I. Rothenberg, chairman and CEO of World Cup USA '94, said it best. "It wouldn't be a World Cup without Brazil," he said. "I would cry if they didn't qualify."

Indeed, it would not be a World Cup without Brazil, because the South American power is the only country to have qualified for all 15 World Cups, although this year's qualifying run was not as smooth and neat as in the past.

But Brazil must be considered one of the legitimate contenders of USA '94 because of its past success in the Americas. In fact, Brazil has lost but once while performing in 5 World Cups in North and South America, compiling an incredible 23–1–6 mark.

In some respects, Brazil has been the victim of its own success. Because many of its most important talented players can earn money elsewhere, they have opted to play overseas. So, when it is time for a vital international match or a World Cup qualifier, a patch-work team sometimes was assembled at the last minute. Sometimes it worked, sometimes it didn't.

Take, for example, Brazil's path to USA '94. The perennial South American powers stumbled early on, tying lowly rated Ecuador in its first match and losing to an unheralded Bolivian side, 2–0, the first time Brazil had lost in 25 qualifying matches. Brazil finally found its range and qualified after coach Carlos Alberto Parreira recalled several players capable of striking at a moment's notice—Romario and Bebeto. Romario, the outspoken and controversial striker who connected for 3 goals in his Spanish First Division debut with Barcelona in September, 1993 could be the missing link that Parreira has been searching for. Not recalled to the team since December, 1992, Romario struck twice in the second half of a 2–0 qualifying win over Uruguay on Sept. 19 to boost the Brazilians into the World Cup.

"It was Parreira who selected Romario and it was God who brought him," Parreira said.

In Brazil (and most of the soccer world, for that matter), God is synonymous with Pele, who was the centerpiece of those great Brazilian championships.

But since its last World Cup victory, Brazil has been hard-pressed to find that magic and just to return to the championship match, let alone bring home the FIFA World Cup trophy. The Brazilians tried to emulate the discipline-oriented European systems in the 1974 and 1978 World Cups and fell short. Then came a string of bad luck as they were eliminated by eventual-champion Italy, 3–2, in a memorable second-round group game in 1982. They were shown the door by France in another unforgettable encounter, losing in penalty kicks in the quarter-finals in 1986. In 1990, the Brazilians used a sweeper for the first time, winning their first 3 matches before they were somehow beaten by a sluggish Argentine side in the quarterfinals, 1–0.

They recently abandoned the sweeper and reverted to their old style of play—flair and improvisation—and it appears to be working. Their Under-20 team captured the World Youth Championship in Japan in 1993, using the same components that have been the corner-stone of the team in the past—flair, artistry and brilliance. As for the World Cup squad, using a 4–4–2 formation in a combination of European-based players and a home-grown core from Sao Paulo, the world club champions, Brazil has the potential to reach the Final Four. If Brazil's performance at U.S. Cup '93, is any indication, soccer fans worldwide will be the winners. The South Americans performed a 90-minute samba against the U.S. in what turned into a 2–0 victory and then played a wild, 3–3 tie with defending world champion Germany, even if they lost a 3-goal halftime advantage.

Even if Brazil does not perform up to its true potential, its fans will be worth the price of admission for the show they put on. Wearing their bright, yellow shirts, Brazilian fans samba before, during and after their team's matches, whether their heroes win, lose, draw or tie-break. They truly know how to throw a party—anywhere.

A bit of interesting information for World Cup history buffs: The only loss Brazil has suffered in 5 World Cups in the Americas since World War II was a 2–1 defeat to Uruguay in the final match of the 1950 tournament. They are 23–1–6 in the Americas.

RUSSIA

POPULATION: 148,000,000

COLORS: White shirts, blue shorts, red socks

WORLD CUP APPEARANCES: Eighth (including 7 as Soviet Union). 15–10–6. 1958 (quarterfinals), 1962 (second round), 1966 (fourth place), 1970 (second round), 1982 (second round), 1986 (second round), 1990 (first round)

World Cup History

Don't let that record fool you. As the Soviet Union, Russia played well in the early rounds, but faded as the competition progressed, in contrast to its Olympic record of 24–6–4, including gold medals (1956, 1988) and 2 bronze medals (1972, 1976, 1980). The Soviets' best World Cup performance came in 1966, where they reached the semifinals before they were beaten by West Germany, 2–1. In the third-place match, the Soviets lost to Portugal, 2–1. Recently, however, they have not fared well at all, being eliminated in the second round in 1986 and in the first round after an abysmal showing in 1990.

How They Qualified

Russia finished second in European Group 5 with a 5–1–2 record and 12 points, scoring 15 goals, allowing 4. The results (home team listed first)—Russia 1, Iceland 0 (Oct. 14, 1992), Russia 2, Luxembourg 0 (Oct. 28, 1992), Luxembourg 0, Russia 4 (April 14, 1993), Russia 3, Hungary 0 (April 28), Russia 1, Greece 1 (May 23), Russia 1, Iceland 1 (June 2), Hungary 1, Russia 3 (Sept. 8), Greece 1, Russia 0 (Nov. 17). The clincher: Sergei Yuran scored the lone goal for Russia in its 1–1 draw with Iceland on June 2.

Players to Watch

Bank on the Sergeis to score a bulk of the goals for the Russians. That's forwards Sergei Kiriakov and Sergei Yuran, who scored 7 of the country's 15 goals in qualifying. Goalkeeper Stanislav Cherchessov is not spectacular, but plays a consistent game.

Probable Lineup

Goalkeeper: Stanislav Cherchessov (Dynamo Dresden). **Defenders**: Yuri Nikiforov (Spartak Moscow), Sergei Gorlukovitch (Bayer Leverkusen, Germany), Victor Onopko (Spartak Moscow), Andrei Ivanow (Spartak Moscow). **Midfielders**: Andrei Kanchelskis (Manchester United), Igor Dobrovolski (Dynamo Moscow), Igor

Shalimov (Inter Milan, Italy). **Forwards**: Sergei Yuran (Benfica, Portugal), Sergei Kiriakov (Karlsruhe), Igor Kolyvanov (Foggia, Italy).

Player Pool

Goalkeepers: Stanislav Cherchessov (Dynamo Dresden), Dmitri Kharine (Chelsea, England), Sergei Ovchinnikov (Lokomotiv Moscow). **Defenders**: Dimitri Galiamin (Espanol, Spain), Sergei Gorlukovitch (Bayern Leverkusen, Germany), Andrei Ivanov (Spartak Moscow), Dimitri Khlestov (Spartak Moscow), Vasili Kulkov (Benfica, Portugal), Andrei Mokh (Espanol, Spain), Yuri Nikiforov (Spartak Moscow), Victor Onopko (Spartak Moscow), Dimitri Popov (Racing, Spain). **Midfielders**: Andrei Afanasiev (Torpedo Moscow), Igor Dobrovolski (Dynamo Moscow), Andrei Kanchelskis (Manchester United), Valeri Karpin (Spartak Moscow), Igor Korneyev (Espanol, Spain), Dmitri Kuznetsov (Espanol, Spain), Igor Lediakhov (Spartak Moscow), Alexander Mostovoi (Benfica, Portgual), Andrei Piatnitcki (Spartak Moscow), Igor Shalimov (Inter Milan, Italy), Vladimir Tartarchuk (Slavia Prague), Omari Tetradze (Dynamo Moscow). **Forwards**: Vladimir Beschastnykh (Spartak Moscow), Igor Kolyvanov (Foggia, Italy), Yuri Matveev (Uralmash), Sergei Kiriakov (Karlsruhe), Dimitri Radchenko (Racing, Spain), Oleg Sergueev (CSKA Moscow), Bakhva Tedeev (Dynamo Moscow), Sergei Yuran (Benfica Portugal)

PLAYER PROFILES
(appearances and
goals through Oct.
28, 1993)

Stanislav Cherchessov, Goalkeeper (Dinamo Dresden, Germany), 5-foot-10, 171 pounds, Born: Sept. 2, 1963, Caps: 20, Goals: 0-Through November, Cherchessov had started 9 of 14 games since the Commonwealth of Independent States became Russia during the summer of 1992, recording a 5–2–2 mark and allowing only 6 goals. He does not make the spectacular saves, but usually plays a consistent game thanks to his agility and ability to dominate the air game in the penalty box. Cherchessov was runner-up for Soviet player of the year in 1990. He performed on the last 3 championship teams, with Moscow Spartak's Soviet crown in 1991, and the first 2 Russian crowns in 1992 and 1993.

Igor Dobrovolski, Midfielder (Dynamo Moscow), 5-foot-11, 163 pounds, Born: Aug. 27, 1967, Caps: 37, Goals: 9-If he can stay away from injuries, which have hampered his international career, Dobrovolski can be an important player for the Russians. He wound up as the leading scorer at the 1988 Seoul Olympics (6 goals), including converting a penalty kick in a 2–1 victory over Brazil in the gold-medal match. He scored a goal in a 4−0 triumph over Cameroon in the 1990 World Cup. And he scored the team's—as the CIS—in a 1−1 draw with Germany. On the other end, he has played for 5 teams in as many countries the past several seasons—Dynamo Moscow 1990−91 and then Castellon (Spain), both in 1990−91, Servette (Switzerland) in 1991−92, Genoa (Italy) in 1992−93 and finally Olympique Marseille (France) in 1993−94.

Sergei Gorlukovitch, Defender (Bayer Leverkusen, Germany), 6-foot, 171 pounds, Born: Nov. 18, 1991, Caps: 28, Goals: 1-Gorlukovitch, who usually plays on the left side, has spent most of his career in Germany at Borussia Dortmund and Bayer after several years at Lokomotiv Moscow and Dynamo Minsk. He was a member of the 1988 Olympic team and played all games in the 1990 World Cup.

Sergei Kiriakov, Forward (Karlsruhe, Germany), 5-foot-8, 154 pounds, Born: Jan. 1, 1970, Caps: 19, Goals: 9-A crafty player—a rarity for a Soviet product—Kiriakov was voted one of the top 24 foreign players in the German First Division. Kiriakov, a small, compact player who has adjusted to playing in the West, scored 3 goals for Karlsruhe in 1992−93, thanks to a powerful shot. He connected for a first-half hat-trick to rally Karlsruhe to a 3−3 tie with Borussia Dortmund in late November, 1993. "When 'Kiki' starts to dribble the ball, my heart begins to sing," Karlsruhe coach Winnie Schafer said. He led Russia in qualifying scoring with 8 goals. He played his entire career at Dynamo Moscow before transferring to the Bundesliga, connecting 11 times in 29 matches for Karlsruhe.

Dmitri Kharine, Goalkeeper (Chelsea, England), 6-foot, 176 pounds, Born: Aug. 16, 1968, Caps: 19, Goals: 0-Kharin isn't afraid to open his mouth, criticizing English soccer in general and his Chelsea teammates in particular in 1993. He has some credentials to back up his words. Kharin, who performed for CSKA Moscow, formerly the Red Army team, played in the 1992 European Championship, after starring for the Soviet Union in its gold-medal squad at the 1988 Olympics.

Victor Onopko, Midfielder, Spartak Moscow, 6-foot-1, 176 pounds, Born: Oct. 14, 1969, Caps: 19, Goals: 1-Onopko was named Russian Player of the Year in 1992 after leading Spartak to the title as the Moscow-based club won by 7 points. He decided to remain at Spartak after getting several offers from European teams. He played with

Shakhtyor Donetsk for 5 years before joining Spartak in 1992. Onopko is part of the need breed of Russian players, driving a Nissan, and being a fan of the rock group Queen and actor Marlon Brando.

Igor Shalimov, Midfielder, Inter Milan (Italy), 6-foot, 158 pounds, Born: Feb. 2, 1969, Caps: 31, Goals: 3-He is the midfielder organizer—he likes to play a short, ground game—who can perform on the left flank or in the middle. Shalimov, who made his international debut against Argentina at Italia '90, learned his trade under former Spartak and Soviet coach Igor Nietto, the first Soviet to play in 50 internationals. He played with Foggia (Italy), scoring 9 goals in 1991–92, before transferring to Inter for a $10 million fee.

Sergei Yuran, Forward, Benfica (Portugal), 5-foot-11, 170 pounds, Born: June 11, 1969, Caps: 26, Goals: 7-As one of the most sought-after Russian players in the past 3 years, Yuran has distinguished himself wherever he has performed. Spartak Moscow and Dynamo Kiev were in the midst of a bidding war for his services in 1990 before Benfica dangled even more money in front of him. After a slow start in Portugal, Yuran scored 22 goals over 52 games, plus another 4 against Hamrun Spartans (Malta) in the European Cup Winners Cup in 1991. Yuran, runner-up to Igor Dobrovolski for Soviet player of the year in 1990, scored 3 times in qualifying, in the 1–0 win over Iceland, the 2–0 victory over Luxembourg and the 3–0 triumph over Hungary.

Coach

On paper, Pavel Fyodorovic Sadyrin might have been tailor-made for this job as he has enjoyed a coaching career transforming also-rans into champions or competitive sides. Born on Sept. 18, 1942, Sadyrin directed Zenit Leningrad to the Soviet championship in 1984, only a year after his appointment. He then guided CSKA Moscow from the Second to the First Division in 3 years, climaxed by winning the title in 1991. Sadyrin was named Russian coach in 1992 after the amalgamation of the Commonwealth of Independent States dissolved and FIFA designated that Russia would be its successor. His playing career wasn't as distinguished as his coaching career, having been a midfielder with Zevdza Perm and Zenit Leningrad.

1994

Will a soccer style Russian Revolution ruin the team's chances at USA '94?

In early December, 14 players from the National Team staged a revolt against coach Pavel Sadyrin, asking for his firing in a letter to Shamil Tarpishchev, President Boris Yeltsin's sports adviser.

"In my opinion Sadyrin doesn't think about the game at all," said forward Sergei Kirarkov, who was quoted in Football, a weekly Russian publication. "We spend our training sessions on some sort of nonsense, and planning for the match takes five minutes, at most. What kind of tactics is that?

"It's all 'Let's go forward and win,' and that's it. But after the game it's a different story. Everyone's to blame, it turns out, except him."

Forward Igor Kolyvanov wanted former national coach Anatoly Byshovets to guide the team. "We don't want to work with Sadyrin any more," Kolyvanov said.

Sadyrin, in turn, blamed Byshovets, saying his predecessor was responsible for the letter. "Most of the players signed the letter, believing it mainly contained financial demands and were unaware of the fact it also demanded the replacement of the coach," Sadyrin said.

Tarpishchev asked the Russian Football Federation to sort out the problems so the team's World Cup chances would not be ruined. At the turn of the new year, nothing had been settled.

Regardless who coaches the team, this could be the last major tournament that Russia appears in, due to the breakup of the Soviet Union. The breakup, however, could bring some beneficial short term effects that could transform the Russians into one of the surprising sides at the cup. For years, the Soviets played machine-like soccer. But because dozens of players have gone on to play for Western European teams since the Iron Curtain was taken down, a variety of styles and tactics could be introduced to the team.

At the other end of the spectrum, with the former Soviet Union falling apart piece by piece, it was difficult enough to get a competitive team together. Satellite republics Latvia, Estonia and Lithuania already have competed as separate entities, while the Ukraine, which traditionally has supplied many players to the Soviet team (12 Dynamo Kiev players were used during the 1986 World Cup in Mexico) is set to move in its own direction for the next cup.

Sadyrin built the team on 3 fronts—using some players from the former republics, a core of players from Spartak Moscow as he mixed them with several foreign-based players. It was more than enough to qualify for the World Cup.

Though a number of Ukrainians decided to play for their homeland, Sadyrin coaxed several to remain with the team, including the

Ukraine's Igor Dobrovolski, who starred in the 1988 Olympics, Belaru's Sergei Gorlukovitch and Valeri Karpine of Estonia.

In keeping with the tradition of the having one team dominate the roster—Sadryin built his team around defending Russian champion Spartak Moscow, with 9 men in the player pool.

Add several players performing abroad—Igor Shalimov of Inter Milan (Italy) and Kiriakov of Karlsruhe (Germany), and Sadyrin had a team, a competitive team at that.

"We know what we're worth and believe in our strength," Sadyrin said. "There's enough first-class players in Russia."

The Russians, who play a 4–3–3 system, sometimes using 3 defenders and 2 defensive midfielders, have been criticized by many for using a sterile gameplan while performing as the Soviet Union. The Soviets have shown a little inclination of coming out of their shell in recent years with a little flair, teasing fans with a second-place finish to the Netherlands at the European Championship in 1988. If the returning players from the Western European clubs bring back some of that much needed individualistic style, the Soviets could wind up as one of the pleasant surprises at USA '94.

A bit of interesting information for World Cup history buffs: Despite its poor World Cup showing, the Soviet Union captured five Olympic medals—two gold and three bronze—the most by any of the 24 World Cup finalists.

CAMEROON
 POPULATION: 11,440,000
 COLORS: Green shirts, red shorts,
  yellow socks
 WORLD CUP APPEARANCES: Third.
  3–2–3 record, 8 goals for, 10 against.
  1982 (first round), 1990 (quarterfinals)

Cameroon's foray into the World Cup has been short, but very sweet. **World Cup History**
The Africans surprised everyone in Spain in 1982, by not losing a
game. The problem was they did not win one either, tying Peru, Poland
and eventual-champion Italy, 1–1, in the opening round. Facing defending champion Argentina in the 1990 opener, Cameroon stunned
the world with a rather improbable 1–0 victory, despite playing a man
down due to an ejection. It was the start of something big as 38-year-old
super-sub Roger Milla scored 4 goals before Cameroon was eliminated
by England in the quarterfinals in one of the most memorable World
Cup matches.

Cameroon won African Group B (first round) with a 2–0–2 record, 7 **How They Qualified**
goals for, 1 against, then captured the Group C (final round) with a
3–1–0 record, 7 goals for, 3 against. The results (home team listed
first): In the first round—Cameroon 5, Swaziland 0 (Oct. 18, 1992),
Zaire 1, Cameroon 2 (Jan. 10, 1993), Swaziland 0, Cameroon 0 (Jan.
17), Cameroon 0, Zaire 0 (March 1). In the final round—Cameroon 3,
Guinea 1 (April 18), Zimbabwe 1, Cameroon 0 (July 4), Guinea 0,
Cameroon 1 (July 18), Cameroon 3, Zimbabwe 1 (Oct. 10). The
clincher: Francois Omam-Biyik scored twice to lead Cameroon to a
3–1 win over Zimbabwe on Oct. 10, 1993.

After being benched for Italia '90, goalkeeper Joseph-Antoine Bell **Players to Watch**
will finally have an opportunity to showcase his talents—blocking
penalty kicks with his uncanny sense of positioning in the penalty area.
Forward François Omam-Biyik has a knack of scoring key goals and
captain Stephen Tataw is a steadying force in the back.

Goalkeeper: Joseph-Antoine Bell (St. Etienne, France). **Defenders**: **Probable Lineup**
Victor-Akem Ndip (Canon Yaounde), Stephen Tataw (Tonnerre
Yaounde), Alphonse Yombi (Canon Yaounde), Dennis Nde (Racing
Bafoussam). **Midfielders**: Marc-Vivien Foe (Fogape), Emile
M'Bouh-M'Bouh (plays in Saudi Arabia), Jean Claude Pagal (Mar-

tiques, France). **Forwards**: David Embe (Rennes, France), François Omam-Biyik (R.C Lens, France), Alphonse Tchami (OB Odense, Denmark).

Player Pool

Goalkeepers: William Andem (Olympic Mvoyle), Joseph-Antoine Bell (St. Etienne, France), Jacques Songo'O (F.C. Metz, France). **Defenders**: Hans Agbo (Olympic Mvoyle), Alexander Bes (Olympique Lyon, France), Victor-Akem Ndip (Canon Yaounde), Jules Onana (Canon Yaounde), Stephen Tataw (Tonnerre Yaounde), Alphonse Yombi (Canon Yaounde). **Midfielders**: Romarin Billong (Olympique Lyon, France), Bertin Ebwelle (Olympic Mvoyle), Stephane Ewane (Excelsior Mouscron), Alexis Eyalla (Racing Bafoussam), Roger Feutmba (Courtrai, Belgium), Marc-Vivien Foe (Fogape), Andre Kana-Biyik (Le Havre A.C., France), Emile M'Bouh (Al Etefag, Saudi Arabia), Cyril Makanaky (Maccabi Tel Aviv, Israel), Richard Njok (Olympique Charleville), Jean Claude Pagal (F.C. Martiques, France). **Forwards**: Daouda Bangura (Rot-Weis Essen, Germany), Olivier Djappa (Rot-Weis Essen, Germany), Ernest Ebongue (C.D. das Aves, Portugal), David Embe (Rennes, France), Samuel Ipoua (Nice, France), Jean-Jacques Misse-Misse (Sporting Charleroi, Belgium), Francois Omam-Biyik (R.C Lens, France), Guy-Noel Tapoko (Stade Lavallois, France), Alphonse Tchami (OB Odense, Denmark).

PLAYER PROFILES
(appearances and
goals through
Dec. 1, 1993)

Joseph-Antoine Bell, Goalkeeper (St. Etienne, France), 5-foot-7, 172 pounds, Born: Oct. 8, 1954, Caps: 83, Goals: 0-Bell might have been Cameroon's MVP on and off the field. Starting the final 4 qualifiers, he allowed only 3 goals. Off the field, he had to negotiate late payments to the team, bonuses and reimbursements for plane tickets, prompting someone to nickname him "Mandela." Bell played a prominent role in helping Cameroon reach Italia '90, but did not play a minute because the Soviet coach decided to go with Thomas N'Kono, hero of the Africans' 1982 World Cup run. Bell, whose strength is stopping penalty kicks, earned Cameroon's Gold Soccer Ball award in 1979, 1984 and 1988. He has played with 10 clubs, including 5 in France.

Stephen Tataw, Defender (Tonnerre Yaounde), 5-foot-8, 176 pounds, Born: March 31, 1963, Caps: 53, Goals: 2-The national captain, Tataw played every minute at Italia '90. He also performed for Olympic Mvolye, which was founded by former national team teammate Roger Milla, as Tataw led the club to victory in the 1992 Cameroon Cup.

Emile M'Bouh, Midfielder (Al Etefag, Saudi Arabia), 5-foot-2, 130 pounds, Born: May 30, 1966, Caps: 52, Goals: 2-He started and played every minute of Cameroon's first 4 games at Italia '90, missing the quarterfinal against England because of a yellow-card suspension. M'Bouh, who made his international debut at 20, has participated in 3 African Nations Cup tournaments (1986, 1988, 1992). The smallest member of the squad—perhaps in the entire World Cup—still manages to make things happen.

David Embe, Forward (Rennes, France), 5-foot-5, 154 pounds, Born: Nov. 13, 1973, Caps: 6, Goals: 2-As one of the stars of the Under-20 World Cup in 1993, Embe played for league champion Racing Bafoussam before transferring to Rennes of the French Second Division.

Francois Omam-Biyik, Forward (R.C Lens, France), 5-foot-8, 172 pounds, Born: May 21, 1966, Caps: 62, Goals: 25-No field player has made more appearances or scored more goals for Cameroon. But Omam-Biyik's most important goal came in the amazing 1–0 upset of Argentina in the opening match of the World Cup, as he scored in the 66th minute. In another important match, Omam-Biyik scored twice in Cameroon's 3–1 triumph over Zimbabwe, which clinched a berth in the World Cup. He has played for 7 clubs since turning pro in 1985, including 3 in France.

Alphonse Tchami, Forward, (OB Odense, Denmark), 5-foot-8, 163 pounds, Born: Feb. 14, 1971, Caps: 24, Goals: 8-His claim to fame was scoring 2 goals—his only 2 in qualifying—in a 3–1 qualifying win over Guinea in April, 1993, despite millions of black butterflies swirling around Yaounde Stadium. Tchami, who performed for Danish Cup winners Odense, also played briefly with Bordeaux and Nantes in France.

Former French coach Henri Michel was named coach of Cameroon earlier in the year. He took over for Jean-Pierre Sadi, who had been the goalkeeper coach. Cameroon also had Philippe Redon, Jules Yenga and Leonard Nseke over a span of 2 years. Nseke became the coordinator of the technical management committee, a 4-man group before Sadi was named 5 days after qualifying. **Coach**

Can Cameroon recapture the magic that made it the darlings of Italia '90? **1994**

Unless 42-year-old Roger Milla comes out of retirement and finds a fountain of youth and unless it gets its coaching situation straightened, it doesn't look like history can repeat at USA '94.

Milla, one of the great revelations at that 1990 World Cup, was utilized as a super sub. He scored 4 goals and created 2 others in only 224 minutes, the equivalent of 2 1/2 games. He has retired—there have been rumors he might put on the red, green and yellow uniform of Cameroon for one more shot at glory—although the attacking style his former teammates play has not been put into mothballs.

The Africans are fun to watch, attacking at will as one of the few qualifiers who use 3 forwards, although their deficiencies on defense usually show through all too easily. Many players seemingly get the man instead of the ball. They survived the opening match of Italia '90, a stunning 1–0 victory over Argentina with rough tactics, but everything caught up to them in the quarterfinals as England's Gary Lineker converted 2 penalty kicks in an entertaining 3–2 game.

Cameroon's success at Italia '90 has allowed 17 national pool players to play abroad in 5 countries, including France, Germany, Portugal, Belgium, Denmark and Israel.

That success is a double-edged sword. The players are able to expand their abilities and horizons, but it is quite difficult to get a full team home for games and training sessions. Perhaps the best place for the National Team to practice is France, where 19 players perform for various clubs.

Perhaps the only team that can beat Cameroon is itself, on and off the field.

When the squad arrived in Harare for a qualifier at Zimbabwe, for example, the team was forced to wait 3 hours at the airport because no one had made hotel reservations.

In early 1993, the team was almost kicked out of its Yaounde, Cameroon, hotel because of a financial crisis. Milla, who was the team manager then, said he could not afford to buy his players mineral water, which cost 72 cents a bottle. Fortunately for the team, sports minister Bernard Massoua and Cameroon Parliament Member Thomas Tobbo Eyoum came up with the money to pay the bills.

Of course, with all this reverse hype, Cameroon could be like a snake in the grass, waiting to attack. With all the pre-tournament attention given to Nigeria as the predicted surprise team, it wouldn't be surprising if Cameroon pulled off another upset or two.

A bit of interesting information for World Cup history buffs: Cameroon became the first group winner in 14 World Cups to have a negative goal differential at Italia '90, scoring 3 goals and allowing 5.

SWEDEN

POPULATION: 8,600,000

COLORS: Yellow shirts, blue shorts, yellow socks

WORLD CUP APPEARANCES: Ninth. 11–14–6 record, 49 goals for, 52 against. 1934 (second round), 1938 (first round), 1950 (second robin-round round), 1958 (second place), 1970 (first round), 1974 (second robin-round round), 1978 (first round), 1990 (first round)

World Cup History

Sweden's glory days in the World Cup are in the past. While the Swedes have qualified for the last 2 competitions, their record since 1974 hasn't been much to boast about—1–7–3, 11 goals for, 15 against, primarily because the Swedish First Division is not a full professional league. Hence, their best players are forced to travel abroad. Their best performance, undoubtedly, came as the hosts in 1958, as they finished second to a talented Brazilian side, losing 5–2 in the final.

How They Qualified

Sweden finished first in European Group 6, finishing with a 6–1–3 record for 15 points, scoring 19 goals, surrendering 8. The results (home team listed first)—Finland 0, Sweden 1 (Sept. 9, 1992), Sweden 2, Bulgaria 0 (Oct. 7, 1992), Israel 1, Sweden 3 (Nov. 11, 1992), France 2, Sweden 1 (April 28, 1993), Sweden 5, Israel 0 (June 2), Sweden 1, France 1 (Aug. 22), Bulgaria 1, Sweden 1 (Sept. 8), Sweden 3, Finland 2 (Oct. 13), Austria 1, Sweden 1 (Nov. 10). The clincher: Martin Dahlin scored twice and Henrik Larsson once in the 3–2 win over Finland in Stockholm.

Players to Watch

If the Swedes are to do anything and silence their critics, it will fall on the shoulders of the 2 front runners, Martin Dahlin and Tomas Brolin. They need to have a big tournament.

Probable Lineup

Goalkeeper: Thomas Ravelli (IFK Gothenburg). **Defenders**: Roland Nilsson (Sheffield Wednesday, England), Jan Eriksson (Kaiserslautern, Germany), Roger Ljung (Admira Wacker, Austria), Pontus Kamark (Vasteras). **Midfielders**: Klas Ingesson (PSV Eindhoven), Netherlands), Jonas Thern (Napoli, Italy), Stefan Schwarz (Benfica, Portugal), Anders Limpar (Arsenal, England). **Forwards**: Martin Dahlin (Borussia Moenchengladbach, Germany), Tomas Brolin (Parma, Italy).

Player Pool

Goalkeepers: Lars Eriksson (IFK Norrkoping), Jonnie Fedel (Malmo FF), Thomas Ravelli (IFK Gothenburg). **Defenders**: Patrik Andersson (Blackburn Rovers, England), Joachim Bjorklund (IRK Gotenburg), Jan Eriksson (Kaiserslautern, Germany), Pontus Kamark (Vasteras), Roger Ljung (Admira Wacker, Austria), Roland Nilsson (Sheffield Wednesday, England), Stefan Petterssen (Ajax, Netherlands). **Midfielders**: Klas Ingesson (PSV Eindhoven, Netherlands), Jan Jansson (IFK Norrkoping), Stefan Landberg (Osters IF), Anders Limpar (Arsenal, England), Mikael Nilsson (IFK Gothenburg), Stefan Rehn (IFK Gothenburg), Stefan Schwarz (Benfica, Portugal), Jonas Thern (Napoli, Italy), Zetterberg (Anderlecht, Belgium). **Forwards**: Kennet Andersson (Lille, France), Tomas Brolin (Parma, Italy), Martin Dahlin (Borussia Moenchengladbach, Germany), Hans Edklund (Osters IF), Johnny Ekstrom (Reggiana, Italy), Magnus Erlingmark (IFK Gothenburg), Hakan Mild (Gothenburg).

PLAYER PROFILES
(Appearances and goals through Dec. 6, 1993)

Tomas Brolin, Forward/midfielder (AC Parma, Italy), 5-foot-10, 166 pounds, Born: Nov. 29, 1969, Caps: 27, Goals: 15-He is emerging as an impact player for the National Team and for Parma, which was battling for the Italian First Division lead with defending champion A.C. Milan, Sampdoria and Juventus during the 1993–94 season. He scored Sweden's lone goal in its 2–1 loss to Brazil in the 1990 World Cup. He finished with 3 goals to tie for the scoring lead—with Germany's Karlheinz Riedle, the Netherland's Dennis Bergkamp and Denmark's Henrik Larsen—at the 1992 European Championship before an injury sidelined him and subsequently hurt Sweden's medal chances. He then recorded a hat-trick—his only 3 qualifying goals—in a 5–0 World Cup victory over Israel on June 2, 1993, which broke a year-long scoring drought. Brolin began his career with GIF Sundsvall, joined IFK Norrkoping for several months before he was transferred to Parma for $1.5 million in 1990. In his first 3 seasons with Parma, Brolin had 15 goals in 89 matches.

Martin Dahlin, Forward, (Borussia Moenchengladbach, Germany), 6-foot-1, 183 pounds, Born: April 16, 1968, Caps: 25, Goals: 16 Dahlin was named 1993 Swedish Player of the Year for his outstanding performance and "for his unselfish attitude and sense of responsibility, which makes him an example to teammates." Dahlin, whose attributes include his quickness, endurance and ability to go up for crosses, led Sweden with 7 qualifying goals, scoring twice in a match only once—in the 3–2 victory over Finland. After being rumored to be going to Bordeaux (France), Dahlin signed a 2-year extension with Borussia, which will take him through the 1995–96 season. The former Malmo star made his international debut in 1988 against Brazil, becoming the first black to play for Sweden.

Jan Eriksson, Defender, (Kaiserslautern, Germany), 6-foot-1, 183 pounds, Born: Aug. 24, 1967, Caps: 31, Goals: 4-His only goal in qualifying came in the 1–0 victory over Austria. Eriksson, who made his international debut against the United Arab Emirates in February, 1990, has performed for IFK Sundsvall, AIK Stockholm and Norrko-ping. He transferred to Kaiserslautern in the summer of 1992.

Klas Ingesson, Midfielder, (PSV Eindhoven, Netherlands), 6-foot-3, 193 pounds, Born: Aug. 20, 1968, Caps: 38, Goals: 9-A former lumberjack, Ingesson started his international career with a bang, coming on as a substitute and scoring both goals in a win over Algeria. His most important goal, however, was the lone score in a 1–0 quali-fying victory over Finland in 1992. He also scored against Israel, breaking a 1–1 tie in a 3–1 win. Ingesson, who is known for his powerhouse style, began his pro career with Gothenburg, then joined Mechelen (Belgium) in 1990.

Anders Limpar, Midfielder (Arsenal, England), 5-foot-8, 153 pounds, Born: Sept. 24, 1965, Caps: 44, Goals: 5-He is probably the best-known Swedish player, having participated at the 1988 Olympics and 1990 World Cup. Playing with Arsenal, Limpar has performed for the 1991 First Division champions, then for the 1993 F.A. Cup champs. Limpars, who was Sweden's Player of the Year in 1991, also has played for Orgryte, Young Boys (Switzerland) and Dremonse (Italy).

Roger Ljung, Defender (Admira Wacker, Austria), 6-foot-1, 175 pounds, Born: Jan. 8, 1966, Caps: 44, Goals: 2-Ljung, known for his strong play in the air, captained Malmo in its championship seasons in 1986 and 1988. Ljung, who performed in the 1988 Seoul Olympics, also played in Switzerland for Young Boys and F.C. Zurich.

Roland Nilsson, Defender (Sheffield Wednesday, England), 5-foot-11, 166 pounds, Born: March 22, 1963, Caps: 57, Goals: 1-He is captain of Wednesday, which lost in the F.A. Cup final in 1993. Nilsson also was a member of the 1988 Olympic and 1990 World Cup teams, while playing for a number of champions—Swedish champions (1983 and 1987), Swedish Cup winners (1983), UEFA Cup winners (1987) and English League Cup winners (1991). He also played for Helsingborgs IF and IFK Gothenburg.

Thomas Ravelli, Goalkeeper (IFK Goteborg), 6-foot-2, 181 pounds, Born: Aug. 13, 1959, Caps: 103, Goals: 0-Although he has been considered to be one of the top keepers in Europe, Ravelli has elected to stay home. As a member of the National Team since 1981—he took over from Ronnie Hellstrom—Ravelli is the Swedes' most capped player. Known for his excellent hands, Ravelli has been a member of 2 Swedish championship teams—with Osters Vaxo in 1980 and 1981 and with Gothenburg in 1990 and 1991. He was Sweden's Player of the Year in 1981. His twin brother Andreas—he is 30 minutes older—played for Osters, Gothenburg and the National Team.

Stefan Schwarz, Midfielder (Benfica, Portugal), 5-foot-11, 168 pounds, Born: April 18, 1969, Caps: 25, Goals: 4-Described as "indispensable" by former club teammates, Schwarz has played at fullback, central defender and midfield for the National Team. Schwarz, known for his quickness and hard left-footed shot, played at Italia '90. He also was a member of Malmo's famous soccer academy, earning a championship medal in 1988 and a cup winners medal the next year.

Jonas Thern, Midfielder, (Napoli, Italy), 6-foot, 175 pounds, Born: March 20, 1967, Caps: 43, Goals: 6-As one of the finest Swedish players produced in the last decade, thanks to his concentration and a powerful shot, Thern has found himself as the National Team captain. Though he did not score in qualifying, Thern set up Martin Dahlin's tying goal against France. Thern has been around the block and then some, starting his career with Malmo, earning Player of the Year honors in 1989. He joined Benfica (Portugal) in 1989 before transferring to Napoli for $5.2 million during the summer of 1992. He also played in the 1988 Olympics and the 1990 World Cup.

Coach   Tommy Svensson has achieved success at virtually every level at which he has participated, whether it has been as coach or player. As a midfielder or forward, he starred for the Swedish National Team from 1967–73, making 39 appearances and playing in the 1970 World Cup.

He also won Sweden Player of the Year honors in 1969, a year afer he led Osters IF to the Swedish title. After playing with Standard Liege (Belgium) from 1971–73, he helped Osters to the Swedish Cup. Born on March 4, 1945, Svensson began his coaching career with Tormso (Norway) in 1978. He returned home to guide Osters IF and Alvest Go IF before taking over as national coach.

Christmas came early for Sweden in 1993, on Oct. 14, to be exact.   **1994** During a team dinner in the early morning hours of that Thursday, hours after they had defeated Finland, 3–2, the Swedes learned they had qualified for the World Cup. Israel had rallied for 2 late goals to stun France in Paris, 3–2.

"This beats everything! Now I believe in Santa Claus," coach Tommy Svensson said.

He wasn't alone. "I think I'm dreaming. It's unbelievable! It's wonderful! This came so suddenly," forward Martin Dahlin said.

The Swedish Soccer Federation rented limos and drove the players to one of Stockholm's popular nightspots. The players, some of whom were draped in American flags, celebrated their good fortune with French champagne until the early hours of the morning.

That was the second major triumph for the Swedes in as many years. They reached the semifinals as one of the revelations of the European Championship in 1992 before succumbing to Germany, 3–2. After a 1–1 tie with heavily favored France, Sweden downed eventual champion Denmark, 1–0, and another favorite, England with a scintillating second-half, 2-1, taking advantage of opportunistic scoring and Svensson's tactical decisions. In the second half against England, for example, he replaced midfielder Andres Limpar with forward Johnny Ekstrom. The Swedes went on the attack, and Jan Eriksson scored 7 minutes into the half and Tomas Brolin with 8 minutes remaining in the match.

Because there is no true full professional league in Sweden, the country's best players are forced to play abroad. When the team does get together, the players must have an interesting reunion. Eight of the starting 11 perform in 6 foreign countries—England, Italy, Germany, Netherlands, Portugal and Austria (and that doesn't include reserve players Kennet Andersson and Pat Zetterberg, who perform in France and Belgium, respectively).

The Swedes, who usually deploy a 4–4–2 formation, revolve around the dynamic duo of Dahlin and Brolin up front. In games either player has scored since May 1, 1991, Sweden is 9–4–3. They will miss

Ekstrom, nicknamed "The Cyclone" because of his sudden burst of speed and non-stop pace, who will not play in the World Cup, it was announced in October, 1993.

For the Swedes to go places in 1994—the Scandanavians lost their 3 first-round matches at Italia '90 by 2–1 scores—they're going to have to continue their opportunistic play they started at the European Championship and play some solid defense.

A bit of interesting information for World Cup history buffs: The 1994 tournament will be the first World Cup since 1938, when Sweden finished fourth and Norway was eliminated in the opening round that those two countries participated in the same Cup. Sweden and Norway are back for USA '94.

GROUP C

GERMANY

BOLIVIA

SPAIN

SOUTH KOREA

GERMANY

POPULATION: 78,700,000

COLORS: White shirts, black shorts, white socks

WORLD CUP APPEARANCES: Thirteenth. 39–14–15 record, 145 goals for, 90 against. 1934 (third place), 1938 (first round), 1954 (champions), 1958 (fourth place), 1962 (quarterfinals), 1966 (second place), 1970 (second-round group), 1974 (champions), 1978 (second-round group), 1982 (second place), 1986 (second place), 1990 (champions)

In recent times, no country has been as successful on a consistent basis as Germany, having reached the championship game in 1966, 1974, 1982, 1986 and 1990 and coming away victorious in 1974 and 1990. In 1954, the West Germans stunned heavily favored Hungary in the championship match, 3–2, after losing an earlier encounter in the first round, 8–3. In 1974, behind the brilliant Kaiser, Franz Beckenbauer, the Germans defeated the Netherlands, 2–1, to capture the cup at home. And in 1990 under the direction of coach Beckenbauer, they emerged as the best team in a rather mediocre tournament, edging Argentina, 1–0, in the championship match.

World Cup History

Germany was an automatic qualifier because it is the defending World

How They Qualified

Cup champion. As West Germany, the team defeated Argentina, 1–0, at Olympic Stadium in Rome, Italy, on July 8, 1990.

Players to Watch

There are so many of them. Start with Juergen Klinsmann, who literally runs circles around his opponents by not running in the traditional up and down the field but in a circle while trying to get open while waiting for the ball. His speed makes him difficult to stop. He is expected to be complemented by Karlheinz Riedle, who is deadly in the air. Lothar Matthaeus, who came back from a knee injury in 1993, has learned a new position-sweeper, but expect him to join the attack once in a while.

Probable Lineup

Goalkeeper: Bodo Illgner (Cologne). **Defenders**: Juergen Kohler (Juventus, Italy), Guido Buchwald (VfB Stuggart), Lothar Matthaeus (Bayern Munich), Stefan Reuter (Borussia Dortmund). **Midfielders**: Stefan Effenberg (Fiorentina, Italy), Thomas Doll (Lazio, Italy), Andreas Moeller (Juventus, Italy). **Forwards**: Juergen Klinsmann (AS Monaco, France), Karlheinz Riedle (Borussia Dortmund).

Player Pool

Goalkeepers: Bodo Illgner (Cologne), Andreas Kopke (Nuremburg). **Defenders**: Manfred Binz (Eintracht Frankfurt), Andreas Brehme (Kaiserslavtern), Guido Buchwald (VfB Stuttgart), Thomas Helmer (Roma, Italy), Juergen Kohler (Juventus, Italy), Lothar Matthaeus (Bayern Munich), Alois Reinhardt (Bayern Munich), Knut Reinhardt (Borussia Dortmund), Stefan Reuter (Borussia Dortmund), Michael Schulz (Borussia Dortmund), Ralf Weber (Bayern Munich), Christian Worns (Bayer Leverkusen). **Midfielders**: Uwe Bein (Eintracht Frankfurt), Thomas Doll (Lazio, Italy), Stefan Effenberg (Fiorentina, Italy), Thomas Haessler (Roma, Italy), Andreas Moeller (Juventus, Italy), Karlheinz Plipsen (Borussia Moenchengladbach), Matthias Sammer (Borussia Dortmund), Heiko Scholz (Bayer Leverkusen), Olaf Thon (Bayern Munich), Thomas Wolter (Werder Bremen), Christian Ziege (Bayern Munich), Michael Zorc (Borussia Dortmund). **Forwards**: Ulf Kirsten (Bayer Leverkusen), Juergen Klinsmann (AS Monaco, France), Bruno Labbadia (Bayern Munich), Karlheinz Riedle (Borussia Dortmund), Andreas Thom (Bayer Leverkusen). goals through Dec. 14, 1993)

PLAYER PROFILES (Appearances and goals through Dec. 14, 1993)

Bodo Illgner, Goalkeeper (Cologne), 6-foot-3, 202 pounds, Born: April 7, 1967, Caps: 43, Goals:0-In the early part of his career, Illgner played in the shadow of former international Toni Schumacher before getting an opportunity to show what he could do in 1990. He stood out in the tie-breaker against England in the semifinals, saving one penalty kick and forcing another player to shoot over the net. He can be erratic, however, being criticized in the 1992 European Championship. In fact, Cologne once gave up a goal with Illgner in the opponents' side of the field. He has been pushed for the job by Andreas Kopke of FC Nuremberg, who finally made it to the National Team at the age of 30.

Lothar Matthaeus, Defender (Bayern Munich), 5-foot-10, 165 pounds, Born: March 21, 1961, Caps: 104, Goals: 19-The big experiment last fall was the switch of long-time midfielder and World Cup captain Matthaeus to sweeper to stabilize a rather shaky defense. Other players have made the transition, and Matthaeus appeared to be adapting. Matthaeus broke the all-time German international appearance record of former coach Franz Beckenbauer (103 caps). He also has played for Borussia Moenchengladbach and Inter Milan (Italy).

Guido Buchwald, Defender (VfB Stuttgart), 6-foot-2, 194 pounds, Born: Jan. 24, 1991, Caps: 68, Goals: 4-No matter what Buchwald does the rest of his career, he forever will be known as the man who marked the great Diego Maradona out of the final match at Italia '90. He also can score once in a while, heading in a goal with 6 minutes left to clinch the 1992 Bundesliga title for VfB Stuttgart.

Juergen Kohler, Defender (Juventus, Italy), 6-foot-1, 185 pounds, Born: Oct. 6, 1965, Caps: 57, Goals: 0-Kohler, who usually is responsible for covering the opposition's leading scorer, has turned into a living, breathing good luck charm. He played a vital role in Mannheim's promotion to the Bundesliga. He was named player of the year in 1988, was a member of Bayern Munich's championship team in 1990 and performed in the World Cup final. He later was transferred to Juventus for $6 million in 1991.

Olaf Thon, Defender (Bayern Munich), 5-foot-7, 147 pounds, Born: May 1, 1966, Caps: 40, Goals: 3-Thon etched his name into German soccer history by recording the clinching penalty kick in a semifinal tie-breaker against England in 1990. He returned to the National Team in 1992 after a 2-year absence.

Andreas Brehme, Defender-Midfielder (Kaiserslautern), Born: Nov. 9, 1960, Caps: 74, Goals: 1-Brehme, who scored the only gaol—a penalty kick against Argentina—of the championship game at Italia '90, retired from international soccer, but it appears he may return to the German squad. He is not known for his man-to-man coverage. Some observers claim he is a one-dimensional, that all he brings to the team is his booming shot. Brehme has returned to Kaiserslautern, for which he scored 34 goals in 150 games in the eighties, after stints with Bayern Muncih and Inter Milan (Italy). His 74 internationals rank Brehme 10th on the all-time German list.

Uwe Bein, Midfielder (Eintracht Frankfurt), 5-foot-10, 154 pounds, Born: Sept. 26, 1960, Caps: 15, Goals: 3-Why isn't this man playing in Italy? He has scored in about a third of his matches, helping Eintracht Frankfurt's revival in 1989–90. Bein, who made his international debut against Finland in 1989, started 4 times at Italia '90.

Thomas Doll, Midfielder (Lazio, Italy), 5-foot-9, 152 pounds, Born: April 9, 1966, Caps: 017 (29 overall, with East Germany), Goals: 1-One of 5 East Germans on the World Cup team, Doll has seen his star rise quickly after reunification. He started his career in East Germany with Hansa Rostock, then moved to Dynamo Berlin and Hamburg in the west in 1990, being named the team's player of the year. After only one season, he transferred to Lazio to become the first East German to perform in the Italian First Division. He teamed with fellow German Karlheinz Riedle at Lazio to form a one-two punch as they were nicknamed, "Romulus and Remus," after the 2 founders of Rome. Doll, a precision passer, refined his heading skills by knocking a ball against a wall on a dairy farm.

Stefan Effenberg, Midfielder (Fiorentina, Italy), 6-foot-1, 180 pounds, Born: Aug. 2, 1968, Caps: 24, Goals: 5-Well, every team has to have one. Effenberg is known as the "enfant terrible" of the World Cup team because of his provacative public comments that have upset his teammates. Still, he is an outstanding defensive midfielder who is not afraid to go forward on occasion.

Andreas Moeller, Midfielder (Juventus, Italy), 5-foot-11, 154 pounds, Born: Sept. 2, 1967, Caps: 33, Goals: 9-It seems every player has a specific role on the German squad. Moeller, who played for Borussia Dortmund and Eintracht Frankfurt, causes the defenses of opposing teams problems with his runs from out of the midfield, which usually are climaxed with a hard shot.

Juergen Klinsmann, Forward (AS Monaco, France), 5-foot-11, 167 pounds, Born: July 30, 1964, Caps: 53, Goals: 18-Klinsmann is like that bunny with batteries in its back. He just keeps on going and going and going . . . He never stops running. He starred in the 1988 Olympics, performed in Germany (Stuttgart Kickers), Italy (Inter Milan) and France (AS Monaco) and played for a world champion (Germany in 1990). Klinsmann, who speaks fluent French, Spanish and English, was a hit with the media at U.S. Cup '93 because of his superb performance and ability to handle the native language.

Karlheinz Riedle, Forward (Borussia Dortmund), 5-foot-10, 156 pounds, Born: Sept. 16, 1965, Caps: 36, Goals: 15-Riedle, who returned home to Borussia Dortmund after spending some time with Lazio (Italy), has blossomed under Vogts, creating havoc in the penalty area because of his opportunistic play. Riedle's specialty is a deadly head shot, as the veteran striker has been described by former German captain Rudi Voeller as "the best header of the ball in Europe." Lazio paid Werder Bremen $6 million for Riedle, who also is a full qualified butcher.

Berti Vogts, born Dec. 30, 1946, has a tough act to follow—a world championship. But everything he has done in his life has prepared him for his greatest challenge—to win a title on the other side of the world. He certainly has the pedigree and background to prepare for the role. As a player, Vogts played his entire career with Borussia Moenchengladbach in a club-record 419 games. Borussia won 5 Bundesliga champions, including 3 straight from 1975–77. He went on to international fame as the third most-capped player in German history behind Lothar Matthaeus and Franz Beckenbauer, with 98 international appearances, including playing on West Germany's world championship team in 1974. After he retired in 1979, Vogts became German youth national coach, guiding his team to a second-place finish to Yugoslavia in the Under-20 World Youth Championship in Chile in 1987. And although he kept on insisting he had no aspirations to coach the national team, he was promoted to assistant and was named Beckenbauer's successor after the 1990 World Cup.

Coach

During the post-game press conference after West Germany captured its third World Cup title, then-coach Franz Beckenbauer gave an advance warning for the 1994 World Cup in the wake of the reunification between his country and East Germany.

1994

"We'll have a broader choice of players, more players to choose from the next time around," he said. "The German team will be unbeatable. I'm sorry about that folks, but it will be tough to beat us."

He wasn't being arrogant and he wasn't kidding, either. The Germans will be tough to beat. The only question is: Can Germany become the first European team to win in the Americas and in the process become only the third country to win back-to-back World Cups? Brazil, a favorite for USA '94, pulled off those two rare feats, winning in Sweden in 1958 and again in Chile 4 years later. Italy won in 1934 and 1938.

The key East Germans added into the mix were midfielders Thomas Doll and Matthias Sammer and forwards Ulf Kirsten and Andreas Thom. Add the core of the 1990 champions, you have one imposing side.

Coach Berti Vogts' biggest lament isn't the quality of his squad, but rather their lack of competitive matches. Because Germany qualified automatically, it did not need to go through the rigors and tension or drama of World Cup qualifying.

So, the Germans welcomed playing in U.S. Cup '93, which it won, against Brazil, England and the U.S. "We took this tournament seriously because we don't have to qualify," said striker Juergen Klinsmann, the cup's MVP.

"For the World Cup, we are one of the favorite teams," he added. "In the World Cup, you have to be in the right place and in the right condition. And in the end you need a little bit of luck."

The Germans also have played a number of friendlies—but exhibition games aren't the real thing. They did participate in the European Championship in 1992, losing to Cinderella Denmark in the finals, 2−0, doing just about everything right in the title match but score.

Scoring, however, hasn't been the Germans' problem, stopping other teams from doing so has been. Brazil and the United States, of all countries, demonstrated that in U.S. Cup '93 by scoring 3 goals apiece on the world champions. Brazil rolled to a 3−0 halftime advantage before the Germans rallied for a 3−3 tie and the Germans grabbed a similar lead against the U.S., before holding off the tenacious Americans, 4−3. Even in its 2−1 win over England, there were holes in the backline.

Vogts' solution? Move World Cup captain Lothar Matthaeus from midfield to sweeper. Matthaeus, who has been slowed down by a knee injury, is expected to stabilize the backline in front of goalkeeper Bodo

Illgner, thanks to his experience. Since Vogts' game plan is for the sweeper to launch the attacks, Matthaeus is expected to fit in well back there in the 4–4–2 formation.

In fact, it is quite bewildering trying to figure out why a team-oriented, disciplined side as the Germans—the forwards go back to defense and the fullbacks overlap well—had defensive problems because of the number of talented players in the back. Guido Buchwald, who entered the global spotlight after marking and stopping Diego Maradona at Italia '90, Juergen Kohler, who is a tight marker, and Olaf Thon, who converted the penalty kick in the tie-breaker that lifted Germany into the World Cup final, and Stefan Reuter, who was the defensive midfielder in the championship game, are among the best in the back.

There also were rumors swirling in the fall that defender Andreas Brehme, who converted the penalty kick against Argentina in the title match, was thinking of returning to international soccer after his retirement.

Vogts was able to make the switch with Matthaeus, because Germany has been blessed with so many able and hard-working midfielders—Thomas Doll, Uwe Bein, Stefan Effenberg, Thomas Haessler and Andreas Moeller, to name a few.

The firepower up front is talented and deep, even without the prolific Rudi Voeller (43 goals), who has retired from international soccer to pursue a career and money in the J-League in Japan. Klinsmann, one of the stars of Italia '90, is expected to be the focal point of the attack, but not the only target man. Karlheinz Riedle has among the best head shots in the world. A new generation also is waiting in the wings—Christian Ziege and Bruno Labbadia of Bayern Munich.

As Beckenbauer said, the Germans are deep.

A bit of interesting information for World Cup history buffs: It will be difficult to keep the Germans out of the semifinals because they have reached the final four of 8 of the last 10 World Cups.

BOLIVIA
POPULATION: 7,500,000
COLORS: Green shirts, white shorts, white socks
WORLD CUP APPEARANCES: Three. 0–3–0, no goals for, 16 against. 1930 (first round), 1950 (first round)

World Cup Histor

Bolivia is still looking for its first victory and first goal. The South Americans have not distinguished themselves in their only 2 appearances, as they did not have to qualify either time. The inaugural World Cup was by invitation. Bolivia dropped both of its first-round games; 4–0 to Yugoslavia and 4–0 to Brazil. In 1950, the Bolivians took a free ride into the tournament as Argentina dropped out during qualifying. They were eliminated in the opening round by Uruguay, 8–0.

How They Qualified

The Bolivians finished second in South American Group B with a 5–2–1 record, scoring 22 goals, allowing 11 The results (home team listed first)—Venezuela 1, Bolivia 7 (July 18, 1993), Bolivia 2, Brazil 0 (July 25), Bolivia 3, Uruguay 1 (Aug. 8), Bolivia 1, Ecuador 0 (Aug. 15), Bolivia 7, Venezuela 0 (Aug. 22), Brazil 6, Bolivia 0 (Aug. 29), Uruguay 2, Bolivia 1 (Sept. 12), Ecuador 1, Bolivia 1 (Sept. 19). The clincher—Bolivia qualified for the very first time with a 1–1 draw with Ecuador in Guayaquil on Sept. 19, 1993, as William Ramallo scored its lone goal.

Players to Watch

Forward Marco Antonio Etcheverry—nicknamed El Diablo or the Devil, who is expected to recover from torn knee ligaments after a freak injury, is a solid finisher. William Ramallo, who led the Bolivians with 7 goals in qualifying, has a lethal shot. Midfielder Erwin Sanchez is one of 6 players on the team from the world-famous Tahuichi Soccer Academy.

Probable Lineup

Goalkeeper: Carlos Trucco (Bolivar). **Defenders**: Luis Cristaldo (Oriente Petrolero), Gustavo Quinteros (San Jose), Miguel Angel Rimba (Bolivar), Marco Sandy (Bolivar). **Midfielders**: Julio Cesar Baldivieso (Bolivar), Carlos Borja (Bolivar), Milton Melgar (free agent), Erwin Sanchez (Boavista, Portugal). **Forwards**: Marco Antonio Etcheverry (Colo Colo, Chile), William Ramallo (Destroyers).

Player Pool

Goalkeepers: Ruben Dario Rojas (Oriente Petrolero), Marcelo Torrico (The Strongest), Carlos Trucco (Bolivar). **Defenders**: Luis Cristaldo (Oriente Petrolero), Miguel Angel Noro (Destroyers), Juan Manuel Pena (Blooming), Roberto Perez (San Jose), Gustavo Quinteros (San Jose), Miguel Angel Rimba (Bolivar), Sergio Rivero (Oriente Petrolero), Marco Sandy (Bolivar), Modesto Soruco (Blooming). **Midfielders**: Julio Cesar Baldivieso (Bolivar), Carlos Borja (Bolivar), Ivan Castillo (Oriente Petrolero), Ramiro Castillo, Milton Melgar (free agent), Juan Carlos Rios (Cicion), Erwin Sanchez (Boavista, Portugal), Johnny Villarroel (The Strongest). **Forwards**: Marco Antonio Etcheverry (Colo Colo, Chile), Jaime Moreno (Blooming), Alvaro Pena (Temuco, Chile), William Ramallo (Destroyers).

Luis Cristaldo, Defender (Oriente Petrolero), Born: Aug. 31, 1969-Considered to be the key player in the defense, Cristaldo scored Bolivia's first goal in its win over Venezuela on July 18.

PLAYER PROFILES (Heights, weights, caps, goals, unavailable, through Nov. 20, 1993)

Marco Antonio Etcheverry, Forward (Colo Colo, Chile), Born: Sept. 26, 1970-Known as El Diablo or The Devil, Etcheverry has bedeviled opponents for years. Take, for example, his debut with Colo Colo (Chile) after a $750,000 transfer on Aug. 11, 1993. He came off the bench to score the final goal in a 4−2 win over Vasco da Gama (Brazil), which tied its foes in the final standings. Etcheverry, who was expected to miss four months leading up to the World Cup with torn knee ligaments after a Universidad Catolica defender accidentally fell on his his leg in a Chilean match in November, 1993. He finished with three goals in qualifying, including two in the 7−0 rout of Venezuela and another in the 3−1 victory over Uruguay on Aug. 22, 1993.

Milton Melgar, Midfielder (free agent), Born: Sept. 20, 1959-Nicknamed "Maravilla"—The Wonder—Melgar was wonderful during qualifying, striking twice in the 7−0 triumph over Venezuela and for a goal in the 3−1 victory over Uruguay on Aug. 8. He has played for River Plate and the Boca Juniors in Argentina and Everton in Chile.

William Ramallo, Forward (Destroyers), Born: July 4, 1963-To defenders, Ramallo certainly has lived up to his nickname—"Fantasma" (The Phantom), becoming a difficult man to catch or stop. Ramallo led Bolivia with 7 qualifying scores. He tallied 4 times in the 7−1 win in Venezuela and the Bolivians' lone goal in their 1−1 draw with Ecuador that clinched a spot at USA '94.

Miguel Angel Rimba, Defender (Bolivar), Born: Nov. 1, 1967-Like it or not, Rimba is best known for being suspended for alleged cocaine use with Brazilian reserve goalkeeper Zetti after the July 15, 1993, qualifying match. The cocaine was traced to a traditional Bolivian tea made from coca leaves, the material from which cocaine is made. The tea, easily available in Bolivia, is used for altitude sickness. Both players were reinstated.

Erwin Sanchez, Midfielder (Boavista, Portugal), Born: Oct. 19, 1969- Sanchez, nicknamed Platini, after the French superstar of the eighties, was a key force in Bolivia's march to the World Cup. He scored 4 times, including a hat-trick against Venezuela. A graduate of the Tahuichi Soccer Academy, Sanchez has performed in Portugal the past 3 seasons. In 1990–91, he helped Benfica capture its 29th league crown. He moved to GK Estoril Praia the next season and wound up as the club's leading scorer with 8 goals in 28 matches. In 1992, he moved to Boavista, which advanced to the Portuguese Cup championship match last year.

Carlos Trucco, Goalkeeper (Bolivar)-As the second oldest player, the 36-year-old Trucco brings a tremendous amount of experience, having performed for clubs in his native Argentina (Independiente de Balnearia and Santa Fe), Bolivia (Destroyers, Oriente Petrolero and Bolivar) and Colombia (Union Magdalena, Blooming and Deportivo Cali). He gained Bolivian citizenship through his 8-year-old daughter Gabriel in 1988, as she was born in Bolivia. Nicknamed "Loco," Trucco used his superb leaping ability to star in the 1–1 tie with Ecuador that clinched a berth.

Coach   Francisco Xavier Azkargorta believes in the power of positive thinking, so it was not surprising that the Spanish-born coach's first order of business upon taking over as coach was to increase the self-esteem of his players. He gave them a psychological test. "Gentleman, our opponents are human just like us," he said. "We won't be beaten by a negative attitude." Bolivia wasn't, reaching its first World Cup in 44 years. His birth certificate might say Spain, but in his heart, Azkargorta is a Bolivian. "I'm a Bolivian in my heart," he said the day Bolivia secured a spot in the World Cup. "I don't need any papers to prove it. I'm a very proud Bolivian today." Because an ankle injury cut short his playing career at an early age, Azkargorta was able to gain valuable coaching experience. By the time he was 30, Azkargorta—born on

Sept. 29, 1953—was coaching in the Spanish First Division, with Espanol. He also has directed Real Valladolid, Sevilla and Tenerife, leaving the latter club in 1991. Azkargorta has been a sports medicine specialist (Diego Maradona has been among his patients), returning to soccer in 1993 as Bolivian coach.

Soccer madness gripped Bolivia, not known for its success at the international level, in the summer of 1993. President Jaime Paz Zamora directed the national team's practice on July 23, 1993. Two days later, the Bolivians upset Brazil, 2–0, handing their South American rivals their first loss ever in World Cup qualifying.

1994

"I want to finish my term of office by seeing Bolivia qualify for the World Cup," said Zamora, who stepped down on Aug. 6, about a month and a half before his country actually qualified.

Depending on your point of view, Bolivia either qualified by skill or by luck.

The national team's supporters will say it was only a matter of several key players maturing from its highly successful youth ranks.

Its critics will claim, however, that the squad's success in matches in the capital of La Paz, 11,000 feet above sea level, had something to do with qualifying for the World Cup. It certainly did not hurt, but, where were all those critics when Bolivia failed to qualify on 10 consecutive occasions from 1954–90?

One reason for Bolivia's sudden success is the Tahuichi Soccer Academy, which started to give Bolivian soccer a higher profile in the late eighties by winning several major international tournament titles, including the Dallas Cup. Tahuichi, which means "Big Bird" in the regional Chiriguano Indian language, was created by Rolando Aguilera in 1978 for soccer players up to the age of 19. The academy has taken boys off the streets, and pointed them in the right direction with the proper education. That includes learning the finer points of soccer as Tahuichi traditionally plays an attacking, efficient and pleasing brand of soccer.

"Tahuichi is more important for Bolivia than other sports organizations to other countries," Aguilera said. "We have lost 100 kilometers in wars with our neighbors. We have been beaten in all our sports. It's important for the youth to change its mind so they can be successful, not just in youth soccer, but in life."

In 1989, Aguilera made a bold prediction: "I think Bolivia will change it's football in 10 years or more."

He was wrong by 5 years, thanks to 6 Tahuichi graduates in the national team pool—forwards Marco Antonio Etcheverry, Erwin Sanchez and Alvaro Pena, and defenders Juan Pena, Luis Cristaldo and Modesto Soruco.

Whether Etcheverry and company—the forward must recuperate from a serious knee injury—can make an impact in a group that includes defending champion Germany, Spain and Nigeria, remains to be seen. As a relatively inexperienced World Cup side—Bolivia hasn't played there since 1950—there are no great expectations. But the Bolivians, who use a 4−4−2 formation, could pull off a surprise or two, not unlike what they accomplished during qualifying.

If nothing else, Bolivia will lead all World Cup teams in nicknames. For example, there's El Diablo (The Devil)—Marco Antonio Etcheverry; Chocolate—Ramiro Castillo, because the color of his skin; Platini—Erwin Sanchez; Correcaminos (The Roadrunner)—Miguel Angel Rimba; and Pichicho—37-year-old midfielder Carlos Borja, the oldest player on the team, among others.

A bit of interesting information for World Cup history buffs: South American countries, other than Brazil, Argentina and Uruguay playing in the tournament, have a 12−26−8 record in 14 appearances, so the Bolivians have their world cut out for them.

SPAIN

POPULATION: 39,000,000

COLORS: Red shirts, blue shorts, blue socks

WORLD CUP APPEARANCES: Ninth. 13–12–7 record, 43 goals for, 38 against. 1934 (second round), 1950 (fourth place in robin-round final round), 1962 (first round), 1966 (first round), 1978 (first round), 1982 (second round), 1986 (quarterfinals), 1990 (second round)

World Cup History

Except for a fourth-place finish in 1950 in Brazil, Spain has had a history of teasing its supporters and proponents. The Spanish are good enough to qualify and get out of the first round, but rarely have made an impact. After a rather discouraging result, when they were the host in 1982, one Spanish newspaper refused to publish the team's lineup, it was so disgusted with the result.

How They Qualified

Spain finished first in European Group 3 with an 8–1–3 record and 19 points, scoring 27 goals, allowing 4. The results (home team listed first)—Latvia 0, Spain 0 (Sept. 23, 1992), Spain 0, Northern Ireland 0 (Oct. 14, 1992), Spain 0, Ireland 0 (Oct. 18, 1992), Spain 5, Lithuania 0 (Feb. 24, 1993), Denmark 1, Spain 0 (March 31), Spain 3, Northern Ireland 1 (April 28), Lithuania 0, Spain 2 (June 2), Albania 1, Spain 5 (Sept. 22), Ireland 1, Spain 3 (Oct. 13), Spain 1, Denmark 0 (Nov. 17). The clincher—Despite playing most of the match a man down after goalkeeper Andoni Zubizarreta was red-carded in the 10th minute, Fernando Hierro scored the lone goal in a 1–0 victory over a difficult and European Champion Denmark in Seville on Nov. 17, 1993.

Players to Watch

Julio Salinas, who came on strong in the later qualifying matches, is skillful up front. Jose Luis Caminero is a defender-midfielder who has a penchant of scoring key goals. Goalkeeper Andoni "Zubi" Zubizarreta is a veteran goalkeeper who has been there before in the World Cup and several European Cup competitions.

Probable Lineup

Goalkeeper: Andoni Zubizaretta (Barcelona). **Defenders**: Albert Ferrer (Barcelona), Rafael Alkorta (Real Madrid), Miguel Angel Nadal (Barcelona), Francisco Camarasa (Valencia), Fernando Giner (Valencia). **Midfielders**: Jose Maria Bakero (Barcelona), Fernando Hierro

(Real Madrid), Luis Enrique (Real Madrid). **Forwards**: Julio Salinas (Barcelona), Andoni Goicoechea (Barcelona).

Player Pool

Goalkeepers: Jose Santiago Canizares (Celta), Alvaro Cevera (Mallorca), Julen Lopetegui (Logrones), Andoni Zubizaretta (Barcelona). **Defenders**: Rafael Alkorta (Real Madrid), Jose Camarasa (Valencia), Jose Luis Caminero (Atletico Madrid), Albert Ferrer (Barcelona), Fernando Giner (Valencia), Miguel Lasa (Real Madrid), Nando (Deportivo Coruna), Roberto Solozbal (Atletico Madrid), Toni (Atletico Madrid), Voro (Deportivo Coruna). **Midfielders**: Guillermo Amor (Barcelona), Thomas Christiansen (Barcelona), Cristobal (Real Oviedo), Fran (Deportivo Coruna), Delfi Geli (Atletico Balompie), Josep Guardiola (Barcelona), Fernando Hierro (Real Madrid), Rafael Martin Vasquez (Real Madrid), Michel (Real Madrid), Miguel Angel Nadal (Barcelona), Juan Vizcaino (Atletico Madrid). **Forwards**: Adolfo Aldana (Deportivo Coruna), Jose Maria Bakero (Barcelona), Claudio Barragan (Deportivo Coruna), Aitor Beguiristain (Barcelona), Emilio Butragueno (Real Madrid), Luis Enrique (Real Madrid), Enrique Estebaranz (Barcelona), Gregorio Fonseca (Espanol), Andoni Goicoechea (Barcelona), Julen Guerrero (Atletico Bilbao), Kiko (Atletico Madrid), Manolo (Atletico Madrid), Alfonso Perez (Real Madrid), Julio Salinas (Barcelona).

PLAYER PROFILES
(Appearances and goals through Dec. 1, 1993)

Jose Maria Bakero, Midfielder (Barcelona), Born: Feb. 11, 1993, Caps: 25, Goals: 7-Bakero, who has been Barcelona's main link between the midfield and front line, has been the most consistent scoring midfielder in the Spanish First Division over 5 seasons from 1988-89 through 1993. He has connected for at least 9 goals a season for a total of 55. He scored several game-winning goals for the Barcas in their quest to win the 1992 European Cup, finding the net against Kaiserslautern (Germany), Sparta Prague (Czechoslovakia) and Benfica (Portugal). His lone qualifying goal came in the 5−0 triumph over Lithuania. Spain coach Javier Clemente said Bakero's presence was "vital to get the whole team going."

Jose Luis Caminero, Defender-midfielder (Atletico Madrid), 5-foot-10, 187 pounds, Born: Nov. 8, 1967-An offensive-minded defender, Caminero has scored a number of vital goals for the National Team and Atletico. He scored in his World Cup qualifying debut in a 5−1 win over Albania on Sept. 22, 1993. He then connected for the important first goal in Spain's 3−1 victory over Ireland in Dublin on Oct. 13, scoring off a throw-in in the 11th minute. Several weeks later, he put in the game-winning goal in Atletico's dramatic 4−3 comeback win over Barcelona on Oct. 31 as his team rallied from a 3-goal deficit.

Albert Ferrer, Defender, Barcelona, 5-foot-4, 143 pounds, Born: June 6, 1970, Caps: 13, Goals: 0-Known as one of the best defenders in Spain, Ferrer played in 11 of the team's 12 qualifying matches. A versatile player, Ferrer was a regular on Spain's gold-medal winning team at the 1992 Barcelona Olympics, starting in five of six matches. Depending on the situation, he can play in one-on-one marking situations, as an attacking fullback or as a defensive midfielder.

Juan Andoni Goicoechea, Forward/midfielder, Barcelona, 5-foot-5, 165 pounds, Born: Oct. 21, 1965, Caps: 43, Goals: 4-Goicoechea hasn't scored many goals at the international level, but his hard work has been an important part of Spain's success. A knee injury suffered during a qualifier against Denmark in March, 1993 sidelined Goicoechea until September. Goicoechea played with Real Sociedad before he joined Barcelona for the 1990-91 season. He is the older brother of Miguel Goicoechea, a member of the 1992 Olympic gold-medal winning team.

Fernando Hierro, Midfielder (Real Madrid), 5-foot-6, 158 pounds, Born: March 28, 1968, Caps: 18, Goals: 6-One of the Spanish First Division's top goalscorers, Hierro scored the lone goal of the 1−0 clinching win over Ireland on Nov. 17. He came into his own for Real Madrid after Hugo Sanchez went down with an injury. He collected a team-high 21 goals in 37 matches in 1991−92, dropping off to 13 in 33 games in 1992−93. Hierro, which means iron in Spanish, comes from a soccer family. His father played in the Third Division, and his 3 brothers, Pepe, Antonio and Manolo, are still playing professionally. He also has played with CD Malaga and Real Valladolid.

Julio Salinas, Forward (Barcelona), 5-foot-11, 180 pounds, Born: Sept. 11, 1962, Caps: 39-He is awkward looking and leggy, but Salinas always gets the job done. He led Spain with 7 goals in 8 qualifiers. A veteran of the 1986 and 1990 World Cups, Salinas came through in a big way in 3 qualifiers, scoring 7 goals. He scored twice—in the 3−1 win over Northern Ireland and in the 3−1 triumph over Ireland—and added a hat-trick in the 5−1 victory over Albania. Salinas, who has earned a reputation with Barcelona as a super-sub, played under national coach Javier Clemente at Atletico Bilbao from 1982–86 and then scored 35 goals for Atletico Madrid from 1986–88.

Andoni Zubizarreta, Goalkeeper (Barcelona), 5-foot-10, 185 pounds, Born: Oct. 23, 1961, Caps: 83, Goals: 0-Another veteran of Mexico '86 and Italia '90, Zubi has made more international appearances than any other Spanish player in history, eclipsing the record by Jose Antonio Camacho (80). Opportunity knocked during the 1985–86 season, when National Team goalkeeper and captain Luis Arconada tore knee ligaments. It was in that year that Zubizarreta earned the Zamora Trophy as the best keeper in the league. He has played for Barcelona in its 3 consecutive First Division titles in 1991, 1992 and 1993. He joined Barcelona for $1.8 million, then a record transfer fee for goalkeepers, from Atletico Bilbao, where he started his career in 1981.

Coach

Javier Clemente took over as coach in the summer of 1992, after a stint as an interim coach at Espanol, trying to transform a national team well known for its skills into one that relies on its strength. The 43-year-old Clemente is one of the more controversial coaches in Spanish soccer, candid and outspoken to the media. A no-nonsense type of person, Clemente is a strong motivator. Clemente began his coaching career at the relatively young age of 25 after an ankle injury ended his playing career. In the next 18 years, he coached in the First, Second and Third Divisions, starting with Arenas de Guecho and guiding Atletico Club to its first First Division title in 27 years in 1982–83. He coached for part of the 1989–90 season under Jesus Gil, the notorious and controversial owner of Atletico Madrid who fires coaches as quickly as he changes underwear.

1994

After playing to consecutive scoreless ties—2 at home—in their first 3 qualifying matches, the Spanish rebounded by winning 5 of their last 6 games, including 3 on the road, to qualify.

In the 4 most recent World Cups, Spain has been something of a tease, entering the competition with great expectations, but leaving rather early with low realizations.

Does one think that USA '94 will be any different? Good question. After much experimenting, coach Javier Clemente has preferred to go with players from perennial Spanish First Division champion Barcelona and sometimes with a physically strong side rather than a traditional one with skills. How that will affect Spain remains to be seen. He also likes to use 5 defenders on the backline, which does not fit into the traditional, Latin, short passing game.

Clemente juggled his lineup more than any coach, using 36 players in 12 qualifying matches to suit the circumstances of each game. He usually has Spain in a 4−4−2 formation that counterattacks to create scoring opportunities.

For now, Clemente decided to go without several veterans, including striker Emilio "The Vulture" Butragueno, who has been a relative disappointment in World Cup matches. He is tied for the Spanish all-time scoring lead with 5 goals, although 4 came in a victory over Denmark in 1986. In other words, he has 1 goal in 8 other games.

Perhaps Julio Salinas, who collected those 7 goals in qualifying, even though he does not play regularly with Barcelona, will emerge as the much-needed scoring star at the World Cup.

A bit of interesting information for World Cup history buffs: Spain has been eliminated from the World Cup by the second round in 5 out of its last 6 appearances, reaching the quarterfinals in 1986.

SOUTH KOREA
POPULATION: 43,200,000
COLORS: Red shirts, red shorts, red socks
WORLD   CUP   APPEARANCES:
Fourth. 0–7–1 record, 5 goals for, 29
against. 1954 (first round), 1986 (first
round), 1990 (first round)

World Cup History

South Korea is the first Asian team to reach 3 consecutive World Cups
and 4 overall, but has struggled when it has reached the final round. In
their World Cup debut in 1954, the Koreans were drubbed by Hungary,
9–0, and Turkey, 7–0. South Korea tied Bulgaria, 1–1, in 1986, and
has lost 2 other matches by one goal.

How They Qualified

South Korea finished first in Asian Group D (first round) with a 7–0–1
record and 15 points, scoring 23 goals and allowing one. Finished
second in the Asian final round with a 2–1–2 record and 6 points,
scoring 9 goals and surrendering 4. The results (first 3 matches in
Beirut, Lebanon, the last 3 in Seoul, South Korea)—In the first round:
South Korea 0, Bahrain 0 (May 9), South Korea 3, India 0 (May 13),
South Korea 3, Hong Kong 0 (May 15), South Korea 2, Lebanon 0
(June 7), South Korea 7, India 0 (June 9), South Korea 3, Bahrain 0
(June 13). In the final round (in Doha, Qatar): South Korea 3, Iran 0
(Oct. 16), South Korea 2, Iraq 2 (Oct. 19), South Korea 1, Saudi Arabia
1 (Oct. 22), Japan 1, South Korea 0 (Oct. 25), South Korea 3, North
Korea 0 (Oct. 28). The clincher—In a rare confrontation of the Koreas,
the South prevailed over the North, 3–0, in neutral Doha, Qatar, on Oct.
28, 1993, to finish second by goal differential over Japan in the
round-robin tournament. Seo Jung-Won, Hwang Sun-Hong and Ha
Seok-Ju scored. Even though they had just registered a solid victory,
the Korean players slumped to the ground, thinking that they had been
eliminated. However, their mood quickly changed to joy after discovering that Iraq had tied Japan, 2–2, on a last-second goal, giving the
Koreans second place on goal differential.

Players to Watch

Midfielder Kim Joo-Sung, an outstanding dribbler, will play in his third
consecutive World Cup. Defender Hong Myung-Bo has started a
number of attacks from the back. Forward Ha Seok-Ju led the team
with 6 qualifying goals.

Probable Lineup

Goalkeeper: Choi In-Young (Hyundai Horang-I). **Defenders**: Chung
Jong-Son (Hyundai Horang-I), Hong Myung-Bo (Posco Atoms), Kim

Pan-Keun (Daewoo Royals), Park Jung-Bae (L.G. Cheetahs). **Mid-fielders**: Choi Moon-Sik (Posco Atoms), Gu Sang-Bum (L.G. Chee-tahs), Kim Joo-Sung (VfL Bochum), Shin Hong-Gi (Hyundai Horang-I). **Forwards**: Hwang Sun-Hong (Posco Atoms), Ko Jon-Woon (Ilhwa Chonma).

Goalkeepers: Choi In-Young (Hyundai Horang-I), Lee Won-Jae (Kyunghee University), Sin Bum-Chul (Daewoo Royals). **Defenders**: Chung Jong-Son (Hyundai Horang-I), Hong Myung-Bo (Posco At-oms), Kang Chul (Yukong Elephants), Kim Pan-Keun (Daewoo Roy-als), Park Cheol (Taegu University), Park Jung-Bae (L.G. Cheetahs). **Midfielders**: Choi Moon-Sik (Posco Atoms), Gu Sang-Bum (L.G. Cheetahs), Ha Seok-Ju (Daewoo Royals), Kim Hyun-Seok (Hyundai Horang-I), Kim Joo-Sung (VfL Bochum, Germany), Lee Tae-Hong (Ilhwa Chonma), Noh Jung-Yoon (Sanfrecce Hiroshima, Japan), Shin Hong-Gi (Hyundai Horang-I). **Forwards**: Hwang Sun-Hong (Posco Atoms), Kim Jeong-Hyeok (Daewoo Royals), Ko Jon-Woon (Ilhwa Chonma), Lee Gi-Bum (Ilhwa Chonma), Seo Jung-Won (L.G. Chee-tahs).

Player Pool

Choi In-Young, Goalkeeper (Hyundai Horang-I), 5-foot-9, 172 pounds, Born: March 5, 1962, Caps: 46-The oldest player on the team, Choi started all 3 matches at Italia '90. He made his international debut in 1984 at the Asian Cup in Singapore.

PLAYER PROFILES
(Appearances
through Dec. 1,
1993, goals
unavailable)

Gu Sang-Bum, Midfielder (L.G. Cheetahs), 5-foot-6, 154 pounds, Born: June 15, 1964, Caps: 88-Gu, the team captain and leader in international appearances, played in the 1988 Olympics and in the 1990 World Cup. He will turn 30 just 2 days before USA '94.

Ha Seok-Ju, Midfielder (Daewoo Royals), 5-foot-5, 156 pounds, Born: Feb. 20, 1968, Caps: 25-Ha led Korea with 6 goals in qualifying. He scored in the 3−0 victory over Iran in the final round and added another in 3−0 win over North Korea, which clinched a spot.

Hong Myung-Bo, Defender (Posco Atoms), 5-foot-8, 161 pounds, Born: Feb. 12, 1969, Caps: 61-Another Italia '90 veteran, Hong was one of South Korea's most valuable players at the final Asian qualify-ing round, being named to the all-star team after he stood out defen-sively and as a playmaker.

Hwang Sun-Hong, Forward (Posco Atoms), 5-foot-9, 174 pounds, Born: July 14, 1968, Caps: 53-Hwang, who scored in the 3–0 World Cup berth clinching victory over North Korea, is a fast forward. He played in the 1990 World Cup in Italy.

Kim Joo-Sung, Midfielder (VfL Bochum, Germany), 5-foot-6, 158 pounds, Born: Jan. 17, 1966, Caps: 81-As one of the most experienced Korean players, Kim has been around the world and then some. He has participated in the 1986 and 1990 World Cups and the 1988 Olympics. He is an excellent dribbler who takes advantage of his speed down the left wing.

Kim Pan-Keun, Defender (Daewoo Royals), 5-foot-4, 147 pounds, Born: March 5, 1966, Caps: 29-If he plays in USA, Kim will complete a unique hat-trick. He participated in the Under-20 World Cup in Mexico in 1983 and played in the 1988 Olympics. He scored once in the final Asian qualifying round.

Ko Jon-Woon, Forward (Ilhwa Chonma), 5-foot-6, 167 pounds, Born: June 27, 1966, Caps: 23-He scored twice in the final Asian qualifying round in Qatar, including the cup-clinching win over North Korea.

Park Jung-Bae, Defender (L.G. Cheetahs), 5-foot-8, 172 pounds, Born: Feb. 19, 1967, Caps: 31-He scored in the opening match of the Asian final qualifying round, a 3–0 triumph over Iran.

Shin Hong-Gi, Midfielder (Hyundai Horang-I), 4-foot-4, 147 pounds, Born: May 4, 1968, Caps: 25-Named the most valuable player of the 2–2 tie with Iraq in the final qualifying round, Shin finished eighth in MVP voting for the entire series, the best ranking of anyone on South Korea.

Coach   Mr. Kim Woo-Chong is the coach. No other information was available.

1994   South Korea, which hosted the 1988 Summer Olympics, has long been an Asian power in soccer, but has not been able to manage to take that last big step to be competitive and win regularly against European and South American sides.

South Korea, which uses the typical 4–4–2 formation, is strong defensively, but has trouble finishing at the highest international, particularly at the World Cup. The Koreans have scored only 5 goals in

8 previous World Cup matches. They need to find someone who can put the ball into the net consistently.

The Koreans tried to improve their squad and chances by petitioning FIFA, world soccer's governing body, to place a combined team—North and South Korea—in the World Cup. It was rejected.

If anything, South Korea is also playing for the future - 2002 World Cup. The Japanese, who never have qualified for the World Cup, and the Koreans are the 2 major candidates. A decent showing—a victory or a spot in the second round—could swing several important votes on the FIFA Executive Committee when the vote comes up in 1996. Would FIFA want to give its grand tournament to a country that never has been able to qualify or one that has been competitive?

A bit of interesting information for World Cup history buffs: Only one Asian team has reached the quarterfinals. That was North Korea in 1966, losing to Portugal, 5–3.

GROUP D

ARGENTINA

GREECE

NIGERIA

BULGARIA

ARGENTINA
  POPULATION: 32,700,000
  COLORS: Light blue shirts, black shorts, white socks
  WORLD CUP APPEARANCES: Eleventh. 24–15–9 record, 82 goals for, 59 against. 1930 (second place), 1934 (first round), 1958 (first round), 1962 (first round), 1966 (quarterfinals), 1974 (second round), 1978 (champions), 1982 (second round), 1986 (champions), 1990 (second place)

World Cup History

Argentina has been one of the most successful countries in recent times, reaching the championship game in 3 of the past 4 World Cups. The 1978 and 1986 titles were well deserved, but had the Argentines defeated Germany in 1990, observers agreed it would have set back soccer years because of the physical, defensive style the team played. The Argentines lost to bitter rivals Uruguay in the first championship match in 1930, 4–2, and it took them 36 years before they got out of the first round, losing to eventual champion England in the quarterfinals in 1966.

How They Qualified

Argentina finished second in South American Group A, with a 3–2–1 record and 7 points, scoring 7 goals, allowing 9. The Argentines then met Australia in a special two-match playoff, outscoring its foes, 2–1. The results (home team listed first)—In South America: Peru 0, Argentina 1 (Aug. 1, 1993), Paraguay 1, Argentina 3 (Aug. 8), Colombia 2, Argentina 1 (Aug. 15), Argentina 2, Peru 1 (Aug. 22), Argentina 0, Paraguay 0 (Aug. 29), Argentina 0, Colombia 5 (Sept. 5). In the special playoff: Australia 1, Argentina 1 (Oct. 31), Argentina 1, Australia 0 (Nov. 17). The clincher: Gabriel Batistuta was credited with a goal—some observers claimed it was an own goal—in a 1–0 victory over Australia on Nov. 17, 1993.

Players to Watch

Argentina's opponents can only hope that they don't go to a penalty-kick tie-breaker because goalkeeper Sergio Goycochea has become one of the best in the world at stopping those spot kicks. Gabriel Batistuta has emerged as the most dangerous goalscorer. Even though he is on the downside of his career, Diego Maradona cannot be ignored because he still has just a wee bit of magic left in his legs and feet.

Probable Lineup

Goalkeeper: Sergio Goycochea (River Plate). **Defenders**: Jose Chamot (Foggia, Italy), Nestor Craviotto (Independiente), Carlos MacAllister (Boca Juniors), Oscar Ruggeri (America, Mexico), Sergio Vazquez (U. Catolica, Chile). **Midfielders**: Diego Maradona (Newell's Old Boys), Hugo Leonardo Perez (Independiente), Fernando Redondo (Tenerife, Spain), Diego Simeone (Seville, Spain). **Forwards**: Abel Balbo (Roma, Italy), Gabriel Batistuta (Fiorentina, Italy).

Player Pool

Goalkeepers: Sergio Goycochea (River Plate), Luis Islas (Independiente), Norberto Scoponi (Boca Juniors). **Defenders**: Ricardo Altimirano (River Plate), Roberto Ayala (FC Oeste), Fabian Basualdo (Newell's Old Boys), Jorge Borelli (Racing), Fernando Caceres (Zaragoza, Spain), Jose Chamot (Foggia, Italy), Nestor Craviotto (Independiente), Carlos MacAllister (Boca Juniors), Oscar Ruggeri (America, Mexico), Julio Saldana (Boca Juniors), Victor Hugo Sotomayor (Velez Sarsfield), Sergio Vazquez (U. Catolica, Chile). **Midfielders**: Leonardo Astrada (Boca Juniors), Diego Cagna (Independiente), Dario Franco (Zaragoza, Spain), Alejandro Mancuso (Boca Juniors), Diego Maradona (Newell's Old Boys), Alberto Marcico (Boca Juniors), Hugo Leonardo Perez (Independiente), Fernando Redondo (Tenerife, Spain), Leonardo Rodriguez (Atalanta, Italy), Diego Simeone (Seville, Spain), Jose Villarreal (River Plate). **Forwards**: Alberto Acosta (Boca Juniors), Abel Balbo (Roma, Italy), Jose Basualdo (Velez Sarsfield), Gabriel Batistuta (Fiorentina, Italy), Claudio Garcia (Racing), Nestor Gorosito (San Lorenzo), Ramon Medina Bello (River Plate), Dario Scotto (Sporting Gijon, Spain), Julio Zamora (Cruz Azul, Mexico),

Gustavo Zapata (Yokohama, Japan), Sergio Fabian Zarate (Nuremberg, Germany).

Abel Balbo, Forward (Roma, Italy), 5-foot-8 176 pounds, Born: June 1, 1966, Caps: 2-He started the first match at Italia '90, but after Argentina was upset by Cameroon, Balbo was benched. He finally caught the eye of coach Alfio Basile, who brought the forward back for the Australia series. After scoring 21 goals for Udinese (Italy), Balboa transferred to Roma.

Gabriel Batistuta, Forward (Fiorentina, Italy), 5-foot-9, 171 pounds, Born: Feb. 1, 1969, Caps: 28-Batistuta seemingly scores all the key goals for Argentina. He connected for the game-winner in the 1991 Copa America championship match, a 2–1 victory over Colombia. He struck for 2 more in the 1993 title victory, a 2–1 win over Mexico. And, not surprisingly, Batistuta scored the lone goal in the 1–0 triumph over Australia that clinched a World Cup berth. Known as "Archangel Gabriel," Batistuta has carried the scoring load since Claudio Caniggia was suspended after testing positive for drugs in Italy in 1993.

Sergio Goycochea, Goalkeeper (River Plate), 5-foot 10, 187 pounds, Born: Oct. 17, 1963, Caps: 51-Goycochea, the backup goalkeeper at Italia '90, was thrust into the spotlight after starter Nery Pumpido broke his right leg. He did not disappoint, starring in 2 consecutive penalty-kick tie-breakers as conservative Argentina reached the finals. Goycochea saved 2 penalties each against Yugoslavia in the quarterfinals and Italy in the semifinals. He repeated his feat against European Champion Denmark in 1993, knocking away 2 more shots. Considered a "stay-at-home" goalkeeper, Goycochea has moved around since turning pro in 1980, playing with seven teams, including Millonarios (Colombia), Brest (France) and Olimpia (Paraguay), before rejoining River Plate for a second time in June, 1993.

Diego Maradona, Midfielder (Newell's Old Boys), 5-foot-8, 170 pounds, Born: Oct. 30, 1960, Caps: 98 Goals: 31-His career has seen better days and he sometimes says the wrong things, but you cannot discount someone with the track record of the controversial Maradona. After all, at times he was a virtual one-man show for Argentina's championship team at the 1986 World Cup, scoring and creating goals from all angles. At Italia '90, Maradona was a mere shadow of himself, playing injured, gesturing for calls by referees and making outrageous comments (he claimed the Mafia was the reason why Argentina lost). Maradona, who is poised to play in his fourth consecutive World Cup, has performed for the Argentinos Juniors and Boca Juniors in his native country, Barcelona (Spain), and Napoli (Italy), leading the club to its first Italian League title in 1987. Banned for 15 months because of failing a drug test, Maradona returned to competitive soccer with Sevilla (Spain), which signed him for $7.5 million. After a season, however, the relationship turned sour and Maradona eventually returned home. Maradona returned to the national side in the Australia series, losing 26 pounds. He set up the Argentines' lone goal in the 1–1 draw in Australia.

Fernando Redondo, Midfielder (Tenerife, Spain), 5-foot-10, 167 pounds, Born: June 6, 1969, Caps: 37-One of Argentina's emerging stars, Redondo has a delicate touch and excellent vision on the field. He made his international debut against Australia on June 18, 1992.

Oscar Ruggeri, Defender (America, Mexico), 5-foot-9, 176 pounds, Born: Jan. 26, 1962, Caps: 103-Ruggeri, the captain of the national team while Maradona was on the sidelines, is the all-time leader in international appearances. Exceptional in the air, Ruggeri is the squad's inspirational leader and has been a fixture at stopper during Argentina's rise to prominence. Ruggeri, who played on the 1986 World Cup championship team, he performed for 6 clubs, including River Plate, Logrones (Spain) and Real Madrid (Spain).

Diego Simeone, Midfielder (Seville, Spain), 5-foot-8, 185 pounds, Born: April 28, 1970, Caps: 39-One of coach Alfio Basile's favorites, Simeone made his international debut at 18. A member of the 1991 and 1993 Copa America championship teams, Simeone has converted the decisive penalty kicks in tie-breaker wins over Denmark in the Europe-South American championship game and against Colombia and Brazil in 1993 Copa America. Tenerife (Spain) offered $4 million for the midfielder, but Sevilla claimed he was worth at least $1 million more. "He's always improving some phase of his game at every practice session," Basile said. "He gets off the plane and wants to go directly to training. I can't think of any comparison. He's special."

Coach

Alfio Basile has 2 tough acts to follow—Cesar Luis Menotti and Carlos Bilardo, who captured World Cup titles in 1978 and 1986, respectively. Basile, born on Nov. 1, 1943, understands the pressure of being the national coach. "Every time you play, you have the whole country behind you," he said. "If you make a mistake at a club, it's serious. But it is multiplied by 10 times when it's the national team." He played with Racing Avellaneda, winning the national championship in 1966 and the Libertadores Cup in 1965. Basile also has coached 8 teams, including Chacarita, Rosario, Racing Club Buenos Aires, Instituto, Huracan, Nacional of Montevideo, Talleres and Velez.

1994

Thank the heavens that coach Alfio Basile has rebuilt the Argentine team and the rest of the world will not be subjected to the same type of negative soccer that was the epitome of Italia '90. He made every effort to shed Argentina of its bruising image.

In fact, the Argentines had not lost since the World Cup final, weaving a 31-game unbeaten streak that saw 2 Copa America titles, in 1991 and 1993. That streak, however, was broken by Colombia in a 2−1 defeat in a World Cup qualifier on Aug. 15, 1993. They lost again to Colombia in an embarrassing 5−0 qualifying loss at home in Buenos Aires on Sept. 5. Argentina went on to defeat Australia in a special playoff to qualify, but those losses were cause for concern.

Was Argentina still the world power everyone thought it was? Or was a situation of not playing well or matching up properly with a team?

The Argentines' 2−1 victory over Germany at the Orange Bowl in Miami on Dec. 15 had to allay some fears. The Germans brought over a team that probably will be the core of its World Cup team, while Basile had to beg to European clubs to release their Argentine players.

"We've given the Argentine people a big Christmas present," said forward Abel Balbo, who scored the game-winning goal. "It was a great game and we played well."

For Argentina to succeed (and reach at least the semifinals), striker Gabriel Batistuta needs to continue scoring at key spots and goalkeeper Sergio Goycochea needs to continue his heroics in tie-breakers. And just another magical pass or goal from Diego Maradona would not hurt, either.

The wildcard could be forward Claudio Cannigia who was to return in May from a drug suspension. His fitness is a big question mark.

Argentina, the top seed in Group D, wound up in a group that includes Bulgaria, Nigeria and Greece. It looked like an easy path to the second round, but Basile was not so sure. "Everybody thinks it is an easy group," he said. "But it is not as straightforward as people think."

Perhaps he was being diplomatic.

A bit of interesting information for World Cup history buffs: In the 4 World Cups in the Americas in which Argentina has participated, it has been to the championship match 3 times, winning twice, with a record of 16−3−3.

GREECE
POPULATION: 10,100,000
COLORS: White shirts, blue shorts, blue
  socks
WORLD CUP APPEARANCES: First

World Cup History
This is Greece's first appearance, qualifying for the first time in 13 tries since 1934.

How They Qualified
Greece finished first in European Group 5 with a 6–0–2 record for 14 points, 10 goals for, 2 against. The results (home team listed first): Greece 1, Iceland 0 (May 13, 1992), Iceland 0, Greece 0 (Oct. 7), Greece 0, Hungary 0 (Nov. 11), Greece 2, Luxembourg 0 (Feb. 17, 1993), Hungary 0, Greece 1 (March 31), Russia 1, Greece 1 (May 23), Luxembourg 1, Greece 3 (Oct. 12), Greece 1, Russia 0 (Nov. 17). The clincher: Greece tied Russia on May 23, 1993, 1–1, to become the first European side to qualify; Anastassios Mitropoulos scored the Greeks' lone goal in Moscow.

Players to Watch
Anastassios Mitropolous, who is the oldest player at 37, is the inspirational force at midfield, while Nikolaos Nioplias is the traffic cop who controls the pace of the game. Defender Apostolakis has excelled at both sides of the field.

Probable Lineup
Goalkeeper: Antonios Minou (Apollon Athens). **Defenders**: Athanassios Kolitsidakis (Panathinaikos), Stylianos Manolas (AEK Athens), Kyriakos Karataidis (Olympiakos Piraeus), Efstratios Apostolakis (Panathinaikos Athens). **Midfielders**: Nikolaos Nioplias (Panathinaikos Athens), Anastassios Mitropoulos (AEK Athens), Panagiotis Tsalouchidis (Olympiakos Piraeus), Nikolaos Tsiantakis (Olympiakos Piraeus). **Forwards**: Nikolaos Mahlas (OFI Crete), Vassilios Dimitriadis (AEK Athens).

Player Pool
Goalkeepers: Antonios Minou (Apollon Athens), Konstantinos Chaniotakis (OFI Crete), Christos Karkamanis (Aris Thessaloniki). **Defenders**: Athanassios Kolitsidakis (Panathinaikos), Stylianos Manolas (AEK Athens), Kyriakos Karataidis (Olympiakos Piraeus), Efstratios Apostolakis (Panathinaikos Athens), Ioannis Kalitzakis (Panathinaikos Athens), Michail Kasapis (AEK Athens), Vasileios Ioannidis (Olympiakos Piraeus), Alexandros Alexiou (PAOK Thessaloniki). **Midfielders**: Nikolaos Nioplias (Panathinaikos Athens), Anastassios Mitropoulos (AEK Athens), Konstantinos Antoniou (Panathinaikos

Athens), Konstantinos Fratzeskos (Panathinaikos Athens), Vasileios Karapialis (Olympiakos Piraeus), Christos Kostis (Iraklis Thessaloniki), Theodoros Zagorakis (PAOK Thessaloniki), Panagiotis Tsalouchidis (Olympiakos Piraeus), Nikolaos Tsiantakis (Olympiakos Piraeus), Panagiotis Gonias (Olympiakos Piraeus), Spyridon Marangos (Panathinaikos Athens), Georgios Toursounids (PAOK Thessaloniki), Alexandros Alexandris (AEK Athens), Vasileios Tsartas (AEK Athens). **Forwards**: Nikolaos Mahlas (OFI Crete), Dimitrios Saravakos (Panathinaikos Athens), Vassilios Dimitriadis (AEK Athens), Georgios Donis (Panathinaikos Athens).

Efstratios Apostolakis, Defender, (Panathinaikos Athens), 5-foot-8, 158 pounds, Born: May 11, 1964, Caps: 55, Goals: 3-One of only 4 players to have played in every minute of the 8 qualifiers, Apostolakis scored the lone goal in the 1–0 win at Hungary on March 31, 1993. Apostolakis, who usually performs at right fullback, has been one of the country's best players in the past 10 years. He overlaps well, has a strong shot and excels at throw-ins. He was a member of the Panathinaikos defense that allowed but 21 goals in 34 matches in 1991–92.

PLAYER PROFILES (Appearances and goals through Dec. 1, 1993)

Vassilios Dimitriadis, Forward (AEK Athens), 5-foot-11, 165 pounds, Born: Feb. 1, 1966, Caps: 25, Goals: 2-He has yet to translate his scoring prowess in the Greek First Division into success at the international level. Dimitriadis led the league in scoring in 1992 and 1993, with 28 and 33 goals, respectively, winning a pair of Toyota Celicas for his achievement. He is a penalty kick specialist, having converted 23 of 29 attempts. Dimitriadis, who scored once in 5 matches in qualifying—in the 2–0 win over Luxembourg—played for Greek national coach Alkis Panagoulias at Aris.

Kyriakos Karataidis, Defender (Olympiakos Piraeus), 6-foot, 165 pounds, Born: July 4, 1965, Caps: 10, Goals: 0-Karataidis' strength is man-to-man coverage. He usually stays back on defense, scoring twice in 170 league appearances.

Athanassios Kolitsidakis, Defender, (Panathinaikos), 6-foot-1, 172 pounds, Born: Nov. 20, 1966, Caps: 7, Goals: 0-As the stopper, Kolitsidakis usually takes on the opposing center forward. Kolitsidakis, who can also play as sweeper, is a superb header of the ball. Not known for his attacking ability, Kolitsidakis, who was the captain of Apollon, has scored only twice in 150 league games.

Nicolaos Mahlas, Forward (OFI Crete), 6-foot, 160 pounds, Born: June 16, 1973, Caps: 5, Goals: 3-Mahlas, who will turn 21 a day before the World Cup starts, is the youngest player on the team and is one of the rising stars of Greek soccer. A strong, aggressive player with good heading ability, Machlas scored in his international debut against Austria on March 10, 1993. He also connected for the lone goal in the 1–0 qualifying win over Russia that clinched the Group 5 crown on Nov. 17, 1993.

Stylianos Manolas, Defender (AEK Athens), 6-foot-2 188 pounds, Born: July 13, 1961, Caps: 64, Goals: 6-As a 14-year veteran with AEK, Manolas is the captain, sweeper and cornerstone of the defense. Manolas played for the AEK amateur team in the late seventies, under the management of former Hungarian great Ferenc Puskas. He played in every minute of Greece's 8 qualifiers. Manolas made his international debut in 1982 and has been a fixture since 1985.

Antonios Minou, Goalkeeper, (Apollon Athens), 6-foot-4, 188 pounds, Born: May 4, 1958, Caps: 12, Goals: 0-Even though he has only a dozen international appearances, Minou has established himself as the No. 1 keeper in Greece, because of his steady play, good positioning and reflexes over the past five years. He starred for AEK Athens' championship teams in 1992 and 1993, playing with U.S. forward Frank Klopas. He has allowed only 238 goals in 260 matches.

Anastassios Mitropoulos, Midfielder (AEK Athens), 6-foot-3, 190 pounds, Born: Aug. 23, 1957, Caps: 68, Goals: 8-It was most appropriate that the oldest player and team captain scored the game-tying goal against Russia on May 23, 1993, a 1–1 draw that clinched Greece's first World Cup berth. Nicknamed Rambo because he plays with much passion, Mitropoulos started his career with Olympiakos, playing an integral part of the team's league and cup championship teams and playing in all 3 major European club competitions. He was a member of AEK's championship team in 1993. He has scored 83 goals in almost 80 league appearances. His 68 caps ranks him third in Greek history, behind Nikos Anastopoulos (73 from 1979-88) and current teammate Dimitrios Savarakos (71).

Nikolaos Nioplias, Midfielder (Panathinaikos Athens), 5-foot-7, 155 pounds, Born: Jan. 17, 1965, Caps: 30, Goals: 1-Nioplias, who gained a reputation for scoring key goals, has combined superb passing and running ability, ball control and a never-say-die spirit to become one of the top players in Greece. He had 34 goals in 257 matches with OFI Crete before joining Panathinaikos for $400,000 in the summer.

Dimitrios Saravakos, Forward (Panathinaikos, Athens), 5-foot-8, 165 pounds, Born: July 26, 1961, Caps: 71, Goals: 21-Saravakos, one of the all-time great Greek players, is poised to surpass Nikos Anastopolous (29 goals in 73 appearances from 1979–88) as the career caps leader. The son of former Greek international Thanassis Saravakos, he has been one of the most prolific scorers in the Greek First Division in the past decade, scoring 159 times in 381 matches. He also captured three scoring crowns (1986, 1990 and 1990) and was on 4 Greek Cup championship teams (1986, 1988, 1989, and 1991). Saravakos, who played in only 2 qualifying matches due to several injuries, scored once, in the 3–1 win at Luxembourg.

Panagiotis Tsalouchidis, Midfielder (Olympiakos Piraeus), 6-foot, 190 pounds, Born: March 30, 1963, Caps: 54, Goals: 11-Even though he is a defensive midfielder, Tsalouchidis has exhibited an offensive presence for his club team and Greece. For example, he scored the game-winner in the 1-0 qualifying win at Iceland, struck for 10 goals during the 1992–93 season and connected twice in the 1992 Greek Cup championship match against PAOK. Tsalouchidis, considered to be one of the most consistent Greek internationals, has missed only 1 NationalTteam match in the past 30, starting all 8 qualifying games.

Nikolaos Tsiantakis, Midfielder (Olympiakos Piraeus), 6-foot, 165 pounds, Born: Oct. 20, 1963, Caps: 40, Goals: 2-As one of the best dribblers on the squad, Tsiantakis has missed only 3 National Team matches since January, 1990. He also played on 2 Greek Cup championship teams, in 1990 and 1992, and played in nearly 250 First Division matches.

Aleketas (Alkis) Panagoulias is a familar name to American soccer fans. He is best known as the coach of Team America, which competed in the North American Soccer League in 1983 and as coach of the U.S. National Team that failed in its bid to reach the 1986 World Cup. He earned his coaching spurs in the U.S., guiding N.Y. Greek-American of the German-American Soccer League (now Cosmopolitan Soccer League) in New York City to an unprecendented 3 U.S. Open Challenge Cup titles, the equivalent to the world-renowned F.A. Cup in

Coach

England. Panagoulias, who has been an American citizen for 25 years, lives part-time in Vienna, VA (during breaks and the off-season) and coaches fulltime in Greece. Born on May 30, 1934, Panagoulias directed the National Team to the final of the 1980 European Championship, the first Greek team to reach the final round.

1994   Coach Alkis Panagoulias has become quite tired of hearing that the only reason why Greece qualified for its first World Cup was because of the break-up of Yugoslavia, which dropped out of the competition due to UN sanctions. He likes to point out that Greece, the only undefeated European team (6–0–2) in qualifying, became the first team on the continent to reach USA '94, tying Russia, 1–1, on May 23, 1993.

Before his side took on Russia for the second time on Nov. 17, which would decide first place in Group 5, Panagoulias told his team: "I'm sick and tired of hearing about your lack of abilities as players and that we are in because Yugoslavia is out. This game is for your own recognition. You're going to the World Cup because you deserve it."

Greece then went out and defeated Russia, 1–0.

The Greeks, who deploy a 4–4–2 formation, use a mixture of youngsters and veterans in an offense that can adapt to the situation. They can play a short or long passing game. The problem, however, is getting someone to consistently score. Greece, which recorded 6 shutouts during qualifying and allowed only 2 goals, scored only 10. Seven players scored during qualifying, as 3 players finished with 2 goals apiece.

Saying that, can the Greeks get past an opening-round group that includes Argentina, Nigeria and Bulgaria? Even the outspoken and optimistic Panagoulias realized that reaching the second round would be difficult.

"National pride spread all over Greece," he said about the aftermath of qualifying. "There was great respectability for the players and myself. And of course, if we do something in the World Cup, if we pass to the second round, it would be quite unexpected."

He had expected Greece to be placed in New York at the World Cup draw, but instead the Greeks will play twice in Boston and once in Chicago in the opening round. Panagoulias, however, still wants to give something back to New York City—he lived there for more than a decade—and train at Adelphi Univesity in suburban Garden City for at least 10 days in late May or early June.

"I want to be close to the Greek-American community," he said.

"I want the players to be close to their compatriots. Plus, it will be good for the players, to have a little distraction."

A bit of interesting information for World Cup history buffs: Of the 26 countries who have made their World Cup debut, 16 have walked away without any victories in their first tournament and only 6 have finished with a .500 record or better.

NIGERIA
POPULATION: 122,500,000
COLORS: Green shirts, green shorts,
    green socks
WORLD CUP APPEARANCES: First

World Cup History   None. Nigeria came close to qualifying in 1990, but Cameroon made it to Italy.

How They Qualified   Nigeria finished first in African Group D (first round) with a 3−0−1 record and 7 points, scoring 7 goals, allowing none, and finished first in African Group A (final round) with a 2−1−1 record for 5 points, scoring 10 goals, surrendering 5. The results (home team listed first)—In the first round: Nigeria 4, South Africa 0 (Oct. 10, 1992), Congo 0, Nigeria 1 (Dec. 20), South Africa 0, Nigeria 0 (Jan. 16, 1993), Nigeria 2, Congo 0 (Feb. 27). In the final round: Ivory Coast 2, Nigeria 1 (May 2), Nigeria 4, Algeria 1 (July 3), Nigeria 4, Ivory Coast 1 (Sept. 25), Algeria 1, Nigeria 1 (Oct. 8). The clincher—Nigeria, which needed only a tie against Algeria in Algiers, earned exactly that on Oct. 8, 1993. Midfielder George Finidi scored his second goal of qualifying for Nigeria in the 19th minute. "It was a dream come true, the fulfillment of a national goal and the crowning on Nigeria's soccer history," Nigerian newspaper, *The Daily Champion* reported.

Players to Watch   Forward Rashidi Yekini scored almost half of Nigeria's qualifying goals. Stephen Keshi, the team captain, is the stablilizing force on defense.

Probable Lineup   **Goalkeeper**: Wilfred Agbonavbare (Rayo Vallecano, Spain). **Defenders**: Benedict Iroha (Vitesse Arnhem, Netherlands), Augustine Eguavon (Courtrai, Belgium), Stephen Keshi (RWD Molenbeek, Belgium), Uche Okechukwu (Roda JC Kerkrade, Belgium). **Midfielders**: George Finidi (Ajax Amsterdam, Netherlands), Adepoju Mutiu (Racing Santander, Spain), Thompson Oliha (Africa Sports, Ivory Coast). **Forwards**: Daniel Amokachi (Brugge, Belgium), Augustine Okocha (Eintracht Frankfurt, Germany), Rashidi Yekini (Vitoria Setubal, Portugal).

Player Pool   **Goalkeepers**: Wilfred Agbonavbare (Rayo Vallecano, Spain), Alloy Agu (Liege, Belgium). **Defenders**: Benedict Iroha (Vitesse Arnhem, Netherlands), Augustine Eguavon (Courtrai, Belgium), Stephen Keshi (RWD Molenbeek, Belgium), Chidi Nwanu (Beveren, Belgium),

Christopher Nwosu (Beerschot, Belgium), Peter Ogaba (Lokeren, Belgium), Uche Okechukwu (Roda JC Kerkrade, Belgium), Andrew Uwe. **Midfielders**: Emmanuel Amonike (Zamalek, Egypt), Sadi Dahiru (Eeklo), Efan Ekoku (Norwich City, England), George Finidi (Ajax Amsterdam, Netherlands), Adepoju Mutiu (Racing Santander, Spain), Thompson Oliha (Africa Sports, Ivory Coast), Samson Siasia (Nantes, France). **Forwards**: Augustine Adejeji (Malines, Belgium), Daniel Amokachi (Brugge, Belgium), Tijani Babangida (Roda JC Kerkrade, Netherlands), Friday Elaho (A.C. B. Lagos), Victor Ikpeba (Monaco, France), Kayode Keshinro (Ostende, Belgium), Mohamed Lawal (Courtrai, Belgium), Sunny Nwachukwu (Racing Genk, Belgium), Mike Obiku (Feyenoord Rotterdam, Netherlands), Christopher Ohen (Compostela, Spain), Bonface Okafor (Hanover 96, Germany), Augustine Okocha (Eintracht Frankfurt, Germany), Godwin Okpara (Eendracht Alost, Netherlands), Sunday Oliseh (Liege, Belgium), Philip Osundu (Anderlecht, Netherlands), Ricky Owubokiri (Boavista, Portugal), Andy Salako (Charlton Athletic, England), Ojokojo Torunarigha (Chemnitz, Germany), Rashidi Yekini (Vitoria Setubal, Portugal).

Wilfred Agbonavbare, Goalkeeper (Rayo Vallecano, Spain), 6-foot, 176 pounds, Born: Oct. 5, 1966, Caps: 19, Goals: 0-Agbonavbare, who started the final 4 qualifying matches, proved his worth in the Spanish First Division match in a scoreless tie with first-place Deportivo Coruna on Jan. 2, 1994. Agbonavbare was brilliant, stopping 3 sure goals, including 2 attempts by Brazilian Bebeto.

PLAYER PROFILES (Appearances and goals through Dec. 1, 1973)

Daniel Amokachi, Forward (Brugge, Belgium), 5-foot-6, 174 pounds, Born: Dec. 30, 1972, Caps: 22, Goals: 2-Amokachi scored twice in qualifying, in victories over Ivory Coast and Algeria. He signed with Brugge at 17, after he scored 5 goals in 3 games during a National Team tour of the Netherlands. He hasn't disappointed, scoring 12 goals in 26 games, as Brugge won the Belgian title in 1991–92. "America will be the biggest stage of all for me, so I'm determined to play there," he said.

Victor Ikpeba, Midfielder-forward (AS Monaco, France), 5-foot-7, 163 pounds, Born: June 12, 1973, Caps: 18, Goals: 4-Though he played in only one qualifer, Ikpeba must be considered potentially one of Nigeria's most dangerous players. In the 1992–93 season, Ikpeba was voted as the top player in Belgium after connecting for 17 goals for Standard Liege. Ikpeba was discovered by Liege during the Under-17

World Cup in Scotland in 1989. After 4 years with Liege, he moved to AS Monaco in the French First Division for 1993–94.

Stephen Keshi, Defender (RWD Molenbeek, Belgium), 6-foot-1, 169 pounds, Born: Jan. 31, 1962, Caps: 75, Goals: 2-The captain of the National Team, Keshi is the current leader in international appearances, having first played for Nigeria in 1980. Keshi, who played 5 years in Belgium with Lokeren and Anderlect and helped Strasbourg gain promotion to the French First Division, is an excellent tackler and has a fine sense of anticipation.

Ricky Owubokiri, Forward (Boavista, Portugal), 5-foot-9, 165 pounds, Born: July 16, 1961, Caps: 26, Goals: 7-Owubokiri, who was a serious volleyball player as a youngster, can put the ball into the net. He has led 3 club teams in scoring—Vitoria Bahia (Brazil) with 15 and 22 goals in 1984–85 and 1985–86, respectively, and Boavista Porto (Portugal) with a league-high 30 in 1991–92. Owubokiri, who also has played in France, scored the game-winning goal for Boavista Porto in the Portuguese Cup.

Rashidi Yekini, Forward (Vitoria Setubal, Portugal), 6-foot, 180 pounds, Born: Oct. 23, 1963, Caps: 67, Goals: 18-He came into his own during qualifying, leading all African players with 8 goals and accounting for 8 of Nigeria's 17 scores in 7 matches. Before that, Yekini had only 10 goals in 60 international appearances. Yekini, who was named African Player of the Year in 1993, scored twice in the 4–1 win over the Ivory Coast and in the 4–0 victory over South Africa.

Coach   Dutchman Clemence Westerhoff, who led Nigeria in its unsuccessful bid to reach Italia '90, returned for USA '94. He replaced German Manfred Hoener. Westerhoff's reign has been controversial, winding up in a spat with the Nigerian Soccer Federation, which claimed the coach had promised payments to the players had the team qualified for the World Cup, without consulting the organization first.

1994   Even though Nigeria has yet to play its first World Cup game, much is expected of the African team. A number of experts have predicted Nigeria will become the first African country to win a World Cup.
          At USA '94, Nigeria has been touted as one of the surprise teams

for 2 reasons—because of its attacking style and success at the international youth level.

The Nigerians have acquitted themselves quite well at the youth level. They captured the Under-17 World Cup in 1985 took second in 1987 and won it in 1993. They also took third in the Under-20 World Cup in 1985 and was second in 1989.

They finally lived up to their promise of the past decade by reaching the World Cup, despite political instability, a presidential election crisis and ethnic division among their citizens.

"It's not surprising," former Nigerian Soccer Federation president John Obakpolor said several years ago of his country's success. "Football has become a part of Nigeria's culture. The groundwork has been done before."

Indeed it has. The groundwork was laid when Nigeria imported several Brazilian coaches in an attempt to increase its level of soccer.

"When we arrived, they played ugly football with the big kick [long ball]," said Amilton Barreto de Barros Junior, one of the Brazilian coaches who taught in Nigeria. "Then they put the ball on the ground. They play a much more beautiful game today."

The Brazilian influence certainly has rubbed off and paid off. The Nigerians play an open, free-flowing game, reminiscent of the Brazilians. In fact, a bongo drum band played at the Under-17 championship match in Toronto, Canada, in 1987, producing sounds familiar to those of a Brazilian samba band.

So it is not surprising that like Italia '90 quarterfinalist Cameroon, Nigeria is not afraid to go on attack. The Nigerians, who scored 17 goals in 8 qualifying matches, are only one of a handful of 24 finalists who use 3 forwards.

Coach Clemence Westerhoff's greatest challenge just might be getting all the players together in one place. His entire starting lineup plays abroad, 10 in Europe. That includes stars George Finidi, a midfielder with Ajax Amsterdam (Netherlands), forwards Rashidi Yekini with Vitoria Setubal (Portugal) and Augustine Okocha of Eintracht Frankfurt (Germany). Westerhoff said he plans to add a member or two of the Under-17 world championship team to the World Cup pool—team captain Wilson Oruma, who signed a 2-year contract with Lens (France), and Nwankwu Kanu, who plays with Ajax Amsterdam (Netherlands).

Despite having the team dispersed throughout Europe, Westerhoff planned to have an extensive preparation schedule, including the Nehru Cup in India in early January and a 4-nation tournament in South

Africa later that month. The Nigerians also participated in the African Nations Cup in Tunisia in late March and early April.

"This is the first time in my four years as Nigerian coach that things have been so organized," Westerhoff said. "I have been in Europe monitoring the form of all the leading Nigerian players and I am pleased things are going well for the players."

A bit of interesting information for World Cup history buffs: Countries making their cup debut since 1934 have compiled a 21–50–22 record, so the Nigerians have their work cut out for them.

BULGARIA

POPULATION: 9,000,000

COLORS: White shirts, green shorts, white socks

WORLD CUP APPEARANCES: Sixth. 0–10–6, 11 goals for, 35 against. 1962 (first round), 1966 (first round), 1970 (first round), 1974 (first round), 1986 (second round)

World Cup History

You don't want to know. The Bulgarians have never won a game in the World Cup, even though they managed to qualify for the second round in 1986, thanks to a pair of ties. They were eliminated by host Mexico, 2–0. In fact, their grandest moment came in the 1986 opener, a 1–1 tie with defending champion Italy, as Naska Sirakov scored the equalized with 5 minutes remaining.

How They Qualified

Bulgaria finished second in European Group 6 with a 6–2–2 record and 14 points, scoring 19 goals and allowing 10. The results (home team listed first)—Finland 0, Bulgaria 3 (May 14, 1992), Bulgaria 2, France 0 (Sept. 9), Sweden 2, Bulgaria 0 (Oct. 7), Bulgaria 2, Israel 0 (Dec. 2), Austria 3, Bulgaria 1 (April 14, 1993), Bulgaria 2, Finland 0 (April 28), Bulgaria 2, Israel 2 (May 12), Bulgaria 1, Sweden 1 (Sept. 8), Bulgaria 4, Austria 1 (Oct. 13), France 1, Bulgaria 2 (Nov. 17). The clincher—Bulgaria got in by the skin of its teeth, as Emil Kostadinov scored his second goal of the match with 10 seconds left for a 2–1 victory over France in Paris on Nov. 17, 1993.

Players to Watch

Hristo Stoichkov is one of the most productive and consistent forwards in the world. Midfielder Luboslav Penev, who set up Emil Kostadinov's goal against France, and his teammate combine to form a solid one-two punch.

Probable Lineup

Goalkeeper: Borislav Mikhailov (Mulhouse, France). **Defenders**: Trifon Ivanov (Real Betis, Spain), Petar Hubchev (Levski Sofia), Emil Kremenliev (Levski Sofia), Tzanko Tzvetanov (Etar Veiko Tarnovo). **Midfielders**: Krasimir Balakov (Sporting Lisbon, Portugal), Yordan Lechkov (Hamburg, Germany), Luboslav Penev (Valencia, Spain), Zlatko Yankov (Levski Sofia). **Forwards**: Emil Kostadinov (Porto, Portugal), Hristo Stoichkov (Barcelona, Spain).

Player Pool

Goalkeepers: Antonio Ananiev (Lokomotiv Sofia), Borislav Mikhailov (Mulhouse, France), Dimitar Popov. **Defenders**: Sasho

Angelov, Nikolai Iliev, Trifon Ivanov (Real Betis, Spain), Petar Khub-chev (Levski Sofia), Illian Kiriakov, Emil Kremenliev (Levski Sofia), Dimitar Mladenov, Zaprian Rakov (Botev Polvdiv), Nikolai Todorov, Tzanko Tzvetanov (Etar Veiko Tarnovo). **Midfielders**: Dean Angelov (Slavia Sofia), Krasimir Balakov (Sporting Lisbon, Portugal), Alexan-dar Dimov (Etar Velika Tornovo), Christo Kolev (Athinaikos, Greece), Yordan Lechkov (Hamburg, Germany), Yordan Mitev (Beroe Stara Zagora), Luboslav Penev (Valencia, Spain), Naska Sirakov (Levski Sofia), Zlatko Yankov (Levski Sofia). **Forwards**: Emil Kostadinov (Porto, Portugal), Hristo Stoichkov (Barcelona, Spain), Kiril Vasilev (Khebar Pazardshik), Velko Yotov (Levski Sofia).

PLAYER PROFILES (through Nov. 16, 1993, caps and goals unavailable)

Krasimir Balakov, Midfielder (Sporting Lisbon, Portugal), 5-foot-9, 159 pounds, Born: April 28, 1966-He scored twice during the qualifying run, the 3–0 victory over Finland, and in the 2–0 win over France. Balakov has been Sporting Lisbon's leading scorer. His specialty is accurate corner kicks, which led to a goal in the victory over France.

Trifon Ivanov, Defender (Real Betis, Spain), 5-foot-11, 156 pounds, Born: July 27, 1965-Ivanov, who plays for the same Spanish Second Division team as U.S. midfielder Tab Ramos, scored Bulgaria's lone goal in its 3–1 qualifying loss to Austria.

Emil Kostadinov, Forward (Porto, Portugal), 5-foot-10, 159 pounds, Born: Aug. 12, 1967-Kostadinov could not have picked a better time to score his third and fourth goals of qualifying, in the 2–1 comeback victory over France in Paris on Nov. 17, 1993. He hadn't scored since Bulgaria's first match, a 3–0 win over Finland. Kostadinov, whose contract with Portuguese champion FC Porto runs through 1995, has scored 26 league goals over the past 3 years.

Borislav Mikhailov, Goalkeeper (Mulhouse, France), 6-foot-1, 165 pounds, Born: Feb. 12, 1962-Mikhailov, the National Team captain, started 9 of the 10 qualifiers, missing only the 1–1 tie with Sweden. He performs in the French Second Division.

Luboslav Penev, Midfielder (Valencia, Spain), 6-foot-1, 183 pounds, Born: Aug. 31, 1966-He is the coach's nephew, but it is more than nepotism that has Penev on the squad. He set up Emil Kostadinov's last-second goal against France with an incredible half-field pass. He also scored twice in the 4–1 triumph over Austria. Penev's participation at USA '94 was placed in serious doubt after a tumor was found in his testicle in February.

Naska Sirakov, Midfielder (Levski Sofia), Born: April 26, 1962- When he plays, Sirakov has teammed with Luboslav Penev and Hristo Stoichkov to form one of the strongest scoring punches in Europe. He scored a second-half goal to help Bulgaria to a 2–2 tie with Irsael.

Hristo Stoichkov, Forward (Barcelona, Spain), 5-foot-8, 161 pounds, Born: Feb. 8, 1966-He is the best player on the team, and one of the best in Bulgarian soccer history. Stoichkov has starred for Barcelona's championship teams in the Spanish First Division (1990–91, 1991–92 and 1992–93) scoring 51 goals in 92 matches, including 20 in 34 games in 1992–93. Stoichkov finished second to the Netherlands' Marco van Basten in European Footballer of the Year in 1992, which upset him; he claimed he should have been first. He led Bulgaria in qualifying, scoring with 5 goals (4 on penalty kicks), including strikes against France, Finland, Israel, Sweden and Austria.

Coach

Dimitar Penev, who was named coach during the summer of 1990, performed in 3 World Cups for Bulgaria as a defender. He played in 1966, 1970 and 1974. Born on July 12, 1945, Penev has a strong family soccer history. His nephew, Luboslav, plays for the National Team. His uncle, also named Luboslav, performed for Sporting Lisbon (Portugal).

1994

The Bulgarians, who qualified for the World Cup by the skin of their teeth, have a reputation to live down. They have never won a game in the World Cup. There a number of teams that suffered a similar fate, but no team has gone 16 matches without a victory.

Heck, even the United States, with all its problems in the international arena through the years, has won 3 World Cup games.

Playing in a group that includes World Cup newcomers Nigeria and Greece, perhaps 1994 will be the year Bulgaria breaks the skid.

Coach Dimitar Penev likes to emphasize defense, using a 4–4–2 formation, but for the Bulgarians to do well, they will have to expect peak production and performance from the attacking trio of Hristo Stoichkov, Emil Kostadinov and Luboslav Penev, who form one of the dangerous frontlines in Europe.

For Stoichkov, it will be an opportunity to put up or shut up. When Dutch master Marco van Basten of A.C. Milan (Italy) was named

European Footballer of the Year in 1992, Stoichkov claimed he was the better player. Here's his chance to prove it. You might say the World Cup's a stage for him. If Stoichkov and his teammates can't do it this time, they might never do it.

Bulgaria, incidentally, had a media image problem during qualifying as its newspapers boycotted the team due to a dispute between Penev and the press.

A bit of interesting information for World Cup history buffs: Bulgaria's 16-game winless streak is the longest in World Cup history. Mexico is next with 13 consecutive matches without a win (0–12–1, from 1930–62).

GROUP E

ITALY

IRELAND

NORWAY

MEXICO

ITALY

POPULATION: 58,000,000

COLORS: Blue shirts, white shorts, blue socks

WORLD CUP APPEARANCES: Thirteenth. 1934 (champions), 1938 (champions), 1950 (first round), 1954 (first round), 1962 (first round), 1966 (first round), 1970 (second place), 1974 (first round), 1978 (second round), 1982 (champions), 1986 (second round), 1990 (third place)

World Cup History

The Italians were the first country to win back-to-back titles and were the second to capture the championship 3 times, after Brazil accomplished the feat. After Brazil and perhaps Germany, no other country has experienced a more glorious World Cup history. Modern fans will remember Italy's amazing run to the 1982 title—the Italians were 14–1 longshots before the competition began—behind the scoring of Paolo Rossi, an impenetrable defense and the solid goalkeeping of Dino Zoff. After a disappointing performance in Mexico in 1986, the Italians, behind Salvatore Schillaci, rebounded with a third-place finish at home 4 years later. For many countries, that would have sufficed. But we're talking about Italy, where nothing less than a champion is accepted.

How They Qualified

Italy finished first in European Group 1 with a 7–1–2 record and 16 points, 22 goals for, 7 against. The results (home team listed first)—Italy 2, Switzerland 2 (Oct. 14, 1992), Scotland 0, Italy 0 (Nov. 18, 1992), Malta 1, Italy 2 (Dec. 19, 1992), Portugal 1, Italy 3 (Feb. 24, 1993), Italy 6, Malta 1 (March 24), Italy 2, Estonia 0 (April 14), Switzerland 1, Italy 0 (May 1), Estonia 0, Italy 3 (Sept. 22), Italy 3, Scotland 1 (Oct. 13), Italy 1, Portugal 0 (Nov. 17). The clincher—Dino Baggio scored with 7 minutes remaining to give Italy a 1–0 victory over Portugal in Milan, Italy, on Nov. 17, 1993.

Players to Watch

Roberto Baggio has emerged into a world-class striker and Paolo Maldini is considered among the best around at left fullback. Sweeper Franco Baresi, who has seen better days, will be in the spotlight because he helps anchor the defense.

Probable Lineup

Goalkeeper: Gianluca Pagliuca (Sampdoria). **Defenders**: Alessandro Costacurta (A.C. Milan), Franco Baresi (A.C. Milan), Antonio Benarrivo (Parma), Paolo Maldini (A.C. Milan). **Midfielders**: Dino Baggio (Juventus), Roberto Donadoni (A.C. Milan), Giovanni Stroppa (Lazio), Roberto Baggio (Juventus). **Forwards**: Giuseppe Signori (Lazio), Pierluigi Casiraghi (Lazio).

Player Pool

Goalkeepers: Luca Marchegiani (Lazio), Gianluca Pagliuca (Sampdoria), Walter Zenga (Inter). **Defenders**: Alessandro Costacurta (A.C. Milan), Franco Baresi (A.C. Milan), Antonio Benarrivo (Parma), Amedeo Carboni (Roma), Massimo Carrera (Juventus), Luigi DeAgostini (Reggiana), Ciro Ferrara (Napoli), Ricardo Ferri (Inter), Andrea Fortunato (Juventus), Marco Lanna (Roma), Paolo Maldini (A.C. Milan), Moreno Mannini (Sampdoria), Roberto Mussi (Torino), Pietro Vierchowod (Sampdoria). **Midfielders**: Demetrio Albertini (A.C. Milan), Dino Baggio (Juventus), Roberto Baggio (Juventus) Nicola Berti (Inter), Alessandro Bianchi (Inter), Fernando DeNapoli (A.C. Milan), Alberto DiChiara (Parma), Roberto Donadoni (A.C. Milan), Stefano Eranio (A.C. Milan), Alberigo Evani (Sampdoria), Luca Fusi (Juventus), Roberto Galia (Roma), Giuseppe Giannini (Roma), Gianluigi Lentini (A.C. Milan), Attilio Lombardo (Sampdoria), Roberto Mancini (Sampdoria), Giovanni Stroppa (Lazio), Gianfranco Zola (Parma). **Forwards**: Francesco Baiano (Fiorentina), Pierluigi Casiraghi (Lazio), Ruggiero Rizzitelli (Roma), Salvatore Schillaci (Inter), Giuseppe Signori (Lazio), Giorgio Venturin (Torino), Gianluca Vialli (Juventus).

PLAYER PROFILES
(Appearances and goals through Nov. 25, 1993)

Dino Baggio, Midfielder (Juventus), 5-foot-9, 158 pounds, Born: July 24, 1971, Caps: 9, Goals: 3-Baggio—no relation to teammate Roberto—scored the goal in the 1–0 victory over Portugal on Nov. 17

that assured Italy of qualifying for USA '94. He made his First Division debut with Torino in 1990, and transferred to Inter for 1991–92 and then to Juventus for 1992–93. Baggio struck for 3 goals in the home-and-home series against Borussia Dortmund (Germany) as Juventus captured the UEFA Cup. He scored 3 goals during qualifying.

Roberto Baggio, Midfielder-forward (Juventus), Born: Feb. 18, 1967, Caps: 32, Goals: 19-It's no wonder Fiorentina fans rioted in Florence in 1990 when Baggio was sold to Juventus for a then world-record $13 million. He is an Italian midfielder who can score goals, lots of goals. He was rewarded for it in 1993, capturing FIFA Player of the Year honors and winning the World Soccer Player of the Year award. He has been severely criticized at Juventus, but he all but silenced his detractors with 2 outstanding seasons, scoring 18 goals in 1991–92 and another 21 in 1992–93, including 15 more in Italian and UEFA Cup competitions. Before the 1993–94 season, Baggio had accumulated 93 First Division goals in 186 matches. The jury is out whether he makes his greatest contributions at forward or midfield. He led Italy with 5 goals in qualifying.

Franco Baresi, Defender (A.C. Milan), 5-foot-6, 155 pounds, Born: May 8, 1960, Caps: 72, Goals: 1-He might have seen better days, but Baresi came out of international retirement thanks to the coaxing of coach Arrigo Sacchi. While he has been prone to mistakes—in one match he scored 2 of his own goals, twice accidentally knocking the ball into his net—his experience and knowledge of the game is virtually unparalleled. Baresi, who is in his 17th professional season, has played his entire career with A.C. Milan, where he captained the two-time European Cup champions in 1988 and 1989. He was the cornerstone of the Italian defense that helped the side to a third-place finish at the 1990 World Cup. His 72 caps is the most among active Italian players.

Alessandro Costacurta, Defender (A.C. Milan), 5-foot-7, 162 pounds, Born: April 24, 1966, Caps: 15, Goals: 1-Though he lived only miles from the Milan training complex, Costacurta grew up wanting to be a basketball player. He finally turned to soccer at the age of 12, and his star has been on the rise ever since. A natural stopper, Costacurta had experienced problems making the transition from the club level to National Team. In Italy's 2–2 tie with Switzerland, for example, he made 2 defensive lapses that led to both Swiss goals.

Gianluigi Lentini, Midfielder (A.C. Milan), 5-foot-7, 159 pounds, Born: March 27, 1969, Caps: 12, Goals: 0-Lentini is lucky to be alive, let alone being a part of the Italian World Cup team. During the summer of 1993, he almost died, suffering serious head injuries after crashing his Porsche. Lentini lapsed into a coma for a while, but he did return for Milan on Nov. 10, 1993. He began his career with Torino in 1986, was loaned to Ancona of the Second Division, transferred back to Torino, then signed with Milan for $16 milion before the 1992–93 season. Torino fans rioted in Turin for several days, and even the Vatican condemned the signing because of the amount of money.

Paolo Maldini, Defender (A.C. Milan), 5-foot-10, 170 pounds, Born: June 26, 1968, Caps: 48, Goals: 2-He is regarded as the finest left fullback in the world because he is fluid, able to move up front and a strong tackler in the back. The son of Cesare Maldini, who performed for the legendary Milan teams of the sixties and now the coach of the Italian Under-21 team, Maldini made his league debut at the age of 16. Maldini, playing in his 10th season, has been on several championship teams—3 Italian championships, 2 European Cup crowns, two European Supercup titles and two World Club championships. He made his international debut as a teenager—against Yugoslavia on March 31, 1988.

Gianluca Pagliuca, Goalkeeper (Sampdoria), 5-foot-10, 170 pounds, Born: Dec. 18, 1966, Caps: 14, Goals: 0-He does not have much international experience, but Pagliuca has forged a reputation as a steady goalkeeper for Sampdoria. He helped the team to its first European trophy ever—the European Cup Winners Cup in 1990. Only a year later, he was a member of Sampdoria's first league championship. He made an important save on German captain Lothar Matthaeus late in the season, securing his team's first-place position. Like national teammate Gianluigi Lentini, Pagliuca almost lost his life in a car accident in 1993. He crashed his car trying to avoid a truck. He suffered a broken collarbone, cuts to his face and minor damage to a lung. He recovered, returned to Sampdoria and did not miss a World Cup qualifier.

Giuseppe Signori, Forward (Lazio), 5-foot-3, 150 pounds, Born: Feb. 17, 1968, Caps: 12, Goals: 4-Signori, who has developed his goal-scoring instincts with several clubs, led Serie A—the Italian First Division—with 26 goals in 1992–93. He started out with Piacenza in the Third Division in 1986–87, joined Trento for 1987–88, moved back to Piaccenza in 1988–89 before he transferred to Foggia. There, he helped the team gain promotion to the First Division, and then joined Lazio. In his international debut, Signori scored on a free kick in a 2-0 victory over Ireland at U.S. Cup '92. He had 3 goals during qualifying.

Coach

After directing A.C. Milan to 2 consecutive European Cup crowns and world club titles in 1989 and 1990, Arrigo Sacchi opted for greater challenges. He found it on Oct. 18, 1991, replacing Azeglio Vicini as coach of the Italian National Team. Born April 11, 1940, Sacchi was named coach of Milan in 1987 and built one of the most successful clubs in modern times behind the Dutch connection of Marco van Basten, Ruud Gullit and Frank Rijkaard and several Italian internationals. Sacchi, who has been described as obsessively neat and meticulous, employs an attacking style of soccer, which is considered revolutionary for a country known for its defense. In fact, he brought the style that made Milan famous—the 4 defenders push up to cut down their opponents' space and midfielders hunt in packs to close down their rivals.

1994

Italy lives by the philosophy that if you don't give up goals, you don't lose games. But there's a flip side. If you don't score yourself, you probably won't win many important games.

That is the predicament Italy faces in the World Cup. The Italians should waltz through the opening round, where points, not victories, are important. But the Italians could be betrayed by their lack of offense later on.

The Italians do attack. They rarely, however, realize their full potential in putting away their chances. The reason is two-fold. The Italian First Division—Serie A—is considered the top league in the world. That, in turn attracts the best players and most dangerous scoring forwards and midfielders. These players—from England, the Netherlands, Germany, Brazil and Argentina—take the role of Italian players who should be refining the craft of scoring goals. It is not surprising that foreign players traditionally dominate the leading scorers. The other reason is homegrown. At a young age, the fastest players usually are placed on defense. So, when a defender is beat up field, he can regain his ground and catch up to his man.

Saying all of that, much is expected of Italy, which will play 2 of its opening-round matches in the next best stadium to Olympic Stadium in Rome—Giants Stadium—in the midst of a huge Italian population in the metropolitan area.

Even though Italy is favored to win Group E, coach Arrigo Sacchi refuses to be complacent. "Our round is not so easy," he said. "We have to start strong. You cannot play a game at 50 percent. You must play every game at 100 percent."

In 2 of the last 3 World Cups, Italy has reached the semifinals thanks to the unexpected scoring heroics of Paolo Rossi (1982) and Salvatore Schillaci (1990).

Who will be the hero this time?

Will it be Roberto Baggio, whose $13 million move from Fiorentina to Juventus caused rioting among the fans of the former club?

Will it be Dino Baggio—no relation—who scored the game-winning goal in the 1–0 clinching victory over Portugal?

Or will it be 26-year-old forward Giuseppe Signori, who led the First Division in scoring with 26 goals in 1992–93?

Depending on how quickly he recovers from a serious car accident suffered during the summer of 1993, midfielder Gianluigi Lentini of Milan could make an impact.

Regardless of what happens, the Italian defense should be the team's strength once again behind the likes of veterans Franco Baresi and Paolo Maldini.

A bit of interesting information for World Cup history buffs: Italy enjoys a winning record when the World Cup is played in the Americas. The Italians, who finished second to Brazil in 1970, are 10–6–6 for 26 points, scoring 31 goals and allowing 25. Germany, which took third in Mexico in 1970, has the best at 11–5–7 for 29 points, scoring 39 goals and surrendering 34.

IRELAND

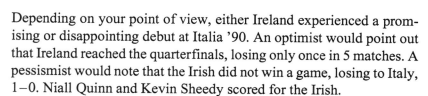

POPULATION: 3,600,000
COLORS: Green shirts, white shorts, green socks
WORLD CUP APPEARANCES: Second. 0−4−1, 2 goals for, 3 against. 1990 (quarterfinals)

World Cup History

Depending on your point of view, either Ireland experienced a promising or disappointing debut at Italia '90. An optimist would point out that Ireland reached the quarterfinals, losing only once in 5 matches. A pessimist would note that the Irish did not win a game, losing to Italy, 1−0. Niall Quinn and Kevin Sheedy scored for the Irish.

How They Qualified

Ireland finished second in European Group 3 with a 7−1−4 record and 18 points, scoring 19 goals, allowing 6. The results (home team listed first)—Ireland 2, Albania 0 (May 26, 1992), Ireland 4, Latvia 0 (Sept. 9, 1992), Denmark 0, Ireland 0 (Oct. 14, 1992), Spain 0, Ireland 0 (Nov. 18, 1992), Ireland 3, Northern Ireland 0 (March 31, 1993), Ireland 1, Denmark 1 (April 28, 1993), Albania 1, Ireland 2 (May 26), Latvia 0, Ireland 2 (June 9), Lithuania 0, Ireland 1 (June 16), Ireland 2, Lithuania 0 (Sept. 8), Ireland 1, Spain 3 (Oct. 13), Northern Ireland 1, Ireland 1 (Nov. 17). The clincher: Only a minute after Jimmy Quinn gave Northern Ireland the lead, second-half substitute Alan McLoughlin scored in the 75th minute to lift Ireland into a 1−1 draw with their rivals in Belfast on Nov. 17.

Players to Watch

Forward John Aldridge has come on strong in the past 2 years. There is a 50−50 chance that the Irish will wind up with a shutout when Packie Bonner is between the posts. Paul McGrath is a solid fixture on defense.

Probable Lineup

Goalkeeper: Packie Bonner (Glasgow Celtic, Scotland). **Defenders**: Paul McGrath (Aston Villa, England), Alan Kernaghan (Manchester City, England), Terry Phelan (Manchester City, England), Dennis Irwin (Manchester United, England). **Midfielders**: Ray Houghton (Aston Villa, England), Roy Keane (Manchester United, England), Andy Townsend (Aston Villa, England), Steve Staunton (Aston Villa, England). **Forwards**: Niall Quinn (Manchester City, England), John Aldridge (Tranmere Rovers, England).

Player Pool

Goalkeepers: Packie Bonner (Glasgow Celtic, Scotland), Alan Kelly (Sheffield United, England), Gerry Peyton (West Ham United, England). **Defenders**: Phil Babb (Coventry City, England), Liam Daish (Cambridge United, England), Chris Hughton (West Ham United, England), Dennis Irwin (Manchester United), Gary Kelly (Leeds United, England), Alan Kernaghan (Manchester City, England), Paul McGrath (Aston Villa, England), Kevin Moran (Blackburn Rovers, England), Chris Morris (Middlesbrough, England), Terry Phelan (Manchester City, England). **Midfielders**: John Byrne (Oxford United, England), Ray Houghton (Aston Villa, England), Roy Keane (Manchester United, England), Eddie McGoldrick (Arsenal, England), Alan McLoughlin (Portsmouth, England), Kevin Sheedy (Blackpool, England), John Sheridan (Sheffield Wednesday, England), Steve Staunton (Aston Villa, England), Andy Townsend (Aston Villa, England), Ronnie Whelan (Liverpool, England). **Forwards**: John Aldridge (Tranmere Rovers, England), Tony Cascarino (Chelsea, England), Tommy Coyne (Tranmere Rovers, England), David Kelly (Wolverhampton Wanderers, England), Mike Milligan (Oldham Athletic, England), Liam O'Brien (Newcastle United, England), Niall Quinn (Manchester City, England), Bernie Slaven (Port Vale, England), Andy Turner (Tottenham Hotspur, England).

PLAYER PROFILES
(appearances and
goals through Nov.
29, 1993)

John Aldridge, Forward (Tranmere Rovers, England), 5-foot-11, 155 pounds, Born: Sept. 18, 1958, Caps: 56, Goals: 13-It took Aldridge 20 games to score his first international goal, against Tunisia in 1988. Since then, Aldridge has been more productive. He led Ireland during qualifying with 6 goals, including a hat-trick over Latvia in a 4–0 win. He also has played for Newport County, Oxford, Liverpool and Real Sociedad (Spain) and Liverpool again. He is the Rovers' captain.

Packie Bonner, Goalkeeper (Glasgow Celtic, Scotland), 6-foot-2, 206 pounds, Born: May 24, 1960, Caps: 69, Goals: 0-As Ireland's most capped goalkeeper, Bonner has registered 36 shutouts in 69 matches. He is closing in on Liam Brady's all-time appearance record of 72. Bonner, who stopped a key penalty kick against Romania in the 1990 World Cup, has played 500 Premier Division matches over 16 seasons for Glasgow Celtic.

Ray Houghton, Midfielder (Aston Villa, England), 5-foot-7, 150 pounds, Born: Jan. 9, 1962, Caps: 56, Goals: 3-Even though he was born in Glasgow, Scotland, Houghton was able to play for Ireland because his father is Irish. He has been an invaluable addition to the squad. Houghton, who earned his first cap in Jack Charlton's first match as coach, scored his first international goal in the 1–1 tie with England at the 1988 European Championship. He was a key member of Liverpool's First Division championship teams in 1988 and 1990 and its F.A. Cup team in 1989. He transferred to Aston Villa in 1992 for $1.1 million.

Dennis Irwin, Defender (Manchester United, England), 5-foot-8, 164 pounds, Born: Oct. 31, 1965, Caps: 24, Goals: 1-He is the first Ireland player to play internationals at 6 levels—schoolboy, youth, Under-21, Under-23, B team and of course, the National Team. Irwin, who scored 5 goals in United's league title winning season in 1992–93, was a member of the 1992 European Cup Winner Cup champions.

Roy Keane, Midfielder (Manchester United, England), 5-foot-10, 164 pounds, Born: Aug. 10, 1971, Caps: 16, Goals: 0-As one of Ireland's few young prospects, Keane moved from Nottingham Forest to Manchester United for $5.25 million in July, 1993. That was quite an investment for Forest, which originally acquired Keane from the Cobh Ramblers for $37,000. He was so impressive at Forest that Keane captured the Young Eagle of the Year award in the 1990–91 season.

Kevin Moran, Defender (Blackburn Rovers, England), 5-foot-11, 182 pounds, Born: April 29, 1956, Caps: 69, Goals: 6-Like it or not, Moran forever will be remembered as the first player to be ejected at an English F.A. Cup final (1985). Moran, the oldest player on the team, needs 3 caps to tie Liam Brady's cap record (72). He has also played with Manchester United and Sporting Gijon (Spain).

Paul McGrath, Defender-midfielder (Aston Villa, England), 6-foot-1, 196 pounds, Born: Dec. 4, 1959, Caps: 63, Goals: 7-McGrath is an incredible success story because his professional career did not start until he was 22, and he has undergone 8 knee operations. McGrath, who is expected to play defense, gives coach Jack Charlton versatility because he also can play midfield or right fullback. McGrath, England's Player of the Year in 1992–93, was Ireland's top player at the 1990 World Cup. He starred for Manchester United until he was transferred to Aston Villa for $600,000.

Niall Quinn, Forward (Manchester City, England), 6-foot-4, 202 pounds, Born: Oct. 6, 1966, Caps: 43, Goals: 10-Quinn has been sidelined for 8 months because of a severe knee injury, putting his participation at USA '94 in doubt. If he does not play, then Ireland will miss one of its key players up front. Quinn, who scored in the 1–1 tie with the Netherlands at the 1990 World Cup, is excellent in the air. Quinn, who also has excelled at hurling, Gaelic football and Australian Rules football, has scored more than 50 goals in 3 seasons with Manchester City. He scored twice during qualifying.

Coach

An Englishman who is celebrated throughout Ireland? That's right. Since taking over as coach in February, 1986, Jack Charlton has worked wonders with the Irish, who have enjoyed their greatest success. They reached the 1988 European Championship for the first time and qualified for the World Cups in 1990 and 1994. Under Charlton, Ireland is 37–10–26. Charlton, the first Englishman to direct Ireland, played on the England team that captured its first and only World Cup in 1966. Born on May 8, 1935, Charlton teamed with his brother, Bobby, to form one of soccer's most famous brother teams. After a 21-year playing career with Leeds United (96 goals in 773 matches), Charlton embarked on a 21-year coaching career that has seen him with Middlesbrough, Sheffield Wednesday, and Newcastle United.

1994

Irish fans like to call the team Jackie's Army, in reference to coach Jack Charlton. But other soccer observers have claimed the squad should be called Jackie's Mercenaries because the team is made up of players who live or play in other countries.

"I . . . think that people who have to go to the extremes of family links to get a place in a team don't have the right feeling for that country," Northern Ireland coach Billy Bingham said.

Ireland has used FIFA's grandfather clause. FIFA, the soccer's world governing body, has allowed countries to use players if a player's parent or grandparent had lived in Ireland or was an Irish citizen. For example, defender Alan Keranaghan, whose grandparents were born in Ireland before 1921, was allowed to play for Ireland. There's midfielder Ray Houghton, who was born in Glasgow, Scotland, but qualified for the team through his Irish father. Forward Tony Cascarino has both Italian and Irish grandparents.

Ireland, which was expected to play in the Foxboro/Boston venue because of its sizeable Irish population, still will be popular in New York. But don't expect the Irish to win new fans with soccer purists. They use a long ball attack that is more hit-or-miss than anything else. Still, it has been effective for the hard-working Irish, who have qualified for the last 2 World Cups and the 1988 European Championship in

Germany, where they upset England in the opening round, 1–0. They were eliminated in that round, but returned home heroes.

Can Charlton's Army duplicate that success?

The Irish face 3 disadvantages right from the start. For one, Ireland has not fared well in the United States in recent years. The Irish played the U.S. to a 1–1 tie in 1991, and lost to the Americans, 3–1, at the U.S. Cup '92. Secondly, several of Ireland's key players are 30 or above, with no new blood in sight, except for midfielder Roy Keane.

And thirdly, with striker Niall Quinn sidelined for 8 months because of a knee ligament injury, another consistent scorer is needed up front if that injury cannot hold up this June and July.

Ironically, Charlton's biggest fears might not be his opponents, but rather the English media, which sometimes has brought tabloid journalism to new depths. Because England, Scotland, Wales and Northern Ireland did not qualify, the tabloids, which like to blow things out of proportion, will focus on the Irish. That has not made Charlton very happy.

An bit of interesting information for World Cup history buffs: Ireland became the only team in history to reach the quarterfinals without winning a game (in Italy in 1990).

NORWAY
POPULATION: 4,300,000
COLORS: Red shirts, white shorts, blue
socks
WORLD CUP APPEARANCES: Sec-
ond. 0−1−0. 1938 (first round)

World Cup History

Norway's history has been short and sweet. The Norwegians played in only 1 game in 1 cup, losing to eventual champion Italy, 2−1, in 1938 in a first-round, single elimination system. Arne Brustad scored their lone goal.

How They Qualified

Norway finished first in European Group 2 with a 7−1−2 record, scoring 25 goals, allowing 5. The results (home team listed)—Norway 10, San Marino 0 (Sept. 9, 1992), Norway 2, Netherlands 1 (Sept. 23, 1992), San Marino 0, Norway 2 (Oct. 7, 1992), England 1, Norway 1 (Oct. 14, 1992), Norway 3, Turkey 1 (April 28, 1993), Norway 2, England 0 (June 2), Netherlands 0, Norway 0 (June 9), Norway 1, Poland 0 (Sept. 22), Poland 0, Norway 3 (Oct. 13), Turkey 2, Norway 1 (Nov. 10). The clincher—Norway blanked Poland in Poznan, 3−0, as Jostein Flo, Jan Age Fjortoft and Renny Johnsen scored on Oct. 13.

Players to Watch

The attack revolves around forward Jostein Flo, who is excellent in the air. Kjetil Rekdal, who led Norway with 5 goals in qualifying, provides some punch from the midfield. Veteran goalkeeper Erik Thorstvedt and sweeper Rune Bratseth are steadying influences in the back.

Probable Lineup

Goalkeeper: Erik Thorstvedt (Tottenham, England). **Defenders**: Henning Berg (Blackburn Rovers, England), Tore Pedersen (Oldham Athletic, England), Rune Bratseth (Werder Bremen, Germany), Stig Inge Bjoernebye (Liverpool, England). **Midfielders**: Gunnar Halle (Oldham Athletic, England), Erik Mykland (Start), Kjetil Rekdal (Lierse SK, Belgium), Lars Bohinen (Nottingham Forest, England). **Forwards**: Jan Age Fjortoft (Swindon Town, England), Jostein Flo (Sheffield United, England).

Player Pool

Goalkeepers: Frode Grodas (Lillestrom), Einar Rossbach (SFK Lyn), Erik Thorstvedt (Tottenham, England). **Defenders**: Henning Berg (Blackburn Rovers, England), Stig Inge Bjornebye (Liverpool, England), Rune Bratseth (Werder Bremen, Germany), Gunnar Halle (Oldham Athletic, England), Roger Nilsen (Sheffield United, England), Tore Pedersen (Oldham Athletic, England). **Midfielders**: Lars

Bohinen (Nottingham Forest, England), Germund Brendesaether (Brann), Kare Ingebrigtsen (Rosenborg), Jahn Ivar Jakobsen (Lierse, Belgium), Oyvind Leonhardsen (Rosenborg), Erik Mykland (Start), Kjetil Rekdal (Lierse SK, Belgium). **Forwards**: Jan Age Fjortoft (Swindon Town, England), Jostein Flo (Sheffield United, England), Jan Ove Pedersen (Lillestrom), Goran Sorloth (Bursapor, Turkey).

Henning Berg, Defender (Blackburn Rovers, England), 6-foot, 166 pounds, Born: Jan. 1, 1969, Caps: 7, Goals: 0-Berg, who was bought by Blackburn from Lillestrom for $600,000 in December, 1992, playing in 2 matches. He also plays with KFUM Oslo and VIF (Valerengens). Berg made 11 appearances with the Norwegian Under-21 team before making his international deubt against the Faroe Islands on May 13, 1992.

Stig Inge Bjornebye, Defender (Liverpool, England), 5-foot-11, 168 pounds, Born: Dec. 11, 1969, Caps: 28, Goals: 1-A former teacher, Bjornebye has been around and then some since he began his career with Strommen in the Second Division in 1987. He joined Kongsvinger IL in the First Division 2 years later before transferring to Rosenborg in 1991. He was a member of Rosenborg's double—league and cup titles—in 1992 before transferring to Liverpool for $900,000 in November, 1992. Bjornebye, who has a powerful left-foot shot, had to wait a month to play while waiting for a work permit. He played in 11 matches for Liverpool in 1992–93.

Lars Bohinen, Midfielder (Nottingham Forest, England), 6-foot-1, 164 pounds, Born: Sept. 8, 1969, Caps: 22, Goals: 7-Bohinen, who was called up to the National Team at the last minute to replace an injured teammate, has become a fixture in the lineup. He scored twice during qualifying—in the 2–0 win over England which left the English closer to elimination, and in the loss to Turkey. Bohinen has also played with FK Langnes, Baerum, Lyn, Vaalerengen and Young Boys (Switzerland). For the Swiss club, he scored 4 times in 22 games in 1990–91 and another 2 goals in 34 appearances the next season.

Rune Bratseth, Defender (Werder Bremen, Germany), 6-foot-4, 188 pounds, Born: Feb. 19, 1961, Caps: 53, Goals: 4-As team captain and sweeper, Bratseth has become the team's most influential player. Most of his success has come with Werder Bremen, for whom he has played more than 200 times since 1987. He played for Bremen's league

PLAYER PROFILES (Appearances and goals through Dec. 6, 1993)

champions in 1988 and 1993, for the German Cup champions of 1991 and in the European Cup Winners Cup in 1992. Bratseth was out of action for 3 months after sustaining a knee injury in June, 1993. As a Christian, he has tried to interest his German teammates in Bible reading. He plans to retire after the World Cup.

Jan Age Fjortoft, Forward (Swindon Town, England), 6-foot-3, 192 pounds, Born: Jan. 10, 1967, Caps: 45, Goals: 15-Fjortoft has filled the nets at every level he has played. He scored 20 goals in 35 matches for Lillestrom. With Rapid Vienna (Austria), he struck 17 times in 1989-90 and for 16 goals apiece the next 2 seasons. Fjortoft, who scored 2 goals in the qualifiers, including one in the clinching win over Poland, moved to Swindon Town for $750,000 before the 1993 season.

Jostein Flo, Forward (Sheffield United, England), 6-foot-4, 203 pounds, Born: Oct. 13, 1964, Caps: 17, Goals: 6-Known as "The Lighthouse" because of his excellent ability to head the ball, Flo is considered to be the mainstay of the Norwegian attack. Flo, Norway's Player of the Year in 1993, scored 7 goals in 25 games for Lierse (Belgium) in 1990−91 and another 8 in just 10 matches for Songdal in the summer of 1991. He played with National Team teammate Kjetil Rekdal at Lierse.

Gunnar Halle, Defender (Oldham Athletic, England), 6-foot, 175 pounds, Born: Aug. 11, 1965, Caps: 42, Goals: 4-Halle has performed for Oldham since 1990—his transfer fee from Lillestrom was $420,000—playing in 68 games and scoring 5 goals through 1992−93. After helping Oldham gain promotion and win the Second Division title in 1990−91, Halle broke his leg on New Year's Day, 1992, and was limited to 10 games. He came back strong in 1992−93, scoring 5 times in 41 appearances. Halle had a hat-trick in the 10−0 trouncing of San Marino, his only 3 goals of qualifying.

Jahn Ivar Jakobsen, Midfielder (Lierse, Belgium), 5-foot-6, 161 pounds, Born: Nov. 8, 1965, Caps: 37, Goals: 5-Nicknamed "Mini" due to his height, Jakobsen has played in Switzerland since 1990, after scoring 17 goals to lead Rosenborg to the Norwegian league and cup crowns. He found the back of the net twice in qualifying, in the second victory over San Marino and in the win over Turkey. Jakobsen, who often has been asked to give after dinner speeches, is an out-

spoken player, as was evidenced in his sometimes controversial auto-
biography.

Erik Mykland, Midfielder (Start), 5-foot-8, 140 pounds, Born: July
21, 1971, Caps: 16, Goals: 1-It's little wonder why his teammates call
Mykland "The Mosquito." When the National Team was given new
suits, Mykland had trouble finding one that fit because they were all too
big. But don't let his size fool you as he played an important role in
Norway's qualifying run, scoring in the rout of San Marino. Mykland,
who works as a part-time chauffeur, also serves with the Norwegian
army.

Tore Pedersen, Defender (Oldham Athletic, England), 6-foot, 177
pounds, Born: Sept. 29, 1969, Caps: 27, Goals: 0-In 1990, he made a
big jump from Fredrikstad in the Norwegian Second Division to IFK
Gothenburg in Sweden. He remained a vital cog in Gothenburg's
championship teams through 1993, when he returned home. Pedersen
performed in 7 of Norway's 8 qualifying games for the 1992 European
Championship, including the 2−1 triumph over Italy.

Kjetil Rekdal, Midfielder (Lierse, Belgium), 6-foot-2, 182 pounds,
Born: Nov. 16, 1968, Caps: 23, Goals: 5-He led Norway in scoring
during qualifying with 5 goals. He had 2 against San Marino, and single
tallies against the Netherlands, England and Turkey. After playing for
Molde and Borussia Moenchengladbach, Rekdal found a home in
Belgium, leading Lierse in scoring for 2 consecutive seasons. He
scored 10 goals in 29 games in 1990−91, 21 in 31 matches in 1991−92
and five in 1992−93.

Erik Thorstvedt, Goalkeeper (Tottenham, England), 6-foot-4, 200
pounds, Born: Oct. 28, 1962, Caps: 78, Goals: 0-Thorstvedt, who is
second on Norway's all-time appearance list, is a perfect example of
persistence. Twice, he tried to get a work permit to play with Tottenham Hotspur and twice he was turned down. The third time was the
charm, when Gothenburg (Sweden) sold him to the London-based club
for $600,000 in 1988. Thorstvedt, who played an important role in
Tottenham winning the F.A. Cup in 1991, has played more than 100
times for the club. He broke his finger against Nottingham Forest the
day after Easter 1993, but he returned for Norway's 2−0 victory over
England on June 2. This won't be Thorstvedt's first appearance in the

U.S., having participated for Norway in the Summer Olympics in 1984, allowing only 1 goal in 3 matches.

Coach

Egil Olsen took over as coach after Ingvar Stadheim resigned in October, 1990. Born on April 22, 1942, Olsen had the perfect background for the job. He coached in the top 5 divisions, the Under-21 team and as assistant of the 1984 Olympic squad before taking over the head role in 1989–90. Nicknamed "Drillo" because of his fantastic dribbling skills, Olsen played for several clubs, including Ostiden, Sarpsborg, Vaalerengen and Frigg, plus 16 times for the National Team. Olsen has earned a reputation as an eccentric because he takes his dog to practice. He is a former Marxist, and is still interested in left-wing politics.

1994

For the first time in 56 years, Norway is going to the World Cup, and the players have no doubts as to why—coach Egil Olsen, who has taken a team known as the laughing stocks of Europe and turned it into one of the World Cup surprises.

"His knowledge of football is phenomenal," team captain Rune Bratseth was quoted in *The European*. "His scientific approach and attention to detail gives us the feeling that we always fully prepare for a match.

"It is important that all players believe in him 100 percent because his unusual ideas and methods don't suit everybody. He analyzes every player's strength and weaknesses through videos and awards plus and minus marks for ball contact, defensive and attacking performance and passing."

Olsen has instilled a winning and festive spirit on the team in a country that is better known for its winter sports. Lillehammer, Norway, hosted the 1994 Winter Olympic Games in February.

Take one good look at the Norwegian roster and you can guess the style the team plays. Eight starters perform in the English Premier Division, so it's not surprising that the National Team is a hardworking side that plays a long ball game. Then again, the weather in Norway isn't conducive to neat playing fields. Instead of following the winter-spring schedule of its European comrades, the Norwegian season runs from May to October, when there is no snow on the ground (heating coils have been built under artificial and grass fields, including the national stadium in Oslo). In fact, more than 60 artificial turf stadiums have been built because snow can be more easily removed.

Norwegian soccer hasn't had much to cheer about at the international level. Norway reached the semifinals of the 1936 Olympics, losing to Italy in the bronze-medal match. Two years later, the Norwegians played in their first and only World Cup, losing to the Italians again, 2–1, in their only match. In 1984, as a late replacement for one of several Communist teams boycotting the Summer Games, Norway wound up at 1–1–1.

So it wasn't surprising that the country went wild when the team qualified. The country's largest newspaper devoted its front page to the victory with a picture of Jan Age Fjortoft in a Viking helmet and "USA" written in big letters. An Oslo tabloid gave 11 pages to the match.

Norwegian Foreign Minister Johan Joergen Holst, who helped bring the historic peace deal between Israel and the Palestine Liberation Organization together, tried to put the soccer team's feat into perspective. "The national team is contributing to put us on the map," he said. "People realize that this small country up in the north is getting itself noticed in several areas."

A bit of interesting information for World Cup history buffs: Of the 24 finalists, Norway has the longest time between appearances—56 years. That tied the record set by Egypt, which also waited 56 years, from 1934 to 1990.

MEXICO
POPULATION: 86,000,000
COLORS: Green shirts, white shorts, red socks
WORLD CUP APPEARANCES: Tenth. 6–17–6, 17 goals for, 27 against. 1930 (first round), 1950 (first round), 1954 (first round), 1962 (first round), 1966 (first round), 1970 (quarterfinals), 1978 (first round), 1986 (quarterfinals)

World Cup History

There isn't much positive information here. The Mexicans were winless in their first 13 matches (0–12–1), which included a World Cup record 9-game losing streak in the process before they defeated Czechoslovakia, 3–1, in 1962 (the Czechs advanced to the final, the Mexicans were eliminated). In fact, Mexico's shining moments came on home turf, reaching the quarterfinals in 1970 and 1986, with records of 2–1–1 and 3–0–2, respectively.

How They Qualified

Mexico had to participate in 2 CONCACAF groups and play 12 games, the most of any World Cup finalist. In Group A, the Mexicans recorded a 4–1–1 mark and 9 points scoring 22, allowing 3 and tying a CONCACAF record with 11 goals against St. Vincent, then won the final group with a 5–1 record and 10 points, scoring 17 and allowing 5. They finished with a 9–2–1 mark, scoring 39 goals, allowing 8. The results (home team listed first)—St. Vincent 0, Mexico 4 (Nov. 8, 1992), Mexico 2, Honduras 0 (Nov. 15, 1992), Mexico 4, Costa Rica 0 (Nov. 22, 1992), Costa Rica 2, Mexico 0 (Nov. 29, 1992), Mexico 11, St. Vincent 0 (Dec. 6, 1992), Honduras 1, Mexico 1 (Dec. 13, 1992), El Salvador 2, Mexico 1 (April 4, 1993), Mexico 3, Honduras 0 (April 11), Mexico 3, El Salvador 1 (April 18), Mexico 4, Canada 0 (April 25), Honduras 1, Mexico 4 (May 2), Canada 1, Mexico 2 (May 9). The clincher—Hugo Sanchez scored 1 goal and set up another by Francisco Javier Cruz for a 2–1 victory over Canada in Toronto on May 9, to become the first team to qualify for the World Cup.

Players to Watch

Hugo Sanchez may be on his last legs, but he proved this past season that he still can find the back of the net. Flamboyant goalkeeper Jorge Campos just might be the legitimate heir to Colombian goalkeeper Rene Higuita when he comes to wandering away from the goal. Luis Roberto (Zaque) Alves might be hard-pressed to duplicate his

7-goal performance against Martinique, but can certainly entertain the crowd.

Goalkeeper: Jorge Campos (UNAM). **Defenders**: Claudio Suarez (UNAM), Juan de Dios Ramirez Perales (Monterrey), Ignacio Ambriz (Necaxa), Miguel Herrera (Atlante), Ramon Ramirez (Santos, Brazil). **Midfielders**: David Patino (Monterrey), Luis Enrique Flores (Atlas), Alberto Garcia Aspe (Necaxa). **Forwards**: Hugo Sanchez (Rayo Vallecano, Spain), Luis Roberto Alves (America).

Probable Lineup

Goalkeepers: Jorge Campos (UNAM), Felix Fernandez (Guadalajara), Pablo Larios (Puebla). **Defenders**: Jorge Rodriguez (Toluca), Ignacio Ambriz (Necaxa), Jose Guadalupe (Cruz Azul), Miguel Herrera (Atlante), Juan de Dios Ramirez Perales (Monterrey), Claudio Suarez (UNAM), Manuel Vidrio (Guadalajara), Ramon Ramirez (Santos), Francisco Ramirez (Necaxa), Abraham Nava (Necaxa), Rual Gutierrez (Atlante), Alberto Coyotte (Leon), Roberto Andrade (Atlante), Carlos Turrubiates (Leon). **Midfielders**: Miguel Espana (UNAM), Marcelino Bernal (Toluca), David Patino (Monterrey), Joaquin Del Olmo (Vera Cruz), Daniel Guzman (Atlante), Benjamin Galindo (Guadalajara), Missael Espinosa (Guadalajra), Luis Enrique Flores (Atlas), Alberto Garcia Aspe (Necaxa), Guillermo Munoz (Monterrey), Jaime Ordiales (Puebla), Jesus Ramirez (Santos). **Forwards**: Luis Roberto Alves (America), Francisco Javier Cruz (Tigres), Luis Garcia (Atletico Madrid, Spain), Ricardo Pelaez (Necaxa), Luis Miguel Salvador (Atlante), Hugo Sanchez (Rayo Vallecano, Spain), Francisco Uribe (America), Ignacio Vazquez (Guadalajara).

Player Pool

Luis Roberto Alves, Forward (America), Born: May 23, 1967-His nickname is Zaque from the Portuguese word zig-zag. He zig-zagged his way to a Mexican-record 7 goals against Martinique in the opening match of the CONCACAF Gold Cup, a 9–0 triumph on July 11, 1993. He finished the tournament with 11 goals. He was seventh in the 1992 "world goal-getter" race with 59. His Brazilian father starred in the Mexican League.

PLAYER PROFILES (Appearances and goals through Nov. 29, 1993)

Ignacio Ambriz, Defender (Necaxa), 5-foot-6, 165 pounds, Born: Feb. 7, 1967, Caps: 22, Goals: 3-Ambriz, who has a lethal, long-range shot, scored his first 3 international goals in Mexico's qualifying run, connecting in 3 successive matches. He tallied in a 3–0 victory against

Honduras on April 11, 1993, in a 3−1 win over El Salvador a week later and once more in a 4−1 triumph over Honduras on May 2.

Jorge Campos, Goalkeeper (UNAM), Born: Oct. 15, 1966, Caps: 20, Goals: 0-Regardless of how Mexico fares, Campos is primed to become one of the more intriguing personalties of the World Cup. He likes to venture out of the net and likes to wear flamboyant jerseys. Campos, who wore a shocking pink shirt in an international friendly against the United States in Washington on Oct. 13, was involved in some controversy when the Mexican federation told him that he had to wear shirts given by the national team's sponsors. As for his forays into the offensive half, Campos follows in the footsteps of Colombian goalkeeper Rene Higuita, becoming a second sweeper. In fact, he was utilized as a field player twice during the CONCACAF Gold Cup. "He does take risks," Mexican coach Miguel Mejia Baron said. "We are fully aware of that. But football is a game of risks and he has the team's and coach's backing."

Francisco Javier Cruz, Forward (Tigres), 5-foot-4, 156 pounds, Born: May 24, 1966, Caps: 8, Goals: 1-Nicknamed "Grandfather," because he was the youngest Mexican player at the 1986 World Cup, Cruz scored in the 84th minute to give Mexico a 2−1 win over Canada, which boosted the side into the 1994 event. After his goal, Cruz ran to the stands to hug Baron, who had been banned from the playing field due to a previous red card.

Luis Flores, Midfielder-forward (Atlas), 5-foot-5, 154 pounds, Born: July 18, 1961, Caps: 14, Goals: 3-Flores, who performed in the 1986 World Cup, played a vital role in Mexico's qualifying run for USA '94. He scored against Honduras in separate matches and added another goal in Canada before a crowd of 120,000 at Azteca Stadium.

Alberto Garcia Aspe, Midfielder (Necaxa), 5-foot-4, 145 pounds, Born: May 11, 1967, Caps: 18, Goals: 3-Another goal-scoring hero for Mexico in the qualifying tournament, Garcia Aspe connected in successive games against Canada and Honduras in April and May. Garcia Aspe, the mastermind of the Mexican midfield, added 2 goals in the quarterfinals of Copa America, the South America championship, in a 4−2 victory over Peru. He was named to the all-tournament team.

Hugo Sanchez, Forward (Rayo Vallecano, Spain), 5-foot-5, 156 pounds, Born: July 11, 1958-He is the best Mexican player of his generation. Sanchez, who played parts of 2 seasons with the San Diego Sockers (North American Soccer League), won 5 Spanish League scoring titles in 7 years with Real Madrid. He also played with Atletico Madrid in Spain. Recalled to the team and made captain by Baron, Sanchez responded with a goal and an assist in the 2−1 victory over Canada on May 9, 1993 that clinched a spot in USA '94. Sanchez usually celebrates a goal with a somersault. He's still celebrating on a fairly frequent basis. At midseason, Sanchez was still among the leaders in the Spanish First Division.

Miguel Mejia Baron took over as coach in January, 1993. He replaced Cesar Luis Menotti, who coached Argentina to the 1978 World Cup championship. Menotti, who had tendered his resignation before the start of Group A matches, returned a week before the Mexicans' first game. However, the dispute between Menotti and the Mexican Soccer Federation became even more bitter and he resigned a second time. Baron, who was born on Sept. 6, 1944, agreed to take over with one stipulation—that he be allowed to keep his job at Monterrey while directing the National Team. Baron gave up a dental practice to coach soccer fulltime. After playing his entire career at UNAM—from 1964−78—Baron was an assistant to coach Bora Milutinovic at the club in the early eighties. He also wound up as an assistant to Bora during the 1986 World Cup.

Coach

If the World Cup was played in 1993, Mexico undoubtedly would have been considered one of the favorites. The Mexicans enjoyed a year to remember, qualifying for the cup, finishing second at Copa America—the South American championship—to Argentina, 2-1, and winning the CONCACAF Gold Cup, avenging a 1991 defeat to the U.S., within a span of less than 3 months.

1994

They were virtually invincible in 1993, registering a 16−4−5 mark (since 1989 Mexico is 37−12−20).

"Together with Colombia, they play the most modern type of soccer," said Italian coach Arrigo Sacchi, whose team will face-off with Mexico in a Group E match.

The Mexicans have played as though they were on a mission during qualifying after missing Italia '90. Ironically, they were banned from playing in the 1990 World Cup because of using an overage player in an Under-20 world championship qualifier, a day after the Americans were awarded the 1994 tournament.

The Mexican squad started to take shape between the 2 qualifying groups. After a poor performance in Europe—a 2–0 loss to Italy and a 1–1 draw with Spain—the public and Mexican media pressured coach Miguel Mejia Baron to invite a number of veterans to the national team camp in Monterrey. Among those recalled were Hugo Sanchez, who performed in the 1986 World Cup along with Juan Flores, and Benjamin Galindo, who was the top scorer of the 1991 CONCACAF Gold Cup. Their infusion into the team worked brilliantly as Sanchez and Flores scored 3 goals apiece.

Baron has had the team play a short passing, attacking game with 5 midfielders and a goalkeeper who sometimes doubles as a forward. That fits in well with keeper Jorge Campos, who has frequently ventured out of the net to aid the attack.

In fact, Baron helped bring the team together, having won over the players after supporting their protest of having one-year professional club contracts without a freedom environment to play in national matches.

"Without Miguel, we would never have achieved what we are achieving now," Sanchez said.

A bit of interesting information for World Cup history buffs: The Mexicans might be the ultimate test of home continent advantage. In cups played in North America, they are 5–1–3. Anywhere else, they are an awful 1–16–3.

GROUP F

BELGIUM

MOROCCO

NETHERLANDS

SAUDI ARABIA

BELGIUM

POPULATION: 10,000,000.

COLORS: Red shirts, red shorts, red socks

WORLD CUP APPEARANCES: Ninth. 7–14–4, 33 goals for, 49 against. 1930 (first round), 1934 (first round), 1938 (first round), 1954 (first round), 1970 (first round), 1982 (second round), 1986 (fourth place), 1990 (second round)

World Cup History

The Belgians did not do much to distinguish themselves in the early years of the cup, but they have been quite a force in the last 3 tournaments. They were the surprise team of both the 1982 and 1986 cups, reaching the second round in the former and eventually losing to France in the consolation match in the latter. Belgium reached the second round at Italia '90, losing to England on a last-minute goal by David Platt in extra time.

How They Qualified

Belgium took second in European Group 4 with a 7–2–1 record and 15 points, scoring 16 goals and surrendering five. The results (home team listed first)—Belgium 1, Cyprus 0 (April 22, 1992), Faroe Islands 0, Belgium 3 (June 3, 1992), Representation of Czechs and Slovaks 1, Belgium 2 (Sept. 2, 1992), Belgium 1, Romania 0 (Oct. 14, 1992), Belgium 2, Wales 0 (Nov. 18, 1992), Cyprus 0, Wales 3 (Feb. 13, 1993), Wales 2, Belgium 0 (March 31), Belgium 3, Faroe Islands (May 22), Romania 2, Belgium 1 (Oct. 13), Belgium 0, Representation of

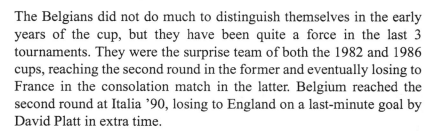

Czechs and Slovaks 0 (Nov. 17). The clincher: Belgium played the Representation of Czechs and Slovaks to a scoreless tie in Brussels, Belgium on Nov. 17. Backup goalkeeper Filip DeWilde, who had played in only 3 internationals before the match, replaced an injured Michel Preud'homme and made an important save to preserve the draw.

Players to Watch

Classy midfielder Enzo Scifo is the motor of the offense with his overall superb play. Marc Wilmots is a proven goalscorer. Philippe Albert is one of the top stoppers in Europe, if not the world. Michel Preud'homme is a solid presence in goal.

Probable Lineup

Goalkeeper: Michel Preud'homme (Mechelen). **Defenders:** Dirk Medved (Club Brugge), Georges Grun (Parma, Italy), Philippe Albert (Anderlecht), Rudy Smidts (Antwerp). **Midfielders:** Frank Van der Elst (Club Brugge), Enzo Scifo (Monaco, France), Danny Boffin (Anderlecht), Lorenzo Staelens (Club Brugge). **Forwards:** Marc Degryse (Anderlecht) Marc Wilmots (Standard).

Player Pool

Goalkeepers: Gilbert Bodart (Standard), Filip DeWilde (Anderlecht), Michel Preud'homme (Mechelen), Danny Verlinden (Club Brugge). **Defenders:** Philippe Albert (Anderlecht), Vital Borkelmans (Club Brugge), Rudy Cossey (Club Brugge), Bertrand Crasson (Anderlecht), Michel DeWolf (Mechelen), Glen DeBoeck (Mechelen), Stephane Demol (Standard), Regis Genaux (Standard), Georges Grun (Parma, Italy), Dirk Medved (Club Brugge), Pascal Plovie (Club Brugge), Rudy Smidts (Antwerp), Johan Walem (Anderlecht), Marc Wilmots (Standard). **Midfielders:** Danny Boffin (Anderlecht), Frank Dauwen (AA Gent), Alain De Nil (AA Gent), Marc Emmers (Anderlecht), Gunter Hofmans (Germinal Ekeren), Enzo Scifo (Monaco, France), Lorenzo Staelens (Club Brugge), Franky Van Der Elst (Club Brugge), Bruno Versavel (Anderlecht). **Forwards** Alain Bettagno (Standard), Alex Czerniatynski (Mechelen), Marc Degryse (Anderlecht), Michael Goosens (Standard), Luc Nilis (Anderlecht), Luis Oliveira (Cagliari, Italy), Stefan Van Der Heyden (Club Brugge).

PLAYER PROFILES
Appearances and
goals through Nov.
25, 1993)

Philippe Albert, Defender (Anderlecht), 6-foot-3, 189 pounds, Born: Aug. 10, 1967, Caps: 27, Goals: 3-Though he played in the 1990 World Cup, Albert's full talents did not emerge until the 1990–91 season. He has become a calm, cool and collected central defender. He has experienced some disciplinary problems, however, on the field, suspended by the Belgian League for 6 weeks for spitting at a player and being ejected in Belgium's last qualifier. Albert, who was selected as Belgian Player of the Year for the 1992–93 season, scored a goal in the 3–0 qualifying victory over Cyprus.

Marc Degryse, Forward (Anderlecht), 5-foot-8, 155 pounds, Born: Sept. 4, 1965, Caps: 45, Goals: 13-Degryse was one of the last cuts from Belgium's European Championship team in 1984 and was not selected for the 1986 World Cup. Instead of blaming others, Degryse attributed it to a lack of effort. He played and worked harder and paid off. He scored 22 goals for Brugge's league championship team in 1988. He also made the Belgian squad for the 1990 World Cup and was named Belgian Footballer of the Year in 1991. Degryse, who missed the final 2 qualifiers with a torn leg muscle, scored once—in the 2–0 victory over Wales.

Georges Grun, Defender (Parma, Italy), 6-foot-1, 163 pounds, Born: Jan. 25, 1962, Caps: 67, Goals: 3-Grun's solid play at Parma has resurrected his international career, although he missed Belgium's final qualifier and 4 months with a serious knee injury. He began his career as a forward with Anderlecht and eventually turned to defense with Parma, as he was an integral part of the Italian team's run into the championship match of the 1993 European Cup Winners Cup. Grun scored the game-winning goal that qualified Belgium for Italia '90.

Michel Preud'homme, Goalkeeper (KV Mechelen), 5-foot-9, 165 pounds, Born Jan. 24, 1959, Caps: 48, Goals 0-Preud'homme had an incredible streak broken in Belgium's last qualifying match, having played every minute of 31 successive games. He had started 33 of 34—from September, 1989, to October, 1993, before a thigh injury. (Filip DeWilde started, instead.) He was named Belgian Player of the Year in 1987 and 1989. Preud'homme, who started his pro career with Standard Liege in 1979, joined Mechelen in 1986. He made his international debut against Austria in 1979.

Enzo Scifo, Midfielder (Monaco, France), 5-foot-9, 155 pounds, Born: Feb. 19, 1966, Caps: 62, Goals: 15-He has only turned 28 and Scifo is already looking toward his third World Cup. It isn't surprising he has done so much at a young age as Scifo scored 432 goals over 4 seasons in the La Louviere youth leagues. He went on to play for Anderlecht and for eventual national coach Paul Van Himst, Inter (Italy), Bordeaux and Auxerre (both France), Torino (Italy) and eventually to Monaco, signing a 5-year contract. Scifo, 1 of the more skillful players around, scored 2 goals in the 1986 World Cup and one at Italia '90. He finished tied for the qualifying lead with 4 goals, incuding 2 in the 3-0 victory over Cyprus and single tallies against the Faroe Islands and Romania.

Marc Wilmots, Forward (Standard Liege), 5-foot-10, 165 pounds, Born: Feb. 22, 1969, Caps: 20, Goals: 8-Wilmots, who relies on his speed and instincts to score, has been an important factor in bringing Standard Liege back to its former glory days and back to the annual European competitions. A member of Belgium's World Cup team in 1990, Wilmots finished fourth in league scoring with 22 in 1992–93, helping Standard to the Belgian Cup. Wilmots, who scored a goal in the 1990 World Cup, finished qualifying with 4 goals, including 2 in the 3–0 win over the Faroe Islands.

Coach   Paul Van Himst, who replaced Guy Thys as national coach in May, 1991, was reluctant to take the job because it can be so pressurized. He had been running a coffee roasting business. Born on Oct. 2, 1943, Van Himst has forged quite a reputation as a player and coach. He made 81 appearances for Belgium, including his international debut at the age of 17 in 1960. He also captured the Belgian Golden Boot award four times. As a coach, he guided Anderlecht to the Belgian crown in 1985 and 1986 and to the UEFA Cup finals in 1984.

1994   Warning to the 23 other finalists: Beware of Belgium, which has been a surprise in the past 2 World Cups.
    In 1986, the Belgians finished a surprising fourth. In 1990, they were eliminated in the second round, by an English team that would go on to take fourth place, on a last-second goal in overtime by David Platt.
    Not bad for a country that boasts a population of 10,000,000.
    The Belgians don't play a particularly pretty style of soccer, using a solid defense and a counter-attacking offense to stifle and surprise its opposition.
    Coach Paul Van Himst has the tools for Belgium to finish first or second in Group F; the Netherlands, Saudi Arabia and Morocco are its foes.
    "Our chances to reach the second round are high," Van Himst said. "Obviously the Netherlands with their world-class strikers will be our strongest opponent."

To go past the second round, however, Van Himst must get the most out of his stars. Enzo Scifo, who is in his prime, Marc Wilmots, a veteran goalscorer, and Marc Degryse must put a few in the net. In the back, defenders Philippe Albert, who must curb his temper, Georges Grun and goalkeeper Michel Preud'homme must keep opposition's chances to a minimum.

An bit of interesting information for World Cup history buffs: Even though they finished fourth in 1986, the Belgians have not fared well in the Americas, going $3-7-1$ in 3 appearances.

MOROCCO
POPULATION: 26,200,000.
COLORS: Red shirts, red shorts, red
socks
WORLD CUP APPEARANCES: 3.
1–3–3, 5 goals for, 8 against. 1970
(first round), 1986 (second round)

World Cup History   It's funny talking about past glories of a country that has won only one
game in the World Cup. But it was a big one, a 3–1 victory over
Portugal in its final opening-round match in the 1986 competition that
secured first place in Group F. So, Morocco became the first African
and Third World country to win a group. Morocco was eliminated on a
late goal in the second round, 1–0, by West Germany, the eventual
champion.

How They Qualified   Morocco finished first in African Group F (first round) with a 4–0–2
record and 10 points, scoring 13 goals and allowing 1, and first in
African Group B (final round) with a 3–1–0 record and 6 points,
scoring 6 goals and surrendering 3. The results (home team listed
first)—In the first round: Morocco 5, Ethiopia 0 (Oct. 11, 1992), Benin
0, Morocco 1 (Oct. 25), Tunisia 1, Morocco 1 (Dec. 20), Ethiopia 0,
Morocco 1 (Jan. 17, 1993), Morocco 5, Benin 0 (Jan. 31), Morocco 0,
Tunisia 0 (Feb. 28). In the final round: Morocco 1, Senegal 0 (April
16), Zambia 2, Morocco 1 (July 4), Senegal 1, Morocco 3 (July 17),
Morocco 1, Zambia 0 (Oct. 10). The clincher—needing a victory to
qualify, Morocco registered a 1–0 win in Casablanca on Oct. 10, 1993,
as Abdeslam Laghrissi scored the lone goal of the match in the 50th
minute.

Player to Watch   Forward Mohammed Chaouch finished the qualifiers with a team-high
5 goals. Midfielder Mustapha Hadji, who had been coveted by France
for its Under-21 team, could be a force, as can defensive midfielder
Rachid Daoudi.

Probable Lineup   **Goalkeepers:** Khalil Azmi (Raja de Casablanca). **Defenders:** Lahcen
Abrami (W.A.C. Casablanca), Abdelkrim El Hadrioui (F.A.R. de Ra-
bat), Ahmet Masbahi (KAC Marrakesh), Nourredine Naybet (F.C.
Nantes, France). **Midfielders:** Rachid Daoudi (W.A.C. Casablanca),
Tahar El Khalej (KAC Marrakesh), Mustapha El Haddaoui (Angers,
France), Mustapha Hadji (Nancy, France). **Forwards:** Mohammed

Chaouch (Nice, France), Aziz El Ouali (Bastia, France), Abdelslam
Laghrissi (W.A.C. Casablanca).

Goalkeepers: Khalil Azmi (Raja de Casablanca), Abdelkader El Brazi
(F.A.R. de Rabat). **Defenders:** Lahcen Abrami (W.A.C. Casablanca),
Rachid Azzouzi (MSV Duisburg, Germany), Abdelkrim El Hadrioui
(F.A.R. de Rabat), Mustapha Khalif (Raja de Casablanca), Ahmed
Masbahi (KAC Marrakesh), Nourredine Naybet (F.C. Nantes, France),
Alaoui-Ashraf Zakaria (KAC Marrakesh). **Midfielders:** Nacer Abdel-
lah (SV Waregem, Belgium), Ismael Audelai (FC Seraing, Belgium),
Rachid Daoudi (W.A.C. Casablanca), Aziz Doufikar (Esphino, Portu-
gal), Mustapha El Haddaoui (Angers, France), Mustapha Hadji
(Nancy, France), Tahar El Khalej (KAC Marrakesh), Radouane Hajry
(SC Farnese, Portugal), Hassan Kachloul, Nimes, France), Moham-
med Lashaf (Standard Liege, Belgium), Karim Mghogi (Germinal
Ekeren, Belgium), Mouloud Moudhaker (Union de Tangier), Nourre-
dine Moukrim (RFC Antwerp, Belgium), Hassan Nader (SC Farense,
Portugal), Maataoui Tijani (Raja de Casablanca). **Forwards:** Moham-
med Achakour (FC Brugge, Belgium), Mohsen Bouhlal (F.A.R. de
Rabat), Abdelmajid Bouiyboud (W.A.C. Casablanca), Mohammed
Chaouch (Nice, France), Aziz El Ouali (Bastia, France), Youssef
Fertout (W.A.C. Casablanca), Abdelslam Laghrissi (W.A.C. Casa-
blanca), Mustapha Mouslim (Rouen, France).

Player Pool

Mohammed Chaouch, Forward (Nice, France), 5-foot-6, 158 pounds,
Born: Dec. 12, 1966, Caps: 33, Goals: 10-He led the squad in scoring
with 5 goals, including 2 each in the 5–0 triumph over Ethiopia and in
the 5–0 victory over Benin. He started his pro career at 16, playing with
Berkane of the Moroccan First Division, and moved to Europe 3 years
later. He wore No. 10—the uniform of former superstar Michel Platini
at St. Etienne (France). He also played for Istres, Metz (he scored 5
goals in his first 5 matches) and Nice.

*PLAYER PROFILES
(Appearances and
goals through Nov.
30, 1993)*

Rachid Daoudi, Midfielder (W.A.C. Casablanca), 5-foot-3, 150
pounds, Born: Feb. 21, 1966, Caps: 39, Goals: 5-Daoudi, who has been
nicknamed "the gentleman gunner," is a rarity for a defensive midfielder. He can score. He finished qualifying with 3 goals, tied for the
second most on the team. On defense, Daoudi usually is asked to cover
the opposition's top forward. He joined W.A.C. Casablanca at the age
of 7, and stayed with the club as a professional.

Mustapha El Haddaoui, Midfielder (Angers, France), 5-foot-8, 167 pounds, Born: July 28, 1961, Caps: 74, Goals: 10-He is the current cap leader, having played for Morocco in 3 African Nations Cup tournaments (1986, 1988 and 1992). He began his career with Raja Casablanca before moving to Europe to play with Servette de Geneva in Switzerland and Nice, Len and Angers in France.

Mustapha Hadji, Midfielder (Nancy, France), 5-foot-9, 165 pounds, Born: Nov. 16, 1871, Cap: 1, Goals: 0-Talk about feast and famine. On the same day he joined the Moroccan team—Oct. 4, 1993—Hadji was selected for the French Under-21 team. Because players are allowed to play internationally for only 1 country, Hadji wound up choosing Morocco. He did not speak any Arabic, but since he was born in Morocco, he picked the African country. It certainly was worth it as he made his debut in the World Cup berth clinching victory over Zambia and was named Man of the Match.

Nourredine Naybet, Defender (F.C. Nantes, France), 5-foot-7, 167 pounds, Born: Feb. 10, 1970, Caps: 49, Goals: 2-He turned 24 recently, but Naybet already had made 49 international appearances. Naybet is excellent in the air.

Coach

Abdellah Blinda took over before Morocco's last qualifying match, a 1–0 victory over Zambia that boosted the squad into the final 24. Morocco goes through coaches very quickly. Blinda replaced German Olk Werner, who had been in charge of the senior, youth and Olympic squads since 1990. He had succeeded Brazilians Faria and Valente, and Italian-Argentine Angelino Angelillo.

1994

Like it or not, Morocco assumed the role of a villian in the world's eyes when it met Zambia in its final World Cup qualifying match on Oct. 10, 1993. The Zambian team had been rebuilt into a competitive side after an April 28 plane crash virtually wiped out the team. A crowd of 80,000 filled Mohammad V Stadium in Casablanca and millions watched on television as Zambia needed only a tie to complete a miracle.

Morocco spoiled the party with a 1–0 win as Abdeslam Laghrissi scored the only goal 5 minutes into the second half—a diving header—to qualify for the third time.

That match was Abdellah Blinda's first as coach and he quickly recognized that the Moroccan government follows the National Team very closely and that King Hassan II is a big fan. "The king has telephone me several times," he said, as quoted in *Soccer America*. "I know already that he will call me at the halftime of the game with Zambia. I already have my answers prepared!"

The Moroccans, who emphasize finesse and passing and use the traditional 4−4−2 system, were placed in a group with Belgium and the Netherlands, 2 European powers. That did not faze Blinda.

"I feel normal about the other teams," he said at the World Cup draw in December. "There are no easy groups. We have to see Belgium and the other teams play but we have 6 months to prepare."

One of the more intriguing match-ups will be against Saudi Arabia at Giants Stadium on Saturday, June 25, the first time 2 Arab teams will meet in the World Cup.

An bit of interesting information for World Cup history buffs: Since Morocco made history in Mexico in 1986, African teams have gone a creditable 4−6−6 at World Cups.

NETHERLANDS
POPULATION: 15,000,000.
COLORS: Orange shirts, white shorts, orange socks
WORLD CUP APPEARANCES: Sixth. 8–6–6 record, 35 goals for, 23 against. 1934 (first round), 1938 (first round), 1974 (second place), 1978 (second place), 1990 (second round).

World Cup History

The Dutch are one of the most unlucky World Cup countries of all time, finishing second twice with 2 of the most talented and entertaining sides. Those teams boasted a world-class player at virtually every position, including Johan Cruyff, Rudi Krol, Robbie Resenbrink and Johnny Rep. In 1974, they were undefeated at 5–0–1 before losing to the host nation in the final, Germany, 2–1. Without the great Cruyff in the 1978, the Dutch reached the final in Argentina, only falling to the home team again, this time in extratime, 3–1.

How They Qualified

The Netherlands finished second in European Group 2 with a 6–1–3 record and 15 points, scoring 29 goals and surrendering 9. The results (home team listed first)—Norway 2, Netherlands 1 (Sept. 23, 1992), Netherlands 2, Poland 2 (Oct. 14, 1992), Turkey 1, Netherlands 3 (Dec. 16, 1992), Netherlands 3, Turkey 1 (Feb. 24, 1993), Netherlands 6, San Marino 0 (March 24), England 2, Netherlands 2 (April 28), Netherlands 0, Norway 0 (June 9), San Marino 0, Netherlands 7 (Sept. 22), Netherlands 2, England 0 (Oct. 13), Netherlands 3, Poland 1 (Nov. 17). The clincher: Dennis Bergkamp scored 2 goals and Frank DeBoer 1 for the Dutch, who needed only a tie to qualify on Nov. 17.

Player to Watch:

There are plenty to watch. Central defender Ronald Koeman is a master at turning free kicks at the edge of the penalty area into goals. Midfielder Ruud Gullit has demonstrated for Sampdoria in the Italian League that he still can dominate a game—from start to finish. Dennis Bergkamp, who shuns the spotlight, but it has been tough to overlook his superb performances. Striker Peter Van Vossen came into his own during World Cup qualifying, leading the team with 6 goals. If Marco van Basten, (career-threatening ankle injury), is healthy the Dutch will be difficult to beat.

Probable Lineup

Goalkeeper: Ed DeGoey (Feyenoord). **Defenders:** Frank De Boer (Ajax), John DeWolf (Feyenoord), Ronald Koeman (Barcelona,

Spain). **Midfielders:** Erwin Koeman (PSV Eindhoven), Jan Wouters (Bayern Munich, Germany), Frank Rijkaard (Ajax), Ruud Gullit (Sampdoria, Italy), Aaron Winter (Lazio, Italy). **Forwards:** Peter Van Vossen (Ajax), Dennis Bergkamp (Inter Milan, Italy).

Goalkeepers: Ed De Goey (Feyenoord), Stanley Menzo (Ajax), Hans van Breukelen (PSV Eindhoven). **Defenders:** Frank De Boer (Ajax), John DeWolf (Feyenoord), Henk Fraser (Feyenoord), Ronald Koeman (Barcelona, Spain), Adri Van Tiggelen (PSV Eindhoven). **Midfielders:** Danny Blind (Ajax), Peter Bosz (Feyenoord), Ruud Gullit (Sampdoria, Italy), Erwin Koeman (PSV Eindhoven), Frank Rijkaard (Ajax), Berry Van Aerle (PSV Eindhoven), John Van't Schip (Ajax), Gerald Vanenburg (Yamaha, Japan), Richard Witschge (Bordeaux, France), Rob Witschge (Feyenoord), Jan Wouters (Bayern Munich, Germany). **Forwards:** Dennis Bergkamp (Inter Milan, Italy), John Bosman (Anderlecht), Ronald De Boer (Ajax), Wim Jonk (Inter Milan, Italy), Erik Meijer (PSV Eindhoven), Marc Overmars (Ajax), Bryan Roy (Foggia, Italy), Gaston Taument (Feyenoord), Marco van Basten (A.C. Milan, Italy), Peter Van Vossen (Ajax), Erik Viscaal (KAA Gent, Belgium), Aaron Winter (Lazio, Italy).

Dennis Bergkamp, Forward (Inter Milan, Italy), Born: May 18, 1969, Caps: 22, Goals: 16-When he was a teen-ager at Ajax, Bergkamp was allowed to practice with the No. 1 team and subsequently signed as a professional at the age of 18. He went on to tie for the Dutch First Division scoring lead with PSV Eindhoven's Romario with 25 goals apiece in 1990–91, led the league with 24 goals in 1991–92, voted as Dutch Players Association Player of the Year, and added a league-high 26 goals in 1992-93. He turned down Real Madrid and then Juventus for the big money abroad—he said he was not ready to live alone in a big foreign city—before settling on Inter Milan because teammate Wim Jonk agreed to come along. He scored 5 goals during qualifying.

John Bosman, forward (Anderlecht, Belgium), Born: Feb. 1, 1965, Caps: 2, Goals: 2-Another Ajax graduate, Bosman played his early years in the shadow of van Basten. After an injury to van Basten, he finally got an opportunity to show what he could do, connecting for 23 goals to finish third in the league in 1986–87, plus another 8 in the European Cup Winners Cup competition. He signed with Mechelen on a 3-year deal, scoring 18 goals to win the Belgian scoring crown. He helped PSV Eindhoven to the Dutch title in 1990 before returning to Belgium, scoring 16 goals for Anderlecht in 1991–92.

Frank DeBoer, Defender (Ajax), Born: May 15, 1970, Caps: 16, Goals: 1-DeBoer, who scored in qualfying wins over San Marino and the clincher against Poland, has played with Ajax since he was a teen-ager. He played on the Ajax squad that captured the 1990 Dutch title and performed in the UEFA Cup victory over Torino (Italy) in 1992. DeBoer and his twin brother, Ronald, who also is a member of the Dutch National Team, both have been timed closed to the European record in the 5,000-meter run.

Ed De Goey, Goalkeeper (Feyenoord), Born: Dec. 20, 1966, Caps: 5, Goals 0-DeGoey, who was capped for the first time in a qualifier vs. Turkey in December, 1992, was in the nets during the Dutch stretch run. He was Sparta Rotterdam's regular goalkeeper for 4 seasons through 1990, moving to Feyenoord. There, he played an important role in the club's Dutch Cup championship sides in 1991 and 1992 and in its league title run in 1993.

Ruud Gullit, Midfielder (Sampdoria, Italy), 6-foot-1, 183 pounds, Born: Sept. 1, 1962, Caps: 65, Goals: 17-He did not play in any of the Netherlands' qualifying matches because of a dispute with coach Dick Advocaat. Gullit would be quite an addition if he continues his strong offensive performances for Sampdoria, which has been among the leaders for most of the Italian First Division season. Gullit, who underwent four knee operations in the late eighties and in 1992, has only recently returned to the form that made him one of the most dangerous attacking midfielders in the game. The dreadlocked player was awesome in his early years, scoring 46 goals in 68 appearances for PSV Eindhoven, which won league championships in 1986 and 1987.

Wim Jonk, Forward (Inter Milan, Italy), Born: Oct. 12, 1966, Caps: 8, Goal: 1-He started out with a bang for his hometown team, Volendam, striking 23 goals in 36 matches before signing with Ajax in 1988. With the Amsterdam-based team, he became as backup to Jan Wouters and Dennis Bergkamp, eventually petitioning the Dutch Players Association in 1991 to help determine why he could not progress. After coach Leo Beenhakker left, Bergkamp was moved into the first team, where he came into his own. Jonk transferred to Inter during the summer of 1993.

Erwin Koeman, Midfielder (PSV Eindhoven), Born: Sept. 20, 1961, Caps: 28, Goals: 2-The older brother of Ronald Koeman, Erwin has been in and out of the National Team lineup since he made his debut in 1983. He performed for a number of championship teams, including Mechelen's victory in the Belgian Cup in 1987, in its European Cup Winners Cup triumph over Ajax in 1988, and PSV Eindhoven's league titles in 1991 and 1992.

Ronald Koeman, Defender (Barcelona, Spain), 5-foot-11, 174 pounds, Born: March 21, 1963, Caps: 66, Goals: 12-Koeman scored one of his patented goals off a free kick early in the second half to start the Dutch on their way to a 2-0 victory over England on Oct. 13, a result that virtually clinched a spot in the World Cup. After he transferred to PSV Eindhoven for more money, leading the team to 3 consecutive league titles in 1987, 1988 and 1989, including the European Cup in 1988, he joined coach Johan Cruyff in a $5 million deal to Barcelona in 1989, helping the Barcas win the Spanish Cup in 1990. After missing the 1990-91 season because of an ankle injury, Koeman bounced back with a 16-goal season in 1991-92, giving Barcelona its first European Cup championship by scoring the lone goal. He played in 3 matches at Italia '90.

Frank Rijkaard, Midfielder (Ajax), 6-foot-2, 176 pounds, Born: Sept. 30, 1962, Caps: 64, Goals: 6-Like it or not, Rijkaard forever will be known for his dismissal from a 1990 World Cup match against West Germany after spitting at Rudi Voeller. That's too bad, because he is an exceptionally talented player who has starred with Ajax, Real Zaragoza (Spain) and A.C. Milan (Italy), as a member of the Dutch trio of Gullit and van Basten from 1988–93. Rijkaard quit international soccer, but returned in 1991. After the 1992–93 season, Rijkaard returned to Ajax to close out his career. "I won't be able to play at the same level," he said. "The future scares me . . . I want to leave Milan, a club which has given me everything, before I start to go downhill."

Marco van Basten, Forward (A.C. Milan, Italy), Born: Oct. 31, 1964, Caps: 58, Goals: 24-Van Basten's participation in the cup is contingent on an ankle that forced him to miss action from December, 1992 through at least early 1994. With healthy, Van Basten has been among the most dangerous players in the world. Just a sampling of his accomplishments: the Golden Boot award for leading Europe in scoring in 1985–86, the top scorer (5 goals) in the 1988 European Championship, won by the Netherlands, 2 consecutive European Cup titles while playing for Milan in 1989 and 1990, and leading the Italian First Division in scoring (25 goals) in 1991–92.

Hans van Breukelen, Goalkeeper (PSV Eindhoven), Born: Oct. 4, 1956, Caps: 73, Goals: 0-At 37, van Breukelen will be one of the oldest players at the cup, and probably one of the fittest if he is selected. He reportedly is a fanatical trainer who has practiced long after the day's sessions have been completed. Nicknamed Positivio because of his optimistic outlook, van Breukelen debuted with Utrecht in 1976, played for Nottingham Forest (England) from 1982–84 and Eindhoven since. He has starred for 6 league championship teams, 3 Dutch Cups and 1 European Cup champion. Van Breukelen is a man for all seasons; he is a trained school teacher and also has been a quizmaster on television.

Peter Van Vossen, Forward (Ajax), Born: April 24, 1968, Caps: 7, Goals: 6-If van Basten can't meet the opening bell, then Van Vossen will do. He scored 6 goals during qualifying, including 2 in his international debut in the 2–2 draw with Poland and another 2 in a 3–1 win over Turkey. Van Vossen has a strong-willed personality. His father refused to allow Van Vossen to play soccer because he considered it to be a sin for his religious family. But Van Vossen, one of 16 children, skipped Bible class and practiced with his team, having one of his brothers fill for him on the class's activities in case his father quized him. It worked out better than he expected. Van Vossen went on to play for Beveren and Anderlecht, which captured the Belgian title in 1993. He signed a 3-year contract with Ajax.

Aaron Winter, Midfielder (Lazio, Italy), 5–foot–8, 159 pounds, Born: March 1, 1967, Caps: 32, Goals: 2-Born in Surinam, Winter moved to the Netherlands as a child. He helped Ajax capture the Cup Winners Cup in 1987 and was a member of the Dutch championship team in 1990. Since joining Lazio, Winter has been the target of racial epithets, prompting Italians soccer authorities and the Italian Players Association to take measures against fans' racism.

Richard Witschge, Midfielder (Bordeaux, France), 5–foot–6, 163 pounds, Born: Sept. 20, 1969, Caps: 19, Goals: 1-No one would have been happier to see Johan Cruyff take the reins of the Dutch squad than Witschge, who played for him at Ajax from 1986–88 and at Barcelona in 1991–92 He had problems after Cruyff left as the coach accused him of being lazy and arrogant. In fact, forner Ajax coach Leo Beenhakker claimed that Witschge was a member of "the French Fries generation," that they eat the wrong food and show little commitment to soccer. He is the younger brother of midfielder Rob Witschge, who plays for Feyenoord and scored 2 goals in a qualifying win over Turkey.

Jan Wouters, Midfielder (Bayern Munich, Germany), 5–foot–9, 165 pounds, Born: Aug. 22, 1966, Caps: 63, Goals: 4-He almost did not get an opportunity to blossom into a star. When he was a small boy, his legs were deformed. A doctor suggested that they be broken so they could grow straight. His father refused, and while it took some time, Wouters became of the Netherlands' leading players. "When I get into a match, something happens to me, a kind of change inside," he said. "I want the ball and I want to win." He starred for Ajax, helping the side to the European Cup Winners Cup in 1987, winning the Dutch Players' Player of the Year in 1990 and transferring to Bayern Munich in the 1991–92 season.

Originally, Dick Advocaat was supposed to direct the Dutch through qualifying and then become an assistant under former Dutch great and current Barcelona coach Johan Cruyff for USA '94. However, Cruyff could not reach a financial settlement with the Dutch Soccer Federation in December, 1993, so Advocaat remained in control. Advocaat's first order of business was to convince several players who did not want to play for him to play, including the talented Ruud Gullit. Advocaat, born on Sept. 27, 1947, might be most familiar with long-time U.S. soccer fans as the defender-midfielder played with the San Francisco Golden Gate Gales (United Soccer Association) in 1967 and for the Chicago Sting (North American Soccer League) as 1978–80. Though he never was selected to the Dutch National Team, Advocaat enjoyed a successful career with AMO Den Haag, Roda, Venlo, Sparta Rotterdam and Utrecht in the Netherlands and Berchem in Belgium. He turned to coaching in 1981 with the amateur team DSVP di Pijnacker, then went on to coach with the Dutch federation staff, Haarlem and SVV Dordrecht before becoming an assistant coach to Rinus Michels at the 1992 European Championship before taking over the reins in September, 1992.

Coach

Potentially, the Netherlands has all the pieces to become world champion—from a solid defense that occasionally provides offense, to

1994

a superior midfield and attacking forward line. But there has always been something to plug up the works.

Many soccer observers touted the Dutch to win the 1990 World Cup, but they wound up as one of the flops of the tournament. They struggled to an 0-0-3 record in the first round—as Marco van Basten experienced a nightmare tourament—before they were eliminated by eventual champion West Germany in the second round, 2–1. Several players blamed the poor performance on the conservative tactics introduced by former coach Thijs Libregts, who was fired several months before the start of the cup. By then, however, the Dutch were so bewildered and split apart they apparently did not recover in time. It was the World Cup's loss, because they usually play attractive, winning soccer.

Since then, the Dutch have begun to reclaim their former glory, reaching the semifinals of the 1992 European Championship before losing to eventual Cinderella champion Denmark in a penalty-kick tie-breaker, 5–4, after a 2–2 tie.

This player pool is loaded with players primarily from 3 home-based teams—Ajax (8), PSV Eindhoven (6) and Feyenoord (6), but the core of the impact players perform abroad, most notably in Italy. The Dutch, who introduced "Total Soccer" to the world during the seventies, used 3 defenders, 5 midfielders and two forwards for many of their qualifying matches.

The midfield of Ruud Gullit, Frank Rijkaard and Jan Wouters is among the best in Europe, if not in the world. Even without van Basten, the forward line has proved to be quite formidable. Peter Van Vossen emerged as a goal-scoring terror during qualifying and Dennis Bergkamp is steady with a number of talented players, including John Bosman and Bryan Roy, in reserve.

And as if the Dutch need any more scoring, there's always defender Ronald Koeman, who is a master at turning free kicks into goals.

A bit of interesting information for World Cup history buffs: The Netherlands is one of two countries that has finished second at successive World Cups—in 1974 and 1978. The other other nation is West Germany, which accomplished that feat in 1982 and 1986.

SAUDI ARABIA

POPULATION: 15,550,000

COLORS: White shirts, green shorts, white socks

WORLD CUP APPEARANCES: First

In its fifth attempt since 1978, Saudi Arabia finally qualified.   How They Qualified

Saudi Arabia finished first in Asian Group E (first round) with a 4−0−2 record and 10 points, scoring 20 goals, allowing 1. Finished first in Asian final group with a 2−0−3 record and 7 points, scoring 8 goals and surrendering 6. The results (first 3 matches of first round in Kuala Lumpur, Malaysia, the final three games in in Riyadh, Saudi Arabia)—Saudi Arabia 6, Macao (May 1, 1993), Saudi Arabia 1, Malaysia 1 (May 3), Saudi Arabia 0, Kuwait 0 (May 5), Saudi Arabia 8, Macao 0 (May 14), Saudi Arabia 3, Malaysia 0 (May 16), Saudi Arabia 2, Kuwait 0 (May 18). The final round (in Doha, Qatar)—Saudi Arabia 0, Japan 0 (Oct. 15), Saudi Arabia 2, North Korea 1 (Oct. 18), Saudi Arabia 1, South Korea 1 (Oct. 22), Saudi Arabia 1, Iraq 1 (Oct. 24), Saudi Arabia 4, Iran 3 (Oct. 28). The clincher—The Saudis, who dominated the match, earned their first World Cup berth with a 4−3 win over Iran in Doha, Qatar, on Oct. 28, 1993, as Hamzah Falatah scored the game-winner.   World Cup History

Forward Saeed Owairan led Saudi Arabia with 7 goals. Midfielder Khalid Al-Muwallid is 1 of the most consistent players.   Players to Watch

Goalkeeper: Mohammed Al Deayea (Al Taie). **Defenders:** Abdullah Al Dosari (Al Etefag), Mohammed Al Khlawi (Al Ettehad), Ahmed Madani (Al Ettehad), Fuad Amin (Al Shabab). **Midfielders:** Mohammed Al Jawad (Al Ahli), Mansour Al Muainea (Al Helal), Khalid Al Muwallid (Al Ahli), Fahad Mehalel (Al Shabab). **Forwards:** Saeed Owairan (Al Shabab), Hamzah Falatah (Ohud).   Probable Lineup

Goalkeepers: Mohammed Al Deayea (Al Taie), Hussein Al Sadig (Al Qadesia). **Defenders:** Salom Al Alwi (Al Shabab), Abdullah Al Dosari (Al Etefag), Mohammed Al Khlawi (Al Ettehad), Abdulrahman Al Roomi (Al Shabab), Ahmed Madani (Al Ettehad), Fuad Amin (Al Shabab), Mohamed Al Jawad (Al Ahli), Saleh Al Dawod (Al Shabab), Mohammed Al Karni (Al Riyadh). **Midfielders:** Mansour Al Muainea (Al Helal), Fahad Mehalel (Al Shabab), Khalid Al Muwallid (Al Ahli),   Player Pool

Mansour Al Mosa (Al Najma), Khalid Al Temawi (Al Helal), Hamzah Saleh (Al Ahli). **Forwards:** Sami Al Jaber (Al Helal), Majed Mohammed (Al Naser), Saeed Owairan (Al Shabab), Nezar Al Abaas (Al Ettehad), Hamzah Falatah (Ohud).

PLAYER PROFILES
(Appearances through Nov. 23, 1993 goals unavailable)

Mohammed Al Khlawi, Defender (Al Ettehad), 5–foot–6, 154 pounds, Born: Sept. 1, 1971, Caps; 16-A left fullback, Al Khlawi is considered to be one of the Saudi's best players. Despite being hampered by injuries in the final round of qualifying, he was one of 3 Saudi players named to the all-star team.

Khalid Al Muwallid Midfielder (Al Ahli), 5–foot–7, 156 pounds, Born: Nov. 23, 1971, Caps: 35-Another key player for Saudi Arabia, Al Muwallid has become a superb passer. One of his specialties is penalty kicks, but Al Muwallid fired one over the crossbar in a 1–1 tie with Iraq, several days after scoring the winning goal in the 2–1 win over North Korea. He finished with 3 qualifying goals.

Majed Mohammed, Forward (Al Naser), 5–foot–7, 156 pounds, Born: Jan. 11, 1959, Caps: 65 The team captain, Mohammed, at 35, is the oldest player of the team.

Fahad Mehalel, Midfielder (Al Shabab), 5–foot–4, 143 pounds, Born Nov. 11, 1970, Caps: 29-Mehalel, who is strong in the air, saved his best for last, scoring 2 of his 3 qualifying goals in the final round. As a substitute, Mehalel connected for a goal in the 2–1 win over North Korea and scored in the 4–3 triumph over Iran. He was the highest-ranked Saudi player in MVP voting.

Saeed Owairan, Forward (Al Shabab), 5–foot–8, 167 pounds, Born: Aug. 19, 1967, Caps: 22-He led Saudi with seven goals, including one in a 1–1 tie with Iraq. He did not play in the final qualifier because of a yellow-card suspension.

Hamzah Falatah, Forward (Ohud), 5–foot–9, 163 pounds, Born: Oct. 9, 1972, Caps: 32-One of the youngest players on the Saudi team, Falatah scored the deciding goal in the 4–3 victory over Iran.

Coach

Former Argentine international Jorge Solari, who was named on Feb. 26, is the third Saudi coach. He has coached Tenerufe (Spain) and several temas in his native country, including Newell's Old Boys, in which Diego Maradona played for him. Solari replaced Leo Beenhak-ker, who directed the Netherlands in the 1990 World Cup. Beenhakker was named coach of Saudi Arabia on Nov. 22, 1993, less than month after the team qualified. He replaced Brazilian Jose Candido, who was sacked for refusing to replace the goalkeeper midway through a match during the final round of Asian World Cup qualifying.

Former coach Leo Beenhakker certainly had his work cut out for him. At the World Cup draw, he admitted he did not know much of his team, which used a 4-4-2 formation and played attacking soccer during the qualifying round.

1994

"At the moment, I know more about my opponents than my own team," he said. "Saudi Arabia are champions of Asia and that has to mean something. But I don't know how to compare the team to European and South American football teams. We've a long way to go and I am still looking for players."

The players who were behind the qualification—including stars Saeed Owairan and Khalid Al Muwallid—received $100,000 each and a Mercedes—for the unprecedented accomplishment.

Encouraged by success at the youth level—the Saudis captured the Under-17 World Cup in 1989—Saudi Arabia has begun to emerge as one of the consistently best Asian teams. It might be a while before it can be competitive against the world powers, although it must be remembered that soccer is a relatively new sport in the Middle Eastern country.

The sport's popularity has grown quite quickly since World War II, thanks to a supportive government in the form of King Fahd and Prince Faisal. They built a state-of-the-art $500 million stadium in Riydah and made certain there were grass fields in a country that has virtually no rainfall.

Saudi Arabia has participated in 1 major soccer tournament in the United States—the 1984 Olympics. The Saudis did not fare too well, losing all 3 first-round matches—3–1 to Brazil, 1–0 to Morocco and 6–0 to West Germany.

In fact, the Saudis were so proud of their accomplishment of just qualifying in 1984, they ran newspaper and TV advertisements in the United States.

A bit of interesting information for World Cup history buffs: Asian teams have compiled a 1-18-4 record in the World Cup, with North Korea registering the only victory, a 1–0 win over Italy in 1966.

Chapter Six

Players to Watch
in the Summer of '94

These players bring some big reputations into the World Cup. Some will live up to them, others will barely get by, while still others will fade away. In alphabetical order, some players to watch during the summer of 1994:

Luis Roberto Alves (Zaque)
Forward, Mexico

Alves achieved international attention during the CONCACAF Gold Cup in 1993, when he scored 7 goals against Martinique. Nicknamed Zaquinho and Zaque, from the Portuguese word zig-zag because of the way he runs, the lanky forward finished the tournament with 11 goals. It was no accident, as the skillful Alves finished seventh in the 1992 World Goalgetter race with 59 goals, playing for Club America (Mexico). His Brazilian father also starred in the Mexican League. Born on May 23, 1967, Alves is expected to form a dangerous forward line with Hugo Sanchez and Luis Garcia.

Roberto Baggio
Midfielder-forward, Italy

The only way Roberto Baggio can top 1993 is by leading Italy to its fourth World Cup title in 1994. He was just about everyone's player of the year, earning FIFA, World Soccer and European Player of the Year honors. He scored 21 goals during the 1992–93 season and helped Juventus capture the UEFA Cup, one of the 3 major European competitions. Baggio, who turned 27 on Feb. 18, 1994, certainly has lived up to his expectations and the $13 million transfer fee that was paid by Fiorentina to Juventus in 1990. Fans in Florence were so upset that they rioted, but about a month later, they were cheering for their former hero as the 5-foot-6, 159-pound Baggio scored a goal off a dazzling individual effort against Czechoslovakia in the World Cup. He combines his talents—speed, a powerful right foot and a master of scoring off free kicks—good looks (he wears a ponytail, too) and outgoing personality into one of Italy's leading personalities—sports or otherwise.

Gabriel Batistuta
Forward, Argentina

While growing up, Batistuta had no delusions of grandeur about becoming a star. He had a poster of Mario Kempes, one of the heroes of Argentina's world championship team in 1978, in his bedroom. "My parents knew nothing of football and I never considered it more than just some fun among my friends," Batistuta said. Fun turned into professionalism for Batistuta, who earned the nicknames "Archangel Gabriel" and "Batigol" for his goal-scoring feats. Batistuta has scored goals in virtually every possible manner, from his right and left feet, head, free kicks and penalty kicks. He turned pro with Newell's Old Boys and never looked back. He blossomed internationally in Copa America in 1991, also honored as South American Footballer of the Year that year before signing with Fiorentina (Italy). Batistuta, who was born Feb. 1, 1969, probably is best known for 4 goals he has scored in 3 matches. He scored the game-winning goal in the 1991 Copa America championship game, a 2–1 victory over Colombia. He connected for 2 more in the 1993 Copa America final, another 2–1 win, over Mexico. And he scored Argentina's lone goal in its 1–0 victory over Australia that clinched a World Cup berth. Batistuta has 18 goals in 27 international appearances. "Bati is an 'inferno' for defenders," Argentine national coach Alfio Basile said.

Bebeto
Forward, Brazil

He is expected to team with Romario to give the Brazilians a difficult one-two punch to stop up front. He can do many things well, whether it is scoring off a free kick—he did so in the waning minutes in Deportivo Coruna's 1–0 victory over Racing Santander in December, 1993—or controlling the ball in the penalty area. Born on Feb. 16, 1964, Bebeto led the Spanish First Division in scoring with 29 goals in 1992–93. That was after he collected 7 goals in 10 international matches in 1992. It isn't surprising, because success has followed Bebeto at virtually every level. He performed for Brazil's silver-medal winning team in the 1988 Olympics. He added 6 of Brazil's 11 goals en route to the Copa America crown in 1989, but played only 7 minutes in the 1990 World Cup.

Dennis Bergkamp
Forward, Netherlands

It has become very difficult to stop Bergkamp, who is excellent in the air, quick and skillful. So, it is not surprising that Inter (Italy) acquired him and Dutch teammate Wim Jonk for the 1993–94 season. Born on May 10, 1969, the rising star began his career at perennial Dutch powerhouse Ajax Amsterdam, and eventually was given special attention from coach Johan Cruyff, who helped to strengthen the striker's self-confidence. It worked because Bergkamp scored 76 goals over a 5-year span before joining Inter. His best seasons came in 1990–91, striking for 25 goals, and in 1991–92, leading the Dutch First Division in scoring with 24 goals, being honored as Dutch Player of the Year and helping Ajax Amsterdam to the UEFA Cup.

Tomas Brolin
Forward/midfielder, Sweden

One of the surprise stars of the 1992 European Championship, Brolin tied for the scoring lead with 3 goals. Ironically, he finished qualifying with as many goals—all scored in a 5–0 triumph over Israel on June 2, 1993. That broke a year-long goalless streak with the national side. Brolin, who scored twice in the 4–0 victory over Morocco in the 1992 Olympics, transferred from IFK Norrkoping to Parma (Italy) for $1.5 million in 1990. Born on Nov. 29, 1969, Brolin had 15 goals in 89 games in his first 3 seasons with Parma.

Jorge Campos
Goalkeeper, Mexico

Depending on your vantage point, Campos will be either the best dressed or worst dressed goalkeeper of USA '94. Thanks to his flamboyant jerseys, Campos certainly will be in the spotlight before he even touches the ball. And when he touches the ball, look at what he does with it. Campos is not afraid of dribbling the ball up the field into the midfield, not unlike Colombian goalkeeper Rene Higuita, who revolutionized the role of the goalkeeper with his penetrating forays. In the 1993 CONCACAF Gold Cup, Campos was moved into the forward position in 2 games, helping to create goals against Martinique and Canada. Not surprisingly, Campos has become one of the most popular players in Mexico, where he stars for UNAM. Campos might be small for a goalkeeper—5-foot-6, 151 pounds—but he compensates with his superb leaping ability and by being sure-handed. Born on Oct. 15, 1966, Campos has made 29 international appearances.

Stephane Chapuisat
Forward, Switzerland

Before he turned pro, Chapuisat had to learn a trade, as is the tradition in Switzerland, and he became a salesman. How appropriate, because Chapuisat has been the best salesman Swiss soccer has had in years, perhaps ever. Borussia Dortmund (Germany) has been sold on the 5-foot-11, 164-pound Chapuisat, who scored 35 goals in his first 2 seasons. In fact, the crafty striker's performance has been so overwhelming that he was named Player of the Year by Bundesliga team captains in 1991 and receives about 50 fan letters a week. His father, Pierre-Albert "Gabet" Chapuisat, also was a soccer player, probably best known for a foul that severed ligaments in a foe's knees. Stephane, however, has been called by the Swiss, "the best soccer ambassador they ever had."

Martin Dahlin
Forward, Sweden

After a non-existent European Championship performance in 1992, Dahlin rebounded well with a team-high 8 goals during Sweden's World Cup qualifying run. Born on April 16, 1968, Dahlin has not been afraid to mix it up with opposing defenders when he isn't beating them with his quickness, strength and leaping ability, usually in the penalty area. During qualifying, Dahlin spaced out his goals over 7 matches, though his 2 most important scores came in the 3–2 victory over Finland on Oct. 13, 1993, which clinched the Swedes a berth. The 6-foot-1, 183-pound Dahlin, the 1993 Swedish Player of the Year, signed a 2-year contract extension with Borussia Moenchengladbach (Germany) in November, 1993. Dahlin became the first black to play for Sweden, making his international debut against Brazil in 1988.

Sergio Goycochea
Goalkeeper, Argentina

The opportunistic Goycochea has made the most out of an opportunity. Starting the 1990 World Cup on the bench, Goycochea replaced Nery Pumpido, who broke his right leg in Argentina's second match. Goycochea turned out to be one of the big heroes of the tournament, twice starring in penalty-kick tie-breakers as the Argentines used mirrors and Goycochea's penalty-kick blocking ability to reach the final. Goycochea, who was born on Oct. 17, 1963, also saved 2 penalties against Denmark in a match between the South American and European champions in February, 1993, and then twice more against Brazil and

Colombia in Copa America later that summer. In fact, his heroics have turned the 5-foot-10, 187-pound Goycochea, a family man, into a sex symbol. "I'm honest, sincere and open," the River Plate goalkeeper said. "What you see is what you get."

Ruud Gullit
Midfielder, Netherlands

In what has become one of the great individual comebacks of soccer, the quality of Gullit's recent performances has reached the heights he had achieved in the late eighties when 4 knee operations turned him from asuperstar to a good player. During the 1993–94 season for Sampdoria (Italy), he has dominated several matches, either scoring goals or setting teammates up for others. Gullit, who connected for 46 goals in 68 matches for perennial Dutch power PSV Eindhoven, made his international debut on his 19th birthday in 1981. He helped A.C. Milan (Italy) win the European Cup in 1989 and 1990 before scoring a goal at Italia '90. At the turn of the year, Gullit's availability for the Dutch national squad for USA '94 was in jeopardy because he does not see eye-to-eye with coach Dick Advocaat. Gullit did not play in the Netherlands' final 4 qualifying matches. When it was announced that former Dutch master Johan Cruyff was to coach the team, Gullit was set to return. But the deal fell through and Advocaat retained his duties. It remains to be seen if Gullit will play under Advocaat.

Gheorge Hagi
Midfielder, Romania

He is called "Maradona of the Carpathians," because of his skill and superb dribbling skills, and he had demonstrated that for Sportul Studentesc of Bucharest, leading the Romanian First Division by scoring with 20 and 31 goals in 1984–85, 1985–86, respectively, and for Real Madrid (joining the Spanish club in a $3.5-million deal), as he collected 12 goals in 1991–92. The 5-foot-8, 156-pound midfielder transferred to Brescia (Italy), scoring only 6 goals in 31 matches. Hagi, who led Romania in scoring with 7 goals during qualifying, connected for the first goal in the 2–1 victory over Wales on Nov. 17, 1993, which clinched a World Cup berth. Born on Feb. 6, 1965, Hagi has 21 goals in 81 international appearances.

Juergen Klinsmann

Forward, Germany

During the final match of U.S. Cup '93 against England, Klinsmann gave a personal demonstration of why it is important to never give up. With the score tied at 1−1 in the 52nd minute, Klinsmann passed the ball to Christian Ziege, who raced in alone on goalkeeper Nigel Martyn. Meanwhile, English defender Gary Pallister pulled Klinsmann down by his shirt. Instead of remaining on the ground, Klinsmann quickly regained his balance and rushed toward the right side of the penalty area as Ziege beat Martyn and fired a shot that hit the left post. The ball bounded in front to Klinsmann, who knocked it into an unattended net for the game-winner. Klinsmann, who was born on July 30, 1964, was criticized for not living up to his potential during his 3-year stay with Inter (Italy). He has had a penchant for scoring important goals, particularly at the international level. He struck 3 times at Italia '90, including the first goal in that memorable 2−1 second-round victory over the Netherlands. Besides his outstanding performance, Klinsmann was one of the most popular players at the U.S. Cup; he speaks fluent English. Klinsmann, who signed a 3-year contract with AS Monaco (France), has scored 18 goals in 53 internationals matches.

Ronald Koeman

Defender, Netherlands

Warning to opponents of the Netherlands: Do not foul any player within 25 yards of the your net, unless you want to pay dearly. The man who makes those teams pay is Ronald Koeman, whose lethal free kicks gives the already talented Dutch squad yet another dimension. Case in point: Koeman connected from a free kick early in the second half in a vital World Cup qualifying match against England on Oct. 13, 1993, as the Dutch registered a 2−0 win, virtually eliminating their rivals. The English claimed that Koeman should have been ejected for a professional foul only minutes before, and he would not have had an opportunity to score. But that's another story. When he isn't performing his heroics for the Dutch national side, Koeman is scoring for 3-time defending Spanish champion Barcelona. Speaking of free kicks, Koeman put in yet another in the 1992 European Cup championship game, a 1−0 victory over Sampdoria (Italy), earning man of the match honors. Entering the 1993−94 season, the 5-foot-11, 174-pound Koeman had scored 47 goals in 4 seasons after joining the First Division team for $5 million in 1989. Koeman, who converted a penalty kick against eventual-champion Germany in a 2−1 second-round loss at

Italia '90, has scored 12 times in 68 internationals appearances. His older brother, midfielder Erwin Koeman (PSV Eindhoven, Netherlands), also is in the national team pool.

Paolo Maldini
Defender, Italy

He is arguably the best left fullback in the world, and it has been difficult to find anyone to argue with that statement. Maldini has combined a tough man-to-man marking with an ability to attack and be a dangerous header on corner kicks to earn those accolades. He was destined to play at perennial Italian power A.C. Milan. His father, Cesare Maldini, played for the legendary Milan teams of the sixties, so there was a lot of pressure on Paolo. Maldini, who was born June 26, 1968, made his First Division debut at 16 and his international debut at 19, and he has never looked back. A 10-year veteran of Serie A, Maldini has teamed with Franco Baresi to form a solid Milan defense that has anchored 3 Italian championships, 2 European Cup titles and 2 World Club crowns. The 5-foot-10, 170-pound Maldini has scored twice in 48 international appearances.

Diego Maradona
Midfielder, Argentina

Like it or not, he's back.

He's the man who claimed the "Hand of God" helped him score a goal.

He's the man who scored one of the most amazing goals ever in the World Cup.

He's the man who made whining, complaining and crying a new art form in soccer.

Maradona is ready to step onto the World Cup stage this summer for his fourth and final cup. All in all, it is a pretty incredible comeback, indeed, for the man known as the anti-Pele, a man many thought had left his international career for dead after serving a 15-month suspension for cocaine use in 1991.

But then came World Cup qualifying. As sharp as the Argentines looked en route to the Copa America title in the summer of 1993, behind Gabriel Batistuta and Sergio Goycochea, they appeared disheveled in a stunning loss at home to Colombia on Sept. 5. With one chance remaining, a 2-game, total-goal series with Australia, coach Alfio Basile turned to his secret weapon. Maradona, who was born Oct. 30, 1960, was not his old brilliant self, but he contributed, setting up

Argentina's lone goal in a 1–1 tie in Sydney before a 1–0 victory in Buenos Aires clinched a World Cup berth.

Whether he can perform the same magic of 1986 or equal his limited accomplishments of 1990 remains to be seen. Maradona, as they might say in another sport, has lost a little off his fastball.

But it is his vision of the game that makes him so dangerous in creating opportunities from virtually nothing. While playing for Napoli in the Italian First Division several years ago, he stood at the top of the right side of the penalty area with his back to the goal. Noticing an open teammate, he blooped a pass to him diagonally across the box. The player scored.

Then there was the simple, non-threatening pass that broke Jorge Burruchaga free for the winning goal in the waning minutes of Argentina's 3–2 World Cup clinching win over West Germany in 1986. But those feats get lost in the shuffle. Soccer fans remember his chicanery and brilliance only minutes apart in the 2–1 cup quarterfinal victory over England in 1986. While leaping for an airball, Maradona "accidentally" punched the ball into the net. The goal incredibly stood. As though he was making amends for his sin, several minutes later Maradona embarked on a 60-yard jaunt that will be difficult to duplicate. He meandered through 6 English players before finally sliding the ball past goalkeeper Peter Shilton.

Argentina won the World Cup, and Maradona was proclaimed the new Pele. He demanded top dollar. With that money he staged a $1-million dollar wedding for himself and wife Claudia, chartering a 747 to bring hundreds of his closest friends to Buenos Aires. Where did he get the money to pay for such extravagant excesses? From his performance on the field. Maradona once earned $250,000 for an exhibition game in Saudi Arabia to celebrate a Saudi prince's birthday—that came to $2,777 a minute; he scored twice in that match.

But it seemingly has been mostly uphill since 1990. There was a mediocre performance with an injured ankle and a sub-par Argentine team at Italia '90. After leading Napoli to its first Italian First Division title in 1987, there was the 15-month suspension after failing a drug test in March, 1991. There was the transfer to Sevilla (Spain) and finally the move to Newell's Old Boys in Argentina in October, 1993.

Maradona has 31 goals in 98 international appearances.

Lothar Matthaeus
Defender, Germany

If Germany is to win a second consecutive World Cup, then its spotty defense must be stabilized. The man in the spotlight was the heart and captain of the 1990 championship team—Lothar Matthaeus, who was moved from midfield to the backline. The jury is still out whether this grand experiment of coach Berti Vogts will work. One of 2 active players who was named to an all-time World Cup team in December, 1993—Argentina's Diego Maradona was the other—Matthaeus turned out to be one of the big stars of Italia '90, finishing with 4 goals. Regardless what transpires at USA '94, Matthaeus, who turned 33 on March 21, has established himself in soccer history as the most capped player in German history (104), surpassing former German great and coach Franz Beckenbauer in a 2–1 victory over Brazil on Nov. 17, 1993. Matthaeus also has earned European and World Soccer Player of the Year Awards in 1990 and was selected as FIFA World Player of the Year in 1991, thanks to his skill, thundering shot and ability to change pace. Matthaeus, who has played for Borussia Moenchengladbach and Bayern Munich (Germany) and Inter (Italy), has scored 19 times at the international level.

Paul McGrath
Defender, Ireland

McGrath's career is one from which movies of the week are made. He did not play pro soccer until the age of 22, enduring 8 knee operations since then. Despite those two obstacles, McGrath has become the mainstay of the Irish defense as a central defender, after playing several positions, and wound up as England's Player of the Year in 1992–93. Of course, he has to show up for the games first. McGrath has a history of missing important matches, reportedly because of personal problems. He did not turn up for Ireland's World Cup trip to Albania in May, 1993, missed Aston Villa's plane to a pre-season tournament in Tokyo and missed the team bus for Villa's F.A. Cup match against Exeter on Jan. 8, 1994. McGrath, who was born in England, was discovered by Manchester United while playing for St. Patrick's Athletic in the League of Ireland in 1982. He stayed with United until 1989, when he was transferred to Villa for $600,000. He was an integral part of Ireland's march to the quarterfinals at Italia '90, anchoring a defense that allowed only 3 goals in 6 matches. McGrath, who has scored 7 goals in 63 international appearances, is strong, an excellent header and has made a career of heading off potentially dangerous situations before they could turn into trouble.

Romario
Forward, Brazil

The sometimes moody, always dangerous Romario has emerged as Brazil's most lethal weapon. He has connected for 20 goals in only 46 international appearances through November 24, including 2 in the 2–0 victory over Uruguay that clinched a World Cup berth on Sept. 19, 1993. It was his first national team appearance in almost a year. Romario's weakness is his mouth. He likes to speak his mind and do what he wants, which has landed him in many a coach's doghouse. Still, it is difficult for coaches to ignore the man known as the Brazilian "Maradona" because of his amazing ball skills. "Together with Marco van Basten, they are the most fabulous strikers in the world," Kees Ploegsma, his former coach at PSV Eindhoven (Netherlands) told *The European*. "The only trouble with Romario is that he is a handful for every coach and his fellow players. I know that the manager who can tame him will turn him into an even better player. In fact, he will then be the best footballer in the world." Romario replied to his detractors. "Players always complain about me," he told *The European*. "They moan and groan about the things I don't do, like defending or working hard, and they claim I do not train hard enough. But they don't talk about the good things I do, about all the goals I have scored. I admit I don't train hard. I save my energy for matches. I go on to the pitch to score goals. And so far I have scored against every team, against every country, against every defender in the world." He led all Olympic scorers with 7 goals during the 1988 Summer Games, leading Brazil to the silver medal, losing to the Soviet Union in the final. He also played one match in the 1990 World Cup, for 65 minutes against Scotland. Born on Jan. 29, 1966, Romario transferred from PSV to Barcelona (Spain) for a reported $4 million during the summer of 1993. Despite undergoing an eye operation to reduce pain that was caused by heat, Romario has emerged as one of the top goalscorers.

Julio Salinas
Forward, Spain

Try to figure this one out. Salinas led Spain in qualifying with 7 goals in 8 matches, but has had trouble making the first team with 3-time defending champion Barcelona in the Spanish First Division. Like it or not, Salinas has become a super-sub for the Barcas, coming off the bench to score late goals that lifted the team into ties or victories. The skilled striker sometimes looks awkward (5-foot-11, 180 pounds) when he plays, but has become a lethal finisher. Maybe it's the influence of national coach Javier Clemente. Under Clemente, Salinas netted 25 goals in 92 matches for Atletico Bilbao from 1982–86. Salinas, who was born Sept. 11, 1962, scored 5 goals in 18 appearances in 1992–93.

Hugo Sanchez
Forward, Mexico

There's still some magic left in the old man's legs after all. Sanchez, who started his storied international career as a teenager in the World Cup, plans to end it on the same stage with a last hurrah at USA '94. He made sure ofthat on May 9, 1993, scoring the first goal and setting up the game-winner of Mexico's 2–1 World Cup berth clinching victory over host Canada in Toronto. USA '94 will be Sanchez's third and last World Cup, having played in the 1978 and 1986 tournaments (scoring against eventual fourth-place finisher Belgium in the opening round). "I hope to finish my professional career at the World Cup in 1994," he said. "It is 90 percent probable I will say goodbye to soccer."

He said hello as a 19-year-old in the 1978 World Cup in Argentina, stopped in San Diego for 2 short stints with the North American Soccer League team in 1979 and 1980 before going on to greater fame with Atletico Madrid and Real Madrid, leading the Spanish First Division in scoring for 5 seasons. Sanchez, who has returned to the First Division with Rayo Vallecano after a year with Club America (Mexico), had accumulated 158 goals in 247 league matches.

He has lost a bit since his heyday—Sanchez captured the Golden Boot as the top scorer in Europe in 1989–90 with 34 goals in 38 matches—the 5-foot-7, 150-pound forward still can be one of the most dangerous players on the field. "When you are seven years older, you lose something, but you win something," said U.S. coach Bora Milutinovic, who coached Sanchez on that 1986 Mexican team. "He loses the speed, but he's smarter." Sanchez, who will celebrate his 36th birthday on July 11, 1994, was at his Real Madrid best that Sunday afternoon in Toronto, hardly touching the ball, especially in the early going, but making a difference when he did. After Canada had taken a 1–0 lead, Sanchez slotted home David Patino's pass in the 35th minute. He raised his hands in triumph, performed one of his patented somersaults and then ran over to the Mexican fans to continue his celebration. As time was running out and the Canadians pushing up, Sanchez fed Francisco Cruz, who scored on the counterattack with 5 minutes left.

Enzo Scifo
Midfielder, Belgium

Scifo can join an elite group of players, including Pele, Grzegorz Lato, Michel Platini and Karl-Heinz Rummenigge, who have scored at least one goal in 3 consecutive World Cups (2 goals in 1986, 1 goal in 1990). For all he has accomplished by the age of 28—he was born Feb. 19, 1966—Scifo has 2 World Cup games he would like to forget. In a 2−2 opening-round tie with Paraguay in 1986, he apparently had scored a goal off a free kick for a 3−1 advantage late in the match. It was nullified because the call actually was an indirect free kick. Another player had to touch the ball before it went into the net. In Belgium's 1−0 second-round loss to England in 1990, Scifo hit the post twice. The 5-foot-9, 155-pound midfielder can make amends at USA '94. One of the most skilled Belgian players, Scifo was a scoring terror as a young player, connecting for 432 goals in 4 seasons in the La Louviere youth leagues. Scifo, the son of Sicilian parents who emigrated to Belgium in 1957, has played for Anderlecht (Belgium), Bordeaux and Auxerre (France), Inter and Torino (both Italy), before leaving the latter for AS Monaco in the French First Division in 1993. Asked why he left the Italian First Division, considered the best league in the world with packed stadiums and enthusiastic fans, Scifo told *The European*, "All that is not important for me. I want to play for a club where I could develop in the best possible way."

Hristo Stoichkov
Forward, Bulgaria

In 1992, Stoichkov finished second to the Netherlands' Marco van Basten in balloting for the European Footballer of the Year in 1992. He claimed he should have won it. Now, the 28-year-old striker has an opportunity to show the entire world how good he really is in the World Cup. European soccer experts already knew how well Stoichkov could play and how prolific he is, as he is considered to be perhaps the finest player to emerge from Eastern Europe in recent years. He was voted Bulgarian Football Player of the Year for 3 consecutive years from 1990−92 (he scored 38 goals with CSKA in Bulgaria in 1989−90), became only the second soccer player to be named Slavic Sportsman of the Year in 1992 and was a member of Barcelona's 3 successive Spanish First Division championship teams (51 goals in 92 matches). Besides the competitive desire, Stoichkov scores thanks to his speed, excellent shot and his ability to work in tight quarters. The 5-foot-8, 161-pound Stoichkov finished with 5 goals during qualifying.

Carlos Valderrama
Midfielder, Colombia

He is one of those rare players who can change the course of a match with the flick of his foot on the ball. Sometimes it is difficult to realize Valderrama's impact on a game because he seemingly spends most of his time walking around the field. Valderrama, who is known as the South American Gullit, stands out in a crowd because of his unusual hairstyle, which looks like a human fright wig. Ironically, Valderrama was born in Santa Marta, the birthplace of Colombian soccer. The 5-foot-9, 161-pound midfielder started to play at the age of 9, refining his skills on the beaches in northern Colombia. Valderrama, who was on born Sept. 2, 1961, has played for several clubs, including Millonarios and Independiente Medellin in Colombia and Montpellier (France).

Marco van Basten
Forward, Netherlands

Not only is van Basten's participation in the World Cup in jeopardy, but so is his career because of an ankle injury he suffered in December, 1992. Van Basten, who will turn 30 on Oct. 31, 1994, has enjoyed a storied career. Just about the only honor that has eluded him has been a successful World Cup. He endured an abysmal Italia '90, not scoring a goal as the Dutch were eliminated in the second round. At the club level, however, there has been no one more reliable in the past decade at scoring. The 6-foot-2, 176-pound van Basten broke in with Dutch power Ajax Amsterdam and scored 128 league goals, capturing the Golden Boot Award after collecting 37 goals in 26 matches in 1985–86 and adding 31 in 1986–87. He joined A.C. Milan in 1987 and continued his scoring feats for 2 European Cup champion teams (1989 and 1990) in what is the best league in the world—the Italian First Division. Van Basten has scored 87 goals in 136 matches, including a league-high 25 goals in 31 matches in the defensive-oriented league during the 1991–92 season. At the international level, van Basten also has been prolific, emerging as the leading scorer at the European

Championship in 1988 with 5. He has scored 24 goals in 58 international appearances. "Van Basten is the best striker in the world," said former Dutch great Johan Cruyff, who now coaches at Barcelona. "Nobody can compete with his talent, his skill and his goals."

They Won't Be There

In a perfect world, all of the world's top soccer players would play in the World Cup. But this is no perfect world.

Among the stars who will be missing in action because their national teams did not qualify:

The crafty and talented **Roberto Cabanas**, who began his career with the New York Cosmos, would have loved to have ended it back in the U.S. with his Paraguayan teammates. Cabanas, who turned 33 on April 11, 1994, starred in the 1986 World Cup with another former Cosmos teammate, J.C. Romero.

Eric Cantona, known as *Enfant Terrible* and *Le Brat* in France because of his outbursts and controversial dealings with coaches and management, has played for 6 teams in the past 6 seasons. Cantona, an integral part of Manchester United's first English championship in 27 years in 1992–93, reads the game well, has an excellent touch and has formed one of the most lethal international scoring duos with Jean-Pierre Papin.

Paul Gascoigne—Gazza as he is known to English soccer fans—is as dynamic on and off the field. Sometimes it can be feast or famine for this Lazio star, who performs in the Italian First Division. But when the controversial Gazza is on his game—he shows a lot of flair for an English player—he is worth the price of admission and then some.

Ryan Giggs, who only turned 20 in November, 1993, has emerged as the top young Welsh and European player over the past 2 years, as his runs and passes have helped spark Manchester United to the top of the English Premier League.

Jean-Pierre Papin, the other part of the French dynamic duo, is one of the most refined players France has known. He scored 13 goals in a limited role with A.C. Milan (Italy) in 1992–93.

Abedi Pele, who was the African Player of the Year in 1992, has been the mainstay of a Ghanan team that has been among the best in Africa the past several years. In one of the early upsets, however, Ghana was eliminated in the first round of qualifying.

David Platt, who scored the game-winning goal for England in its second-round victory over Belgium at Italia '90, is the flip side of Gascoigne. Platt, who currently stars for Sampdoria (Italy), is one of the most classiest players around.

Robert Prosinecki, who plays for Real Madrid (Spain), has been called the Slavic Maradona. Prosinecki was expected to turn Yugoslavia into one of the more dominant European teams of the nineties, with teammates Zvonimir Boban (A.C. Milan) and Davor Suker (Sevilla, Spain). But because of its breakup and the UN sanctions imposed against the country, Yugoslavia, or what is left of it, cannot compete in the World Cup.

Ian Rush, a key component of Liverpool's great teams since 1980–81 (208 English League goals through the 1992–93 season) probably won't get another chance at a World Cup because of his age. He will turn 33 on Oct. 20, 1994.

Peter Schmeichel, who was the star of Denmark's victory over Germany in the final match of the 1992 European Championship, is regarded as one of the best, if not the best, goalkeeper in the world.

Anthony Yeboah, another member of the star-studded Ghanan team, wound up tied for the scoring lead (20 goals for Eintracht Frankfurt) in the German First Division in 1992–93.

The list goes on and on. There's also Zimbabwe goalkeeper Bruce Grobbelaar, who once played for the Vancouver Whitecaps (North American Soccer League), and must be content to enjoy his glory days with Liverpool (England), the talented Laudrup brothers of Denmark, Brian and Michael, Uruguay's Ruben Sosa and Enzo Francescoli, and England striker Gary Lineker, who has gone on to greater fame and fortune in the new J-League in Japan.

Chapter Seven

How the U.S. Got It

It certainly was an innocuous and curious place—the lobby of a boy's domitory at the Indiana Central University during the National Sports Festival (now called the Olympic Sports Festival) in Indianapolis on July 30, 1982—to announce one's intentions to host the world's greatest sporting spectacle. A sportswriter from the *Rochester [NY] Democrat and Chronicle* put the question to U.S. Soccer Federation President Gene Edwards: How much interest did the USSF have in hosting the World Cup?

While there were rumors of the U.S. putting in a bid to host the 1986 and 1990 World Cups, the federation actually had its sights set toward 1994. The USSF had filed an application to host the 1990 edition, which eventually was awarded to Italy in 1984.

"We did it to show an interest to host it at some time," Edwards said. "We realize it goes back to Europe in 1990. I would say our chances in 1994 would be very good."

Not surprisingly, Edwards's statement did not exactly grab front-page headlines in the U.S. or around the globe because, let's face it, 12 years is a long, long time to plan for something. In these quick-paced days of short attention spans, thanks to videos, the MTV generation and virtual reality, 12 years could be construed as a generation or two.

In the months ahead, the USSF would drift off course from that plan just a bit because an opportunity to host the 1982 cup was dangled in front of the federation. Colombia, which was selected to organize the event when it included 16 teams, dropped out in October, 1982, after failing to overcome problems trying to find enough first-class stadiums for a tournament that was upgraded to 24 teams.

U.S. soccer officials wanted that World Cup badly because professional soccer was faltering and falling fast in the early eighties. The U.S.'s predominant professional league, North American Soccer League, was teetering toward extinction. After boasting as many as 24 teams in 1980, sparked by the presence of Pele in the late seventies, the league had dwindled to 12 teams for 1982 with a rather bleak future staring at it. A number of soccer officials thought the World Cup would give the league a boost and save the sport.

More important international soccer decision-makers, however, had other ideas.

The contenders and pretenders emerged, including Brazil, Mexico, U.S. and Canada. The process turned into an embarrassing fiasco for the United States, which seemed to go out of its way to irritate FIFA—Fédération Internationale de Football Association, world soccer's governing body—virtually every step of the way. At one time or another, the USSF insulted FIFA, demanding that the

---

How to Do It Right
The U.S.'s Success in Securing the World Cup in 1987 and 1988

The bidding process to host the 1994 World Cup was an arduous one. Follow the United States, its opponents and FIFA down the long and winding road:

Jan. 19, 1987 FIFA mails invitations to national associations for the right to host the 1994 World Cup.

Feb. 28 The deadline for interested national associations to notify FIFA of their intentions to host the World Cup.

March 10 FIFA mails the terms of reference to interested national associations.

April 15 The USSF notifies FIFA that it has begun the bid process to host the World Cup, in a letter from USSF President Werner Fricker. Brazil, Chile and Morocco are confirmed as the other candidates.

July 2-5 At the USSF's 71st annual general meeting in Colorado Springs, CO, the organization an-nounces that it has hired Eddie Mahe Jr. and Associates to prepare its World Cup bid. The USSF eventually creates World Cup USA 1994, a subsidiary of the organization that is responsible for the bid.

Sept. 30 USSF Treasurer Paul Stiehl, Rey Post Jr. of Eddie Mahe Jr. and Associates and Jim Trecker, who is serving as World Cup USA 1994's public relations director, deliver the U.S. bid to FIFA at its headquarters in Zurich, Switzerland.

Nov. 5 Chile will drop out of the bidding, *Soccer Week*, a New York City area publication, announces in an exclusive report.

Nov. 12 Chile drops out, saying its candidature was viable only in the event Brazil did not pursue its application.

Nov. 19 U.S. President Ronald Reagan meets FIFA President Dr. Joao Havelange, FIFA General

organization fly over an inspection team to look at its stadiums, making ridiculous threats, wailing about every decision that FIFA ruled against it and claiming that an agreement between FIFA and Mexico was made in secret.

"FIFA is run a bit like a country club," said Clive Toye, the former New York Cosmos general manager who signed Pele in 1975. "They have to get to know you before you're accepted . . . If you're going to join a club, you abide by the club's rules. When you become president, you can change them. But you don't change them by stand-

(How to Do cont.)

Secretary Joseph S. Blatter and Fricker in the Oval Office at the White House.

Dec. 10–12 Fricker and the U.S. delegation host FIFA executive committee members at a reception in Zurich, Switzerland, during the qualifying draw for the 1990 World Cup in Italy.

Jan. 19, 1988 Stiehl is named director of World Cup USA 1994, Inc.

Feb. 29 World Cup USA 1994 announces the creation of its 94-member Founders Club. Miami Dolphin's owner Joe Robbie is named Founders Club chairman.

March 3 FIFA announces that it has changed its decision date from June 30 to July 4, U.S. Independence Day, making some soccer observers feel the U.S. has the nod. "There's no significance," USSF spokesman Thom Meredith says. "It's just an administrative thing. Octavio Pinto Guimaraes, Brazilian Soccer Confederation president responds. "The United States applying to stage a world soccer cup is the same as Brazil vying to host a world baseball championship. It would not make any sense."

March 21 A World Cup Advisory Committee is formed by World Cup USA 1994. Former U.S. Secretary of State Henry A. Kissinger is named chairman.

April 10–18—FIFA's 5-man technical inspection group visits 16 stadiums in 13 cities in the U.S. The FIFA officials, who included Horst Schmidt of West Germany, Walter Gagg, head of FIFA's technical department, Guido Tognoni, FIFA's press officer, Ernie Walker, secretary of the Scottish Football Association, and Augustin Dominguez, secretary of the Spanish Football Association.

May 19–20 Stiehl meets with FIFA officials in Zurich to talk about television rights and contractual agreements that have already been made.

July 4 The U.S. is awarded the 1994 World Cup after a vote by the FIFA executive committee in Zurich, Switzerland. The tally: U.S. 10; Morocco 7; Brazil 2.

ing outside the door, kicking at it, and then spitting in the eye of the man who opens it."

In other words, you don't mess around with FIFA if you want to play international soccer. At last count, FIFA's membership had reached 168 members, including a number of emerging nations so small that each could be put in Rhode Island's back pocket. Based in Zurich, Switzerland—the country of ultimate neutrality—FIFA is one of the most powerful sports organizations, in the world.

"Violence, political and racial reasons have bothered or damaged other sports," FIFA General Secretary Joseph (Sepp) Blatter said. "Since 1972, there have been problems in the Olympic Games. We have not had such problems in FIFA. There never has been a boycott."

If FIFA were the United Nations, there would be no, or few, wars. All battles and arguments would be settled on the soccer field. If a country does not like a FIFA decision, it could quit the organization and sacrifice playing the sport on the international level. "We have power—that's important; respect and power," states FIFA Press Officer Guido Tognoni.

How much respect and power?

In 1973, the Soviet Union refused to play Chile in a World Cup qualifying match because of political reasons. The Soviets were fined $50,000 and Chile was awarded a forfeit. Had it been the UN, the Soviets might have gotten away without paying their dues.

"Nobody must play football in FIFA," Blatter said. "If they want to play association football, they must abide. It's like you're in a family. You respect the rules of the family or leave the family."

The family was started officially on May 21, 1904, when representatives of 7 countries—France, Belgium, the Netherlands, Spain, Sweden, Switzerland and Denmark—met in Paris. A number of statues were laid down and FIFA was formed. Robert Guerin, secretary of the French Football Department, was elected the first president, serving for two years. In 1932, FIFA moved to Switzerland.

England joined the family in 1905, followed by Italy (1906) and the United States (1913), among others.

Despite being a member for 70 years, the U.S. felt, at times, as if it were on the other side of the window looking in, and the Americans would do anything to become one of the boys. So, it was rather surprising that in 1983, the U.S. did not help itself one iota by presenting a flimsy, 92-page bid with color photos and access routes to the proposed stadium. The USSF did estimate a conservative ticket revenue of $42 million, more than twice what Spain took in 1982, according to Werner Fricker, USSF vice president and World Cup committee chairman. It all looked nice, but FIFA wanted some substance with that style. And there were no governmental guarantees that Mexico had managed to get in on time.

"Sure we can blame FIFA,"said Guy DiVencenzo, USSF treasurer and member of the organization's World Cup executive committee. "Let's face it, we blew it ourselves . . . I think the sloppy handling of it helped make it easier for FIFA to say no.

"The application we presented to FIFA on March 11 was frivolous, glossy, and transparent, and probably deserved the treatment it received. We proved that FIFA was correct in describing our application as 'superficial' when we sent a supplement on May 12. It was like taking a test in school, failing, and then asking the teacher if we could try again."

FIFA, worrying about putting the Cup in what was essentially a non-soccer country, started to favor Mexico, which had staged the event in 1970. Brazil? It had dropped out because of severe financial problems. Canada never was taken very seriously (there was talks of the U.S. and Canada putting together a joint bid, but FIFA would never go for countries as co-hosts).

Edwards, the USSF president, tried to put the fiasco into perspective. "In retrospect, what would have happened if we got it," said Edwards after the rejection "We could have easily messed it up."

In retrospect, it certainly appears it turned out for the best.

"FIFA is looking for us [to host the World Cup]," Edwards said. "Yes, it [Soccer] is popular, but it has competition here [from other sports]. In other countries, it's a way of life and a religion. Although we have the biggest stadiums and the best press, parking and medical facilities, there are none laid out just for soccer. There was a question of whether a baseball team would give up a month or six weeks during the middle of their season opener to soccer. They [FIFA] feel it's a little premature at this time.

"Put everything aside, the pros and cons. On deadline, we did not include the government guarantees [of visas and foreign exchange, for example] and stadium guarantees. It did not meet a requirement. It had to be for everybody. Mexico did it."

On May 20, 1983, in Stockholm, Sweden, FIFA announced Mexico as the home country to the 1986 World Cup. "Mexico is a real soccer country," said Dr. Joao Havelange, FIFA president. "The United States and Canada are not ready for such a competition."

Not only did the U.S. not get the opportunity to host the 1986

World Cup, it could not qualify, further solidifying FIFA's reasoning.

First, the struggling NASL went belly up after the 1984 season. Ironically, the Americans were eliminated from the qualifying competition exactly a year to the day to the start of Mexico '86 in a 1–0 loss to Costa Rica in Torrance, CA. on May 31, 1985.

But the seeds that the great Pele planted had started to sprout hundreds of thousands of children playing soccer in the most unlikely of places—suburbia. Finally, a substantial base was being established from which to build. But as organizers discovered the hard way, players did not necessarily mean fannies in the seats. There was an audience from which to build that was not associated with its tradi-

How To Do It Wrong: The U.S.'s Failure in 1983

Oct. 25, 1982 Colombia drops out as host, citing ecomonic problems.

Dec. 31 The USSF announces it will make a bid for the World Cup.

Jan. 20, 1983 Team America, which is expected to house many of the national team players, is formed. Werner Fricker, USSF vice president, says the announcement is "not intended to be a message or a signal to FIFA." Fricker says he expects FIFA to note "we have taken major steps to be competitive in 1986."

Feb. 15 Economic problems don't rule out Mexico and Brazil as hosts, FIFA general secretary Joseph S. Blatter says.

March 10 Citing economic problems, Brazil drops out of the race. The USSF announces it has made its bid to FIFA. "We feel very confident that after our offer is received, there should be no other choice but us," says Fricker, who adds that the U.S. would double the $20 million gate receipts at the 1982 World Cup in Spain.

March 11 Canada makes its bid.

March 17 Pele endorses the U.S. "Having the 1986 World Cup in the United States would be the best thing for soccer," he said. USSA president Gene Edwards says the U.S.'s chances of hosting the finals have improved.

March 18 FIFA says a special 5-member committee will make inspection visits to the U.S., Canada and Mexico.

March 23 President Ronald Reagan pledges his support to secure the World Cup.

March 25 New York Cosmos defender Franz Beckenbauer, captain of the 1974 West German world champions, endorses the U.S. bid.

March 30 Blatter says the U.S., Canada and Mexico will each receive a cable informing them "if and when" a FIFA inspection team will visit. Blatter's statement leaves open the possibility that FIFA could decide not to

tional ethnic roots (the number broke 1 million in 1984 and is at 2.2 million and counting today in affiliated leagues). However, it would take some time for those roots, despite how plentiful they were, to take hold.

In 1984 the U.S. hosted the Summer Olympics, which included soccer. And in perhaps the most Orwellian of ironic twists, soccer's version of Big Brother—FIFA—was watching. It walked away rather pleased, not just with the quality of play, but also the numbers. Soccer, of all sports, led all others in attendance: 1,421,627 fans—an average of 44,426 per match—showed up for 32 games. Track and field was next at 1,129,463. Total attendance was 5,797,923.

(How To Do It Wrong: cont.) visit one of the candidates.

March 31 FIFA rejects the bids by the U.S. and Canada, claiming insufficient stadiums and tremendous traveling distances contributing to the rejection. "I am truly outraged at FIFA's announcement that they would only consider Mexico . . . without even making inspection tours of the U.S. and Canada," North American Soccer League president Howard Samuels said.

April 1 The USSF sends a strongly worded statement to FIFA, asking for its bid to be reconsidered. "It's unacceptable," Fricker said. Edwards, who doesn't approve of the telegram, objects to the strong language. "You don't throw gasoline on a smoldering fire," he said.

April 2 English officials say that Mexico will be unable to meet FIFA's standards. "With the heat and the current inflation in that country, I feel it could be moved elsewhere, " said Ted Crocker, secretary of the English Football Association.

April 3 FIFA President Dr. Joao Havelange says, "Mexico is a real soccer country; it appears fully capable of staging the Cup."

April 7 FIFA may reverse its decision and reconsider the U.S. as a candidate, says Fricker, who has talked to Blatter by telephone. He adds that the door is open to dispatch a committee to examine U.S. facilities. . . . Henry Kissinger, Pele and Beckenbauer testify before the House of Representatives, asking for support.

April 8 Rep. James J. Florio (D-NJ) believes Congress will act quickly to support the USSF's efforts.

April 15 The USSF says a FIFA delegation will visit the last week in April to review its ability to organize the World Cup.

April 16 Herman Neuberger, head of FIFA's World Cup Committee, says Mexico is more likely to host the tournament than the U.S. or Canada. He adds that

The tournament was encompassing, with 16 teams and not only one stadium or area. Not even the Rose Bowl in Pasadena, CA, could hold all of the teams and matches. So the tournament branched out to Stanford Stadium in Palo Alto, CA to Harvard Stadium in Cambridge, MA, and to the Navy-Marine Corps Memorial Stadium, Annapolis, MD, under the auspices of the soccer commissioner—Los Angeles attorney Alan I. Rothenberg. Remember that name.

While the crowds did not break any records in the East, although they were at or close to capacity level, an amazing story unfolded some 3,000 miles to the west. The tone was set early. In its July 29 opener at Stanford Stadium in Palo Alto, the U.S. won its first Olympic match in 60 years, defeating Costa Rica, 3–0, as 78,265 curious souls watched. On July 31 a crowd of 63,624 at the Rose Bowl watched the U.S. drop

(How To Do It Wrong: cont.)
he has no plans to visit the U.S.

April 21 The Senate Commerce Committee votes unanimously to support the USSF's bid. The panel says the U.S. already is capable of meeting all the requirements expected of the host country . . . FIFA reaffirms its refusal to inspect proposed sites in the U.S.

April 25 FIFA rejects pleas from the U.S. and Canada to inspect proposed sites. Blatter says the decision is final.

April 26 The USSF formally appeals to FIFA for an inspection. "We are simply seeking a fair and equal opportunity for all three candidates . . . to be considered," Fricker said. The House Energy and Commerce Committee votes unanimously to support the bid.

April 27 NASL Commissioner Phil Woosnam, says, contrary to reports, that Havelange assured him that FIFA will inspect U.S. facilities. Blatter, however, claims FIFA won't inspect the sites.

May 1 Kissinger enlists the help of former Secretary of State Cyrus Vance in a final effort to secure the tournament.

May 3 Mexico will host the 1986 World Cup, Havelange says. "The United States and Canada are not yet ready for such a competition," he said. The House of Representatives endorses the USSF's efforts.

May 5 The U.S. World Cup organizing committee says it will send a 10-man delegation to Stockholm, Sweden to state its case to FIFA on May 20.

May 6 Congress adopts a resolution declaring the goverment's support of the USSF's effort to secure the World Cup.

May 20 FIFA awards the 1986 World Cup to Mexico.

a 1-0 decision to Italy. A day later, Brazil edged West Germany 2-1, before 75,249 at Stanford.

The U.S. did not get out of the opening round, yet attendances continued to rise or be impressive. For instance, in the semifinals, France defeated Yugoslavia 4-2, before 97,451 at the Rose Bowl on Aug. 6. Two days later Brazil downed Italy, 2-1, in the other semifinal before "only" 83,642 at Stanford.

There still was room for growth.

On Aug. 10, a consolation match—a rather meaningless affair in soccer history, although a bronze medal was at stake—attracted an incredible 100,374 at the Rose Bowl as Yugoslavia edged Italy, 2-1. That was a hard act to follow, but France and Brazil topped that in a 2-0 gold-medal triumph for the French as 101,799 jammed into the Rose Bowl for that encounter. The record still stands today as the largest crowd in U.S. soccer history. It is not expected to be broken for the 1994 World Cup because as many as 5,000 seats at the Pasadena-based stadium are expected to be used for the media or for security reasons.

Perhaps it was the Olympics or the international lure that accounted for it. The bottom line was that people had watched the matches, and FIFA took notice.

"FIFA and the world of sports were equally surprised: The Olympic Football Tournament surpassed the keenest hopes," Blatter wrote in his organization's official report of the Summer Games.

He was not alone. "All in all, Pasadena was a tremendous success for FIFA, of which they can be justifiably proud, and certainly augurs well for the future of association football in the United States," International Olympic Committee Member Dr. Kevin O'Flanagan reported in the same publication. "One evening well into the competition, I saw president Havelange standing alone . . . with a satisfied smile on his face. It seemed to me he was glowing with inward pride at the success he saw all around him."

Suddenly, the U.S.'s stock as an international organizer of soccer events was on the rise. So were its World Cup aspirations. Because the 1990 Cup was scheduled to return to Europe, hosting that tourney was out of the question, but 1994 was certainly a viable possibility.

In one sense, the U.S.'s chances did not look very promising. There was no true coast-to-coast pro league. On the international level, the U.S. continued to struggle against the medium powers; forget about the superpowers.

Buoyed by optimism, the U.S., along with Brazil, Chile and

Morocco, threw their collective hats into the World Cup ring for a chance to stage the 1994 showcase. The Americans had learned from their mistakes. World Cup USA 1994, a non-profit subsidiary of the U.S. Soccer Federation, was formed in 1987 to prepare the bid and eventually organize the cup.

Instead of a frivolous application, World Cup USA 1994 handed in to FIFA a 381-page document that cost $500,000 to compile. "Phone books," Werner Fricker, who was by that time federation president, liked to call it.

Those phone books encompassed a tremendous number of documents of federal government guarantees, including the government allowing players, coaches and representatives of hostile countries such as Iran and Iraq to obtain visas for the tournament, a selection of 18 stadiums, transportation system (road, train and plane routes and maps), tickets and media and marketing.

"There is a strong desire by FIFA and most people to have the World Cup come to the United States," Fricker said after the application was completed. "A lot of people see the United States as a white spot on the map of soccer in the world. . . . They [FIFA] would very much like to see development in soccer in the United States and to see it grow in a very big way."

Toye, who is now the New York/New Jersey host chairman for World Cup USA 1994, was privy to both the 1986 and 1994 bids. "The big thing this time is the manners care, superb, minute detail, which FIFA wants," he said. "The document is thicker than *Tolstoi's War and Peace* and will put you to sleep a lot faster. It's been approached with greater dignity than arrogance. The U.S. made itself a contender by the professionalism and dignity of its approach."

As it turned out, of the 18 stadiums listed in the application, only 5 are among the 9 venue sites for USA '94: RFK Stadium (55,000) in Washington, D.C.; Soldier Field (66,260) in Chicago; Cotton Bowl (72,000) in Dallas, TX; Rose Bowl (103,553) in Pasadena, CA; and Citrus Bowl (50,843) in Orlando, FL.

The others? In the Northeast region, there was JFK Stadium (90,000) and Franklin Field (61,000) in Philadelphia; Palmer Stadium (45,000) in Princeton, NJ; and the Navy-Marine Corps Memorial Stadium (30,000) in Annapolis, MD. In the Southeast region: Orange Bowl (75,355) in Miami, FL; Joe Robbie Stadium (74,990) in Fort Lauderdale, FL; and Tampa Stadium (74,317) in Tampa FL. In the Midwest region: Arrowhead Stadium (78,065, artificial turf) in Kansas City, MO; and Minnesota Sports Stadium (45,000, under construction;

proposed 1994 capacity: 90,000) in Blaine, MN. And in the West region: Coliseum (92,516) in Los Angeles, CA; Husky Stadium (72,484) in Seattle, WA; Parker Stadium (40,593) in Corvallis, OR and Sam Body Silver Bowl (30,000) in Las Vegas, NV.

The stadium criteria included a grass field, which had to be 115 by 75 yards. The capacities varied, from 30,000–40,000 for opening group matches to 60,000–80,000 for the opening match, semifinals and finals.

On Sept. 30, 3 U.S. representatives—USSF Treasurer Paul Stiehl, who later would become director of World Cup USA, the first of several leaders of that organization, Rey Post Jr. of Eddie Mahe Jr. and Associates, which includes among its clients, the Republican National Committee, which prepared the application, and former Cosmos and NASL Public Relations Director Jim Trecker, who was brought in as a part-time public relations director—flew to FIFA headquarters in Zurich, Switzerland, to present the application to FIFA. The U.S. bid,

At the stately English stadium in Middlesborough, the North Koreans stun the Italians with an upset victory during the first round in 1966.

along with its rivals, was given to the 27-member World Committee of FIFA, which reviewed them. The race for the World Cup was underway.

Over the ensuing months, World Cup USA and the federation would be in constant communication with FIFA, making sure every "i" was dotted at least once and every "t" crossed.

In December, 1987, each of the candidates made a verbal presentation at the qualifying draw for the 1990 World Cup in Italy, with the U.S. presenting a video. Next, FIFA sent a delegation to each of the remaining 3 countries to inspect stadium sites and facilities (the U.S. was inspected from April 10–18, 1988).

In fact, Havelange met with President Reagan in late 1987 in what was called a hopeful summit. Reagan threw his support behind the bid, and Havelange, who hadn't had many nice things to say about U.S. soccer, in general, and the USSF, in particular, over the years, offered some encouraging words. "Holding the championship in this country would clearly be a way of promoting the sport more effectively in this part of the globe," he said.

As for the U.S.' rivals, Chile dropped out early, saying it had taken the chance to ensure South American representation had Brazil not decided to pursue hosting the cup. But Brazil had serious problems of its own. Despite its long, storied history in soccer, the country of Pele's birth and 3 world championship teams had experienced in 1987 and 1988 a seemingly endless list of problems in international soccer. The Brazilian Soccer Federation reportedly was disorganized and so out of touch with contemporary sport that 13 leading teams had threatened to secede from the association and start its own playoffs before a compromise was reached. And on the global level, the Brazilian national teams had accomplished very little to distinguish themselves in recent years. At the Under-16 World Cup in Canada during the summer of 1987, Brazil was eliminated in the opening round without scoring a goal—a humiliating setback—and was ousted by Chile, not exactly a world soccer power, in the first round of Copa America, the South American championships.

Then there was the economic consideration. Brazil owed U.S. banks somewhere in the neighborhood of $10 billion, which many institutions feared they would never see. In addition, Brazil's stadiums were is disrepair and would cost millions of dollar to rebuild or renovate, according to a FIFA source. Building new structures was out of the question, given the country's financial crisis.

And there was the bid itself. The formal written portion was sloppy and in places handwritten. Brazilian officials were also late in arriving for the 1990 World Cup qualifying draw and its December gathering. With FIFA, neatness, punctuality and attendance count.

So does the number of stadiums. While FIFA took Morocco's bid seriously, the emerging soccer country—it became the first Third World and African nation to win its group and qualify for the second round of the World Cup in Mexico in 1986—had only one stadium that met FIFA's standards, a source said. Morocco probably is years away, 2006 at the earliest, before it receives the nod.

So, not surprisingly, there was the feeling that things were going the Americans' way as the bid gained support throughout the world.

"It is important for football to have the World Cup in the United States," said Pele, a Brazilian. "I love Brazil. Everybody knows that Brazil is in a bad financial situation. In the United States, it would be good for the game because it would change in the World Cup. We played in 1970 in Mexico, but soccer doesn't change a thing. If there is a World Cup in Brazil, it doesn't change anything. It [the United States] is something new."

Even FIFA gave some hints. "We cannot all the time choose a football country—soccer country, but we have to promote the game and bring soccer to this country," FIFA Technical Director Walter Gagg said. "And I think bringing soccer to this country, the enthusiasm will come at the same time."

Peter Velappan, a member of FIFA's World Cup Committee, agreed. "I think the time is now right to bring the U.S. soccer group under the wings of FIFA," he said. "I do not know whether it is wise to keep them away until 1998, by which time people get frustrated."

Originally, the day of decision was set for June 30, 1988. But on March 3, FIFA changed it to July 4, U.S. Independence Day, making some soccer observers feel the U.S. was a shoo-in.

The U.S. was hardly a shoo-in. While its bid was solid, there were a number of concerns and minuses. There was a question of whether grass could be placed over the artificial turf football fields. There was no strong, national pro league. There was the question if the USSF could find a television network or networks, possibly a cable concern, to originate a strong signal for not only the games in the states but for the rest of the world.

With all that in mind, the U.S., Brazil and Morocco had one last meeting with the FIFA Executive Committee at the Movenpick Hotel in Zurich the morning of July 4. Finally, at 1:21 P.M. that day—7:21

A.M. EST—FIFA Executive Vice President Harry Cavan announced that the U.S. would host the 1994 World Cup.

The final tally of the vote, though a secret, card ballot was the U.S. 10, Morocco 7 and Brazil 2. Most of the U.S. support came from the officials from Europe and CONCACAF (Confederation of North, Central American and Caribbean Association Federations), of which the U.S. is a member. Morocco received 6 votes from the African and Asian members of the committee, and 1 from Europe. Brazil received 1 to 2 votes from its South American colleagues. (Two Brazilians on the committee—Havelange and Abilio D'Almedia—declined to vote so there would be no conflict of interest.)

Cavan, who chaired the executive committee meeting, tried to measure the World Cup's impact on soccer in the U.S.

Countdown to the Big Announcement

So what exactly happened on July 4, 1988, the day the United States was awarded the World Cup in Zurich, Switzerland? A blow-by-blow account of the key moments:

9 A.M. The FIFA Executive Committee begins its session in the Regulus Room at the Movenpick Hotel. The committee holds a draw to determine the order of the final presentations. Three egg shells are placed in an oversized brandy sifter. The order: Brazil, Morocco and the U.S.

The committee also outlines the procedure it will follow through the next 4 hours. "We stuck fairly rigidly to it," says FIFA senior vice president Harry Cavan, who chaired the meeting. FIFA President Dr. Joao Havelange, a Brazilian, does not chair the meeting of vote so that there would be no conflict of interest.

The committee receives a report from the technical committee and takes a break to read it.

10 A.M. The Brazilian delegation, including Brazilian Soccer Confederation President Octavio Pinto Guimares and Confederation Administrator Moacir Peralta, gives its presentation. Each delegation is limited to 30 minutes.

Cavan later says, "We had quite a bit of emotion collectively from all three, least of all from the United States."

The U.S. delegation, Cavan adds, is "very level voiced, very quietly put and very effectively put."

10:40 A.M. The Moroccan delegation, including Minister of Sport Abdellatif Semlali, meets the committee.

Semlali says that he urged FIFA to continue helping the development of soccer in Third World countries. "I tried to prove that the United States does not need such competitions," he says. "They have so many already."

"I think obviously it will have a tremendous development on United States football," he said.

In fact, progress already might have taken place. "I noticed this morning, if I am allowed to repeat something, I noticed the delegation of the United States used the word football," he said. "I was quite happy about that because I have for years been trying to get them to do it."

Added Fricker: "We now have the timetable set for us. We do not have the privilege to say, 'We'll do it someday.' We must do it now.' "

(Countdown to cont.)

11:25A.M. The U.S. delegation is called in and gives a 22-minute presentation, including a 2-minute speech on videotape by President Reagan. The 5 men who meet with the Executive Committee include U.S. Soccer Federation President Werner Fricker, World Cup USA 1994 Director Paul Stiehl, former USSF President Gene Edwards, World Cup USA 1994 Counsel Scott LeTellier and Rey Post of Eddie Mahe Jr. and Associates.

"It was exactly, give or take a minute, how long we thought the presentation would be," Stiehl says. "We didn't want to make it so long that it would have bored everybody to death. At the same time, we couldn't cut it too short.

"We were all very satisfied. It think we were able to optimistically read some of the faces."

1:05P.M. The 3 of the delegations heads, including Fricker, are called into the executive committee meeting, and they are told the news. Fricker, showing no emotion, walks back to the U.S. waiting room, where he slams the door. "He's stone-faced," Stiehl says. "He's very good at that."

Once inside the room, Fricker put his right thumb up to signify victory. (One observer later says that Fricker had such a sour look on his face, it was as though FIFA told him not only won't the U.S. host this World Cup, it will never host one).

Several minutes later, the Brazilian and Moroccan delegations walk over to the U.S. room to congratulate the Americans.

1:21P.M. Before about 100 members of the international media, FIFA president Dr. Joao Havelange lets Cavan make the big announcement.

"After very careful and very responsible consideration of all the information that has been brought to us today," Cavan says, "the executive committee of FIFA has, in a very democratic way, arrived at a conclusion that I am happy to announce on behalf of the president of FIFA, the executive committee of FIFA, the following results.

"It was a card vote, a secret vote. It resulted as follows: Brazil 2, Morocco 7, the United States 10.

There are cheers from the audience.

(Countdown to cont.)

Cavan continues, "I declare on behalf of FIFA that the host country for the 1994 World Cup will be the United States of America."

A number of hours later, several members of the U.S. delegation gathered together in the lobby of the Zurich Hilton. Champagne was passed around, and Fricker lifted his glass in a toast.

"It was very nice to work with a wonderful group of people and thanks for all your support from the people back home," he said. The really hard work was only just beginning.

Chapter Eight

The Great Stadium Chase

When World Cup USA 1994 announced it was taking bids from stadiums for sites on January 9, 1990, there were many doubting Thomases, home abroad, critics snickering in the background that it would be difficult to find 12 venues that were interested or qualified in hosting the games.

Surprise, surprise.

By the time the May 1, 1991, deadline arrived, a total of 27 communities had filed formal bids.

Alan I. Rothenberg, CEO and chairman of World Cup USA 1994, said "remarkable interest exists . . . to host games or events," after the first of a series of tours of propsective venues.

In alphabetical order, the candidates: Atlanta, Boston/Foxboro, Charlotte, Chicago, Columbus, Dallas, Denver, Detroit/Pontiac, Honolulu, Houston, Kansas City, Knoxville, Las Vegas, Los Angeles/Pasadena, Miami, New Haven, New Jersey, New York, New Orleans, Orlando/Kissimmee/St. Cloud, Philadelphia, Phoenix, Portland/Corvallis, San Francisco Bay area (Palo Alto), Seattle, Tampa Bay and Washington, D.C.

The unofficial early line had the Rose Bowl in Los Angeles/Pasadena as one of the obvious favorites not only to host matches, but also to be the site of the opening and final matches. It would be difficult to argue with that reasoning because of its success during the 1984 Olympics. Chicago and Soldier Field, which was to become the new home of the U.S. Soccer Federation in late 1991, was considered another favorite. Dallas, because of its huge youth soccer population and the fact that it was the home of the Dallas Cup, one of the most prestigious youth tournaments in the world, also was placed with the haves.

Florida was bound to get at least one venue. Miami, with state-of-the-art Joe Robbie Stadium, would certainly be a perfect place to play as many as 7 or 8 World Cup matches. In fact, FIFA officials were so enamored of the stadium's facilities, there was serious speculation that the opening or final matches could be played there. Tampa Stadium and the Citrus Bowl in Orlando could be paired with Miami, or used as a backup if Robbie could not be used.

Then there was New York, the financial and media capital of the world. It was an obvious choice for a venue, but there was one slight problem—there was no proper facility in the metropolitan area or in the city.

In the city itself, there were Yankee and Shea stadiums, solid facilities, but baseball parks. FIFA did not want its jewel to be played on a baseball field with players celebrating the winning goal near the pitcher's mound. Somehow, it would not look right to the rest of the world. There was rundown Downing Stadium on Randalls Island, which could hold maybe 20,000 fans, but it had seen better days when the Cosmos first played there in the early seventies. Then there was a desperate, half-cocked plan by local officials to build a temporary stadium and stands on the infield of Aqueduct Raceway in Elmont, Long Island. Fortunately, that idea did not get to the drawing board, let alone off of it.

Across the Hudson River there was a gem of a facility—Giants Stadium—where the Cosmos attracted capacity crowds of 70,000 or more on several occasions during their heyday and where the great Pele closed out his amazing playing career; the place the rest of the world associated with American soccer in the late seventies and early eighties. But there were two slight problems: artificial turf and the width of the field. The stadium missed FIFA's minimum requirements of 75 yards by a mere 7 or 8 yards. One possible solution had FIFA building a platform above the artificial turf, not unlike building a stage for a rock concert. About 5,000 seats would be lost because the platform would spill into the first 6 rows; but for the players, 10 extra yards of field would be created. About 8 inches of sod and grass would have been placed on the platform, which would be surrounded by dasher boards. The cost was estimated at $3 million, which would be paid for by the organizing committees (although with construction costs the way they are in the New York City area, $6 million might have been the final bill, informed sources said).

"It is very pragmatic," FIFA Press Officer Guido Tognoni said. "I'm quite positive we can resolve the technical problems with this stadium."

As it turned out, stadium officials and FIFA did resolve the technical problems, but not by adopting the platform idea.

Some 70 miles to the north, a group calling itself the New York/New Haven Bid Committee had entered the fray with the 70,896-seat Yale Bowl in New Haven, CT. While the Yale Bowl did not need as extensive renovations as Giants Stadium, it needed improvements in several other areas, including media and VIP facilities, concession stands, rest rooms, doping control center, locker rooms and FIFA official offices, Tognoni said. "Today I saw a stadium that needs a makeover," he said after an inspection tour. "Everybody knows it."

Although World Cup officials would not say it publicly, New Haven was a good safety valve if Giants Stadium did not pan out.

Somehow, some way, New York would wind up as part of the mix.

The same could not be said of Honolulu, the first community to place a bid, Knoxville, Charlotte or Las Vegas. They were considered longshots.

The most intriguing bids came from Detroit/Pontiac (Pontiac Silverdome), Kansas City (Arrowhead Stadium), New Jersey/New York (Giants Stadium), New Orleans (Superdome) and Philadelphia (Veterans Stadium). All had artificial turf. No World Cup game—except for a couple of qualifiers between the U.S. and Canada in 1976—had ever been played on artificial turf.

The stadiums in Detroit/Pontiac and New Orleans had taken it a step farther. They all had domes.

Eventually, officials from the Hoosier Dome in Indianapolis and the Tacoma Dome also placed bids.

"It is feasible to grow grass indoors," said Scott LeTellier, the organization's managing director and chief operating officer. "With the right type of lighting, grass will grow very well in a domed stadium."

Not surprisingly, when the announcement of artificial turf and domed stadiums was made during the 1990 World Cup in Florence, Italy, many European sportswriters scoffed at the idea.

"We talk about tradition the way it is played on the pitch, it is completely different from 40 to 50 years ago," U.S. Soccer Federation President Werner Fricker said. "And it has changed for the best, not the worst."

The 8 criteria for selection included stadium, civic/government support for the cup, local soccer interest, population, geography, community infrastructure, space availability for a main press center, and miscellaneous items such as climate and legal aspects.

The selection process took more than 2 years to complete, starting with the Jan. 9, 1990, announcement that venue specification packages be sent to the prospective venue communities, with the final announcement scheduled for New York City on March 23, 1992.

Inbetween those two dates, were several stadium tours, a trip to Italy, lots of planning and plenty of speculation from the media.

A trip to Italy? That's right—to Italia '90 to see how the 1990 World Cup functioned inside the stadiums and out. Most of the delegations were made up of city officials, community soccer leaders and coaches and some unusual personalities—former Dallas Cowboys coach Tom Landry, who was a member of the Dallas delegation. A total of 205 people flew over to see what the World Cup was all about.

Grass Experiment Has a Silver(dome) Lining

Pontiac, MI. The grand experiment got a green thumb's up from soccer officials and players.

The real star of Germany's 2–1 victory over England in the U.S. Cup '93 finale on June 19 was not the teams or players, but rather the grass field that was placed over the artificial turf in the Silverdome. It was the first match—domestic or international—that was played under such conditions. And, it received good grades.

"It was one of the best football pitches that we could have had," FIFA Technical Director Walter Gagg said. "The top grass was of good quality. For the players, there were no problems to control the ball or to drive the ball."

FIFA Senior Press Officer Guido Tognoni also was pleased. "If every pitch in the world were like this one, we would never have a problem," he said. "It was a little question mark because it was a unique event and an experiment, but the grass was even better than expected. There is no question now.

"The main thing is how even it is. You could play golf on it . . . If nobody steals the grass in the winter, we'll have four great games next year."

German striker Juergen Klinsmann, who was named Cup MVP (Most Valuable Player) after scoring the winning goal, said no one had any problems with the turf. "The field and grass were perfect," he said. "We never expected such perfect conditions."

German coach Berti Vogts, who a day before the match called the field "a miracle," reiterated his feelings afterwards. "The pitch is perfect, and this is something like a stadium of the future. It has everything."

Everything that a player needs and wants. "This field behaves like any other grass pitch I've played on," German forward Karlheinz Riedle added.

A weeding-out process was needed. Before its final selection tour from Oct. 29 to Nov. 9, World Cup USA 1994 named 19 priority venues it was going to visit. The lucky 19: Atlanta (Bobby Dodd Stadium, 45,000), Boston/Foxboro (Foxboro Stadium, 61,000), Chicago (Soldier Field, 66,814), Columbus (Ohio Stadium, 86, 071), Dallas (Cotton Bowl, 72,000), Denver (Mile High Stadium, 76,123), Detroit/Pontiac (Pontiac Silverdome, 72,794), East Rutherford, NJ (Giants Stadium, 76,891), Kansas City (Arrowhead Stadium, 78,065), Los Angeles/Pasadena (Memorial Coliseum, 92,000 and Rose Bowl, 104,091), Miami/South Florida (Joe Robbie, 73,000 and Orange Bowl, 75,500), New Haven (Yale Bowl, 70,896), New Orleans (Superdome,

(Grass Experiment cont.)

Two days later, the U.S. Women's National Team and its Canadian counterparts played a second match on the grass under the dome and the grass still was in superb condition.

"The field was beautiful," U.S. goalkeeper Saskia Webber said after a 3–0 American victory. "It was better than I expected. It was soft, not dry and very easy to play on. It will be a great field for the World Cup."

The field, which consisted of 1,988 pieces of sod (in modules) installed at a cost of about $1 million, was removed and preserved for 4 games for the 1994 World Cup.

The grass, 65 percent Kentucky bluegrass and 35 percent perennial ryegrass, was developed at Michigan State University by Trey Rogers, assistant professor of crop and soil sciences at the school. A 6,500-square foot "Silverdome West" was built at the school with the same kind of Teflon dome to use as a research facility. The grass was grown in southern Californian and trucked here three months before the U.S. Cup. It was installed a week before the match and was mowed and brushed daily.

"Me and my co-workers have put our heart and soul and blood into this," Rogers said. "We've put our personal lives on hold. It's like our baby is going in for testing."

After the game, the modules were reassembled in the stadium parking lot, repaired and then maintained in a special nearby facility for the Cup. Similar grass will be used over the artificial turf at Giants Stadium.

"A few years ago, you wouldn't think it was possible," English captain David Platt said. "It was just like playing on a normal grass field. "The ball held up a little, but I think that was because it was very dry."

Speaking of dry, ironically, a thunderstorm hit the area during the game, but no one under the dome noticed.

73,000), Orlando/Kissimmee/St. Cloud (Citrus Bowl, 70,500), Philadelphia (Veterans Stadium, 61,000), San Francisco Bay (Candlestick Park, 61,000 and Stanford Stadium, 86,019), Seattle (Husky Stadium, 72,000), Tampa (Tampa Stadium, 74,317) and Washington, D.C. (RFK Stadium, 57,000).

"The fact we had . . . [so many] communities come forward with applications for games demonstrates the depth of commitment that soccer enjoys in the United States," Rothenberg said. "Needless to say, we had to make some very difficult and painful decisions in the process.

"I wish there was some way we could stage a World Cup in 26 cities because everybody was really wonderful. It's amazing that merely a year and a half ago there were skeptics who were saying we

---

(Grass Experiment cont.)

If there was a downside, it was the humidity in the building, which hovered at 92 percent. Mixed with 78-degree temperatures inside the dome, life was uncomfortable for some spectators, if not the players, at times.

"It was humid and not easy to play," Klinsmann said.

Gagg admitted that the humidity was the only major problem encountered, but added, "there was much more humidity in Washington than here."

There were a few divots during the match, but no patches of turf were dug up. The divots were repaired with sand dressing. "The field came out in as good a shape as we expected," Rogers said.

On Friday, June 25, the grass was placed on trucks bound for a turf farm in Ventura, CA, where it will grow and strengthen until spring 1994. Then it will be brought back here for 4 first-round matches—June 18, 22, 24 and 28.

And if the grass holds up, domed stadiums could very well become the wave of the future, especially in the colder climates of northern Europe. Japanese soccer officials have also inquired about domed stadiums with grass.

"We wanted to leave some sort of indelible American touch to the World Cup, a piece of American ingenuity, and maybe this is it," said U.S. Cup Press Officer Jim Trecker, who is in a similar capacity as a vice president with World Cup USA 1994. "Not only did we think it could be done, we proved it can be done. This was not just an international football match, it was a moment with some potentially considerable historical importance for the game."

Only time will tell.

wouldn't even get eight qualified bidders to host the World Cup. The United, as always, has shown those doubters to be wrong."

To facilitate the inspection process, the tour was broken into two groups—northern and southern.

The northern group included Augustin Dominguez of Spain, former secretary general of Real Madrid and of the Spanish Football Federation; Guido Tognoni of Switzerland, the FIFA media officer and press director; Hugo Salcedo of Los Angeles, a former U.S. Olympic player who has served FIFA in various capacities; and Guillermo J. Canedo of Mexico, the FIFA World Cup organizing committee's deputy chairman, who could not make the first three inspection dates because of commitments in his native country. The tour started on Oct. 29 in Philadelphia and continued through East Rutherford, NJ (Giants Stadium), New Haven, Boston/Foxboro, Chicago, Detroit/Pontiac, Columbus, Seattle and ended in San Francisco.

FIFA Vice President Hermann Neuberger of Germany, President of the FIFA World Cup organizing committee Walter Gagg of Switzerland, FIFA Technical Director Horst Schmidt of Germany and Wolfgang Niersbach of Germany comprised the southern delegation. That tour encompassed 9 sites, starting on Oct. 29, with Washington, D.C., with stops in Atlanta, Miami/South Florida, Orlando, New Orleans, Dallas, Kansas City, Denver and Los Angeles/Pasadena.

Officials said all the right things, never a negative word about any of the venues. For example, when the northern delegation visited Giants Stadium: "I cannot figure that the image of the U.S. would be the same without New York," Tognoni said. "FIFA would be very happy if we could include the New York area in the program. We will be missing something if we do not include New York.

"Our President Dr. Havelange and General Secretary Sepp Blatter have told the organizing committee we want very much to play in New York. We're very convinced that soccer's revival in this country has to start in New York."

The average tour at each stadium lasted from two to two and a half hours. The inspectors rated the facilities (fields, locker rooms and press box) from 1 to 10, with 10 being the highest rating. After touring a stadium they met with Tognoni to compare notes. Salcedo's most important criteria? There were the field dimentions, dressing rooms, security for the players, medical doping control and comfort for the fans. "We have to make sure we look at everything to give it the proper perspective," he said.

At the end of the tour, on Nov. 7, the two groups met and debriefed in Los Angeles. Final recommendations were made.

"I don't want to be at the local organizing committee when they announce the seven that didn't make it," Salcedo said. "It will be difficult because there will be seven disappointed communities."

In late November, 1991, World Cup officials started to figure that the World Cup might not necessarily be cheaper by the dozen. Organizers started to consider the possibility of using 8 venues instead of 12 to save in the neighborhood of $50 million.

Depending on who you believed, the U.S. had either climbed out of its months of recession, or it was still mired in it. The bottom line was that many regions of the country were still hurting economically.

Costs of preparing stadiums for soccer and returning them to their original condition and of providing telephone and broadcasting linkages might be prohibitive, even for the organizing committees.

"None of us wants to do that [8 venues]," Rothenberg said. "Unlike other World Cups, we don't have government support or a rich uncle. We have to be fiscally prudent."

There was concern that 8 venues could hinder the exposure of soccer, which has struggled to find acceptance in the States. Remember, the World Cup was supposed to broaden soccer's appeal in the U.S.

"We would love to use 12 venues if we can," Rothenberg said. "The purpose of the World Cup is to sell the excitement of the sport."

Finally, on March 23, 1992, Rothenberg, with 9 sealed envelopes in hand, made the announcement at the Hotel Waldorf-Astoria in New York City. The winners: New York/New Jersey, Orlando, Washington, D.C., Boston/Foxboro, Detroit/Pontiac, Chicago, Los Angeles/Pasadena, San Francisco and Dallas.

At a later date, the 9 were divided into 3 groups of 3—New York/New Jersey, Washington, D.C. and Orlando in one group, Boston, Chicago, Dallas in another, and Los Angeles, San Francisco and Detroit/Pontiac in the third.

"Some of the bids were outstanding," Rothenberg said. "I wish we could have had more venues."

There were a number of surprises. Giants Stadium did get the nod, as FIFA moved back its width requirements several yards to accommodate New York City.

"For FIFA, it was a must to play in New York," Blatter said. "We could not bring the World Cup to the United States and not play in New York."

In an unconventional move in contrast to its conservative image for the first time, FIFA selected an indoor stadium—the Silverdome. "This is an innovation that shows so-called conservative FIFA has some open-minded spirit," Blatter said.

If successful, indoor grass stadiums could be the wave of the future, Rothenberg said. "I can't read FIFA's mind, but if it works, it could be a solution where weather isn't good in the northern parts of Europe," he said.

In perhaps the closest call, Orlando won out over Tampa and Miami as the Florida site. Miami, with Robbie Stadium, lost out when an expansion baseball team—the Florida Marlins—was named to play at the stadium, starting in 1993.

The tournament was divided into 6 groups of 4 teams each. Two groups were assigned to each 3-city cluster. For example, if Italy was seeded at Giants Stadium, it would play 2 matches there and 1 game in Washington, D.C. Traditionally, seeded teams would play all their matches at the same stadium. But as we have discovered, the 1994 World Cup does not seem as if it will be a traditional World Cup.

So, what do we know about these 9 stadiums?

LOS ANGELES/PASADENA
Rose Bowl
Capacity: 102,083
Field dimensions: 115.6 by 75.3 yards
Schedule: First round: June 18, 19, 22, 26; Second round: July 3; Semfinal. July 13; Third-place match: July 16; Final: July 17.
If it hadn't been for the 1984 Olympics, the U.S. probably would not have gotten a decent shot to host the 1994 World Cup. The Rose Bowl was in the middle of the excitement during the tournament, as it attracted 3 crowds of more than 97,000, including 100,374 for the bronze-medal game and 101,799 for the gold-medal match. The stadium, built in 1922, is located about 7 miles from downtown Los Angeles.

Los Angeles has hosted a number of tournaments, particularly teams with Hispanic backgrounds and Mexican Clubs.

SAN FRANCISCO/PALO ALTO
Stanford Stadium
Capacity: 86,019
Field dimensions: 115.6 by 75 yards
Schedule: First round: June 20, 24, 26, 28; Second round: July 4;
Quarterfinal: July 10.
Stanford Stadium pulled in some impressive numbers during the 1984 Olympics, including a near-capacity 83,642 for the semifinal match. It also was the site of the largest crowd to watch the U.S. National Team in the U.S.—61,132 in a 3–1 loss to the Soviet Union on Feb. 24, 1990.

The stadium is located in Palo Alto, 27 miles south of San Francisco.

DETROIT/PONTIAC
Pontiac Silverdome
Capacity: 72,794
Field dimensions: 112 by 72 yards
Schedule: First round: June 18, 22, 24, 28.
In one of its most daring moves ever, FIFA decided to play with a roof over its head. Since then, it has been proven that grass can be grown and sustained indoors, during U.S. Cup '93, when tournament champion Germany defeated England, 2–1, on June 17. There were no problems reported with the turf.

The stadium, opened in 1978, is located in Pontiac, Michigan, 18 miles northwest of Detroit.

CHICAGO
Soldier Field
Capacity: 66,814
Field dimensions: 115 by 75 yards
Schedule: First round: June 17, 21, 26, 27; Second round: July 2.
Chicago, which is headquarters of the U.S. Soccer Federation, has a long, storied soccer history, from the amateurs to the professional ranks. It was the home to the Chicago Sting, perennial contenders and champions of the North American Soccer League in 1991.

The stadium is located on the shores of Lake Michigan.

BOSTON/FOXBORO
Foxboro Stadium
Capacity: 61,000
Field dimensions: 115 by 75 yards
Schedule: First round: June 21, 23, 25, 30; Second round: July 5;
Quarterfinal: July 9.

With New York and Philadelphia, Boston is considered the cradle of soccer in the U.S., producing a number of legendary stars from the Portuguese communities of the Fall River and New Bedford areas. More recently, Harvard Stadium hosted first-round matches of the 1984 Olympics to near-capacity crowds, and Foxboro Stadium has been the site of 2 important games—the U.S. 1–1 tie with Ireland that attracted 54,743 in 1991 and the Americans' 2–0 upset of England on June 9, 1993.

The stadium, built in 1970, is located halfway between Boston, MA and Providence, RI.

DALLAS
Cotton Bowl
Capacity: 72,000
Field dimensions: 115 by 75 yards.
Schedule: First round: June 17, 21, 27, 30; Second round: July 3;
Quarterfinal: July 9.

The Cotton Bowl, which is more accustomed to American football, will be the focal point of another brand of football for a month—soccer. The city also annually hosts the Dallas Cup, one of the most prestigious youth soccer tournaments.

The Cotton Bowl, built in 1930, is located in Dallas' historic Fair Park.

NEW YORK/NEW JERSEY (East Rutherford)
Giants Stadium
Capacity: 76,891
Field dimensions: 112 by 72 yards.
Schedule: First round: June 18, 23, 25, 28; Second round: July 5;
Quarterfinal: July 10; Semifinal: July 13.

When you talk of pro soccer in the U.S., you think immediately of Giants Stadium, home of the world-renowned New York Cosmos, who dominated the North American Soccer League from 1977 to 1984. It attracted several capacity crowds, including 77,691 for a playoff game in 1977 and 77,002 for Pele's farewell game in October, 1977, although officials later admitted more than 80,000 fans packed the stadium (they did not list that as the official attendance because of fire laws). New York, because of its ethnic diversity and population, has one of the most storied soccer histories in the country.

The stadium, located 10 miles from New York City, was built in 1976.

WASHINGTON, D.C.

RFK Stadium

Capacity: 56,500

Field dimensions: 115 by 75 yards

Schedule: First round: June 19, 20, 28, 29; Second round: July 2. Can there be a World Cup without the nation's capital? The smallest of the 9 stadiums, which precludes it from hosting later-round matches, was the home to the Washington Diplomats (NASL) and Johan Cruyff and the 1980 Soccer Bowl between the New York Cosmos and Fort Lauderdale Strikers, which drew 50,768. The Washington area is another region that has a long soccer legacy.

The stadium, built in 1961, is located about 20 blocks east of the Capitol.

ORLANDO

Florida Citrus Bowl

Capacity: 70,188

Field dimensions: 115 by 75 yards

Schedule: First round: June 19, 24, 25, 29; Second round: July 4. The Citrus Bowl is a relative newcomer to international soccer, but it is situated in the middle of the entertainment capital of the world, which includes Walt Disney World, Universal Studios and Sea World. The bowl hosted the U.S. National Team games against Australia and Russia in 1992 and 1993, respectively, and was scheduled to be the site of at least one other international match in 1994.

The stadium, built in 1976, is located 1 mile west of downtown Orlando.

Chapter Nine

A Few Precious Moments in Soccer's Promised Land

Depending on your point of view, the United States' participation in the World Cup—qualifying and the finals—has been either fabulous or abysmal.

If you are a died-in-the-wool optimist, there is the semifinal finish in the very first World Cup in 1930 and the incredible upset of England in 1950.

If you are a pessimist—some people might call it a realist in this case—the team has performed miserably, particularly in the qualifying rounds. The U.S. has participated in 4 World Cups—1930, 1934, 1950 and 1990.

Let's face it. Getting there has been the problem. Once the U.S. reaches soccer's promised land, the Americans have had a way of winding up in the middle of some important soccer history.

The headline in the July 21, 1930, edition of *The New York Times* said it all: "U.S. Favorite to Win World's Soccer Title."

That was no misprint. Thanks to its 2 opening round victories, the Americans had qualified for the semifinals and had been given a fighting chance to take home the Jules Rimet Trophy. They didn't, dropping a 6–1 decision to Argentina, and, as it turned out, that was the closest they had come to winning the competition.

Because the first World Cup was a new tournament—only 13 teams made it to Uruguay because of the long boat ride across the Atlantic Ocean from Europe to South America—the Americans had their best chance to win the cup.

In what started an ill-advised tradition that, unfortunately, has been followed for too many years to mention, the U.S. picked its squad through 3 tryouts. By the time the team was ready to board the *S.S. Munargo* for a 14-day voyage to parts south, coach Robert Millar had assembled his team that included representation from New York (goalkeeper Jimmy Douglas, defender George Moorehouse, mid-

A Promising Start
(1930)

fielder James Gallagher, forward James Brown); Providence, RI (midfielder Andrew Auld); New Bedford, MA (forwards Thomas Florie and Arnie Oliver); Fall River, MA (forwards Bert Patenaude and Bill Gonsalves); and Philadelphia (James Gentle), and St. Louis (Frank Vaughn and midfielder Raphael Tracey); Cleveland (Michael Bookie) and Detroit (defender Alexander Wood and Bart McGhee).

The team, nicknamed the "Shot-putters" by the French because of the large size of several players, left for Uruguay without having played together, another ill-advised tradition that was to be followed through some lean years.

Perhaps the worst part of the experience was the journey—a 14-day boat ride from Hoboken, NJ to South America. Many team members succumbed to seasickness.

The team arrived in Montevideo on July 1, 12 days before its first match, so the players had plenty of time to acclimate to the less-than-favorable weather conditions. It had rained almost every day for the past 3 months and there was a touch of snow on the day of the opening match. The U.S. team marched into Central Park, home of Nacional F.C., singing the *Stein Stong*, the theme song of entertainer Rudy Vallee, who might be best known for his rendition of *Westminster Cathedral.*

Now, that pre-game ritual should have been followed down through the years because the U.S. recorded a 3–0 victory over Belgium as McGhee, Florie and Patenaude scored on a field that had countless pools of water before an encouraging crowd of 10,000,

It was almost more of the same in the second contest, a 3–0 triumph over Paraguay that clinched the Group 4 title before only 800 people on July 17. Patenaude, a 21-year-old French-Canadian born in Massachussets, was credited with 2 goals, midfielder Gonsalves—was credited with accidentally knocking the ball into his own net. Had it counted, Patenaude would have recorded the first World Cup hat-trick.

That also meant the Americans had qualified for the semifinals and a chance to take on Argentina. It never was a match, as the Argentines used a short-passing game to win 6–1 before 80,000 at Centenary Stadium. Actually, the U.S. had made a game of it in the opening 45 minutes, winding up with a 1–0 halftime deficit on a goal by Luis Monti. But there were problems, major problems. Although he did not realize it at the time, Tracey had broken his leg 10 minutes into the match. Douglas came up lame in the nets, and just about everything collapsed in the second half.

"We played 10 players against 11," said Oliver, a Hall of Famer

who passed away in October, 1993. "That's like the Red Sox paying without a shortstop or centerfielder."

Also not helping matters was the huge field—100 by 138 yards. "We never played on such a wide field before," said Brown, the only living member of the 1930 team. "It affected our game. We couldn't play our style of wing-to-wing passes and our crosses from the wing to the center kept falling short."

Uruguay takes 1–0 lead on Pablo Dorado's goal in its 4–2 win over Argentina in the first World Cup final in 1930

Single elimination (1934)

Imagine traveling 4,000 miles to play an elimination game before the start of the tournament, losing and having to turn around and go home the next day. That's what happened to Mexico. The U.S., behind Buff Donelli's 4 goals, registered a 4−2 triumph over the Mexicans in Rome.

The U.S. had not put in its entry until after the qualifying groups had been drawn up. So, it was decided that the Americans would play the winner of Group 1—Mexico (which prevailed over Cuba and Haiti). That type of decision-making would not be tolerated by FIFA today.

As it turned out, it would be the last time the U.S. would defeat Mexico in World Cup qualifying competition for 46 years, or until a 2−1 triumph in Fort Lauderdale, FL, on Nov. 23, 1980, which broke a 15-game winless streak.

As it turned out, politics reared its ugly head on the U.S. squad, as the New England and St. Louis players had wanted to keep Donelli out of the lineup. Gonsalves went to coach Elmer Schroeder and said, "If you don't play Donelli, I'm not playing," Gonsalves was quoted in *U.S. Soccer vs. The World.*

But like Mexico, the U.S.'s stay was too short and bittersweet as the Italians, heavily favored to win the World Cup, rolled to a 7−1 victory in the single-elimination first round. Monti, who scored the first goal for Argentina in the 1930 semis, came back to haunt the U.S. on the Italian side, limiting Donelli to a goal.

"Monti! I can still see him, he was on top of me," Donelli said in *U.S. Soccer vs. The World.* "You know, because I scored four goals against Mexico, Monti would not let me alone."

A No-Show (1938)

Because of the tense political storm clouds over Europe at the time, the U.S. decided not to attend the tournament in France, the only time it did not attempt to qualify.

The Great Upset (1950)

Perhaps *Soccer Week* said it best in 1989: "In a galaxy far, far away, a long time ago . . . the United States qualified for a World Cup."

The story referred to the last time before the 1990 World Cup that the Americans had actually qualified on the field for the finals—in 1950.

That team included midfielder Walter Bahr, defender Harry Keough and forward Joe Gaetjens, among others, who would go on to make some history in the World Cup.

"We were a jovial, outgoing group," said U.S. Soccer Hall of Famer Jack Hynes, a forward on the team that qualified. "We had a lot of fun. We had no regrets, that's for sure. We went night-clubbing a lot."

They also found time to play soccer, usually for a local factory or steel mill, or in Hynes' case, the original American Soccer League.

After a 12-year layoff because of World War II, FIFA wanted to re-organize its new international tournament, the World Cup. Brazil was selected as host. The North American-Caribbean area would get 2 berths, and 3 countries were interested—the U.S., Mexico and Cuba. So the U.S. Soccer Federation sent a team to Mexico City to play in a qualifying tournament. It wasn't too much of a big deal, because the United States had appeared in two of the first three World Cups.

"I wasn't fully cognizant of the whole thing," Hynes said. "We played on so many all-star teams in those days, it was like another game or tournament. "We were just going to another country. It wasn't until later on that it hit me."

The team, as was the case in that era, hardly practiced together.

"We did not have a first-class coach," Hynes said. "There was no set way of training. No advice, no technical advice." "Walter Bahr and I led most of the training. We did gymnastics outside the hotel. It was the first time we trained together. It was a farce."

So was the opener against Mexico, a 6–0 victory for the home team before 60,000 fans on Sept. 4, 1949.

"They got a penalty," Hynes remembered. "They didn't take it. They rolled it to the goalie. It was a gesture. I didn't like it . . . We were outclassed, completedly outclassed."

Ten days later, the U.S. played Cuba to a 1–1 tie. On Sept. 18, Mexico rolled to a 6–2 triumph over the U.S.—John Souza and Ben Wattman scored. But the Americans completed the tournament with a 5–2 victory over Cuba on Sept. 21. Pete Matetich (two goals), Frank Wallace, Souza and Bahr found the back of the net.

"The game had some rough play," Hynes said. "It was an indication of how we improved. We finally blossomed."

The Cubans were to play Mexico in a couple of days, yet the U.S. squad was so confident the Mexicans would vanquish the Cubans, it went out to a restaurant in Mexico City called Los Globos and celebrated reaching the World Cup, even though the U.S. had only a 1–2–1 record.

"We were on our way," Hynes said. "We had a victory party."

The U.S. left the country before the match was played, which was a 2–0 Mexican triumph. "We found out about the score after we returned home," Hynes said.

"We accepted it. You didn't have TV. There were no replays. There were no movies [of the game back then]. You're lucky to get pictures of the games."

So the U.S. was off to the World Cup in Brazil. The Americans, mostly amateur players, were seeded in the same group as Spain, England and Chile.

The Americans enjoyed an encouraging start, taking a 1–0 lead on a goal by Gino Pariani and keeping it until the 80th minute before the Spanish burst their bubble with 3 goals in the final 10 minutes in Curtiba.

Next was the English, for whom the Americans had a tremendous amount of respect. The English were playing in their first World Cup. Still, coach Walter Winterbottom had an array of stars to choose from—the team reportedly had been insured by Lloyd's of London for $3 million, a tremendous sum in those days—even if a couple of players here and there were lost to touring teams. Stanley Matthews, arguably the greatest English player, did not start against the U.S. in that June 29 encounter.

"We went into the game hoping to keep the score down," goal-keeper Frank Borghi said. "If we could have held them to five or six goals, we would have called it a moral victory."

"It was like the Yankees losing to an amateur team from Mass-apequa, NY," defender Joe Maca said.

"We were 70–1 underdogs. I should have bet $10 on the game," midfielder Charles Colombo said with a laugh.

The U.S., though, held its own and scored the lone goal in the 37th minute. Gaetjens, now presumed dead as a political prisoner in his native Haiti, headed in a Bahr pass past the English goalkeeper. In Associated Press reports, Ed Souza was credited with the goal.

The English press said that Gaetjens' goal was an accident; that he misjudged the shot and deflected the ball off the top of his head, not his forehead, into the net.

The U.S. team did not buy that.

"I had taken a shot from 25 yards out," Bahr said. "Gaetjens was a highly skilled [player]. He turned my shot to the left-hand post and into the right-hand corner."

Accident or not, the U.S. had an improbable 1–0 lead.

"Now, I thought, they're going to bury us," defender Harry Keough said. "We just woke up a sleeping lion."

It never happened.

Somehow, the Americans managed to hold on, although there

were a number of heart-stopping moments. With 20 minutes remaining, Charles Colombo, the midfielder who wore gloves, made the defensive play of the match when he stopped English great Stan Mortenson from going in alone on Borghi to tie the score. Colombo tackled Mortenson at the edge of the penalty area, and England protested for a penalty kick. Instead, the English were awarded a free kick just outside the area, but nothing came of it.

"I dove headlong and tackled him," Colombo said. "He got a step on me and was going in on goal. If they scored one, they would have scored six. After I had tackled him, the referee, who was Italian, shouted at me, 'Bono, bono, bono,' which means good in Italian. The English thought he was giving me hell."

Afterwards, the English press complained about the field ("narrow, rutted and stony," one journalist reported) and about the 3 non-citizens who performed for the U.S.—Gaetjens, Maca (Belgium) and midfielder Ed McIllveny (Scotland). They were residents of the U.S., and residents allowed to play at the time. Nowadays, a player must be a citizen.

"We never should have of played," Maca said. "At that time, they didn't ask any questions . . . If we hadn't beaten England, no one would have said anything."

The U.S. players were carried off the field by Brazilian fans.

Lost in the afterglow of the upset was the fact that the U.S. dropped a 5–2 decision to Chile 3 days later in Recife (Souza and Pariani had the goals) and was eliminated. So were the English, who lost to Spain, 1–0.

The Lean Years, Part I (1954-1966)

As positive as the 1950 performance and the upset of England had been, soccer did not take off. In fact, the Americans have only just ended a lean period, one that lasted 4 decades and 2 generations.

If there was a constant roadblock in the U.S.'s hopes of reaching a World Cup, it was Mexico. Every time the U.S. tried to qualify, the Mexicans appeared.

Counting the 2 losses in the 1950 qualifying, the U.S. registered a 0–12–3 mark until it managed to topple the Mexicans in a 1982 qualifier, 2–1, in what was an inconsequential match in Fort Lauderdale, FL, in November, 1980. Nine of those matches between the U.S. and Mexico came during this period. Usually the scenario would go like this: The U.S. would struggle against Mexico and gain better results, usually a victory or tie, against an inferior country.

For 1954, for instance, the U.S. dropped a pair of decisions to the Mexicans—4–0 and 3–1—but rebounded with victories over

Haiti—3–2 and 3–0. But because Mexico defeated Haiti, 4–0 and 8–0, Mexico qualified for the World Cup in Switzerland.

It did not help matters that the USSF, then known as the U.S. Soccer Football Association, agreed to play both games in Mexico City in January, 1954, because of climatic reasons. There were more problems. The U.S. team, made up of players not yet citizens, was selected in tryouts in New York and Chicago. But the Mexican Soccer Federation claimed the U.S. had to comply with FIFA rules that required native-born or naturalized citizens play. The team was dismantled.

For the 1958 qualifiers, why bother playing? The U.S. team showed up in Mexico City 2 days before its match, with groups flying in from New York, Chicago and Los Angeles. Not surprisingly, the players had never played together. Mexico pounded the U.S., 6–0.

U.S. soccer officials claimed it would be different in the return match in Los Angeles, and they were correct. The U.S. lost, 7–2, and never did regain its balance, losing as well to Canada, 5–1 and 3–2.

For the 1962 cup, Mexico grabbed a 3–0 lead after 30 minutes and won by the same score in Mexico City, although the U.S. managed to hold Mexico a scoreless tie for a moral victory in Los Angeles.

In preparation for the 1966 competition, the U.S. actually enjoyed a headstart, training for 12 days and 4 matches in Bermuda. Even though the end results were the same, the U.S. made 2 games of it, with a 2–2 draw in Los Angeles before Mexico bounced back in its capital 5 days later, with a 2–0 win. The Americans were still alive, but could not sweep Honduras, winning the first encounter, 1–0 and tying the second, 1–1.

The Lean Years, Part II (1970-1982)

Finally, there was no Mexico to stand in the way of the U.S. The Mexicans hosted the 1970 tournament, so there could be no excuses this time because there was much more and better preparation. There were, however, only more frustrating losses.

After splitting with Canada—losing the opener, 4–2, but winning the return trip in Atlanta, 1–0—the U.S. had few problems with Bermuda, with 6–2 and 2–0 victories. But Haiti became this qualifying run's nemesis, winning twice, 2–0 and 1–0.

The Americans' No. 1 nemesis returned for the 1974 cup. After missed opportunities with Canada—a 3–2 defeat in St. John's, Canada and a 2–2 tie in Baltimore—the U.S. stumbled to a 3–1 loss in Mexico City, followed by a 2–1 defeat in Los Angeles, and another seat on the sidelines.

It was more of the same for the 1978 World Cup in Argentina, only the torture lasted 5 games. This time the U.S. got off to a

promising start, tying Canada in Vancouver on Sept. 24, 1976, 1–1, and Mexico in Los Angeles, on Oct. 3. In Puebla, Mexico, the Americans fell, 3–0, but they rebounded with a historic 2–0 victory over Canada in the Kingdome in Seattle—the first time a World Cup qualifier was played indoors and on artificial turf. Because the U.S. and Canada were tied, a special tie-breaker was played in Port-au-Prince, Haiti on Dec. 22, with the Canadians emerging victorious, 3–0.

Walter Chyzowych, the coach of the U.S. team, remembered how poor the conditions were in Mexico in his 1982 book, *The World Cup*.

"The bus that was to take us to the training round arrived one hour late," he wrote. "Upon arriving at the field, the gate was locked, and the players were forced to climb the wall. The team had a 35-minute workout

West German goalkeeper Toni Schumacher watches a diving header by striker Paola Rossi sail into the net in Italy's 3–1 victory in the title match of the 1982 World Cup.

before darkness set in—hardly enough. We were told the game would be played at noon the next day. Prior to departure, the kickoff time was changed to 3 P.M. Upon arriving at the stadium at 1:30 P.M., the Canadian referee, in a rush, informed us that we had 30 minutes to prepare for kickoff, which was apparently now at 2 P.M. After a frantic dressing and taping scene in the American locker room, the team made the official kickoff time without a warmup and was down 2–0 within 20 minutes."

For the 1982 World Cup in Spain, the number of berths were increased from 16 to 24, so CONCACAF would get 2 instead of 1. So, the U.S. would finally qualify, right? Wrong.

Could there be even more disappointment? There sure was, with a scoreless tie and 2–1 victory with Canada. But the U.S. was trounced, 5–1, in Mexico City before that 2–1 U.S. triumph over the Mexicans in Fort Lauderdale. By then, it was too little and too late, as Mexico advanced to the next round. Ironically, even though favored Mexico did not reach Spain, finishing third behind Honduras and El Salvador, there was some justice, only the U.S. did not mete it out.

No Mexico, but still no cigar (1986)

After failing miserably in its attempt to host the 1986 World Cup, the U.S. thought it got a break when Mexico was awarded the tournament—no Mexico in the qualifiers.

However, there was only one berth left for CONCACAF, so the U.S. wound up struggling again against Caribbean and Central American teams.

In fact, only 4 days after qualifying began, the North American Soccer League unknowingly had played its last game. The Chicago Sting defeated the Toronto Blizzard, 3–2, on Oct. 3, 1984. Several months later, with a number of teams dropping out, the NASL folded.

This time, the U.S. had a year's worth of preparation as Team America, which supposedly had the country's best native-born and naturalized citizens, played as a team based out of Washington, D.C. in the NASL. Not surprisingly, not every team wanted to give up its top Americans, and some of the players themselves did not want to leave their club teams. On paper, it was a great idea. On the field, it was something else altogether.

Team America started out 8–5, but collapsed to finish at 10–20. Still, the concept was a bold move. "No country has ever placed its national team in a professional league," USSF President Gene Edwards said. "It will serve as an important first step towards making the United States a viable force in international competition."

Its coach was Alketas (Alkis) Panagoulias, an outspoken and

controversial gentleman who most recently had directed Olympiakos of the Greek First Division and was a former coach of the Greek National Team. Moreover, he had coaching experience in the U.S., directing N.Y. Greek-American of the then-German American Soccer League to 3 consecutive U.S. Open Challenge Cup titles in 1967, 1968 and 1969.

"We're not that far away—really," Edwards said. "We have to walk before we can run. Building a strong program takes time. It takes patience."

The latest attempt to reach the World Cup started off on a promising note with a scoreless tie in Curaco, the Netherlands Antilles, on Sept. 29, 1984, before rolling to a 4–0 victory in St. Louis as Ade Coker connected twice and Earhardt Kapp and Angelo DiBernardo once apiece. That set up a round-robin, home-and-home series with Trinidad & Tobago and Costa Rica in the spring.

Because of several restrictions, the U.S. was forced to play those 4 final matches over a 16-day period, a rather unhealthy situation for World Cup qualifying.

Those restrictions?

"The most important goal of my career," Pele said of his game winning (1–0) first goal in World Cup competition against a very tough Welsh defense.

- There were players still competing in the Major Indoor Soccer League—defenders Gregg Thompson and Mike Jeffries with the Minnesota Strikers and goalkeeper Jim Gorsek, defender Kevin Crow and midfielders Jacques Ladouceur and Jean Willrich with the San Diego Sockers.
- There were players still going to school—defender Paul Caligiuri had to return to UCLA to take final exams.
- And there also were players trying to earn a living outside of league play. Defender Jeff Durgan was in New Jersey, giving soccer clinics. Goalkeeper Winston DuBose was in Tampa, working as a salesman.

"It is frustrating because I'm not getting the players," Panagoulias said. "Being on the other side of the world [he coached in Greece, including the National Team for 10 years], and seeing the potential [in the U.S.] makes me upset and mad. Everybody keeps telling me that this is America and we have to live with American standards.

"That's why I'm very outspoken for everyone. That's what the national coach has to do, sometimes be outspoken. We deserve a better place in international soccer."

Despite those obstacles, the first 3 results were rather positive. The U.S. stopped Trinidad in St. Louis, 2–1, on a goal by Mark Peterson with 100 seconds left (Chico Borja scored the first goal) on May 15, 1985, edged Trinidad, 1–0, on Caligiuri's goal—remember that name—in Torrance, CA, 4 days later, and played Costa Rica to a 1–1 draw in San Jose, Costa Rica behind a John Kerr tally on May 26.

Those results placed the U.S. atop the group with a 2–0–1 record and 5 points, a point ahead of Costa Rica (1–0–2, 4) setting up a confrontation in Torrance on May 31, exactly a year to the day of the start of the World Cup.

The U.S. needed only a tie. It got only more frustrating in a match that could have been played in Costa Rica because the crowd of 11,800 at El Camino College was mostly Hispanic and rooted for the visitors.

Still, the Americans played hard, creating a number of scoring opportunities, but the Costa Ricans cashed in on one of theirs—on a goal by Evaristo Coronado in the 35th minute and wound up with a 1–0 victory and qualification to the final round with Canada and Honduras (Canada wound up qualifying for the cup).

It turned out to be a lucky goal. Jorge Chevez sent a free kick into the penalty area that goalkeeper Arnie Mausser tried to punch away. A

Costa Rican player, however, headed the ball to the right side, where Coronado knocked it into the net at 34:50.

"The goalkeeper misjudged the distance," Panagoulias said. "He wanted to punch the ball. He should have caught the ball."

U.S. captain Rick Davis appeared to be devastated by the defeat. For a good half hour afterward, he sat at his locker with his head down.

"We can't play much better than that," he said. "It's a shame. It wasn't supposed to end this way . . . We were playing for U.S. soccer—for its reputation and recognition in our country. It's another setback. We missed a golden opportunity."

Added defender Dan Canter: "It's a disaster. To stumble like this, there are no excuses."

Panagoulias offered none. "Costa Rica beat us because of tradition," he said. "We outplayed them, but they did what they had to do. They scored on a break. They stalled. They played hard. They did everything they had to do.

"This is one of the most frustrating days in my life. The boys played their hearts out. I'm frustrated, very frustrated . . . We created so many chances. The team deserved to win."

For the ninth consecutive time, the U.S. failed to reach soccer's promised land, and although it looked rather dark for soccer in the United States, there was some light at the end of the tunnel, even if the other side of the tunnel looked light years away.

Consider possible irony.

Only 40 days after the United States qualified for the 1994 World Cup as host of the event, it faced elimination from the 1990 competition.

The U.S., which automatically secured a berth in the 1994 World Cup when it was named host by FIFA on July 4, 1988, needed a victory over Jamaica in St. Louis on Aug. 13 to advance to the final round of 5 teams. The top 2 teams from that round would gain a berth at Italia '90.

After the Americans played host Jamaica to a scoreless tie in Kingston in the first leg of the home-and-home series on July 24, a tie other than a 0–0 result would bounce the U.S. (in FIFA qualifying, away goals were counted double if the total goals were tied).

"The whole world is looking at us now because we are the host team," U.S. defender Brian Bliss said. "The pressure definitely has increased. Before, we were not expected to win a game. Now everybody is looking at us to be a dominant team, at least in the CONCACAF region."

Finally . . . (1990)

With that added pressure, the U.S. scored 4 goals in the second half to break a 1–1 tie to record a 5–1 victory over the Jamaicans.

"This was the most important game we've played so far," said forward Frank Klopas, who led the way with 2 goals. "If we lose the game, there is no international soccer in the United States for the next 3 years."

And it would have given the country's critics another valid reason to ask for the competiton to be moved from the U.S. But Bliss, Klopas and their teammates made sure that was not going to happen. After Bliss had given the U.S. a 1–0 lead in the 18th minute, the Jamaicans equalized off a goal by Alton Sterling in the 54th minute.

Was the U.S. facing elimination? Maybe.

Some 14 minutes later came the play that changed the direction of the match when midfielder Hugo Perez, who came on for the ailing Mike Windischmann at the half, was tripped in the penalty area by defender Dave Brooks. It looked like Perez added some acting of his own to accentuate the call, but it was ruled a penalty kick by Canadian referee David Brummit.

"Hugo might have gotten a 9.8 on that one, but it was definitely a penalty," U.S. Coach Lothar Osiander said.

There was no monkeying around on the penalty kick as Perez decisively booted it to the right of goalkeeper Paul Campbell for a 2–1 lead.

"The ball goes in, that's it. They're finished," Davis said. "They were a completely different team."

The U.S. was not finished. In the 76th minute, Klopas converted a short pass from substitute Bruce Murray, who needed to be taken to Chicago the night before the match for a new passport (passports are used as means of identification at World Cup qualifying matches). Murray's old passport was just that—old—and he needed a new one for the game, under FIFA regulations.

It was a good thing Murray was there, because 2 minutes later he crossed the ball to Paul Krumpe, who headed it in for a 3-goal advantage. Klopas closed out the scoring with his second goal in the 86th minute.

"I am very delighted that we won," Osiander said. "For us, it means we can continue. I am totally confident that we will make the last two teams of the competition. It means in the future we will have a competitive team in 1994."

The victory propelled the Americans into the final round along with Costa Rica, Trinidad & Tobago, Guatemala and El Salvador. Of that group, only the U.S. and El Salvador had participated in the World Cup.

The top 2 teams would qualify for Italia '90, and Mexico wasn't part of the final group. Ironically, only a day before the U.S. had been awarded the 1994 tournament, Mexico was banned from international soccer—including the World Cup—for two years.

If soccer observers did not know any better, it appeared FIFA was giving the U.S. a red carpet to the 1990 World Cup, although at times, it seemed that the U.S. was about to have the carpet pulled out from under it.

During the winter, the U.S. Soccer Federation, looking for a fulltime coach, named Bob Gansler as the new National Team coach on Jan. 16. Gansler, 47, at the time of his appointment, was the coach of the U.S. Under-20 team that was about to participate in the FIFA U-20 World Championships in Saudi Arabia, coach at the University of Wisconsin-Milwaukee and a staff coach with the USSF since 1975.

"It's going to be a heck of a challenge," Gansler said. "I think I'm looking forward to it."

Osiander, who was the maitre d' at a San Francisco restaurant, would not quit his job. Because of coaching instability at the international level, Osiander realized he probably would be out of a fulltime job; he remained as a USSF staff coach and wound up as the 1992 Olympic coach. He did the right thing.

The players might not have been as sure about that, because there was a lot of apprehension from the very beginning when Gansler met with the senior players on the team at a week-long training camp at the University of California-Irvine. When Davis, the U.S. captain, was asked about the players' reaction to Gansler's appointment, Davis replied: "First of all, right up front, the questions for Gansler have not been answered yet . . . I think the players approached our only opportunity with him with a certain amount of apprehension."

Gansler and the U.S. got off on the wrong foot on April 16, dropping a 1–0 decision to Costa Rica in San Jose, Costa Rica. Midfielder Gilberto Rhoden scored the only goal 14 minutes into the match before 26,271 at Estadio National.

"We didn't play that well," U.S. Captain Windischmann said. "There are really no excuses to be made."

Exactly 2 weeks later, the Americans exacted their revenge in a 1–0 victory at the St. Louis Soccer Park in Fenton, MO, but it was not without its drama.

First, they waited until the 72nd minute to score—midfielder Tab

Ramos fired a shot from just outside the top of the penalty area that glanced off a defender's foot and into the corner of the net.

Second, Costa Rica had 2 apparent goals, both shot by midfielder Hector Marchena, called back by Honduran referee Rodolfo Meija Martinez. In the eighth minute, one of Marchena's goals was called back because of an offside call, and in the 77th minute, his diving header was disallowed because of a handball.

And with time running out in the match, U.S. goalkeeper David Vanole raced off his goal line to meet a cross and let the ball slip through his hands. Defender Steve Trittschuh, covering Vanole's back on the goal line, stopped the resulting shot by Alvaro Solano with his hands and a penalty kick was whistled.

Vanole, benched in the San Jose match, tried his best to disrupt the penalty-kick shooter, defender Mauricio Montero. He walked up and stood in front of Montero before the Costa Rican took the shot.

Montero's poor attempt was hit straight on, and Vanole did not have to move too far to block in, sending the overflow crowd of 8,500 into a frenzy.

"I tried to psyche the guy, but he wouldn't look at me, and maybe his not looking meant I had him," Vanole said. "I felt I knew exactly what he'd do, and the ball came at me like a pumpkin. It was huge. It was probably coming at me at hundred miles an hour, but it was in slow motion to me."

A funny thing happened to the Americans in what they thought was going to be a 1–0 victory over Trinidad & Tobago on May 13; they gave up the tying goal in the waning minutes, a goal that almost came back to haunt them. Instead of walking away with 2 points, the Americans had to split them with their rivals from the Caribbean.

The U.S. was clinging to a 1–0 lead behind a goal by Trittschuh with 2 minutes left. U.S. forward Peter Vermes cleared the ball into the Trinidad half of the field. Trinidad's Brian Williams took control and knocked a long pass toward Hudson Charles, who ran into open space, drawing Trittschuh with him.

Two players raced for the ball—Windischmann with an out-stretched foot and Trinidad forward Marlon Morris, who got there first to head it gently to Charles. He had only Vanole to beat. No last-minute heroics this time.

"We kind of had a letdown," Trittschuh said. "I don't know why. We weren't tired, but I could feel us letting down."

It was still early and the U.S. got an opportunity to redeem itself against Guatemala in New Britain, CT, on June 17—a 2–1 victory behind goals by Eric Eichmann and Murray.

"You could say it was huge," said Vanole, explaining the importance of the match. "I think even if we had tied this game, it would have been disappointing."

The victory left the U.S. with a 2–1–1 record and in second place in the tournament. Costa Rica (3–2–1; 7) led, with Guatemala (1–2; 2), Trinidad & Tobago (0–2–1; 1) and El Salvador (0–0–0; 0) trailing.

Next up was El Salvador on July 9.

"It's going to be like hell going down to El Salvador in July," Murray said. Or so everyone thought.

The Americans' match in El Salvador was postponed until Sept. 17, to be played at a neutral site in Tegucigalpa, Honduras, because unruly fans had stopped El Salvador's qualifier on June 25 with Costa Rica, which enjoyed a 4–2 advantage with 6 minutes remaining. Fans from the capacity crowd of 50,000 threw fruits, bottles and pennants onto the field to protest their team's poor performance.

Due to the postponement, Gansler was able to experiment with the lineup and decided to use 20-year-old Tony Meola, a University of Virginia sophomore who had acquitted himself well in the Marlboro Cup, an exhibition tournament, against the Peru National Team and Benfica (Portugal). Meola, who eventually captured the Hermann Trophy as college soccer's top player in 1989, split his time between the National Team and Virginia, helping the Cavaliers to a share of the NCAA Division I championship with Santa Clara in December, 1989.

Meola, an excellent ballhandler for a goalkeeper, could not, however, give the U.S.A. a needed lift offensively. The Americans did manage to get by El Salvador, 1–0, on a free kick by Perez.

The U.S. could not have planned a worse time for a scoring drought, playing host Guatemala on Oct. 8 and El Salvador at the St. Louis Soccer Park on Nov. 5 to back-to-back scoreless ties.

On Oct. 8, the U.S. outplayed Guatemala and had several serious scoring opportunities, but had trouble putting them away.

"Our Achilles' heel showed again," Gansler said. "We had difficulty putting it in."

The U.S. (3–1–2; 8) remained in third place behind Costa Rica (5–2–1; 11), which clinched a berth with the result, and Trinidad & Tobago 3–1–3; 9).

"It feels like a loss," said Murray, who had 2 of the best scoring chances for the U.S. during a 5-second span in the first half, but goalkeeper Ricardo Piccinini made a pair of bang-bang saves on point-blank shots. "I'm just disappointed. We came down to get two points and we didn't get them. We're going to need them for the stretch run."

Meola agreed. "I'm as depressed as if we lost," he said. "The most depressing thing about it was we have an incentive for Italia '90, they didn't."

For a team eliminated in September and rebuilt within the ensuing couple of weeks, Guatemala (1–4–1; 3) acquitted itself quite well. There wasn't much local interest in this match, as one newspaper headlined the game *"Futbol de la consolacion"*—consolation soccer.

Although ticket prices were as low as 80 cents, $2 and $3.20, a crowd of only 4,723 turned up at the 45,000-seat Estadio Nacional Mateo Flores that featured a field better suited for growing rice than playing soccer because of torrential rain during the past several weeks.

It was more of the same against El Salvador at the St. Louis Soccer Park on Nov. 5. El Salvador, which had been eliminated, brought in what was an experimental team, but played the Americans to a scoreless tie.

So, that set up THE GAME—the deciding match in Port of Spain, Trinidad, on Nov. 19.

"It's a very big game," Trittschuh said at the time. "The whole nation is on our shoulders. If we qualify, the next four years will be big. There is pressure on us. We know what to do.

"The whole world doesn't have a lot of respect for us. If we don't qualify, people will say, 'Why did the U.S. get the cup? There is pressure on us. Nobody talks about it. It's there. You read it in the papers. We know that it is about the future of soccer in this country."

It wasn't going to be easy. The U.S. had not won a World Cup qualifier on the road—not at a neutral site—in more than 21 years, when the Americans defeated Bermuda in Hamilton, 2–0, on Nov. 10, 1968.

Trinidad wasn't about to role over and die.

In fact, they painted the town red for the game after a govenment asked its citizens, especially Port of Spain residents to show their support by reveling in that color, whether it was in clothes, drapes or flags.

Calypso ballads also were composed, singing the praises of coach Everett Cumming, who once played for the New York Cosmos, of the team, and even of the 88th-minute goal that Trinidad scored to secure that 1–1 tie back on May 13.

Osvaldo Ardiles eludes Dutch players Johan Nesskens (ground) and Robbie Rensenbrink during Argentina's 3–1 extratime victory in the 1978 champion-ship encounter.

"When the Yankees come to the stadium, we're going to beat them like bongs," said one of the songs composed by a musician called Super Blue.

"It's soccer madness," said Mervyn Wells, managing editor of Trinidad Express. "It [the country] hasn't been keyed up like this for anything at all."

The madness was for football, as it is known in this tiny Caribbean country, which needed only a tie to become the smallest country—1.2 million population—to reach Italia '90.

"That's what all the people are talking about in the streets, nothing else," Wells said. "They're wondering how they're getting a ticket, what team they're going to put on the field, who's going to be put on the sidelines."

On Sunday, National Stadium was a sea of red, as an overflowing crowd of more than 30,000 word red as popular calypso stars sang songs about the road to the World Cup two hours before the kickoff. Fans arrived six hours before the match to make sure they would get a seat.

Everything was geared for a Trinidad tie or victory, but someone forgot to tell the U.S.

It was far from a beautifully played game. It started slow and eventually picked up steam.

The U.S.'s unlikely hero was Caligiuri, a surprise starter and defensive midfielder who had not started an important international in more than a year—or since the 1988 Olympics. Gansler decided to start Caligiuri instead of John Stollmeyer, a midfielder with strong ties to Trinidad—his father was born there and his great uncles were world-class cricket players there—who had not missed a minute in the seven previous qualifying matches. "I felt his quickness was better suited for [Russell] Latapy and [Dwight] Yorke," Gansler said of the two dangerous Trinidad midfielders.

Caligiuri made the most of his opportunity 31 minutes into a scoreless tie. He gathered in the ball about 30 yards on the left side from the Trinidad goal, took a step or two and then lofted a 25-yard shot that hooked into the right side and into the net past goalkeeper Michael Maurice. It was only Caligiuri's second goal in 24 international appearances—both against Trinidad. His first came in May, 1985, the lone score of a 1–0 U.S. World Cup qualifying win that helped eliminate Trinidad from that competition.

The same thing happened this time as the Americans held on for a 1–0 victory.

"This game will have a tremendous impact on the sport in the United States," Caligiuri said in a locker room that was part New Year's Eve and part Mardi Gras. "It was the single most important game we ever won. It proves to the rest of the world we can play and we can qualify. We all knew what was on the line for the future of soccer in the United States."

He received little argument from his comrades.

Before he opened the locker room to the media, U.S. coach Bob Gansler told his troops, "Now we've gotten where we want to go, now we can dream a little bit."

When they were not drinking or spilling champagne over each other and chanting, "USA, USA," or "Italia '90," Caligiuri's teammates and U.S. soccer officials talked about the victory's significance.

"I'm especially pleased that the team went out there and did the job," U.S. Soccer Federation President Werner Fricker said. "We needed it very badly. It was most important. Had the U.S. not won today, some of the players would have not gotten another chance."

Some of the players put it more succinctly. "It's the greatest feeling in the world," Windischmann said. "It's just an awesome feeling."

Added Murray: "I'm sky-high right now. It's been a long, hard grind."

Walter Bahr, who set up Joe Gaetjens' goal in the 1950 shocker over England, was on the sidelines when Caligiuri scored his. "Our goal was a well-kept secret," Bahr said. "The World Cup has grown so much in stature since 1950 that this was big for U.S. soccer. That goal will be heard around the world and in the States."

Next stop was Rome, Italy, for the World Cup draw on Dec. 9, when the U.S. discovered its 3 foes: host Italy and two fairly solid European sides—Czechoslovakia and Austria. British bookmakers made the Americans as 500–1 longshots to win the cup.

"The idea, of course, is to look to qualify for the second round," Gansler said. "History tells us that three points got four teams into the second round the last time and two points got two of the four teams into the second round. Somewhere between that we're going to have to set our goals."

On the way to Italia '90, Gansler made 2 possible blunders by not including 2 key U.S. players on the squad—Hugo Perez, who had been the center of the attack, but he was recovering from a broken leg, and one-time team captain Davis, who was healthy.

There was talk, serious talk, that Gansler did not want the influence of Davis on the team because the younger players—the U.S.'s average age was 24.2, the lowest of the 24 finalists—would go to him before they would go to the coach. Gansler said that wasn't the case, that he had to pick the 22 best players he felt could help the team.

Very little went right against Czechoslovakia, a plodding team, in its opening match on June 10. Quite simply, it was men against boys. The game ended nothing short of a complete disaster against a team that was expected to struggle to reach the second round. The Americans' 5–1 loss to the Czechs exposed their every weakness to the world: They were slow. They lacked a physical presence. And they showed their inexperience in the way of soccer savvy.

They were outshot, 23–7. They gave up 2 goals off corner kicks, another from the penalty spot. They also had a player ejected. One of the few bright spots was Caligiuri, who defied the experts and odds-makers by scoring a goal for the U.S.

Believe it or not, it could have been worse, much worse. The Czechs seemingly fired at will at the U.S. goal and Meola had to save a penalty kick in the 89th minute to save any further embarrassment before 32,226 at Estadio Communale in Florence.

In other words, it was a game to forget.

"It wasn't like you wanted to swap jerseys and put it on the wall with 5–1 written on it," U.S. substitute forward Chris Sullivan said. "You could call it a team's biggest nightmare."

Gansler's spin on the match? "Obviously, our inexperience showed in a number of facets of the game," he said. "I thought we started reasonably well with a measure of confidence. But we gave up a couple of soft goals. I think we will have the determination to regroup and do well in our next game."

The Czechs probed the American defense for soft spots and weaknesses in the early going. Finally, in the 25th minute, the Czechs went into high gear when midfielder Lubos Kubik raced through the U.S. midfield, past defender Stollmeyer on the left side and crossed the ball to Tomas Skuhravy, who surged into the penalty area to beat Meola from just about the penalty spot.

They continued to attack, and the U.S. continued to make mistakes. Trittschuh's inability to clear the ball in the area led to the second goal. Windischmann, the sweeper, got possession of the ball and then lost it to Ivan Hasek, whom he tripped while reaching for the ball. On the ensuing penalty kick, Meola guessed correctly, diving to his right, but Michel Bilek still powered it into the upper corner for a 2-goal advantage.

It went from bad to worse.

In the 51st minute, Hasek headed home Frantisek Straka's corner kick from the near post while U.S. defenders played statues, standing around and watching.

Two minutes later, midfielder Eric Wynalda was given a red card for retaliating against midfielder Lubomir Moravcik, who had stepped on his foot, and became the first U.S. player to be ejected from a World Cup match.

"It's called paying your dues," Gansler said. "Eric got baited. No. 11 stepped on his foot and he pushed back. And a lot of times the first foul is not seen. It's a matter of inexperience."

Despite playing a man down, Caligiuri raced down the right wing, eluded a couple of defenders, and pulled goalkeeper Jan Stejskal out of the net to score from 12 yards in the 61st minute. It was the U.S.'s first World Cup goal since John Souza scored in a 5–2 loss to Chile in Recife, Brazil, on July 2, 1950.

"At 3–0, you have to take risks," Caligiuri said.

The Czechs were not finished. Skuhravy headed in his second goal, this time from 3 yards in the 79th minute, and substitute Milan Luhovy closed out the scoring in the 92nd minute, 2 minutes into injury time.

Sandwiched between those 2 goals was a penalty kick awarded after midfielder John Harkes tripped a player in the box. Again Bilek took the kick, trying to embarrass the U.S. by blooping it into the upper-right corner. Again, Meola guessed correctly, this time catching it in mid air.

"I had a feeling he was going to try to beat me with something tricky," Meola said.

Several minutes later, referee Kurt Roethlisberger of Switzerland mercifully whistled an end to the rout.

"The most frustrating thing is we made all the oddsmakers look like kings," Meola said. "This team doesn't deserve that."

With that result in mind, it looked like the U.S. was going to be fed to the lions (Italy) in Rome, but the Americans had some ideas of their own, managing to turn the pro-Italian crowd against the home team on June 14. The Americans' conservative tactics had the partisan crowd of 73,423 at Stadio Olympico whistling their displeasure in the early going. By the final whistle of Italy's 1–0 victory, however, the crowd still was whistling, but against the Italians' disappointing performance and poor finishing.

"They wouldn't let us play," Italian captain and defender Giuseppe Bergomi said. "They stayed in their half. They added a defender. It was difficult for us to do anything."

The Italians struck first—on a goal by Giuseppe Giannini in the 12th minute after he broke through the American defense and past Harkes and Windischmann.

The U.S. did have one chance at destiny—in the 68th minute—after Meola saved Gianluca Vialli's penalty kick in the 34th minute, when midfielder Riccardo Ferri was slapped with a yellow card for elbowing Murray 22 yards from the net. On the free kick, Murray fired a shot that goalkeeper Walter Zenga dived to his right to knock away. The ball came to Peter Vermes, who blasted a shot that Zenga saved. This time the ball squirted loose and was bounding toward an open net before Ferri barely cleared it.

"I tried to put it high," Vermes said. "I think I should have put it in the back of the net. He made a nice save. I had an opportunity, it didn't happen."

Gansler wasn't surprised by the team's improvement. "You might call me a blooming optimist, but we tried for a point tonight," he said. "We showed our real face tonight."

Five days later on June 19, the U.S. reverted back to its opening-game antics in its third and final match against Austria in Florence.

The game's turning point came in the 33rd minute. Referee Jemal Al-Sharif red-carded Austrian defender Paul Artner for brutally fouling Vermes at midfield. The U.S. was hopeful, Austria was concerned. Some 57 minutes of playing time later, Austria was ecstatic, the U.S. stunned.

Despite playing with a man advantage, the U.S. exited its first World Cup in 40 years in embarrassing fashion via a 2–1 loss to Austria.

Just Two Feet from Glory

Rome, Italy—The United States turned out to be 2 feet from a miracle on June 14, 1990. Had forward Peter Vermes converted Bruce Murray's rebound past goalkeeper Walter Zenga, the Americans would have tied Italy, 1–1, in what would have been one of the biggest surprises in World Cup history.

As it was, the Americans acquitted themselves quite well before a partisan crowd of 73,423 at Rome's Stadio Olympico, losing a Group A first-round match, 1–0.

Keeping the score close turned out to be quite an accomplishment, considering every serious soccer fan on this planet expected a *batosta*—a rout. But the U.S. surprisingly kept it close to the vest, using conservative tactics.

"You might call me a blooming optimist, but we tried for a point tonight," U.S. Coach Bob Gansler said. "We showed our real face tonight."

On June 10, American faces were red after an embarrassing 5–1 defeat to Czechoslovakia. Four days later, they were smiling after regaining their self respect even though they were on the verge of elimination with a 0–2 record. Italy, meanwhile, clinched a spot in the second round.

"I think we created a lot of character today," midfielder Tab Ramos said. "I never feel good about a defeat. I can't tell you that today. What I feel good about is that we did what we wanted."

Well, almost. The Americans wanted to score a goal and that nearly happened in the 68th minute after Italian midfielder Riccardo Ferri received a yellow card for elbowing Murray some 22 yards from the goal. On the ensuing free kick, Murray ripped a shot that Zenga dived to his right to knock away. The bouncing ball came to an onrushing Vermes, who rifled a shot that

It wasn't the fact the Americans lost to Austria, it was the way the deed was accomplished. Imagine: The U.S. enjoyed a one-man advantage for almost 1 hour and allowed not 1, but 2 goals in a physical match that saw Al-Sharif award 10 cards, including 9 yellows, before a crowd of 34,857 at Stadio Comunale.

(Just Two Feet cont.)

Zenga stopped. The ball squirted loose and headed toward the open goal before Ferri cleared it just a couple of feet from destiny.

"I tired to put it high," Vermes said. "I think I should have put it in the back of the net. He made a nice save. I had an opportunity, it didn't happen."

The U.S. never had a better opportunity to tie the score.

The Italians, who were severely criticized by their fans and media for the result, scored in the 12th minute on a goal by Giuseppe Giannini. He broke through the U.S. defense past John Harkes and sweeper Mike Windischmann, who fell down, and beat goalkeeper Tony Meola with a 14-yard shot.

Then came a turning point in the 34th minute when Italy was awarded a penalty kick after midfielder Paul Caligiuri tripped midfielder Nicola Berti in the penalty area. "It was a questionable call," Ramos said.

Gianluca Vialli's ensuing penalty kick hit the left post with Meola going the wrong way before the ball was cleared.

"The missed penalty kick was heavy for us," Italian captain and defender Giuseppe Bergomi said.

And a lifesaver for the Americans. Had Vialli converted it, Italy would have relaxed and the game would have opened up.

Instead, the U.S. was given a second chance at gaining at least a point. The Americans pulled into a defensive shell and waited for their moment to strike. In fact, they started to dictate the tempo of the match, slowing it down. The U.S.'s strategy—you might call it an 11-corner offense—worked almost to perfection. The Americans' passes were square or went back to Meola. When they had the ball in their end, defenders Windischmann and Marcelo Balboa would have their own private catch and then dump it back to Meola. Anything to waste precious seconds here and there.

That made the Italian team more anxious and its fans—who whistled their displeasure—quite angry.

"We dictated the tempo of things," Ramos said. "We tried to slow the game down, then stick one in in the final 15 or 20 minutes. We wanted to take the fans out of the game. If you can make them impatient, hopefully you can take them out of the game."

The U.S. did just about everything it could do, but win.

"It was a very frustrating for us to have a man advantage and give up two goals," said defender John Doyle, one of the U.S.'s bright spots in the World Cup. "Everybody's hurting a little."

And for good reason. With a victory, the Americans had a chance—albeit a long one—of reaching the second round. Still, a victory—even a tie—would have put a nice finishing touch on the tournament.

"We're disappointed with the results," Gansler said. "I thought we had the ability to do it [win] . . . The difference between the other nations and ourselves is not as great as we would believe."

The wheels for this loss were put into motion in the 33rd minute when Artner kicked Vermes after he took him down at midfield. Artner was ejected and left the field while the meager crowd of Americans sang, "Hey, hey, goodbye."

The Austrians managed to end the half unscathed. It was a matter of time before they cracked. Or was it?

At halftime, they replaced their scoring leader, an ineffective Toni Polster (no goals in the cup) with Andreas Reisinger.

"A team with 10 men works harder," Harkes reminded his teammates.

It went in one ear and out the other because only 5 minutes into the second half, it was the U.S. that became unwound. Austrian forward Andreas Ogris picked up a loose ball after an American corner kick, outran defenders Jimmy Banks and Desmond Armstrong in the midfield and Windischmann before beating Meola with a 12-yard bloop shot.

The U.S. never was the same.

"It was very frustrating because we were playing well," Ramos said. "We were close to getting a 1–0 lead.

The Austrians utilized a counterattack for their second goal. Ogris raced down the right side and crossed the ball to Gerhard Rodax, who scored off a 10-yarder.

Finally, in the 83rd minute, the Americans struck as Murray put the ball through goalkeeper Klaus Lindenberger's legs from 10 yards. But like Caligiuri's goal in the opening loss to the Czechs, it was too little and too late.

For Ramos, best just wasn't good enough in Italy.

"We have the best American players here, nothing better," he said. "As a team, we're just not good enough. There's absolutely nothing we can do about it. We can play with a lot of heart and intensity and hope for the best. Technically, we're overwhelmed and physically not as talented as these teams.

"You have to remember where we're at and at what level the Italians are at. I'm not saying we're going to shut them down. We could beat them 1–0, but it's very unlikely it's going to happen."

There is a world of difference between the U.S., the Italys, Brazils and Germanys of the world. "In other countries, they would shut down their businesses to watch the World Cup," said Ramos, who along with Harkes and Doyle were the U.S. standouts. "If they lose, they cry and don't go to work the next day. If they win, they celebrate and they don't go to work the next day.

"The other teams have no idea of our situation. We'll come home and at Kennedy Airport, no one will know who we are."

Catching up to the rest of the world won't happen overnight, Ramos said. It could take time, lots of time. A professional league must develop in the U.S. and the best players must play overseas at the highest level.

Before the cup, several Americans already were playing in Europe—Vermes with FC Voldendam (the Netherlands) and Sullivan with Raba Eto Gyor (Hungary). But having just a handful of players abroad would not turn around the U.S. fortunes overnight.

"It won't be enough because we need 20–30 players," Ramos said. "It's a matter of playing in Europe, adjusting for a year and becoming one of the best players. That's how you become competitive in the World Cup."

Ramos and the U.S. will have another shot in 1994.

Chapter Ten

The Most Memorable, Most Forgettable Matches

The best thing about the World Cup is the memories it has generated, the outstanding performances, the beautiful goals and the unforgettable matches. With that in mind, presenting a list of the top 10 games that will be remembered as long as the sport is played.

THE MOST UNFORGETTABLE

United States 1, England 0
June 29, 1950
Belo Horizonte, Brazil

Has there been a more stunning result in World Cup history? When the score appeared on the wire services, editors thought it was a mistake, that a 1 had been dropped off of the English score. Some 44 years later, however, it is considered by many experts to be the greatest victory in U.S. soccer history, if not the greatest upset in World Cup history.

"There never has been an upset of that measure," U.S. defender Harry Keough said.

The American team was made up of European immigrants and a handful of native-born citizens, and was considered to be a heavy underdog.

"We went into the game hoping to keep the score down," U.S. goalkeeper Frank Borghi said.

The U.S. did. The English pounded away at the American goal, but could not score. The game's only goal was scored by Haitian native Joe Gaetjens, who headed home a long pass by Walter Bahr in the 37th minute.

Not surprisingly, some critics and embittered English fans

claimed the ball hit Gaetjens rather than the forward hitting the ball. But the goal stood.

As it turned out, Gaetjens was not a U.S. citizen at the time—he had a Haitian passport. Under current World Cup rules, Gaetjens would not have been eligible to play for the U.S.

"We shouldn't have played," said the late Joe Maca, who was a U.S. resident, but a Belgian citizen. "At that time they didn't ask any questions. Now in order to play for a national team, you have to be full-fledged citizen. If we hadn't beaten England, no one would have said anything.

"It was like the Yankees losing to an amateur team."

West Germany 3, France 3
(Germany advanced on penalty kicks, 5–4)
July 8, 1982
Barcelona, Spain

Someone had to lose in what perhaps was the greatest World Cup game played—if you counted the drama, the quality of both teams, and what was at stake: a place in the finals.

"Surely, it was the craziest match I ever played," said West German star Karl-Heinz Rummenigge, one of the heroes.

The Germans connected in the 18th minute on Pierre Littbarski's goal but the French equalized on Michel Platini's penalty kick in the 27th minute after Dominique Rocheteau was held back by Bernd Forester. He kissed the ball—soccer's version of the French kiss—placed it down and then booted it past goalkeeper Toni Schumacher.

The game remained even until 12 minutes into the second half when a controversial play changed the course of the match. French substitute François Battiston raced into the German end and fired a shot that missed the net by inches. Still in stride, Battiston was leveled by Schumacher. Battiston was replaced by Christian Lopez, and Schumacher remained in the game, although many observers felt that the goalkeeper should have been red-carded. Others claimed the collision wasn't intentional. The Germans were able to play at even strength into extratime.

If this was sudden death, the match would have been over after Marius Tresor scored off a volley for France 2 minutes into the first extra period. Teammate and midfielder Alain Giresse connected sev-

eral minutes later and the French seemingly had a commanding 3–1 advantage. Seemingly.

There were 22 minutes remaining, plenty of time for a German miracle. The thrust toward victory began in the first extratime when Rummenigge, who did not start because of a leg injury, was inserted into the match after the French's first extra-time goal.

It worked. Rummenigge cut the margin to a goal in the 102nd minute and Klaus Fischer equalized in the 107th minute, so for the first time in the World Cup a match—a semifinal—would be decided by penalty kicks.

Giresse led off for France, and he put his attempt through, as did Manfred Kaltz. Manuel Amoros and Paul Breitner converted theirs for a 2–2, but the French took a 3–2 lead as Rocheteau connected and Uli Stielike shot straight at goalkeeper Jean-Luc Ettori. France was in the drivers' seat, but Didier Six missed his attempt and Littbarski scored for a 3–3 tie. Platini and Rummenigge made it 4–4 to force sudden death. Schumacher saved Jean-Luc Bossis' attempt and Horst Hrubesch calmly put his shot into the back of the net and the Germans survived an incredible match.

"We had the luck immediately to score the second goal," Rummenigge said. "Secondly, we have the lack of tradition of losing to French teams. I think we never have lost important games against the

Germany's Rudi Voeller scored on a header from Berthold in the 1986 final against Argentina.

French National Team. Combined with that, we were physically better prepared than the French team."

England 4, West Germany 2
July 30, 1966
London, England

Traditionally, World Cup finals rarely have lived up to the hype of the entire tournament. But then again the British and West Germans threw away the script in an incredible see-saw match that included dramatic comebacks and controversy that will be talked about until the end of time.

Helmut Haller lifted the West Germans into a 1–0 edge 13 minutes into the match, but Geoff Hurst tied it with the first of his 3 goals in the 19th minute. Martin Peters gave the hosts a 2–1 lead in the 78th minute off an Alan Ball corner kick. Hurst fired a shot that was cleared by the defense, but the ball rolled to Peters.

The score remained that way until the final minute. Jack Charlton fouled Siegfried Held. Lothar Emmerich's ensuing free kick rebounded to Wolfgang Weber, who beat goalkeeper Gordon Banks to the far post for a 2–2 tie with 15 seconds remaining in regulation.

It was a disheartening goal for the English. Before his team entered the pitch before the first extra time, English coach Alf Ramsey told his team: "You've beaten them once this afternoon. Now go out and do it again."

Ramsey's message obviously reached its mark. Hurst made sure of that, scoring what proved to be a controversial goal when his shot bounded off the crossbar into the goal. Or was it?

The Germans claimed it wasn't a goal, but linesman Tofik Bakhramov of the Soviet Union ruled the ball had indeed crossed the line and the goal stood.

"I believe the goal was in," Hurst said in 1993. "When you play in the final, you believe the goal was in . . . I don't think anyone has proved the goal didn't cross the line.

"It is one of the most, if not most controversial moment in world sports. It is still talked about today."

Hurst connected for his third goal in the waning minutes to become the first and only player to have scored 3 goals in a World Cup championship game.

North Korea 1, Italy 0
July 19, 1966
Middlesbrough, England
and
Portugal 5, North Korea 3
July 23, 1966
Liverpool, England

Another David *vs.* Goliath encounter as David won the game.

The entertaining North Koreans ran circles around the heavily favored Italians. Their efforts and hard work paid off in the 43rd minute, when Pak Seung-zin beat Giovanni Rivera on a clearance and headed the ball toward the goal. Pak Doo Ik got the ball at the edge of the area and scored from 15 yards for what turned out to be the only goal of the game.

The Italians? They returned home disgraced and they were pelted with vegetables at the Rome airport.

The North Koreans? They had to wait 24 hours before discovering if they had qualified for the quarterfinals—thanks to the Soviet Union's 2–1 win over Chile—where they met heavily favored Portugal. Twenty-four minutes into quarterfinals, it appeared the North Koreans were headed toward yet another upset, holding a 3–0 advantage. But the great Eusebio picked this day to score 4 goals, in the 27th, 42nd, 55th and 58th minutes—2 via penalty kicks—Jose Augusto added a fifth goal—to lead a stirring comeback en route to a 5–3 Portuguese victory.

North Korea has never been heard from again in serious international soccer.

England 3, Cameroon 2
July 1, 1990
Naples, Italy

Cameroon, the saviors and darlings of Italia '90, came close to pulling off a stunning result. In a World Cup devoid of goals and memorable moments, this match stood out. And why not? It had a little bit of everything—a flair for the dramatic, heroics, lead changes and even goals in a tournament starved for excitement.

Two of the goals were by striker Gary Lineker—the last a penalty kick in the first extra time period—that put England into the semifinals for only the second time.

"We pulled it out of the fire," England Coach Bobby Robson said.

Cameroon had enjoyed a 2–1 lead in the hard-fought match with 7 minutes remaining in regulation in front of 55,205 at Stadio San Paolo as its not-so-secret weapon, 38-year-old substitute Roger Milla (4 goals), set up goals by Emmanuel Kunde and Eugene Ebwelle. "At one time I thought we were on the plane home," Robson said.

It was up to Lineker to pull his teammates off that plane, even though he was in the midst of a miserable World Cup, having injured a toe after kicking a Dutch player earlier in the tournament.

In the 83rd minute, Lineker was tripped in the penalty area by defender Benjamin Massing. He converted his kick, beating goalkeeper Thomas N'Kono to the lower right for a 2–2 tie.

As time was running out in the first extra period, Lineker broke in alone on N'Kono, who tripped him for another penalty. This time the striker placed the ball into the middle while N'Kono dived to his right.

Uruguay 2, Brazil 1
July 16, 1950
Rio de Janeiro, Brazil

This is just another example of a soccer team counting its soccer trophies and winners' medals before they are handed out.

As hosts of the 1950 World Cup, Brazil was considered the overwhelming favorite—it was a 1–10 favorite by the oddsmakers—to capture its first world championship. The 1950 World Cup, the first since 1938 and first since World War II, had an unusual set up. Instead of having a planned championship, 4 teams were placed in a final-round group—Brazil, Uruguay, Sweden and Spain.

As it turned out, the 2 highest point-getters, Brazil and Uruguay, played in the final match. The hosts led with a 2–0–0 mark and 4 points and needed only a tie, while the Uruguayans (1–0–1; 3 points) needed a victory.

So, a World Cup record crowd of 199,854 packed newly built Maracana Stadium (the world's largest) for one big celebration party. There was one roadblock—Uruguay, the first champions in 1930, had other ideas.

The Brazilians went out and attacked, but could not solve Uruguay's solid defense in the scoreless first half. But, only 2 minutes into the second half, Friaca scored off an Ademir feed for a 1–0 lead.

Instead of playing more defense—coach Flavio Costa had ordered Jair to drop back on defense, but the instructions never reached him—Brazil continued to attack.

Uruguay leveled the score in the 66th minute as Alcide Elgardo Ghiggia connected off a pass from captain Obdulio Varela. With the Brazilian defense expecting Ghiggia to center another pass, the right winger ran toward the goal and beat goalkeeper Moacyr Barbosa to the near post.

The Brazilian fans took this loss hard, crying in the stadium and on the streets of Rio.

West Germany 2, Netherlands 1
June 24, 1990
Milan, Italy

In a match worthy of a semifinal or even a final, the West Germans outlasted the Dutch, 2–1, in a second-round encounter as intense as a World Cup match that has ever been played.

Both teams never stopped running and that included into each other. In the 21st minute, Dutch defender Frank Rijkaard was given a yellow card for tripping forward Rudi Voeller, who received a yellow himself for arguing that his opponent deserved more punishment. On the ensuing free kick, Voeller ran into Dutch goalkeeper Hans Van Breukelen. Rijkaard came over and spat at Voeller and both were ejected by referee Juan Loustau of Argentina.

The Germans scored in the 49th minute as Juergen Klinsmann put in a left-wing cross by midfielder Guido Buchwald from 12 yards, and Buchwald created the second goal with six minutes remaining, setting up defender Andreas Brehme, who scored from the top right of the area. The Dutch came back in the 88th minute on Ronald Koeman's penalty kick.

"Today was just not a football match between two countries," Klinsmann said. "This is one of the best matches I ever played in my life."

Italy 3, Brazil 2
July 5, 1982
Barcelona, Spain

You might be better off to say it was Paolo Rossi 3, Brazil 2, because the Italian striker put on one of the great individual scoring displays in World Cup history.

Every time the Brazilians came within striking distance of Italy, destiny's darlings of the tournament, Rossi would come back with a goal of his own.

Rossi, who had just returned from a 2-year ban because of his involvement in a game-fixing scandal, began his amazing run of 6 goals in the final 3 matches. Rossi struck first, 5 minutes into the game, heading in Antonio Carbrini's cross before 44,000 spectators at Sarria Stadium.

For the Brazilians, who had come from behind to defeat the Soviet Union and Scotland, it was business as usual. They tallied in the 12th minute as Socrates scored on a great individual effort off a Zico feed.

A defensive mistake by Brazil allowed Rossi to score again in the 25th minute, but Falcao tied it in the 68th minute.

But 7 minutes later, Rossi hit his third goal after Junior did not clear a corner kick.

France 1, Brazil 1
(France advanced on penalty kicks, 4-3)
June 21, 1986
Guadalajara, Brazil

It was a game for the ages as 2 talented and skillful opponents slugged it out for 120 minutes before the match was decided by penalties in the mid-day Mexican heat.

Brazil grabbed a 1–0 lead in the 18th minute, when Careca connected from 15 yards, but the French equalized with 4 minutes remaining in the half on a goal by the great Michel Platini off two fine passes by Alain Giresse and Dominique Rocheteau past Brazilian goalkeeper Carlos, who allowed his first goal in 401 minutes.

The second half featured end-to-end action, but no goals. Zico, who replaced Muller in the 70th minute, had a grand opportunity to put the Brazilians in front with a penalty kick in the 74th minute Branco had been brought down by goalkeeper Joel Bats, who saved the attempt.

Then came the drama of penalties. Socrates missed his kick and Yannick Stopyra put home his to give the French the lead. Brazil's Alemao and Manuel Amoros traded kicks. The Brazilians drew even when Zico converted his and France's Bruno Bellone fired his try off the post. Platini missed his attempt as did Julio Cesar for Brazil. Luis Fernandez ended this madness, converting his kick to win the tie-breaker, 4–3, and the French were into the semifinals against West Germany, setting up a rematch of the 1982 semis.

Brazil 6, Poland 5
June 5, 1938
Strasbourg, France

There were tons of goals and plenty of drama in this encounter, including 2 outstanding individual performances. Leonidas da Silva of Brazil, who better known as Leonidas, and Ernst Willimowski of Poland each scored 4 goals, the only time in which 2 players have scored 2 goals in a World Cup match.

By halftime, Leonidas, who was nicknamed the Black Diamond already, had connected for a hat-trick to give the Brazilians a seemingly safe 3 – 1 lead at Stade de la Meinau (no crowd was recorded). But in the second half, the Polish midfield took over as Willimowski connected 3 times as the teams entered extratime tied at 4-4. (Berjum Peracio also scored for Brazil).

Not surprisingly, Leonidas and Willimowski each had a goal in overtime. But surprisingly, the game-winner did not come from either player as midfielder Romeo settled this wild affair 3 minutes into extratime.

As it turned out, this was not the highest scoring match in World Cup history. Austria and Switzerland combined for 12 goals — a 7 – 5 Austrian victory — in the 1954 quarterfinals.

FORGETTABLE GAMES

It seems for every great game there seems to be 10 clunkers. In fact, here are examples of 10 games World Cup officials would rather not remember.

Hungary 4, Brazil 2
June 27, 1954
Berne, Switzerland

The game appropriately is called the Battle of Berne; and everyone thought that Switzerland was a neutral country. Think again when it comes to World Cup soccer.

This might have been the most disgraceful World Cup game ever played. There were 42 free kicks, which meant there was a minimum of 42 fouls called (no telling how many fouls were not whistled because of the advantage rule), 3 ejections, 2 penalty kicks and a locker room fight in a quarterfinal match before a crowd of 40,000 at Wankdorf Stadium.

The game started to unravel in the opening minutes as Hungarian defender Gyula Lorant was slapped with a yellow card by referee Arthur Ellis of England. Lorant, who laughed at Ellis' decision, was fortunate he was not given another yellow card for dissent, which would have meant his dismissal.

The Brazilians were off their game because of the wet field conditions, and it showed early on as Nandor Hidegkuti scored in the fourth minute as his shorts were ripped from his body. Hidegkuti turned playmaker 4 minutes later, setting up Sandor Kocsis' header.

The 2–0 deficit sparked Brazil to find its game in a match that saw both sides tackling aggressively. Brazilian Indio felt the brunt of it in the 18th minute, as he was hammered in the penalty area, which set up a penalty kick by defender Djalma Santos to slice the lead to 2–1. The score stayed that way until the second half when Ellis awarded Hungary a questionable penalty kick after Kocsis and Santos had collided in the penalty area. Hungary was expecting a free kick, but was surprised when Ellis awarded a penalty. Mihaly Lantos converted for a 3–1 advantage.

The Brazilians were furious at the decision, and the game got out of hand. Julinho cut the margin to 3–2, but tempers flared as Nilton Santos and Jozsef Bozsik fought and were sent off. They needed a police to escort them off the field.

With 4 minutes remaining, Brazil's Humberto was given his marching orders for kicking Lorant violently. With one minute left, Kocsis headed in a Zoltan Czibor cross for the final goal.

The game was over, but the battle continued on the way to the locker room. One story had the Brazilians hiding and attacking the Hungarians in the tunnel to the locker rooms. Another had the great Hungarian captain Ferenc Puskas, who did not play because of an injury, throwing a bottle at the Brazilians as they came off the field. Regardless where it began, a bloodbath ensued as bottles and soccer cleats were swung in anger. Hungary's Gustav Sebes had his cheek cut open and Ellis was escorted to his locker room by armed guards in the World Cup's lowest moment.

West Germany 1, Austria 0
June 25, 1982
Gijon, Spain

Of course, not every bad match included an ugly scenario. Some were just downright boring, others suspicious.

While no one can prove that it was collusion, a 1–0 result in favor of West Germany was what both countries needed to reach the second round at the expense of Algeria.

Horst Hrubesch headed home a Pierre Littbarski cross in the 10th minute and then both sides literally quit playing. Much of the game was played in the midfield before a disappointed crowd of 41,000 at El Molinon Stadium. French Coach Michel Hildalgo, who scouted the match, but did not take a note. He did suggest, however, that both teams be awarded the Nobel Peace Prize for their unaggressive play.

One West German fan was so disgusted with his country's performance that he set fire to the German flag in the stands.

Algerian fans, who claimed the match was fixed, booed and heckled both sides. In what might have been the most aggressive action associated with the match, Algeria protested to FIFA that the game was fixed and called for both countries to be disqualified. Nice try. FIFA turned it down.

Former New York Cosmos and West German World Cup star and coach Franz Beckenbauer could not believe what he had seen.

"Later many people asked me whether there had been a previous deal on the score," Beckenbauer wrote in his book, *World Cup Espana 82*. "I know this was not the case. But of course there exists in soccer something of a 'tacit' agreement that comes about in the course of the game. What remains is an unpleasant memory. This was not a game worthy of the World Cup and it has done great harm to the prestige of German soccer.

Chile 2, Italy 0
June 2, 1962
Santiago, Chile

This confrontation—named the Battle of Santiago—started to boil over well before these 2 teams met. Italian journalists fired things up at the outset by criticizing the Chilean living and playing conditions. The story made it back to Chile, which was bent on revenge in the match.

The game was televised live worldwide, and attended by 66,057 at Estadio Nacional. Only 8 minutes into the rough game, Giorgio Ferrini was ejected for retaliating for being kicked from behind by Chilean striker Honorino Landa. Referee Ken Aston of England red-carded Ferrini, but he refused to leave the field. Ferrini finally left the field 10 minutes later, but not before FIFA officials and police were called in.

Some 5 minutes before the half, Italian Humberto Maschio took Leonel Sanchez down on a bad foul. Sanchez then broke Maschio's nose with a left hook that would have done Muhammad Ali proud. Everyone in the stadium—plus that TV audience—saw the punch, everyone but Aston, whose back was turned, and the two linesmen. Sanchez never was ejected (years later in newspapers accounts of the incident, Sanchez proudly described the punch) and even set up Chile's first goal, by Banda Ramirez in the 74th minute. Sanchez Toro scored 2 minutes from time.

Another Italian, Mario David, was ejected for tackling Sanchez around his neck.

Not surprisingly, Aston needed a police escort off the field, and never officiated another World Cup match.

Brazil 1, Czechoslovakia 1
June 12, 1938
Bordeaux, France

Before there was Santiago and before there was Berne, there was Bordeaux, as in the Battle of Bordeaux.

The body count included a broken leg, a broken arm, a stomach injury and 3 ejections in a match that was chosen as the showpiece of the opening of Parc de Lescure, Bordeaux's new stadium.

Only moments into the game, Brazil's Zeze Procopio kicked Czech forward Oldrich Nejedly for no apparent reason, and subsequently was given his marching orders by referee Paul Van Hertzka of Hungary in the quarterfinal match in front of 25,000 spectators.

There was some soccer played, too, as Leonidas da Silva connected for the Brazilians in the 30th minute. It looked as though the teams would escape the half without any further incidents when Jan Riha and Brazil's Machado were sent off for fighting.

The Czechs got an opportunity to equalize in the 64th minute when defender Domingos—the father of 1950 Brazilian World Cup star Ademir—was called for a handball in the penalty area. Nejedly,

Joe Gaetjens'
header passes
England's goal-
keeper Bert Will-
iams to score one
of the biggest
upsets in the his-
tory of soccer
(1–0).

who was still standing—he eventually left the match with a broken leg—converted the penalty.

Amid more rough stuff later on, Czech goalkeeper Frantisek Planicka had his arm broken.

The rematch—the Brazilians used 9 new players, the Czechs 6—had no such incidents in what was a 2–1 victory for Brazil.

Argentina 1, France 0
July 15, 1930
Montevideo, Uruguay

Actually, it was nothing the players did that made this match forgettable. Blame it on an overzealous and miscalculating referee named Almeida Rego.

Late in the second half, the Argentines enjoyed a 1–0 lead with the French threatening to score when Rego suddenly whistled the game was finished. Or was it? The French rightfully protested, claiming there were 6 minutes left. As mounted police entered the field to restore order, Rego talked with his linesman, and it was decided there were 6 minutes remaining. The game was restarted, but Argentine midfielder

Cierro fainted. The Argentines held on for the victory, but it was not without repercussions.

The Uruguayans, who attended the match, claimed that France should have won. The Argentines, arch-enemies of Uruguay on the soccer field, complained about the game to the World Cup Organizing Committee and threatened to pull out of the Cup. The Argentines did reach the championship match, to lose to Uruguay, 4–2.

West Germany 1, Argentina 0
July 8, 1990
Rome, Italy

In a match that was hardly befitting a final, the West Germans managed to score a goal and defeat the defending champion Argentines, 1–0.

It was a disgraceful game as the Germans came to play soccer, but most of the time were unsuccessful at it. The Argentines came to play something, but it wasn't soccer. Argentina somehow made it to the final using mirrors, a record 20 players and an ailing Diego Maradona, who would rather complain than play the game.

Defender Andreas Brehme converted the lone goal—a penalty kick in the 84th minute—before 73,603 fans and a worldwide TV audience estimated at 1.5 billion. They deserved better.

"It wasn't a very good final," German coach Franz Beckenbauer said. "It was just too bad the Argentines didn't participate in the game. They wanted to destroy."

Argentina acutally got within striking distance of the German goal in the 38th minute when Guido Buchwald tripped midfielder Jose Basualdo 20 yards from the net on the right side. Maradona's free kick sailed over the goal and goalkeeper Bodo Illgner, who touched the ball only once, when a teammate passed it back.

The Argentines did get a piece of soccer history. Referee Edgardo Codesal of Mexico red-carded Pedro Monzon and Gustavo Dezotti, the first players to be sent off in a World Cup final in the 65th and 87th minutes, respectively.

The bitterly disappointed Argentines continued to argue with Codesal after the final whistle. Argentine coach Carlos Bilardo had to run onto the field to pull his players away from the referee.

The game ended disgracefully, with the Argentines complaining to the game officials and crying.

Brazil 2, Bulgaria 0

July 12, 1966

Liverpool, England

Bulgarian midfielder Zhechev is not a name etched in World Cup lore. He holds the distinction of finding a way to stop the marvelous Pele—injure him. He did so in the opening half, but not before Pele fired in a free kick to become the first player to score in 3 consecutive tournaments. Pele, who at 25 was at his prime, was taken down brutally in the first half by Zhechev. "Pele won't finish the World Cup," a French journalist was quoted in *The Sunday Times History of the World Cup*. "It's amazing he hasn't gone mad."

Brazil and Pele were never the same, failing to reach the next round. Without Pele, Brazil went down to Hungary 3 days later, 3−1. And even with the great one in the lineup, Brazil was not its former self, losing to Portugal, 3−1, on July 19.

France 4, Kuwait 1

June 21, 1982

Valladolid, Spain

How often does a referee reverse his decision and take a goal away from a team after the opposition complains? In the World Cup, fortunately, it does not happen very often, but it occurred in this first-round match.

With France enjoying a 3−1 lead with 15 minutes remaining, Soviet referee Miroslav Stupar awarded the French a goal when Alain Giresse scored from in close as the Kuwaiti defenders did not move.

The Kuwaitis claimed they had heard a whistle and stopped. Prince Fahid, the Kuwaiti Football Association president, walked from the stands onto the field—which usually meant automatic expulsion—to protest and argue the decision. Kuwait appeared ready to walk off the field, but Stupar did a 180-degree turn on his original decision, upsetting the French.

By the time the matter had been settled, the match had been held up for 8 minutes in front of 30,034 at Nuevo Estadio Jose Zorrilla.

The French got a measure of revenge and the goal back in the final minute as Maxime Bossis scored.

And oh yes, FIFA slapped Kuwait with a $12,000 fine, which had to be loose change for Fahid, one of the world's richest men.

Argentina 3, Chile 1
July 22, 1930

Montevideo, Uruguay

Before there was even the Battle of Bordeaux, there was the under-publicized mini-battle of Montevideo between these two South American neighbors in the very first World Cup, which certainly had more than its share of growing pains.

Guillermo Stabile had scored twice for the Argentines in the opening half and Asgorga Subiabre for Chile before a crowd of 1,000 at Centenary Stadium. Several minutes before halftime, however, a fight broke out between the teams. It got so ugly that police had to come onto the field to separate the brawlers.

Incredibly, the second half was free from incident as both teams decided to play soccer. Mario Evaristo closed out the scoring for the winners.

France 3, Mexico 2
June 19, 1954

Geneva, Switzerland

There were 2 major incidents at the 1954 World Cup.

Actually, this first-round game before 19,000 spectators at Les Charmilles was just playing out the string as neither team could advance to the next round. France won the match on a late penalty kick by Raymond Kopa with only 2 minutes remaining, which prompted several Mexican players to attack referee Manuel Asensi of Spain. There were no reports on how Asensi survived this disgraceful incident.

Chapter Eleven

Amazing Facts
World Cup Trivia

It will be intriguing to see if Jeopardy! will add a category or two about USA '94, in honor of the World Cup. If the game show doesn't, there still is plenty to talk about, and you don't have to put your response in a question.

There's a First Time for Everything

First game: Mexico vs. France in Montevideo, Uruguay, on July 13, 1930. France won, 4–1.

First goal: By Lucien Laurent of France in the first half against Mexico.

First multiple-goal game: By Andre Maschinot of France, as he scored twice in the opener.

First hat-trick: By Guillermo Stabile of Argentina in a 6–3 victory over Mexico on July 19, 1930.

First penalty kick: By Mexico's Manuel Rocquetas Rosas in the 38th minute of Argentina's 6–3 win in 1930.

First penalty kick miss: By Argentina's Fernando Paternoster in the 6–3 triumph over Mexico.

First tie: Italy 1, Spain 1 on May 31, 1934, in Florence, Italy.

First replay: Italy edged Spain, 1–0, on June 1, 1934, after the first tie.

First scoreless tie: Brazil 0, England 0 on June 11, 1958, in Stockholm, Sweden.

First own goal: By Ernst Loertscher for Switzerland vs. Germany on June 4, 1938, in Paris.

First yellow card: In Mexico's scoreless tie with the Soviet Union on May 31, 1970.

First red card: Chile's Carlos Caszely for kicking West Germany's Berti Vogts (who will coach Germany in the 1994 cup) in the 67th minute in the Germans' 1–0 win over June 14, 1970.

First ejection: Peru captain Mario de Las Casas by Chilean referee Alberto Warken in a 3–1 loss to Romania on July 14, 1930.

First substitute: The Soviet Union's Albert Shesterniev was replaced by Anatoly Pusatch at halftime in the 1970 opener, a scoreless tie with host Mexico on May 31.

First player to replace a substitute: Mexico's Juan Basaguren, who replaced Salgado Lopez, who had replaced Garcia Borja in a 3–0 first-round victory over El Salvador on June 7, 1970.

First player to score as a substitute: Mexico's Juan Basaguren scored in the 83rd minute of that win over El Salvador.

First substitution of a goalkeeper: Romania's Steve Adamache had to come out after an injury in the 29th minute of a 3–2 loss to Brazil on June 10, 1970. He was replaced by Necula Raducanu.

First injury: To French goalkeeper Alex Thepot, who had to be replaced in his country's 4–1 1930 opening victory 10 minutes into the match after a Mexican player kicked him in the jaw. Augustin Chantrel, a midfielder, replaced him.

First final: Uruguay vs. Argentina on July 30, 1930 in Montevideo. Uruguay won, 4–2.

First televised game: Yugoslavia vs. France in Lausanne, Switzerland, on June 16, 1954.

First time a goal was scored a minute or less into a match: By Emile Veinante of France, who scored 40 seconds into the game of his country's 3–1 victory over Belgium on June 5, 1938, in Paris.

First time penalty-kick tie-breakers were used: In 1982 as West Germany took on France. The teams were tied after extra time, 3–3, but Germany prevailed in the tie-breaker, 5–4.

The first time a final was decided by a shutout: West Germany 1, Argentina 0 on July 8, 1990.

First World Cup mascot: World Cup Willie at the 1966 cup in England. It was a lionlike boy.

The teams that participated in the first World Cup (13): Argentina, Brazil, Uruguay, Paraguay, United States, France, Mexico, Chile, Yugoslavia, Bolivia, Romania, Peru and Belgium.

West German forward Hans Schaeffer charging Czech goalkeeper Dolejsi. A goal was given by the referee over Czech protests. This 1958 first round game ended in a tie.

First time a non-European or non-South American country played: Egypt in 1934.

Countries that are participating for the first time at USA '94: Nigeria, Saudi Arabia.

Fast, Faster, Fastest

The fastest goal in World Cup history was scored by England's Bryan Robson, after only 27 seconds of a 3 – 1 victory over France on June 16, 1982, exactly 44 years to the day that Olle Nyberg of Sweden struck after 30 seconds against Hungary in the 1938 World Cup. The third fastest goal was scored by Bernard Lacombe of France, 31 seconds into a 2 – 1 loss to Italy on June 2, 1978.

Fastest substitution: Italy's Mauro Bellugi was replaced by Antonello Cuccureddu 6 minutes into a 1 – 0 triumph over Argentina on June 10, 1978.

The Only Time

The only occasion 4 teams from the British Isles qualified: 1958, when England, Scotland, Northern Ireland and Wales made it to the final 16.

The only time a host country had to qualify: Italy, in 1934.

The only players who have participated in the World Cup before

and after World War II: Switzerland's Alfred Bickel and Sweden's Erik Nilsson played in the 1938 and 1950 tournaments.

The only time a player scored in consecutive World Cup championship games: Vava, who accomplished the feat in 1958 and 1962.

The only player to have participated in 5 World Cups: Mexican goalkeeper Antonio Carbajal tended goal in 1950, 1954, 1958, 1962 and 1966.

The only time 2 countries met twice in the same World Cup (other than replays): West Germany vs. Hungary in 1954. Hungary won the first matchup, 8–3, when the Germans rested 6 regulars. They met again in the final, with the Germans at full strength and emerging victorious, 3–2.

The only time a player recorded a hat-trick in a championship game: By Geoff Hurst for England in a 4–2 victory over West Germany on July 30, 1966, at Wembley Stadium in London.

The only countries to lose back-to-back finals: The Netherlands and West Germany. The former lost to the host countries, West Germany and Argentina in 1974 and 1978, respectively, the later to Italy and Argentina, in 1982 and 1986, respectively.

The only players to have scored in 2 World Cup championship matches: Brazil's Vava and Pele and West Germany's Paul Breitner are the only 3 players who have accomplished that feat. Vava is the only player to have done it in 2 consecutive finals—1958 and 1962—while Pele scored in 1958 and 1970, and Breitner in 1974 and 1982.

The only player to have scored 5 or more goals in two World Cups: Peru's Teofilio (Nene) Cubillas scored 5 goals in each of the 1970 and 1978 tournaments.

The only team to win out of its hemisphere: Brazil, which won in Sweden in 1958.

The only brothers to play for a champion: Fritz and Otmar Walter of West Germany in 1954 and Jack and Bobby Charlton of England in 1966.

The only father and son combination: Domingus Da Guia of Brazil played in the 1938 cup and his son, Ademir Da Guia, performed in the 1974 event. Interesting note: There was an uncle-nephew combination. In 1930, Jose Andrade competed for Uruguay. Some 20 years later, his nephew, Rodrigeuz Andrade payed for the World Cup champions.

The only times a player with a hat-trick played on a losing team: Poland's Ernst Willimowski, who scored 4 goals in his side's 6–5 loss to Brazil in the opening round on June 5, 1938, and Igor Belanov in the Soviet Union's 4–3 loss to Spain in the second round on June 15, 1986.

The only time brothers have coached in the World Cup: Zeze Moreira coached Brazil in 1954 and brother Aimore directed the team in 1962.

The only time brothers were a goalkeeping tandem on the same team: Viktor and Vyacheslav Chanov for the Soviet Union in the 1982 World Cup.

The only time a country won its group with a negative goal differential: Cameroon (2-1-0), which captured Group B at Italia '90. The Africans scored 3 goals and allowed 5 for a negative goal differential of 2, after a 4–0 loss to the Soviet Union. As it turned out, they finished with the worst differential of their group. Romania (1-1-1) was at plus one, Argentina (1-1-1) at plus one and the Soviet Union (1–2) was even.

The only four players who have played for 2 countries in the World Cup: Luis Monti (Argentina in 1930 and Italy in 1934), Ferenc Puskas (Hungary in 1954 and Spain in 1962), Jose Santamaria (Uruguay in 1954 and Spain in 1962) and Jose Mazzola (Brazil in 1958 and Italy in 1962). (The rules have been changed since then, limiting players to one country.)

The only country to have participated in every World Cup: Brazil, which will make in 15 in 1994.

It's Never Happened—Yet

No player has captained a championship team twice, but 2 came close. West Germany's Karl-Heinz Rummenigge did it twice as a loser in the final—1982 and 1986. Argentina's Diego Maradona was the captain of the 1986 champions and the 1990 runners-up.

Olympian Feats

Only 8 players can claim the feat of being Olympic and World Cup champions. Jose Nasazzi, Jose Leonardo Andrade, Hector Scarone and Pedro Cea from Uruguay's 1924 and 1928 Olympic gold-medal winning teams and the 1930 World Cup champions, and Alvaro Gestidio in 1928 and 1930. Italy's Alfredo Foni, Pietro Rava and Ugo Locatelli played for the 1936 Olympic titlists and the 1938 World Cup champions.

There have been 24 players who have played in an Olympic and World Cup final: Jose Nasazzi, Jose Leandro Andrade, Hector Scarone and Pedro Cea played for Uruguay in the 1924 and 1928 Olympics, and the 1930 World Cup. Fellow countryman Alvaro Gestidio did the same in 1928 and 1930; Italy's Alfredo Foni, Pierto Rava and Ugo Locatelli played in the 1936 Olympic title match and for the 1938 World Cup title; Argentina's Fernando Paternoster, Juan Evaristo, Luis Monti and Manuel Ferreira played in the 1928 Olympics and the 1930 World Cup (Monti also played for Italy in the 1934 World Cup final); Sweden's Nils Liedhold and Gunnar Gren played in the 1948 Olympics and the 1958 World Cup final; Hungary's Gyula Groscis, Jeno Buzansky, Mihaly Lantos, Jozsef Bozsik, Gyula Lorany, Jozsef Zakarias, Zoltan Czibor, Sandor Kocsis, Nandor Hidegkuti and Ferenc Puskas.

Only 3 players have scored in Olympic and World Cup finals: Uruguay's Pedro Cea, who did it in the 1924 Olympics and 1930 World Cup, and Hungary's Ferenc Puskas and teammate Zoltan Czibor, who accomplished the feat at the 1952 Olympics and the 1954 World Cup.

There have been 3 stadiums to host Olympic and World Cup championship matches: Wembley Stadium, London, England (1948 Olympics and 1966 World Cup), Olympic Stadium, Munich, Germany (1972 Olympics and 1974 World Cup) and Azteca Stadium, Mexico City, Mexico (1968 Olympics and 1970 and 1986 World Cups). The Rose Bowl, the site of the 1984 Olympic final, will join the group in 1994, as it will be the home for 8 matches, including the July 17 championship match.

Brotherly Love

There have been several sets of brothers who have performed in the cup. Perhaps the best known were Bobby and Jack Charlton, starters and key players on England's world championship side in 1966. Fritz and Otmar Walter starred for West Germany, the 1954 champs. They each scored a goal in the 6–1 semifinal victory over Austria. Then there were the Van der Kerkhof twins—Rene and Willy—of

second-place Netherlands in 1978. Ironically, they each scored in the 83rd minute against West Germany (Rene) and Austria (Willy) in second-round group matches.

The first brother combination was Fernando and Manuel Rosas of Mexico, who played in the very first World Cup match against France on July 13, 1930.

Other brother combinations include: Juan and Mario Evaristo (Argentina, 1930), Zlatko and Zeljko Cajkovski (Yugoslavia, 1950), Albert and Robert Koerner (Austria, 1954), Antonio and Francesco Lopez (Paraguay, 1950), Anatoliy and Viktor Ivanov (Soviet Union, 1958), Piotyr and Emil Kozlicek (Austria, 1958) and John and Mel Charles (Wales, 1958).

Hurst's shot hit the crossbar down to the line. Or did it? The Germans said not, but linesman Tofik Bakhramov said yes. The English won the 1966 final 4–2.

It's Not Always Fair

These 4 countries finished undefeated in the World Cup, but for some reason, they did not advance to the next round:

- **Scotland** In 1974, the Scots compiled a 1-0-2 record and out-scored their opposition, 3–1, but did not qualify for the second round because the country it was tied with—Brazil—had a better goal differential (3 goals for, 0 against).

- **Brazil** In 1978, the South Americans recorded a 3-0-3 mark, but could not make it into the semifinals. They tied Argentina for first place in that group with a 2-0-1 record, but the Argentines had the better goal differential (8 to Brazil's 5).

- **Cameroon** In 1982, Cameroon had not lost a first-round game, but did not advance. Italy did not win a game, but did reach the second round. They were in the same group and finished with the same records (0-0-3), but Italy scored 2 goals in its first-round games, Cameroon 1.

- **England** And again in 1982, England recorded an impressive 3-0-2 mark, only to be sent packing after the second round. The English tied both their second-round matches, finishing second to West Germany in Group B.

For the Ages

The youngest player to participate in a World Cup: Northern Ireland's Norman Whiteside, who was 17 years, 42 days old, when he played in the 1982 World Cup. Pele was the youngest player to perform in a championship game as a 17-year-old in 1958. He was 17 years, 237 days old.

The oldest player: Northern Ireland goalkeeper Pat Jennings, who was 41-years-old when he played in his final match against Brazil in the 1986 World Cup.

The oldest player on a championship team: Italy's Dino Zoff, who, at 40, was the goalkeeper of the 1982 cup-winning team.

The oldest player to score at a World Cup: Cameroon's Roger Milla, 38, who connected 4 times at Italia '90.

Of Coaches and Kings

The king who would be coach was Romanian King Carol II. For the very first World Cup in 1930, Carol made sure his country was represented in Uruguay. Originally, the invitation was rejected because the Romanian players could not get 3 months off from work to take the roundtrip boatride and stay in South America. Carol intervened, making sure each player would have his job—at full pay—when he returned. Romania was eliminated after only 2 matches. In 1940, Carol was overthrown and he fled to South America, where he was remembered as the "football-mad" king.

The most successful coach has been Vittorio Pozzo of Italy, who directed championship teams in 1934 and 1938. He is the only coach to have guided teams to a pair of World Cup crowns. Honorable mention goes to West Germany's Helmut Schoen, who directed his country to a second-place finish in 1966, a third-place finish in 1970 and the title in 1974.

The most successful player-coaches were Brazil's Mario Zagalo and West Germany's Franz Beckenbauer, who are the only men to have played on and coached World Cup championship squads. Zagalo played for the 1958 and 1962 champions and guided Brazil to the 1970 crown. Beckenbauer played in the 1966 final and for the 1974 champions, and directed Germany to a final appearance in 1986 and to the title in 1990.

Having coaching license, will travel: Rudolf Vytlacil, Blagjoe Vidinic, Bora Milutinovic and Carlos Alberto Parreira are the only men who have coached 2 different countries in a World Cup. Vytlacil, a Czech, coached his native country in 1962, when it finished a surprising second to Brazil in Chile, and guided Bulgaria 4 years later. Vidinic, a Yugoslav, directed Morocco in 1970 and Zaire in 1974. Bora, another Yugoslav, coached Mexico to a quarterfinal finish in 1986 and first-time qualifier Costa Rica into the second round in 1990. And Parreira, a Brazilian, guided Kuwait in 1982 and United Arab Emirates in 1990. Barring a major calamity, Bora and Parreira will become the first men to coach teams in 3 different countries in 1994. Bora will direct the U.S. fortunes, while Parreira will guide his native Brazil.

Paraguayan coach Cayetano Re became the first coach to be thrown out of a World Cup match, getting tossed in the waning minutes of a 2–2 opening-round tie with Belgium in 1986. He was wandering too close to the field.

Uruguyan coach Omar Borras became the first coach to coach from the stands in cup history. He was not allowed to sit on the bench for his team's 1–0 second-round loss to Argentina on June 16, 1986. He called French referee Joel Quiniou "a murderer" after a scoreless tie with Scotland.

Zeze and Aimore Moriera are the only brothers to have coached the same country in the World Cup. Zeze guided Brazil in 1954 and Aimore in 1962.

Some Shirt Tales

The trading of shirts at athletic competitions, most common in soccer, probably began during the 1954 World Cup in Switzerland, according to Prof. Julio Mazzei, confidant of Pele and former coach of the New York Cosmos. "Since then it has become a tradition," Mazzei said. "Some players start collecting special shirts from special idols, such as Pele."

In the 1986 World Cup, however, FIFA had a rule prohibiting the trading of shirts because the organization did not want players to bare their chests on the field, but several players traded shirts anyway.

Some interesting shirt tales:

- The first time numbers were used on shirts were in the 1938 competition in France.

- Brazilian star Tostao gave his shirt and World Cup medal to the surgeon in Houston who had performed 2 operations on a detached retina in his eye before the 1970 tournament.

- Early in the second half of Uruguay's 1–1 tie with West Germany in the 1986 cup, referee Vojtech Christov of Czechoslovakia noticed that teammates Jose Batista and Miguel Bossio were wearing each other's jerseys. So, he had the Uruguayan players switch shirts on the field. He could have given each a yellow card for being out of uniform.

- After France dropped a 2–0 decision to West Germany in the 1986 World Cup, French players Michel Platini and Jean Tigana, instead of trading shirts with the victors, threw their jerseys into the stands in Jalisco Stadium in Guadalajara, thanking fans for their support.

- At the same competition, Portuguese players threatened to wear their shirts inside out if their World Cup bonuses were not doubled from $2,000 a match.

- And then there were Guadalajaran prostitutes, who, after Brazil's 1–0 victory over Spain in 1986, wore yellow shirts—Brazil's color—to celebrate the victory and attract joyful customers.

What's in a Name?

The most appropriate name in World Cup history must belong to South Korean goalkeeper Oh Yun-Kyo, who participated in the 1986. That's oh, as in zero, or a shutout.

Early in the second half of England's 3–0 second-round victory over Paraguay in 1986, Gary Andrew Stevens replaced Peter Reid at midfield. There was nothing unusual about that, except that there was a Gary Stevens in the lineup already for the English—defender Gary Michael Stevens—which drove several radio and television announcers crazy.

Is it Roger Milla or Roger Miller? Actually it's both. The Cameroon star changed his name to Milla to sound more African.

The players with the shortest names were Paraguay's Cayetano Re in 1958 and Argentina's Francisco Sa in 1974.

A total of 66 players have performed for Bulgaria in 16 matches and every player has had his name end in a v, except for Milko Gaidarski, who played in the 1970 World Cup.

Then there was Argentine Julio Olarticoechea. Try to pronounce that. ESPN announcers called him Julio. He just might have had the most intimidating name at the 1986 cup.

Incredible But True

After Hungary lost to Italy in the 1938 final in Paris, Hungarian goalkeeper Antal Szabo said: "I have never felt so proud in my life." Say what? "We may have lost the match, but we have saved 11 lives. The Italian players received a telegram from Rome before the game which read, 'Win or die!' Now they can go home as heroes." The telegram reportedly came from Mussolini.

Sometimes celebrating can be hazardous to your health. After Uruguayan Juan Hohberg scored the tying goal in the 87th minute against Hungary in the 1954 semifinals, his teammates jumped on him and knocked him out. He did recover and hit the post with a shot in overtime, but Hungary registered a 4–2 victory.

After Argentina was eliminated in the 1958 finals in Sweden—3–1 loss to West Germany and a 6–1 defeat to Czechoslovakia—its players experienced a rude welcome at Buenos Aires airport as fans threw rotten tomatoes, stones and fruit at them.

After Italy was bounced by North Korea, 1–0, fans at the airport in Rome pelted the team with vegetables. Italian fans were more into psychological warfare in 1986. When the team arrived at Rome airport after elimination, the Italians were welcomed with the sign, "Italy Vomits on You."

Oops

In the 1934 World Cup championship game, Italy's Raimondo Orsi scored a brilliant goal against Czechoslovakia: He curled a shot into the goal. The day after, Orsi attempted to repeat the feat more than 20 times for photographers in a posed situation, but could not do it.

As he scored a penalty kick in Italy's 2–1 semifinal victory over Brazil in 1938, captain Peppino Meazza lost his shorts, torn earlier in the match, and they fell to the ground. His teammates gathered around him as a new pair was produced.

As he left his locker room for a match against Brazil in 1950, Yugoslav midfielder Rajko Mitic walked into an iron girder and knocked himself out at Maracana Stadium. His 10 teammates walked out onto the field and tried to walk back to the locker room to delay the kickoff, but referee Mervyn Griffiths of Wales demanded they start the match on time. By the time Mitic, who was heavily bandaged, returned, the Yugoslavians had a 1–0 deficit. Brazil went on to win, 2–0.

Mexican goalkeepers proved to be a superstitious lot at the 1966 cup. Ignacio Calderon knelt underneath the crossbar before 2 matches and Antonio Carbajal kissed both goalposts for luck. It must have worked because Mexico played Uruguay to a scoreless tie.

They almost began the World Cup without the proper field markings in the 1974 World Cup in West Germany, of all places. After a spectacular opening ceremony before Brazil and Yugoslavia tussled, officials had to quickly put in the corner and center flags while the referee delayed the start of the match.

During Italy's 1–1 draw with Peru in 1982, West German referee Walter Eschweiler ran into a Peruvian player, was knocked on his back and lost his whistle in the process.

After he allowed a goal in a 1–1 draw with Honduras in 1982, Spanish goalkeeper Luis Arconada later was roughed up by a Valencia policeman who mistook him for a burglar.

A computer in the Soviet Union predicted that Brazil would win the

1982 World Cup, defeating West Germany in the final, 1–0. The computer was half-right. Brazil did not reach the semifinals, but the West Germans did lose in the finals to Italy, 3–1.

During the 1986 World Cup in Mexico, a soft drink commerical showed that Mexican star Hugo Sanchez converted a penalty kick. In real life, Sanchez missed an important penalty in the final moments of the 1–1 first-round tie with Paraguay, much to the amusement of his critics.

He was 20-years-old at the time, but there was no excuse for what happened to Belgian Enzo Scifo in a 2–2 opening-round draw with Paraguay in 1986. He apparently had scored a goal off a free kick for a 3–1 advantage late in the match—or so he thought. It was nullified because the call actually was an indirect free kick. Another player had to touch the ball before it went into the net.

Iraqi defender Barmeer Shaker was given a 1-year suspension from international matches by FIFA for spitting at the referee during a 2–1 first-round defeat to Belgium in 1986.

English midfielder Ray Wilkins threw the ball at referee Gabriel Gonzalez (Paraguay) during a 0–0 draw with Morocco in 1986. He was given a red card and a 2-game suspension by FIFA.

Forward Branko Segota showed up late for Canada in the 1986 World Cup because his visa had expired.

Uruguayan defender Jose Batista was hit with the fastest red card in cup history. He was ejected only 53 seconds into a scoreless draw with Scotland in the opening round of the 1986 cup.

Gianluca Vialli experienced one of the most embarrassing matches in Italy's 1–0 victory over the United States in 1990, registering a unique hat-trick. He missed a penalty kick, had a goal called back because of an offside call and looked terrible when he attempted and missed a bicycle kick in the penalty area.

At Italia '90, Japanese journalists Juzuru Saito and Isoyama Katsuni were attacked by English hooligans while filming fans on the street near the main railroad station in Cagliari, Sardinia. Saito received a cut in an eyebrow when he was hit by a rock and Katsuni received severe chest bruises from a beating.

Alain Lammortain, a 26-year-old Belgian, was mistaken as a hooligan and was attacked by youths in Latina, about 30 miles south of Rome at the 1990 World Cup.

Fans

Manuel Gonzales. In 1962, Manuel Gonzales, a 17-year-old bellboy who was adopted by the Uruguayan team as its mascot at the hotel where the team stayed in Arica, Chile, suffered a heart attack and died after a 3–1 loss to Yugoslavia. The team attended Gonzales' funeral.

Paul Connell. The Englishman had to be the most unlikely fan at the 1982 World Cup in Spain. Only 2 weeks after he fought and then wounded in the Falklands, he attended England's match against Czechoslovakia.

Domingo Padilla. The Honduran native, who was so upset over the "unjust" elimination of his team, shot and killed himself during the 1982 World Cup.

English fans. They taunted Argentine fans over the surrender of the Falkland Islands during the 1982 competition. They chanted, "How does it feel to lose the war?" in England's 2–0 victory over Czechoslovakia.

Sarajevo, Yugoslavia fans. They destroyed the car of Yugoslavian player Safet Susic because of his and the team's disappointing first-round performance in 1982.

Brazilian fans. Five people died and more than 650 were injured during celebrations of a Brazilian victory in 1986.

Mexico City fans. After each of Mexico's 3 victories during the 1986 World Cup, the fans celebrated into the night at Independence Monument downtown, causing damage in the hundreds of thousands of dollars.

A Haitian policeman. He shot and killed his neighbor, Rodriguez Mouval, 23, after they argued over which team—Argentina or England—would reach the championship match in 1986.

Pedro Gatica. The 52-year-old man from Argentina bicycled hundreds of miles to Mexico City for the 1986 cup. When he arrived, however, he found the tickets too expensive. And then thieves stole his bike.

Abdul Razzaq. The 45-year-old Iraqi fan died from a heart attack brought on by a referee's decision to disallow a goal against Paraguay in a 1–0 loss on June 4, 1986.

Joseph Oscar. He was 76 at the 1986 World Cup, and he hadn't missed a World Cup since 1958. He gave a toot on his horn after France scored a goal.

Xia Qianli. This 17-year-old Chinese man strangled his father in Wenzhou, Zhejiang, because he was not allowed to watch the opening ceremony of the 1990 competition.

Banu Begum. The 30-year-old Bangladesh woman committed suicide on July 1, 1990, after Cameroon had been eliminated by England. Before hanging herself, Begum left a suicide note that read: "Now that Cameroon has left the World Cup, I am leaving this world."

Andrea Mantovan. The 17-year-old Italian died on June 23, 1990, after receiving a severe head injury after falling from a car during a post-match celebration in Merano, Italy.

The Money Game and Other Incentives

In 1982, Kuwaiti players could have earned $200,000 each if the team reached the second round. It didn't.

In 1990, Khalid Ismail Mubarak scored the United Arab Emirates' first World Cup goal ever in its 5–1 loss to West Germany on June 9. He received a Rolls Royce for his feat.

In 1990, the Royal Dutch Soccer Federation said it would pay bonuses of $65,220 to each player if the Netherlands won the title (it didn't). That prompted the team's 3 leading players—Ruud Gullit, Marco van Basten and Frank Rijkaard—to offer their bonuses to their

Netherlands Johnny Rep heads a ball over Daniel Passarella in the 1978 final which Argentina won 3–1 with two goals in extratime.

teammates. Gullit called them "the lowest players' bonuses around." There's more. Italian players would have received $370,000 apiece if they had won. Each Belgian player had been promised $105,000 and the United Arab Emirates, technically amateur, received $135,000 each from President Sheik Zayed bin Sultan Ali Nahyan just for qualifying. Businessmen and rulers of the 7 emirates (states) also gave the players and coaches a number of gifts.

And then there's Egypt, which would pay $600 a victory and $300 for a tie.

Medicine Men

Players who were banned because of drug use: Haiti's Ernst Jean-Joseph in 1974 and Scotland's Willie Johnston in 1978.

Illegal drugs were found in the system of Spanish player Ramon Caldere at the 1986 cup, but he was not banned from playing because the team doctor mistakenly gave him the drugs. The Spanish Soccer Federation was fined $13,000 for the incident.

It's Not Always a Grand Old Flag

During West Germany's controversial and lackluster 1–0 victory over Austria in 1982, which qualified both countries for the second round, Algerian fans burned West German flags in protest of the less-than-exhuberant performances by both sides.

Four years after the Falkland Wars, Argentine fans burned English flags during the quarterfinal confrontation between the 2 teams at the 1986 World Cup.

All God's Creatures, Large and Small

During France's 1–0 victory over Canada in 1986, an overzealous French fan threw a rooster—the national team's symbol—onto the field. The rooster was removed by the referee.

A dog ran onto the field in Peru's scoreless tie with Cameroon in the 1982 cup. The dog was on the field for several minutes. Finally, the game was held up to clear out the pooch.

And speaking of animals, the all-time best mascot had to be Kuwait's live camel at the 1982 cup.

Odds and Ends

Pele, not surprisingly, has played for 3 champions. Ten other players have taken the victory lap twice. They are Giovanni Ferrari (Italy, 1934, 1938), Giuseppe Meazza (Italy, 1934, 1938), Didi (Brazil, 1958, 1962), Garrincha (Brazil, 1958, 1962) Gilmar do Santos Neves (Brazil, 1958, 1962), Djalma Santos (Brazil, 1958, 1962), Nilton Santos (Brazil, 1958, 1962), Vava (Brazil, 1958, 1962), Mario Zagalo (Brazil, 1958, 1962), Zito (Brazil, 1958, 1962).

Cesar Zavala just might have had the hardest shot at the 1986 World Cup. The Paraguayan midfielder fired the ball barely over the crossbar midway through the first half of a 1−1 opening-round draw with Mexico. The power of the shot deflated the ball, which was replaced.

The best performance by a substitute was by Hungary's Laszlo Kiss, who scored 3 goals after coming on in the second half of his country's 10−1 romp over El Salvador in 1982.

The most unusual souvenir of all-time at a World Cup had to be the official World Cup '82 bagpipes, which were sold in Gio and La Coruna in Spain.

Scalpers in Valencia, Spain made a killing for the Spain-Honduras match in 1982. They sold $9 tickets for $100. Then there were 42 would-be scalpers in Seville, who were arrested trying to sell 1,060 tickets for the Scotland-Soviet Union match.

Brazilian coach Tele Santana lost 6 1/2 pounds because of his team's tough workouts in the heat (more than 90 degrees) in 1982.

Algeria enjoyed a memorable Independence Day celebration at the 1982 World Cup. On the 20th anniversary of the country's birth—June 16—Algeria jolted West Germany, pulling off a 2−1 upset.

When Czechoslovakia gained the 1934 championship match, the squad was made up of 11 players from only 2 teams—Sparta and Slavia. No other finalist has had such a small club representation.

Before qualifying for USA '94, Bolivia advanced to the World Cup on two occasions, doing so without playing a qualifier. The 1930 tournament was by invitation only, and the Bolivians road to Uruguay in 1950 was after Argentina dropped out.

John Charles, who scored for Wales in its 1−1 tie with Hungary in 1958, arrived in Sweden only a day before that match after the Italian

Football Federation gave him last-minute permission to be released from commitments with Juventus.

The most frequent surname in the World Cup is Gonzales or Gonzalez, of which there has been 14 players with that name. Lopez is next with 11.

Italy has provided the most referees and linesmen to the World Cup—15. The Italians are followed by England (12) and France and West Germany, with 11 apiece.

Bulgaria has never won a game despite participating in 16 matches over 5 cups. The Bulgarians are 0-10-6.

Poland's Leslaw Cmikiewicz made 6 appearances for his country as a substitute in the 1974 World Cup. Cmikiewicz played all of 102 minutes. His longest stint was 33 minutes vs. Yugoslavia. He replaced Robert Gadocha (vs. Argentina), Zygmunt Maszcyzk (vs. Haiti) and Andrzej Szarmach (vs. Italy) in the opening round, Szarmach (vs. Yugoslavia) and Henryk Kasperczak (vs. Germany) in the second round and Kasperczak (vs. Poland) in the third-place match. The only match he did not appear in was a second-round encounter vs. Sweden.

Brazil used only 12 players—a record—in 6 matches in its march to the championship in 1962. Had Pele not been injured—he was replaced by Amarildo in the second game—the Brazilians would have used an unchanged lineup.

The Last Time

The last goal: By West Germany's Andreas Brehme in the 85th minute of a 1–0 victory over Argentina in the championship match on July 8, 1990.

The last penalty kick: By Brehme on July 8, 1990.

The last goal, other than a penalty kick: Salvatore Schillaci for Italy in its 2–1 victory over England in the third-place match on July 7, 1990.

The last own goal: By South Korea's Cho Kwang-rae in Italy's 3–2 victory on June 10, 1986.

The last hat-trick: By Tomas Skuhravy in Czechoslovakia's 4–1 second-round victory over Costa Rica on June 23, 1990.

The last ejection: Argentina's Gustavo Abel Dezotti in West Germany's 1–0 victory on July 8, 1990.

The last match decided by a penalty-kick tie-breaker: West Germany vs. England on July 4, 1990. The teams played to a 1−1 tie and the West Germans won the tie-breaker, 4−3.

The last scoreless tie: Argentina vs. Yugoslavia in the quarterfinals on June 30, 1990. The Argentines advanced on penalty kicks.

The last scoreless tie (not decided by penalty kicks): Egypt vs. Ireland on June 17, 1990.

Chapter Twelve

Beyond the World Cup

The 1994 World Cup is supposed to leave a legacy for soccer in the United States—a national pro league—or as Alan I. Rothenberg put it, "the cherry on the icing on the cake."

At the World Cup draw in Las Vegas in December, 1993, the U.S. Soccer Federation unveiled its plans for a 12-team pro league that will begin operation in 1995.

It took the U.S. Soccer Federation more than 5 years to get its act together. When the U.S. was awarded the rights to the 1994 World Cup on July 4, 1988, it was with the stipulation that a professional league be formed. For one reason or another, it wasn't.

So, on Dec. 17, 1993, USSF President Rothenberg, who also happened to be the CEO and chairman of World Cup USA 1994, announced plans—remember, they were only plans—for a pro league. The USSF national board of directors approved the new league, 18-5, over 2 other proposals—by the American Professional Soccer League, which already has Division II status, and Chicago entrepreneur Jim Paglia, who plans to pursue a 12-team national league anyway. Paglia's league—called League 1 America—which will include entertainment malls built around soccer stadiums, could turn out to be a "unaffiliated pirate league," but there is precedent for that in U.S. soccer history.

The new league endorsed by the USSF, called Major League Soccer, is supposed to have 12 cities and run from April to September. The league will be run by a single entity that will own all the players and teams, similar to a fast-food chain that franchises out its restaurants.

Each team will be restricted to 3 foreign players, although Rothenberg said he hoped that the number could be increased in the first seasons to boost its attractiveness and ensure top-class teams. An estimated $100 million will be needed to start and fund the league, which would be used to improve stadiums or build new ones, buy back

American players' contracts from their European teams and provide competitive salaries. There also was a television contract being negotiated.

"We believe the time has never been more right for a professional league to succeed," Rothenberg said. "The level of participation in soccer in this country has been growing by leaps and bounds. We have proved in the organizing the World Cup that we can convert participants into spectators. I have no doubt a league like this will be successful."

The new league also got the approval of FIFA, which had been urging the USSF to form a league since 1988. "FIFA was very pleased to receive the excellent report from Major League Soccer," FIFA General Secretary Joseph Blatter said. "We are optimistic about the future of soccer in the United States."

Still, there seemed to be more questions than answers about the new league.

Where will the teams be located?

League officials could not name which cities were among early candidates (Rothenberg at one time wanted to use the 9 World Cup cities as a core), but for a coast-to-coast pro league to be viable, teams are a must in the 3 largest cities—New York, Los Angeles and Chicago.

"Why 12? The feeling is less than 12 [would] raise the question of not being a national league," Rothenberg said. "More than 12, it dilutes our player talent."

Where will they play?

The league wants stadiums with capacities of 20,000–25,000 (during its best days, the North American Soccer League averaged in the neighborhood of 15,000 fans per game), which could prove problems for the major metropolitan areas. In New York, for example, there are no stadiums smaller than 50,000. Two possibilities are the 76,000-plus capacity Giants Stadium, home of the New York Cosmos from 1977-1984, or Rutgers Stadium, which will hold 50,000 after its renovation is completed in the spring of 1994.

How much will the players be paid?

While salaries will not come close to the multi-million dollar contracts found in other sports, they should be enough to live on, averaging about $70,000 per player, said Mark Abbott, an attorney for

Major League Professional Soccer, Inc., the MLS's corporate entity. Rothenberg said the league was prepared to pay more for the European-based players—for example, midfielder John Harkes reportedly earns in the neighborhood of $200,000 from Derby County in the English First Division—to maintain the quality of the league.

"We want to lure back the top players and have competitive salaries," Rothenberg said.

Even though soccer is a strong participation sport in the U.S., can those players be turned into paying spectators?

"In our experience, there is enough hunger for soccer in this country," Rothenberg said. "Player participation has never been so high. We have showed we can successfully convert players into spectators."

The other investors could come from corporate America or from foreign concerns. There has been speculation that foreign-owned clubs could place developmental teams in the U.S. Italian champion A.C. Milan approached the USSF about sponsoring a team, according to USA TODAY. Perhaps other strong European clubs—Manchester United (England), Barcelona (Spain) and Bayern Munich (Germany)—will back teams. There has also been speculation that some teams from the J-League, which made a popular and successful debut in Japan in 1993 with a number of aging international stars (Brazil's Zico and England's Gary Lineker, to name a few), could eventually invest in U.S. teams. J-League teams are backed by major corporations with deep pockets.

Bruce Arena, coach of 4-time NCAA Division I men's champion, the University of Virginia, said he would not mind foreign-sponsored clubs, even as farm teams, as long as a minimum of 8 American players were on the field at all times.

"We're better for it," he said. "In this country, we can throw out 120 players and mix in foreign players. It gives them the mentality of playing overseas."

To some people, it's only a matter of time. Seton Hall University Coach Manfred Schellscheidt, who has coached two national championship youth teams and the U.S. Olympic team, said he felt the day is coming when soccer enthusiasts—soccer millionaires, as he calls them—will have money to spend and burn while owning a soccer team.

"These are people who are big-time executives, and they could care less how much money they will lose," he said. "In time, whether you like it or not, they will come."

Six years was certainly long enough to wait for a pro league. Why the long wait? There always seemed to be an excuse. On that July day back in 1988, Werner Fricker, then president of the USSF, talked about some ambitious plans for a 3-tier league, which would not be unlike the structure of European soccer. Those original plans called for 32 teams in a national league (Division I), 64 in regional leagues (Division 2) and 128 in local leagues (Division 3), with promotion and relegation for the top and bottom clubs of each division.

Fricker said such a setup "will create an ideal environment for the American soccer player to develop and become a highly skilled and competitive player at the world-class level."

That league was supposed to be in place by 1991.

But the Fricker administration dragged its heels and eventually was voted out of office in 1990. Rothenberg, who replaced Fricker as USSF president, said staging the World Cup was the primary focus. The league was put off until 1994 and then until 1995.

Professional soccer isn't new to the United States, as it has been alive and kicking in one incarnation or another since the 1920s. The original American Soccer League, which began in 1921, lasted only a handful of years. It had franchises in Fall River, MA, Jersey City, NJ and Brooklyn, NY (Todd Shipyard). The second version of the ASL was born in 1933 and likewise was an East-coast league made up of teams representing mills and businesses. It expanded into the Midwest and to the West and before it went out of business after the 1983 season, falling one year short of celebrating its 50th anniversary. The United Soccer League, organized by a band of owners disgruntled by the way the ASL was operated, was formed in 1984. But that league fizzled out after only a couple of years.

In 1960, the International Soccer League, under the sponsorship of the ASL and sports promoter Bill Cox, was formed as teams from Europe and South America visited the U.S. and played in a tournament, usually at the Polo Grounds in New York City, in an attempt to test the support of American soccer fans for first-class soccer. It lasted until the mid-sixties.

Ironically, another World Cup gave birth to the modern version of pro soccer. The 1966 World Cup, particularly England's 4−2 overtime victory over West Germany in the championship match, stirred so much interest in the U.S. that not one, but 2 leagues were born in 1967. There was the United Soccer Association, which brought over teams from Europe and South America to play in 12 cities (the Los Angeles Wolves, the league champion, were represented by Wolverhampton of England), which was given approval by the USSF. Another league, the National Professional Soccer League, which was not sanctioned by FIFA, was formed. It had 10 teams, many in the same cities as the USA.

After an $18-million lawsuit was filed by the NPSL, the two leagues got together and merged into the NASL in 1968. The NASL became the dominant pro soccer league until its demise after the 1984 season. At its height (1978–80), the NASL, which was patterned after the National Football League, boasted 24 teams in all the major cities. Some of the world's greatest stars played in the NASL, including Pele, Franz Beckenbauer, Johan Cruyff and Giorgio Chinaglia. However, huge financial losses, small attendances and a slow plan to Americanize the teams (at one time, believe it or not, there was a quota of one North American per team) were among the reasons why the league went out of business.

As the NASL was fading, the Western Soccer Alliance, comprised of teams on the West Coast, was born. The league eventually changed its name to the Western Soccer League. On the East Coast, the American Soccer League popped up. Those 2 leagues came together to form the American Professional Soccer League in 1991. The APSL had only 7 teams for 1993—the champion Colorado Foxes, Fort Lauderdale Strikers, Los Angeles Salsa, Montreal Impact, Tampa Bay Rowdies, Toronto Blizzard and Vancouver 86ers—and only 4 in the U.S.

Don't go away. There's more: The U.S. Interregional Soccer League, a self-described minor league planned 71 franchises in large and small markets across the U.S. in 1994. Calling itself a minor league has given the USISL instant credibility in a sport where owners and promoters called anything major league (The Greensboro Dynamo captured the 1993 USISL title).

During the heydays of the NASL, a number of hardy businessmen and investors took a chance on indoor soccer.

The Major Indoor Soccer League was formed as a 6-team league in 1978, had as many as 14 franchises in both the 1982–83 and 1984–85 seasons before going out of business after the 1991–92 season. The American Indoor Soccer Association was formed as a midwestern league in 1984. It has expanded slowly to the east and eventually switched its name in 1990 to the National Professional Soccer League. The NPSL had 12 teams for the 1993–94 season—Baltimore Spirit, Buffalo Blizzard, Canton Invaders, Cleveland Crunch, Dayton Dynamo and Harrisburg Heat in the American Division and Chicago Power, Detroit Rockers, Kansas City Attack, Milwaukee Wave, St. Louis Ambush and Wichita Wings in the National Division.

In 1993, a group of owners from the National Basketball Association got together, having noticed that their arenas were vacant during the summer months. So they formed the Continental Indoor Soccer League, which premiered during the summer of 1993, with 7 franchises—the champion Dallas Sidekicks, Arizona Sandsharks, L.A. United, Monterrey La Raza, Portland Pride, Sacramento Knights and San Diego Sockers. The league was expected to expand for the 1994 season.

As for soccer in the U.S., it will be around for a very long time. More than 15 million people are involved as either players, coaches, parents, administrators and game officials. More than 2.2 million youths play in organized leagues. That number could be as much as two times greater because many children and teen-agers play in leagues that are not affiliated or are run by the YMCA, police athletic clubs, churches, city parks, ethnic leagues and other unaffiliated groups.

Some of those leagues feed into a host of amateur and semi-pro leagues, which boast a high quality level of soccer, ironically due to the lack of a pro league. There is also high school and college soccer (women's soccer is the fastest growing sport at the collegiate level), although those seasons are 2, maybe 3 months at the most.

And fans will not have to wait very long for the next big international tournament, although it does not hold the same prestige as the World Cup. The Summer Olympics are scheduled for Atlanta in 1996 with the gold-medal matches at the University of Georgia. Soccer fans will be in for an extra treat because women's soccer will be part of the Olympics for the first time. The U.S., whose women's National Team captured the very first FIFA world championship in China in 1991, is expected to be one of the favorites. The U.S. women first will have to defend their world title in Sweden in June, 1995.

As for the World Cup itself, the 1998 tournament was awarded to France in 1992, and it will be held there, even though the French did not qualify for its second successive World Cup. The 2002 cup is expected to be held in Asia, with Japan and South Korea as the leading candidates. Japan, with its highly successful J-League, was considered to be the early front-runner, but its cause suffered a blow when its national team could not qualify for the 1994 World Cup. Japan never has reached the

World Cup, while rivals South Korea, host of the 1988 Olympics, has qualified for 3 straight cups. It looks like an intriguing race.

There has even been some talk of 2006, as Germany has expressed interest although FIFA President Dr. Joao Havelange said an African country could wind up as host. 1998? 2002? 2006? We're getting way ahead of ourselves. Let's enjoy USA '94 while it lasts.

Appendix A

The Best and
The Brightest

The World Cup has always been a showcase of the planet's greatest talent. Presenting 40 players who distinguished themselves in the world's greatest sporting spectacle:

Gordon Banks, England (1966, 1970)—He starred for the 1966 champions, giving up only three goals in six matches, including two in the final victory over West Germany. The Germans managed to solve Banks four years later, but not before he produced what many consider to be the greatest save in World Cup, denying Pele a goal in a 1-0 defeat to Brazil in Mexico in 1970. Pele headed the ball toward the corner of the net and Banks, standing at the far post, miraculously knocked the ball out of harm's way with one hand. Banks, born Dec. 30, 1937, performed for Chesterfield, Leceister City, Stoke City in the English League and for Morton in Scotland. After an automobile accident cost him his right eye, Banks completed his playing career with the Fort Lauderdale Strikers of the North American Soccer League from 1977-78.

Gilmar, Brazil (1958 and 1962)—He is the only goalkeeper to have played on two winning World Cup sides. Gilmar and Brazil allowed four goals in six matches in Sweden in 1958 and five goals in six games in Chile in 1962. Gilmar's World Cup record is 10-0-2. Born on Aug. 22, 1930, Gilmar performed for the Corinthians and Santos in his native country, from 1951 to 1969. He made 93 appearances for the Brazilian National Team.

Sepp Maier, West Germany (1970, 1974)—One of the all-time greats, Maier anchored Germany's world championship team in 1974. Maier had a thing about streaks. The acrobatic keeper set a World Cup record for keeping the opposition off the scoresheet (475 minutes) that eventually was broken by Italy's Walter Zenga in 1990 and played an incredible 442 successive West German First Division matches from 1966 to 1979 with Bayern Munich. Maier, who was Feb. 28, 1944, also was voted West German Footballer of the Year on three occasions. He made 95 international appearances.

Dino Zoff, Italy (1974, 1978, 1982)—The book on Zoff in his later years was that he could be beaten by long shots, although it was a longshot to put a goal past this crafty veteran. He once went 1,145 minutes without allowing a goal, between September, 1972 and June, 1974. Born on Feb. 28, 1942, Zoff was 40-years-old when Italy captured its third World Cup in 1982. He was magnificent in the nets, becoming the oldest captain on a World Cup championship team. Zoff, who starred for Mantova, Napoli and Juventus, made 112 appearances for his country. He later coached Juventus to the UEFA Cup in 1990 and now directs Lazio.

Defenders

Carlos Alberto, Brazil (1970)—Trivia question: Which position did Alberto play when Brazil took home its third and last World Cup? Would you believe right fullback? That's right the Brazilian captain, who was better known as a sweeper during his heydays with the New York Cosmos, patrolled the right side for the 1970 champions. He helped steady a defense that wasn't overworked very much because Brazil controlled the ball for long periods of time. Alberto scored only one World Cup goal—the exclamation point of the tournament—the final goal in the 4-1 championship win over Italy. Born on June 17, 1944, Alberto starred also played for four North American Soccer League champions with the Cosmos (1977-80, 1982), with a year's stint with the California Surf in 1981. Alberto, whose son Carlos Alexandre is a defender for Fluminense, played in 73 international matches. He will celebrate his 50th birthday on the day of the World Cup final.

Franz Beckenbauer, West Germany (1966, 1970, 1974)—Before his accomplishments as a coach, in which he reached the final twice, and captured one title (1990), Beckenbauer was the mainstay of the great West German machine a generation ago. That German team took second to England in that controverisal 1966 final, that finished in the Final Four in Mexico (The Kaiser played despite a painful shoulder injury) and captured the crown in 1974. Beckenbauer, who revolutionized the sweeper position by attacking from the back, also captained West Germany to the European Championship in 1972 and sparked Bayern Munich to the European Cup title in 1974-76. Beckenbauer, who was born Sept. 11, 1945, starred for the Cosmos from 1977-80 and 1983, before returning to his homeland to finish his career with Hamburg. He made 103 international appearances.

Paul Breitner, West Germany (1974, 1978, 1982)—It's easy to get lost in the shuffle on a teams that included Franz Beckenbauer and Gerd Mueller, but Breitner established himself domestically with Bayern Munich internationally with the West German national side. Breitner is considered one of the most inventive fullbacks of modern times, excelling for the 1974 world champions with a powerful shot. Born on Sept. 5, 1951, Breitner also performed for Real Madrid (Spain) and Eintracht Frankfurt. Breitner, who writes a controversial column for a German newspaper, often clashed politically with Beckenbauer because of his Maoist views. He scored 10 goals in 48 international appearances, including goals in the 1974 and 1982 championship matches.

Giancinto Facchetti, Italy (1966, 1970, 1974)—Although he never played on a champion—he was Italy's captain in the 1970 final against Brazil—the 6-foot-3 Facchetti made his mark in international soccer as an attacking defender, usually from the stopper position. In fact, Franz Beckenbauer drew his inspiration from Facchetti. Born on July 18, 1942, Facchetti was the cornerstone of the Inter attack for many years. He scored three goals in 94 appearances.

Rudi Krol, Netherlands (1974, 1978)—He could do it all in the back as Krol stood out on the flanks or as a central defender on a Dutch team that finished second twice. He was the captain of the 1978 squad. He is fluent in German, English and Italian. Born on March 24, 1949, Krol played for Ajax, Vancouver Whitecaps (NASL), Napoli (Italy) and Cannes (France). He scored twice in 83 appearances for the Netherlands.

Bobby Moore, England (1962, 1966 and 1970)—One of the all-time greats. Moore, who died of cancer in February, 1993 at the age of 51, was a member of three consecutive World Cup teams, anchoring the defense on the 1966 championship side. The former England captain completed a unique hat-trick when he climbed those famous steps at Wembley to collect the World Cup trophy. As West Ham captain in

1964, he took the same route to lift the F.A. Cup and a year later, history repeated when he picked up the European Cup Winners Cup. Born April 12, 1941, Moore played the central defender position unemotionally. Moore, who was named the outstanding player of the 1966 World Cup, was capped 106 times.

Daniel Passarella, Argentina (1978, 1982, 1986)—He was captain of Argentina's 1978 championship squad, the rock of a solid defense and the initiator of many of the Argentines' attacks. He also moved up into attacking position, scoring three career World Cup goals. Passarella, born on May 25, 1953, played for River Plate, Fiorentina (Italy) and Inter (Italy). He scored 24 goals in 69 international appearances.

Djalma Santos, Brazil (1954, 198, 1962 and 1966)—It's almost an oxymoron—a Brazilian defender among World Cup greats? Aren't the Brazilians more famous for their attacking abilities? They sure are, but Santos contributed to four World Cup teams and two world champions, as a superb overlapping right fullback. Born on Feb. 27, 1929, Santos starred for Portoguesa, Palmeiras and Atletico Parana in Brazil. Santos, who was capped 101 times, was known for his quick tackling.

Nilton Santos, Brazil (1958, 1962, 1966)—Santos, no relation to Djalma Santos, played both ends of the field equally well. Whether it was keeping his cool during a foes' offensive onslaught or over-lapping from his left fullback position, Santos was an impact player on a team of impact players. In the 1958 final against, Sweden, for example, Santos shut down the home team's top threat, Kurt Hamrin. He played 22 years for Botafogo, until his retirement in 1970. Born on May 16, 1927, Santos scored three goals in 75 appearances for Brazil.

Midfielders

Jozsef Bozsik, Hungary (1954 and 1958)—Considered the greatest midfielder Hungary produced, Bozsik was a member of the Magic Magyars of the fifties. He usually set up the legendary Ferenc Puskas and Sandor Kocsis. Born on Nov. 22, 1925, starred for Kispest and Honved. He scored 11 goals in 100 international appearances.

Bobby Charlton, England (1962, 1966, 1970)—A classy man and player, on and off the field. He was a forward in the 1962 tournament and returned as a creative force in England's quest for the trophy four years later. Charlton, one of the survivors of the horrific Manchester United plane crash in Munich in 1958, was capped 106 times for England. Former England international Jimmy Greaves called his one-time teammate, — like a Nureyev on grass. — Born on Oct. 11, 1937, Charlton scored a record 49 goals for England. He is now a spokesman for MasterCard, a World Cup sponsor.

Johan Cruyff, Netherlands (1974)—Though he participated in but one World Cup, Cruyff, nicknamed El Flaco—The Thin Man—made his presence felt in West Germany, masterfully guiding the Dutch to a second-place finish. He did not play on the 1978 squad that also finished second, although observers felt if he had played, the Dutch would have been champions. Born on April 25, 1947, Cruyff led Ajax to the European Cup crown three times before joining Barcelona and the Los Angeles Aztecs and Washington Diplomats (NASL). He scored 33 goals in 48 international matches. Cruyff coaches champion Barcelona of the Spanish First Division.

Didi, Brazil (1954, 1958, 1962)—Another member of those great Brazilian championship teams, Didi wound up as the midfield architect of the 1958 and 1962 squads. The midfielder, known as Waldir PereiraDidi, helped originate the boomerang free kicks, which were called the folha seca (dry leaf). When he wasn't distributing the ball to Pele, Did managed to score 24 goals in 72 international appearances. Born on Oct. 8, 1928, he almost had his right leg amputated when he was 14 after a serious injury. But it wasn't, and Didi went on to star for Fluminese, Real Madrid (Spain), Valencia (Spain) and Botafogo. He also coached Peru at the 1970 World Cup and later in Saudi Arabia.

Gerson, Brazil (1966, 1970)—After an rather impressive performance in one start in the 1966 World Cup in England, Gerson—whose full name is Gerson de Oliveira Nunes-was the midfield schemer for the world champions four years later in Mexico. Gerson, who played for Flamengo and Botafogo, was not a particularly big fan of practice and reportedly smoked 40 cigarettes a day. Born on 1941, Gerson made 84 international appearances for Brazil.

Mario Kempes, Argentina (1974, 1978, 1982)—The 1978 World Cup was a showcase for Kempes, who connected for six goals in seven matches, including a goal in the 3-1 triumph over the Netherlands in the final. Known for his flowing air, Kempes was equally effective at midfield or forward. Born on July 15, 1954, Kempes played for Rosario Central, Valencia (Spain), River Plate and Sankt Polten (Austria). He scored 20 goals in 42 international appearances.

Josef Masopust, Czechoslovakia (1962)—He was the key to the Czech attack in the team's second-place finish to Brazil in Chile. His only goal came in the final—the first goal of what turned into a 3-1 Brazilian win. Still, he was named Europe's Footballer of the Year in 1962. Born on Feb. 9, 1931, Masopust played for Teplice, Dukla Prague, which was the Czech Army team, and Royal Molenbeek (Belgium). He scored 10 times in 63 international matches.

Michel Platini, France (1978, 1982, 1986)—Platini actually distinguished himself more in European and club competitions, thanks to his incredible vision and skills. Still, he guided France to a third-place finish in 1982 after the French blew a 3-1 lead to West Germany in extratime in the semifinals. Born on June 21, 1955, Platini played in the 1976 Olympics in Montreal, starred for Nancy, St. Etienne and Juventus (Italy). Platini, who mastered the free kick, scored the lone goal for Juventus in the team's 1-0 victory over Liverpool in the 1985 European Cup final in Brussels, Belgium, the same game that saw 39 Italian fans die in pre-game rioting with English supporters. He scored 41 goals in 72 international appearances. Most recently, Platini coached the French to a rather disappointing finish at the 1992 European Championship. He resigned almost immediately after the competition, and joined the French World Cup Organizing Committee for 1998.

Johan Neeskens, Netherlands (1974, 1978)—Neeskens was one of the driving forces behind the Dutch's two consecutive second-place finishes (only West Germany has duplicated that feat, in 1982 and 1986). Neeskens scored the Dutch's first goal, off a penalty kick, in the 1974 final vs. the West Germans. Neeskens, who began his professional career with Ajax, went on to play for Barcelona (Spain) and the New York Cosmos (NASL). Born Sept. 15, 1951, Neeskens scored 17 goals in 49 appearances for the Netherlands.

Juan Schiaffino, Uruguay (1950, 1954)—He was a frail-looking player who could dominate the game with his dribbling and passing. Schiaffino—nicknamed Pepe—scored the tying goal in the 1950 World Cup final, which Uruguay eventually won over Brazil, 2-1. He finished the competition with five goals. Born on July 28, 1925, Schiaffino performed for Penarol and A.C. Milan (Italy), leading the club to three league championships and the 1958 European Cup crown, and AS Roma (Italy). He made 45 international appearances for Uruguay, and four for Italy (before the rule was established limiting players to one country).

Fritz Walter, West Germany (1954 and 1958)—Only one can wonder how great his career would have been had there were no World War II. Still, it wasn't too bad as Walter, behind his exceptional vision and technical skill, captained the 1954 world champions, scoring twice in the 6-1 semifinal win over Austria. His international career got off to a rousing start as a 19-year-old in July, 1940, as Walter scored three goals in a 9-3 romp over Romania. He did not play with the National Team from 1942 through 1951 because of the war. Born on Oct. 31, 1920, Walter played for Kaiserslautern. He scored 33 goals in 61 international matches.

Forwards

Zito, Brazil (1958, 1962)—Zito—whose full name was Jose Eli de Miranda—helped make Brazil's offensive-minded 4-2-4 formation click en route to a pair of world championships, behind his imaginative passing and tackling ability. Born in 1974, Zito played with Pele at Santos, including on two Brazilian title teams in 1959 and 1963. He scored three goals in 45 international matches.

Jose Leandro Andrade, Uruguay (1930)—He was among the first World Cup stars, setting up several goals behind his exceptional sklls and keen sense of positioning for the champions in the very first competition. After staring on Uruguay's gold-medal winning teams at the 1924 and 1928 Olympics, Andrade retired from international soccer. He was coaxed out of retirement for the World Cup. Born on Nov. 20, 1901, Andrade performed for Bellavista, Nacional, Penarol, Atlanta and the Wanderers. His nephew, Victor Rodriguez Andrade, was a member of the second Uruguayan side to win a World Cup—in 1950. Andrade made 43 international appearances. He died in 1954.

Teofilo (Nene) Cubillas, Peru, 1970, 1978, 1982)—Considered Peru's finest player ever, Cubillas he is the only player to have scored five goals in two World Cups—five in 1970 and five more in 1978 thanks to an explosive shot—tying for fifth on the career scoring list. He played another three matches in the 1982 competition, but he failed to score. Born March 8, 1949, Cubillas starred for Alianza and eventually for the Fort Lauderdale Strikers (NASL) 1979-83. In fact, Cubillas settled in South Florida, playing for amateur teams and helping the growth of the game in his new home. He scored 38 goals in 88 international appearances.

Leonidas Da Silva, Brazil (1934 and 1938)—Legend has it that Leonidas wanted to play without his cleats against Poland in the 1938 World Cup because the field was too muddy. The referee would not allow this and he went out and scored four goals—three in the opening half—in a 6-5 Brazilian victory. Nicknamed the Black Diamond, Leonidas' specialty was bicycle kicks. Born Sept. 6, 1913, Leonidas must have been the original free agent as he played for eight clubs during his 19-year career. The seemingly endless list includes Sao Cristovao, F.C. Sun America, Bomsucesso, Penarol (Uruguay), Vasco da Gama, Flamengo, Boca Juniors (Argentina) and Sao Paulo. He scored 22 goals in 19 international matches.

Eusebio, Portugal (1966)—Another one of those one-cup wonders, but again, what a cup! Eusebio struck for nine goals in Portugal's first appearance. His most memorable performance came in the quarterfinals against an upstart North Korea side that had stunned and eliminated Italy, 1-0, and that had taken a 3-0 lead over the Portuguese. But Eusebio took things into his own hands, so to speak, and scored four goals—including two penalty kicks—in an amazing 5-3 comeback victory. Born Jan. 25, 1942 in Mozambique, Eusebio starred for Benfica (313 goals in 291 games) before crossing the Atlantic to lead the Toronto Metros-Croatia to the 1976 NASL title; he also performed for the Boston Minutemen and Las Vegas Quicksilvers. His full name Eusebio da Silva Ferreira. Eusebio had 41 goals in 64 international matches.

Just Fontaine, France (1958)—He played in just one World Cup, but it was an unforgettable performance by Fontaine, who scored a record 13 goals as the French finished third in Sweden. He had a hat-trick in his World Cup debut in a 7-3 win over Paraguay, two in a 3-2 loss to Yugoslavia and another in a 2-1 victory over Scotland, all in the opening round. Fontaine, who profited from his understanding with French midfield general Raymond Kopa, connected for two goals in a 4-0 quarterfinal triumph over Northern Ireland and one in a 5-2 defeat to Brazil before he closed out his amazing one-man show with four goals in the third-place match, a 6-3 victory over West Germany. Fontaine, incidentally, was one of only a handful of players who scored in each game of a World Cup. Born on Aug. 18, 1933 in Morocco, Fontaine played for USM Casablanca (Morocco), Nice, Reims and the French Army. His playing career as a prolific goalscorer, however, ended prematurely with his second fracture of his left leg in early, 1961, at the age of 28. He finished with one of the best goals-per-games average in international history, connecting for 30 goals in only 21 appearances.

Garrincha, Brazil (1958, 1962, 1966)—His left leg was shorter than the other because of being born a cripple, but the man known as Little Bird ws a big man when it came to the World Cup, standing out on two championship teams. While Pele received much of the international accolades, Garrincha was known to tear a defense apart with his incredible runs and skills down the wing. After his teammates begged the coach to play him in Sweden in 1958, Garrincha did not disappoint, creating Brazil's first two goals in the championship match. He scored five World Cup goals. Born as Manoel dos Santos Francisco on Oct. 23, 1933, Garrincha bounced around with several clubs, including Botafogo, Corinthians, Flamengo, Bangu, Portuguesa Santista and Olaria. He scored 12 goals in 41 international appearances. He died in January, 1983 at the age of 50.

Jairzinho, Brazil (1966, 1970, 1974)—He proved to be a worthy successor to Garrincha, thanks to his speed and uncanny shooting ability. In Mexico in 1970, he became the only player to score in every World Cup match, including the final. Born Jair Ventura Filho in 1944, he played for Botafogo, Olympique Marseille (France) and also for clubs in Venezuela and Bolivia. He was capped 80 times for Brazil.

Sandor Kocsis, Hungary (1954)—Kocsis, who was called the—The Man With The Golden Head,—led the 1954 World Cup with 11 goals, including a couple of headers in overtime in Hungary's 4-2 semifinalvictory over Uruguay. His seven hat-tricks tied him with

Pele at the top of the international list. A member of the magnificent Magical Magyars teams of the fifties, Kocsis scored 75 goals for Hungary. Born Sept. 21, 1928, Kocsis led the Hungarian League in scoring on three occasions, playing with Honved and as a member of Hungary's 1952 gold-medal winning team. He also performed with Young Boys (Switzerland) and Barcelona (Spain). He scored an incredible 75 times in 68 international matches. He died in 1980.

Giuseppe Meazza, Italy (1934, 1938)—The brilliant, elusive forward starred for the Italians' back-to-back champions, captaining the 1938 side. He scored twice in 1934 and once in 1938. Born on May 4, 1949, Meazza played for Ambrosiana, A.C. Milan, Juventus, Atalanta and Inter Milan, collecting 261 goals in 443 league matches. Stadio Meazza, home of both Milan sides, was named after him. He scored 33 goals in 53 international appearances. He died in 1979.

The Pele file

There is no question that Pele is the greatest soccer player. His performance in the World underscores that:

* He is the only player to have played on three World Cup champions.
* He scored 12 goals in 14 matches, making him third on the all-time list behind Germany's Gerd Mueller, who scored 14 goals in two cup appearances and France's Just Fontaine, who recorded 13 goals in only one cup.
* Brazil was 8-0 whenever Pele scored a goal and was 12-1-1 when he was in the lineup. The only blemishes were a scoreless tie with Czechoslovakia in 1962 and a 3-1 loss to Portugal in 1966.
* Pele played in all of Brazil's matches only once—in 1970.

A breakdown of the World Cup goals he has scored:

1958 (Sweden)
June 15 (opening round)—Brazil 2, Soviet Union 0—no goals
June 19 (quarterfinals)—Brazil 1, Wales 0—one goal
June 24 (semifinals)—Brazil 5, France 2—three goals
June 29 (final)—Brazil 5, Sweden 2—two goals

1962 (Chile)
May 30 (opening round)—Brazil 2, Mexico 0—one goal
June 2 (opening round)—Brazil 0, Czechoslovakia—no goals

1966 (England)
June 12 (opening round)—Brazil 2, Bulgaria 0—one goal
June 19 (opening round)—Portugal 3, Brazil 1—no goals

Gerd Mueller, West Germany (1970, 1974)—Just the mention of his nickname—Der Bomber—would make opponents quake in their cleats. And why not? He finished with a career-record 14 goals over two tournaments. In Mexico in 1970, Mueller led everyone with 10 goals, including consecutive hat-tricks, no mean feat, which earned him European Footballer of the Year. He also led the continent in scoring twice to capture the Golden Boot. Mueller, who eventually went on to play for the Fort Lauderdale Strikers (North American Soccer League), did not look like a classic striker—many clubs thought he was too short and too stocky. Tell that to opposing goalkeepers. He finished with 628 goals. Born Nov. 3, 1945, Mueller scored a German record 68 times in only 62 appearances.

Pele, Brazil (1958, 1962 and 1970)—The man who was born on Oct. 23, 1940 as Edson Arantes do Nascimento is the only player to have performed for three world champions. He is considered the greatest player to have played the game because of prolific scoring ability, artistry leading up the goal and his ability of setting up his teammates. Pele, who stole the spotlight when he strolled onto the international stage with a sterling performance as a 17-year-old in Sweden in 1958, scored 12 goals in 14 matches for Brazil Although he missed most of the 1962 tournament in Chile (scoring once in two games) because of an injury and was butchered for most of the 1966

(The Pele file cont.)

1970 (Mexico)

June 3 (opening round)—Brazil 4, Czechoslovakia 1—one goal
June 7 (opening round)—Brazil 1, England 0—no goals
June 10 (opening round)—Brazil 3, Romania 2—two goals
June 14 (quarterfinals)—Brazil 4, Peru 2—no goals
(June 17 (semifinals)—Brazil 3, Uruguay 1—no goals
June 21 (final)—Brazil 4, Italy 1—one goal

Qualifying

He has performed for three champions, but Pele has participated in just one qualifying series because Brazil twice automatically qualified as the defending champion.

His only qualifying appearance occurred in 1989, for the 1970 World Cup in Mexico.

The Black Pearl played in six matches during that run, scoring as many goals as Brazil defeated Colombia, Venezuela and Paraguay, outscoring its foes, 23–2.

Pele was not the top scorer for the Brazilians. Tosato was, connecting for 10 goals.

competition in England (one goal in two games), Pele bounced back with a brilliant individual performance in the 1970 cup in Mexico (four goals in six matches). Pele, who played 19 years for Santos, joined the New York Cosmos (NASL) in a multi-million dollar deal for three years starting in1975. Pele finished his career with 1,281 goals in 1,363 matches. He scored 97 times in 111 international appearances.

Ferenc Puskas, Hungary, Spain (1954, 1962)—Was there ever a player with a better left foot than Puskas? The Galloping Major, as English fans dubbed him, Puskas was a vital part of the Magical Magyars of the fifties. He helped Hungary reach the final of the 1954 World Cup in Switzerland, only to see his side lose, 3-2. Puskas might be partly to blame for the defeat because he had insisted on playing, although he was not fully recovered from an ankle injury. He had four goals in that tournament. After defecting to Spain because of the Hungarian Revolution in 1956, Puskas went on to star for Real Madrid (242 goals in 269 matches) and played for Spain in the 1962 World Cup and Vancouver Royals (National Professional Soccer League). Born April 2, 1924, Puskas scored 85 goals in 84 international matches.

Roberto Rivellino, Brazil (1970, 1974, 1978)—He found the back of the net three times for the 1970 champions, then captained a pair of teams that fell short the next two tournaments. Rivellino, who had one of the strongest shots around, also scored another three goals in 1974. Born on Jan. 1, 1946, Rivellino performed for the Corinthinians, Sao Paulo, Fluminese and Hillal Al Riyad (Saudi Arabia). He scored 25 goals in 96 international appearances.

Paolo Rossi, Italy (1978, 1982)—If you want to get technical, Rossi's contribution to World Cup folklore lasted all of three games in 1982. But what a memorable three games. After sitting out two years for his involvement in a game-fixing scandal, Rossi caught fire in a quarterfinal-round match against favored Brazil, in which he scored all of Italy's goals in a 3-2 victory. He scored both goals in the 2-0 semifinal triumph over Poland and the first in the 3-1 championship victory over West Germany. Incredibly, Rossi did not play a minute in 1986, and Italy subsequently was given the boot in the second round by France. Born on Sept. 23, 1956, Rossi played in the Italian First Division for Como, Vicenza, Perugia, Juventus, Milan and Verona. He scored 20 goals in 48 international games.

Guillermo Stabile, Argentina (1930)—Stabile was a prolific goalscorer, even though he was not included in the Argentine squad until captain

Ferreira was not available. He made sure he was not taken out of the line, registering the first hat-trick in World Cup history in a 6-3 victory over Mexico. Stabile wound up as the tournament's leading scorer with eight goals. Born on Jan. 17, 1906, Stabile played for Huracan, Genoa (Italy), Napoli (Italy) and Red Star Paris (France). He made 31 international appearances.

Behind every successful team there is a coach, or manager, as they say in the rest of the world. Presenting four World Cup coaches of note (in alphabetical order):

Managers/Coaches

Franz Beckenbauer, West Germany (1986, 1990)—He was the first and only player to have captained a championship team (1974) and then coached the Germans to the world title in 1990. His finest coaching job, ironically, was in 1986, when the West Germans finished second to the more talented Argentina, losing in the final with five minutes left, 3-2. Beckenbauer moved players in and out of the lineup to just reach the final.

Carlos Bilardo, Argentina (1986, 1990)—There was no question Bilardo had an easy task in 1986 because he had the greatest player on the planet on his side. But Diego Maradona was hardly himself four years later in Italy, and Bilardo juggled his lineup through injuries and suspensions (he used 20 players) and probably used mirrors to get Argentina into the finals, a place they had no reason being.

Vittorio Pozzo, Italy (1934, 1938)—He is the only man to coach a country to a pair of World Cup titles—consecutive ones at that. Cynics will claim that Pozzo directed the Italian squad during a time when the World Cu lacked much of the luster that goes with it today, but try winning successive championships at the international level. Italy was 65-15-17 during Pozzo's rein. Pozzo, incidentally, helped form the Torino Club, studied in England and directed Italy in the 1912 Olympics. He died on Dec. 21, 1968.

Helmut Schoen, West Germany (1966, 1970, 1974, 1978)—Just keeping a job for one World Cup is difficult enough. Schoen coached the West Germans to the 1966 final against host England, to the semifinals in Mexico in 1970 and finally to the world championship in 1974. Born on Sept. 15, 1915, Schoen made 16 international appearances as a player.

Appendix B

Qualifying Results—1994

EUROPE/ISRAEL

13 teams qualified
2 from each group (*)
plus Germany, as current champions

Group 1

Estonia, Italy, Malta, Portugal, Scotland, Switzerland

August 16, 1992	Estonia 0, Switzerland 6
Sept. 9, 1992	Switzerland 3, Scotland 1
Oct. 14, 1992	Italy 2, Switzerland 2
Oct. 14, 1992	Scotland 0, Portugal 0
Oct. 25, 1992	Malta 0, Estonia 0
Nov. 18, 1992	Scotland 0, Italy 0
Nov. 18, 1992	Switzerland 3, Malta 0
Dec. 19, 1992	Malta 1, Italy 2
Jan. 24, 1993	Malta 0, Portugal 1
Feb. 17, 1993	Scotland 3, Malta 0
Feb. 24, 1993	Portugal 1, Italy 3
Mar. 24, 1993	Italy 6, Malta 1
Mar. 31, 1993	Switzerland 1, Portugal 1
Apr. 14, 1993	Italy 2, Estonia 0
Apr. 17, 1993	Malta 0, Switzerland 2
Apr. 28, 1993	Portugal 5, Scotland 0
May 1, 1993	Switzerland 1, Italy 0
May 12, 1993	Estonia 0, Malta 1
May 19, 1993	Estonia 0, Scotland 3
June 2, 1993	Scotland 3, Estonia 1
June 19, 1993	Portugal 4, Malta 0

Sept. 5, 1993	Estonia 0, Portugal 2
Sept. 8, 1993	Scotland 1, Switzerland 1
Sept. 22, 1993	Estonia 0, Italy 3
Oct. 13, 1993	Italy 3, Scotland 1
Oct. 13, 1993	Portugal 1, Switzerland 0
Nov. 10, 1993	Portugal 3, Estonia 0
Nov. 17, 1993	Italy 1, Portugal 0
Nov. 17, 1993	Malta 0, Scotland 2
Nov. 17, 1993	Switzerland 4, Estonia 0

Standings

1. **Italy*** (7-1-2, 22-7, 16)
2. **Switzerland** * (6-1-3, 23-6, 15)
3. Portugal (6-2-2, 18-5, 14)
4. Scotland (4-3-3, 14-13, 11)
5. Malta (1-8-1, 3-23, 3)
6. Estonia (0-9-1, 1-27, 1)

Group 2

England, Netherlands, Norway, Poland, Turkey, San Marino

Sept. 9, 1992	Norway 10, San Marino 0
Sept. 23, 1992	Norway 2, Netherlands 1
Sept. 23, 1992	Poland 1, Turkey 0
Oct. 7, 1992	San Marino 0, Norway 2
Oct. 14, 1992	England 1, Norway 1
Oct. 14, 1992	Netherlands 2, Poland 2
Oct. 28, 1992	Turkey 4, San Marino 1
Nov. 18, 1992	England 4, Turkey 0
Dec. 16, 1992	Turkey 1, Netherlands 3
Feb. 17, 1993	England 6, San Marino 0
Feb. 24, 1993	Netherlands 3, Turkey 1
Mar. 10, 1993	San Marino 0, Turkey 0
Mar. 24, 1993	Netherlands 6, San Marino 0
Mar. 31, 1993	Turkey 0, England 2
Apr. 28, 1993	England 2, Netherlands 2
Apr. 28, 1993	Norway 3, Turkey 1
Apr. 28, 1993	Poland 1, San Marino 0
May 20, 1993	Poland 3, San Marino 0
May 29, 1993	Poland 1, England 1
June 2, 1993	Norway 2, England 0
June 9, 1993	Netherlands 0, Norway 0
Sept. 8, 1993	England 3, Poland 0

Sept. 22, 1993	Norway 1, Poland 0
Sept. 22, 1993	San Marino 0, Netherlands 7
Oct. 13, 1993	Netherlands 2, England 0
Oct. 13, 1993	Poland 0, Norway 3
Oct. 27, 1993	Turkey 2, Poland 1
Nov. 10, 1993	Turkey 2, Norway 1
Nov. 17, 1993	San Marino 1, England 7
Nov. 17, 1993	Poland 1, Netherlands 3

1. **Norway** * (7-1-2, 25-5, 16)   Standings
2. **Netherlands** * (6-1-3, 29-9, 15)
2. England (5-2-3, 26-9, 13)
4. Poland (3-5-2, 10-15, 8)
5. Turkey (3-6-1, 11-19, 7)
6. San Marino (0-9-1, 2-46, 1)

Group 3

Albania, Denmark, Ireland Republic, Lithuania, Latvia, Northern Ireland, Spain

Apr. 22, 1992	Spain 3, Albania 0
Apr. 28, 1992	Northern Ireland 2, Lithuania 2
May 26, 1992	Ireland Republic 2, Albania 0
June 3, 1992	Albania 1, Lithuania 0
Aug. 12, 1992	Latvia 1, Lithuania 2
Aug. 26, 1992	Latvia 0, Denmark 0
Sept. 9, 1992	Northern Ireland 3, Albania 0
Sept. 9, 1992	Ireland Republic 4, Latvia 0
Sept. 23, 1992	Lithuania 0, Denmark 0
Sept. 23, 1992	Latvia 0, Spain 0
Oct. 14, 1992	Denmark 0, Ireland Republic 0
Oct. 14, 1992	Northern Ireland 0, Spain 0
Oct. 28, 1992	Lithuania 1, Latvia 1
Nov. 11, 1992	Albania 1, Latvia 1
Nov. 18, 1992	Northern Ireland 0, Denmark 1
Nov. 18, 1992	Spain 0, Ireland Republic 0
Dec. 16, 1992	Spain 5, Latvia 0
Feb. 17, 1993	Albania 1, Northern Ireland 2
Feb. 24, 1993	Spain 5, Lithuania 0
Mar. 31, 1993	Denmark 1, Spain 0
Mar. 31, 1993	Ireland Republic 3, Northern Ireland 0

Apr. 14, 1993	Denmark 2, Latvia 0
Apr. 14, 1993	Lithuania 3, Albania 1
Apr. 28, 1993	Ireland Republic 1, Denmark 1
Apr. 28, 1993	Spain 3, Northern Ireland 1
May 15, 1993	Latvia 0, Albania 0
May 25, 1993	Lithuania 0, Northern Ireland 1
May 26, 1993	Albania 1, Ireland Republic 2
June 2, 1993	Denmark 4, Albania 0
June 2, 1993	Lithuania 0, Spain 2
June 2, 1993	Latvia 1, Northern Ireland 2
June 9, 1993	Latvia 0, Ireland Republic 2
June 16, 1993	Lithuania 0, Ireland Republic 1
Aug. 25, 1993	Denmark 4, Lithuania 0
Sept. 8, 1993	Albania 0, Denmark 1
Sept. 8, 1993	Northern Ireland 2, Latvia 0
Sept. 8, 1993	Ireland Republic 2, Lithuania 0
Sept. 22, 1993	Albania 1, Spain 5
Oct. 13, 1993	Denmark 1, Northern Ireland 0
Oct. 13, 1993	Ireland Republic 1, Spain 3
Nov. 17, 1993	Northern Ireland 1, Ireland Republic 1
Nov. 17, 1993	Spain 1, Denmark 0

Standings

1. **Spain*** (8-1-3, 27-4, 19)
2. **Ireland*** (7-1-4, 19-6, 18)
3. Denmark (7-1-4, 15-2, 18)
4. Northern Ireland (5-4-3, 14-13, 13)
5. Lithuania (2-7-3, 8-21, 7)
6. Latvia (0-7-5, 4-21, 5)
7. Albania (1-9-2, 6-26, 4)

Group 4

Belgium, Cyprus, Czechs and Slovaks (RCS), Faroe Islands, Romania, Wales

Apr. 22, 1992	Belgium 1, Cyprus 0
May 6, 1992	Romania 7, Faroe Islands 0
May 20, 1992	Romania 5, Wales 1
June 3, 1992	Faroe Islands 0, Belgium 3
June 16, 1992	Faroe Islands 0, Cyprus 2
Sept. 2, 1992	RCS 1, Belgium 2
Sept. 9, 1992	Wales 6, Faroe Islands 0

Sept. 23, 1992	RCS 4, Faroe Islands 0
Oct. 14, 1992	Belgium 1, Romania 0
Oct. 14, 1992	Cyprus 0, Wales 1
Nov. 14, 1992	Romania 1, RSC 1
Nov. 18, 1992	Belgium 2, Wales 0
Nov. 29, 1992	Cyprus 1, Romania 4
Feb. 13, 1993	Cyprus 0, Belgium 3
Mar. 24, 1993	Cyprus 1, RCS 1
Mar, 31, 1993	Belgium 2, Wales 0
Apr. 14, 1993	Romania 2, Cyprus 1
Apr. 25, 1993	Cyprus 3, Faroe Islands 1
Apr. 28, 1993	RCS 1, Wales 1
May 23, 1993	Belgium 3, Faroe Islands 0
June 2, 1993	RCS 5, Romania 2
June 6, 1993	Faroe Islands 0, Wales 3
June 16, 1993	Faroe Islands 0, RCS 3
Sept. 8, 1993	Wales 2, RCS 2
Sept. 8, 1993	Faroe Islands 0, Romania 4
Oct. 13, 1993	Romania 2, Belgium 1
Oct. 13, 1993	Wales 2, Cyprus 0
Oct. 27, 1993	RCS 3, Cyprus 0
Nov. 17, 1993	Belgium 0, RCS 0
Nov. 17, 1993	Wales 1, Romania 2

1. **Romania*** (7-2-1, 29-12, 15)   Standings
2. **Belgium*** (7-2-1, 16-5, 15)
3. RCS (4-1-5, 21-9, 13)
4. Wales (5-3-2, 19-12, 12)
5. Cyprus (2-7-1, 8-18, 5)
5. Faroe Islands (0-10-0, 1-38, 0)

Group 5

Greece, Hungary, Iceland, Luxembourg, Russia[1], Yugoslavia[2]

May 13, 1992	Greece 1, Iceland 0
June 3, 1992	Hungary 1, Iceland 2
Sept. 9, 1992	Luxembourg 0, Hungary 3
Oct. 7, 1992	Iceland 0, Greece 1
Oct. 14, 1992	Russia 1, Iceland 0
Oct. 28, 1992	Russia 2, Luxembourg 0
Nov. 11, 1992	Greece 0, Hungary 0

Feb. 17, 1993	Greece 2, Luxembourg 0
Mar. 31, 1993	Hungary 0, Greece 1
Apr. 14, 1993	Luxembourg 0, Russia 4
Apr. 28, 1993	Russia 3, Hungary 0
May 20, 1993	Luxembourg 1, Iceland 1
May 23, 1993	Russia 1, Greece 1
June 2, 1993	Iceland 1, Russia 1
June 16, 1993	Iceland 2, Hungary 0
Sept. 8, 1993	Hungary 1, Russia 3
Sept. 8, 1993	Iceland 1, Luxembourg 0
Oct. 12, 1993	Luxembourg 1, Greece 3
Oct. 27, 1993	Hungary 1, Luxembourg 0
Nov. 17, 1993	Greece 1, Russia 0

Standings

1. **Greece*** (6-0-2, 10-2, 14)
2. **Russia*** (5-1-2, 15-4, 12)
3. Iceland (3-3-2, 7-6, 8)
4. Hungary (2-5-1, 6-11, 5)
5. Luxembourg (0-7-1, 2-17, 1)

[1]Formerly Commonwealth of Independent States and Soviet Union
[2]Excluded due to UN sanctions

Group 6

Austria, Bulgaria, Finland, France, Israel, Sweden

May 14, 1992	Finland 0, Bulgaria 3
Sept. 9, 1992	Bulgaria 2, France 0
Sept. 9, 1992	Finland 0, Sweden 1
Oct. 7, 1992	Sweden 2, Bulgaria 0
Oct. 14, 1992	France 2, Austria 0
Oct. 28, 1992	Austria 5, Israel 2
Nov. 11, 1992	Israel 1, Sweden 3
Nov. 14, 1992	France 2, Finland 1
Dec. 2, 1992	Israel 0, Bulgaria 2
Feb. 17, 1993	Israel 0, France 4
Mar. 27, 1993	Austria 0, France 1
Apr. 14, 1993	Austria 3, Bulgaria 1
Apr. 28, 1993	Bulgaria 2, Finland 0
Apr. 28, 1993	France 2, Sweden 1
May 12, 1993	Bulgaria 2, Israel 2
May 13, 1993	Finland 3, Austria 1
May 19, 1993	Sweden 1, Austria 0

June 2, 1993	Sweden 5, Israel 0
June 16, 1993	Finland 0, Israel 0
Aug. 22, 1993	Sweden 1, France 1
Aug. 25, 1993	Austria 3, Finland 0
Sept. 8, 1993	Bulgaria 1, Sweden 1
Sept. 8, 1993	Finland 0, France 2
Oct. 13, 1993	Bulgaria 4, Austria 1
Oct. 13, 1993	France 2, Israel 3
Oct. 13, 1993	Sweden 3, Finland 2
Oct. 27, 1993	Israel 1, Austria 1
Nov. 10, 1993	Austria 1, Sweden 1
Nov. 10, 1993	Israel 1, Finland 3
Nov. 17, 1993	France 1, Bulgaria 2

1. **Sweden*** (6-1-3, 19-8, 15)
2. **Bulgaria*** (6-2-2, 19-10, 14)
3. France (6-2-2, 17-10, 13)
4. Austria (3-5-2, 15-16, 8)
5. Finland (2-7-1, 9-18, 53)
6. Israel (1-6-3, 10-27, 5)

Standings

CONCACAF

(Confederation of North, Central American and Caribbean Association
Football—2 qualify including U.S. as hosts)

Caribbean Association

Antigua, Barbados, Bermuda, Dominican Republic, Guyana, Haiti, Jamaica, Netherlands Antilles, Puerto Rico, St. Lucia, St. Vincent/Grenadines, Surinam , Trinidad & Tobago

Central American Association

Costa Rica, Guatemala, El Salvador, Honduras, Nicaragua, Panama

North American Association

United States, Canada, Mexico

Pre-preliminary Round

March 21, 1992	Dominican Republic 1, Puerto Rico 2
March 22, 1992	St. Lucia 1, St. Vincent/Grenadines 0
March 29, 1992	Puerto Rico 1, Dominican Republic 1
Puerto Rico advances	
March 29, 1992	St. Vincent/Grenadines 3, St. Lucia 1

St. Vincent & the Grenadines advance

April 19, 1992	Barbados 1, Trinidad 2
April 19, 1992	Netherlands Antilles 1, Antigua 1
April 26, 1992	Antigua 3, Netherlands Antilles 0
Antigua advances	
April 26, 1992	Bermuda 1, Haiti 0
April 26, 1992	Guyana 1, Surinam 2
May 23, 1992	Jamaica 2, Puerto Rico 1
May 24, 1992	Haiti 2, Bermuda 1
Bermuda advances	
May 24, 1992	Surinam 1, Guyana 1
	Surinam advances
May 30, 1992	Puerto Rico 0, Jamaica 1
Puerto Rico advances	
May 31, 1992	Trinidad 3, Barbados 0
Trindiad & Tobago advances	
June 14, 1992	Antigua 0, Bermuda 3
July 4, 1992	Bermuda 2, Antigua 1
Bermuda advances	
July 5, 1992	Trinidad 1, Jamaica 2
July 19, 1992	Nicaragua 0, El Salvador 5
July 23, 1992	El Salvador 5, Nicaragua 1
El Salvador advances	
July 26, 1992	Honduras 2, Guatemala 0
Honduras advances	
Aug. 2, 1992	Surinam 0, St. Vincent 0
Aug. 16, 1992	Jamaica 1, Trinidad 1
Jamaica advances	
Aug. 16, 1992	Panama 1, Costa Rica 0
Aug. 23, 1992	Costa Rica 5, Panama 1
Costa Rica advances	
Aug. 30, 1992	St. Vincent 2, Surinam 1
St. Vincent advances	

Second Round

Group A—Costa Rica, Mexico, Honduras and St. Vincent.
Group—Jamaica, Bermuda, Canada and El Salvador.

Group A

Nov. 8, 1992	Costa Rica 2, Honduras 3
Nov. 8, 1992	St. Vincent 0, Mexico 4
Nov. 15, 1992	Mexico 2, Honduras 0
Nov. 15, 1992	St. Vincent 0, Costa Rica 1
Nov. 22, 1992	Mexico 4, Costa Rica 0
Nov. 22, 1992	St. Vincent 0, Honduras 4
Nov. 28, 1992	Honduras 4, St. Vincent 0
Nov. 29, 1992	Costa Rica 2, Mexico 0
Dec. 5, 1992	Honduras 2, Costa Rica 1
Dec. 6, 1992	Mexico 11, St. Vincent 0
Dec. 13, 1992	Costa Rica 5, St. Vincent 1
Dec. 13, 1992	Honduras 1, Mexico 1

Standings

1. Mexico (4-1-1, 22-3, 9)
2. Honduras (4-1-1, 14-6, 9)
3. Costa Rica (3-3-0, 11-9, 6)
4. St. Vincent (0-6-0, 0-29, 0)

Group B

Oct. 18, 1992	Bermuda 1, El Salvador 0
Oct. 18, 1992	Jamaica 1, Canada 1
Oct. 25, 1992	Bermuda 1, Jamaica 1
Oct. 25, 1992	El Salvador 1, Canada 1
Nov. 1, 1992	Canada 1, Jamaica 0
Nov. 1, 1992	El Salvador 4, Bermuda 1
Nov. 8, 1992	Canada 2, El Salvador 3
Nov. 8, 1992	Jamaica 3, Bermuda 2
Nov. 15, 1992	Canada 4, Bermuda 2
Nov. 22, 1992	Jamaica 0, El Salvador 2
Dec. 6, 1992	Bermuda 0, Canada 0
Dec. 6, 1992	El Salvador 2, Jamaica 1

Standings

1. El Salvador (4-1-1, 12-6, 9)
2. Canada (2-1-3, 9-7, 7)
3. Jamaica (1-3-2, 6-9, 4)
4. Bermuda (1-3-2, 7-12, 4)

Third Round

April 4, 1993	Honduras 2, Canada 2
April 4, 1993	El Salvador 2, Mexico 1
April 11, 1993	Canada 2, El Salvador 0
April 11, 1993	Mexico 3, Honduras 0
April 18, 1993	Canada 3, Honduras 1
April 18, 1993	Mexico 3, El Salvador 1
April 25, 1993	Honduras 2, El Salvador 0
April 25, 1993	Mexico 4, Canada 0
May 2, 1993	Honduras 1, Mexico 4
May 2, 1993	El Salvador 1, Canada 2
May 9, 1993	Canada 1, Mexico 2
May 9, 1993	El Salvador 2, Honduras 1

Standings
1. **Mexico*** (5-1-0, 17-5, 10)
2. Canada (3-2-1, 10-10, 7)
3. El Salvador (2-4-0, 6-11, 4)
4. Honduras (1-4-1, 7-14, 3)

Mexico qualified while Canada advanced to special playoff with Oceania champion, Australia.

OCEANIA

No team qualified (one team could have qualified)
Group 1: Australia, Tahiti and Solomon Islands.
Group 2: New Zealand, Fiji, Vanuatu.

June 7, 1992	New Zealand 3, Fiji 0
June 27, 1992	Vanuatu 1, New Zealand 4
July 1, 1992	New Zealand 8, Vanuatu 0
July 17, 1992	Solomon Islands 1, Tahiti 1
Sept. 4, 1992	Solomon Islands 1, Australia 2
Sept. 11, 1992	Tahiti 0, Australia 3
Sept. 12, 1992	Fiji 3, Vanuatu 0
Sept. 19, 1992	Fiji 0, New Zealand 0
Sept. 20, 1992	Australia 2, Tahiti 0
Sept. 25, 1992	Vanuatu 0, Fiji 3
Sept. 26, 1992	Australia 6, Solomon Islands 1
Oct. 9, 1992	Tahiti 4, Solomon Islands 2

Group 1
1. Australia (4-0-0, 13-2, 8)
2. Tahiti (1-2-1, 5-8, 3)
3. Solomon Islands (0-3-1, 5-13, 1)

Group 2
1. New Zealand (3-0-1, 15-1, 7)
2. Fiji (2-1-1, 6-3, 5)
3. Vanuatu (0-4-0, 1-18, 0)
Second Round
May 30, 1993   New Zealand 0, Australia 1
June 6, 1993   Australia 3, New Zealand 0
Australia advances, will meet Canada in home-and-home series

SPECIAL PLAYOFF
First Round
July 31—Canada 2, Australia 1
Aug. 14–Australia 2, Canada 1
Australia wins series on PKs, 4-1

Second Round
Oct. 31—Australia 1, Argentina 1
Nov. 17—Argentina 1, Australia 0
Argentina qualified for the World Cup

AFRICA

3 teams qualified
Group A   Algeria, Ghana, Burundi (Uganda withdrew)
Group B   Cameroon, Zaire, Liberia, Swaziland
Group C   Egypt, Zimbabwe, Togo, Angola (Sierra Leone with-
             drew)
Group D   Nigeria, Congo, South Africa (Libya, Sao Tome with-
             drew)
Group E   Ivory Coast, Niger, Botswana (Sudan withdrew)
Group F   Morocco, Tunisia, Benin, Ethiopia (Malawi withdrew)
Group G   Senegal, Gabon, Mozambique (Mauritania withdrew)
Group H   Zambia, Madagascar, Namibia (Tanzania and Burkina
             Faso withdrew)
Group I   Kenya, Guinea, Mali (Gambia withdrew)

First Round
Group A

Oct. 9, 1992	Algeria 3, Burundi 1
Oct. 25, 1992	Burundi 1, Ghana 0
Dec. 20, 1992	Ghana 2, Algeria 0
Jan. 17, 1993	Burundi 0, Algeria 0
Jan. 31, 1993	Ghana 1, Burundi 0
Feb. 26, 1993	Algeria 2, Ghana 1

Standings

1. Algeria (2-1-1, 5-4, 5)
2. Ghana (2-2-0, 4-3, 4)
3. Burundi (1-2-1, 2-4, 3)

Group B

Oct. 18, 1992	Cameroon 5, Swaziland 0
Oct. 25, 1992	Swaziland 1, Zaire 0
Jan. 10, 1993	Zaire 1, Cameroon 2
Jan. 17, 1993	Swaziland 0, Cameroon 0
Jan. 31, 1993	Zaire vs. Swaziland (cancelled)
Feb. 28, 1993	Cameroon 0, Zaire 0

Standings

1. Cameroon (2-0-2, 7-1, 6)
2. Swaziland (1-1-1, 1-5, 3)
3. Zaire (0-2-1, 1-3, 1)

Group C

Oct. 9, 1992	Zimbabwe 1, Togo 0
Oct. 11, 1992	Egypt 1, Angola 0
Oct. 25, 1992	Togo 1, Egypt 4
Dec. 20, 1992	Zimbabwe 2, Egypt 1
Jan. 10, 1993	Angola 1, Zimbabwe 1
Jan. 17, 1993	Togo 1, Zimbabwe 2
Jan. 18, 1993	Angola 0, Egypt 0
Jan. 31, 1993	Zimbabwe 2, Angola 1
Jan. 31, 1993	Egypt 3, Togo 0
Feb. 14, 1993	Angola vs. Togo, cancelled
[3]Feb. 28, 1993	Egypt 2, Zimbabwe 1
Feb. 28, 1993	Togo 0, Angola 1

[3]Match replayed on April 15, 1993, in a neutral site in France because of fan violence in Egypt, and Zimbabwe played the Egyptians to a scoreless tie and qualified for the next round.

1. Zimbabwe (4-0-2, 8-4, 10)   Standings
2. Egypt (3-1-2, 9-3, 8)
3. Angola (1-2-2, 3-4, 4)
4. Togo (0-5-0, 2-11, 0)

Group D
Oct. 10, 1992   Nigeria 4, South Africa 0
Oct. 24, 1992   South Africa 1, Congo 0
Dec. 20, 1992   Congo 0, Nigeria 1
Jan. 16, 1993   South Africa 0, Nigeria 0
Jan. 31, 1993   Congo 0, South Africa 1
Feb. 27, 1993   Nigeria 2, Congo 0

1. Nigeria (3-0-1, 7-0, 7)   Standings
2. South Africa (2-1-1, 2-4, 5)
3. Congo (0-4-0, 0-5, 0)

Group E
Oct. 11, 1992   Ivory Coast 6, Botswana 0
Oct. 25, 1992   Niger 0, Ivory Coast 0
Dec. 20, 1992   Botswana 0, Niger 1
Jan. 1, 1993   Botswana 0, Ivory Coast 0
Jan. 31, 1993   Ivory Coast 1, Niger 0
Feb. 28, 1993   Niger 2, Botswana 1

1. Ivory Coast (2-0-2, 7-0, 6)   Standings
2. Niger (2-1-1, 3-2, 5)
3. Botswana (0-3-1, 1-9, 1)

Group F
Oct. 11, 1992   Morocco 5, Ethiopia 0
Oct. 11, 1992   Tunisia 5, Benin 1
Oct. 25, 1992   Benin 0, Morocco 1
Oct. 25, 1992   Ethiopia 0, Tunisia 0
Dec. 20, 1992   Ethiopia 3, Benin 1
Dec. 20, 1992   Tunisia 1, Morocco 1
Jan. 17, 1993   Ethiopia 0, Morocco 1
Jan. 17, 1993   Benin 0, Tunisia 5
Jan. 31, 1993   Tunisia 3, Ethiopia 0
Jan. 31, 1993   Morocco 5, Benin 0
Feb. 28, 1993   Morocco 0, Tunisia 0
Feb. 28, 1993   Benin 1, Ethiopia 0

Standings   1. Morocco (4-0-2, 13-1, 11)
2. Tunisia (3-0-3, 14-2, 9)
3. Ethiopia (1-4-1, 3-11, 3)
4. Benin (1-5-0, 3-19, 3)

Group G
| | |
Oct. 11, 1992 | Gabon 3, Mozambique 1
Oct. 25, 1992 | Mozambique 0, Senegal 1
Dec. 19, 1992 | Gabon 3, Senegal 2
Jan. 17, 1993 | Mozambique 1, Gabon 1
Jan. 30, 1993 | Senegal 6, Mozambique 1
Feb. 27, 1993 | Senegal 1, Gabon 0

Standings   1. Senegal (3-1-0, 10-4, 6)
2. Gabon (2-1-1, 7-5, 5)
3. Mozambique (0-3-1, 3-11, 1)

Group H
Oct. 11, 1992 | Madagascar 3, Namibia 0
Oct. 25, 1992 | Namibia 0, Zambia 4
Dec. 19, 1992 | Tanzania 2, Namibia 0
Dec. 20, 1992 | Madagascar 2, Zambia 0
Jan. 17, 1993 | Namibia 0, Madagascar 1
Jan. 31, 1993 | Zambia 4, Namibia 0
Feb. 28, 1993 | Zambia 3, Madagascar 1

Standings   1. Zambia (3-1-0, 11-3, 6)
2. Madagascar (3-1-0, 7-3, 6)
3. Namibia (0-4-0, 0-12, 0)

Group I
Oct. 11, 1992 | Guinea 0, Mali 3 (forfeit)
Dec. 20, 1992 | Guinea 4, Kenya 0
Feb. 27, 1993 | Kenya 2, Guinea 0
Note: Mali withdrew after one match

Standings   1. Guinea (1-1-0, 4-2, 2)
2. Kenya (1-1-0, 2-4, 0)

All 9 group winners advanced to the second round.

Second Round

Group A

April 16, 1993	Algeria 1, Ivory Coast 1
May 2, 1993	Ivory Coast 2, Nigeria 1
July 3, 1993	Nigeria 4, Algeria 1
July 18, 1993	Ivory Coast 1, Algeria 0
Sept. 25, 1993	Nigeria 4, Ivory Coast 1
Oct. 8, 1993	Algeria 1, Nigeria 1

1. **Nigeria*** (2-1-1, 10-5, 5)   Standings
2. Ivory Coast (2-1-1, 5-6, 5)
3. Algeria (0-2-2, 4-6, 2)

Group B

April 18, 1993	Morocco 1, Senegal 0
May 2, 1993	Senegal vs. Zambia, postponed
July 4, 1993	Zambia 2, Morocco 1
July 17, 1993	Senegal 1, Morocco 3
Aug. 8, 1993	Senegal 0, Zambia 0
Sept. 26, 1993	Zambia 4, Senegal 0
Oct. 10, 1993	Morocco 1, Zambia 0

1. **Morocco*** (3-1-0, 6-3, 6)   Standings
2. Zambia (2-1-1, 6-2, 5)
3. Senegal (0-3-1, 1-8, 1)

Group C

April 16, 1993	Cameroon 3, Guinea 1
April 30, 1993	Guinea 3, Zimbabwe 0
July 4, 1993	Zimbabwe 1, Cameroon 0
July 18, 1993	Guinea 0, Cameroon 1
Sept. 26, 1993	Zimbabwe 1, Guinea 0
Oct. 10, 1993	Cameroon 3, Zimbabwe 1

1. **Cameroon*** (3-1-0, 7-3, 6)   Standings
2. Zimbabwe (2-2-0, 3-6, 4)
3. Guinea (1-3-0, 4-5, 2)

SOUTH AMERICA

4 teams qualified

Group A

Argentina, Colombia, Paraguay, and Peru.

Aug. 1, 1993	Colombia 0, Paraguay 0
Aug. 1, 1993	Peru 0, Argentina 1
Aug. 8, 1993	Paraguay 1, Argentina 3
Aug. 8, 1993	Peru 0, Colombia 1
Aug. 15, 1993	Colombia 2, Argentina 1
Aug. 15, 1993	Paraguay 2, Peru 1
Aug. 22, 1993	Argentina 2, Peru 1
Aug. 22, 1993	Paraguay 1, Colombia 1
Aug. 29, 1993	Colombia 4, Peru 0
Aug. 29, 1993	Argentina 0, Paraguay 0
Sept. 5, 1993	Argentina 0, Colombia 5
Sept. 5, 1993	Peru 2, Paraguay 2

Argentina qualified by defeating Oceania champion, Australia, in a special playoff.

Standings

1. **Colombia*** (4-0-2, 13-2, 10)
2. Argentina (3-2-1, 7-9, 7)
3. Paraguay (1-1-4, 6-7, 6)
4. Peru (0-5-1, 4-14, 1)

Group B

Brazil, Uruguay, Ecuador, Bolivia, and Venezuela

July 18, 1993	Ecuador 0, Brazil 0
July 18, 1993	Venezuela 1, Bolivia 7
July 25, 1993	Bolivia 2, Brazil 0
July 25, 1993	Venezuela 0, Uruguay 1
Aug. 1, 1993	Uruguay 0, Ecuador 0
Aug. 1, 1993	Venezuela 1, Brazil 5
Aug. 8, 1993	Bolivia 3, Uruguay 1
Aug. 8, 1993	Ecuador 5, Venezuela 0
Aug. 15, 1993	Bolivia 1, Ecuador 0
Aug. 15, 1993	Uruguay 1, Brazil 1
Aug. 22, 1993	Bolivia 7, Venezuela 0
Aug. 22, 1993	Brazil 2, Ecuador 0

Aug. 29, 1993	Brazil 6, Bolivia 0
Aug. 29, 1993	Uruguay 4, Venezuela 0
Sept. 5, 1993	Brazil 4, Venezuela 0
Sept. 5, 1993	Ecuador 0, Uruguay 1
Sept. 12, 1993	Uruguay 2, Bolivia 1
Sept. 12, 1993	Venezuela 2, Ecuador 1
Sept. 19, 1993	Brazil 2, Uruguay 0
Sept. 19, 1993	Ecuador 1, Bolivia 1

1. **Brazil*** (5-1-2, 20-4, 12)   Standings
2. **Bolivia*** (5-2-1, 22-11, 11)
3. Uruguay (4-2-2, 10-7, 10)
4. Ecuador (1-3-4, 7-7, 5)
5. Venezuela (1-7-0, 4-34, 2)

ASIA
(2 teams qualified)

First Round Groups

Group A	China, Iraq, Jordan, Yemen, Pakistan
Group B	Iran, Syria, Oman, Chinese Tapei, Myanmar
Group C	North Korea, Qatar, Singapore, Vietnam, Indonesia
Group D	South Korea, Bahrain, Hong Kong, Lebanon, India
Group E	Saudi Arabia, Kuwait, Malaysia, Macao
Group F	United Arab Emirates, Japan, Thailand, Sri Lanka, Bangladesh

Group A
In Amman, Jordan
May 22, 1993—Jordan 1, Yemen 1
May 22, 1993—Pakistan 0, China PR 5
May 24, 1993—Jordan 1, Iraq 1
May 24, 1993—Yemem 5, Pakistan 1
May 26, 1993—Jordan 0, China PR 3
May 26, 1993—Yemen 1, Iraq 6
May 28, 1993—Pakistan 0, Iraq 8
May 28, 1993—Yemen 1, China PR 0
May 30, 1993—Iraq 1, China PR 0
May 30, 1993—Jordan 3, Pakistan 1

In People's Republic of China
June 12, 1993—China PR 3, Pakistan 0

June 12, 1993—Yemen 1, Jordan 1
June 14, 1993—Iraq 4, Jordan 0
June 14, 1993—Pakistan 0, Yemen 3
June 16, 1993—China PR 4, Jordan 1
June 16, 1993—Iraq 3, Yemen 0
June 18, 1993—China PR 1, Yemen 0
June 18, 1993—Iraq 4, Pakistan 0
June 20, 1993—China PR 2, Iraq 1
June 20, 1993—Pakistan 0, Jordan 5

Standings   1. Iraq (6-1-1, 28-4, 13)
2. China (6-2-0, 18-4, 12)
3. Yemen (3-3-2, 12-13, 8)
4. Jordan (2-3-3, 12-15, 7)
5. Pakistan (0-8-0, 2-36, 0)

Group B
In Iran
June 23, 1993—Chinese Taipei 0, Syria 2
June 23, 1993—Iran 0, Oman 0
June 25, 1993—Iran 6, Chinese Taipei 0
June 25, 1993—Oman 0, Syria 0
June 27, 1993—Iran 1, Syria 1
June 27, 1993—Oman 2, Chinese Tapei 1

In Syria
July 2, 1993—Oman 0, Iran 1
July 2, 1993—Syria 8, Chinese Taipei 1
July 4, 1993—Chinese Tapei 0, Iran 6
July 4, 1993—Syria 2, Oman 1
July 6, 1993—Chinese Tapei 1, Oman 7
July 6, 1993—Syria 1, Iran 1

Standings   1. Iran (3-0-3, 15-2, 9)
2. Syria (3-0-3, 14-4, 9)
3. Oman (2-2-2, 10-5, 6)
4. Chinese Taipei (0-6-0, 3-31, 0)

Group C
In Qatar
April 9, 1993—N. Korea 3, Vietnam 0
April 9, 1993—Qatar 3, Indonesia 1
April 11, 1993—N. Korea 2, Singapore 1
April 11, 1993—Qatar 4, Vietnam 0
April 13, 1993—N. Korea 4, Indonesia 0
April 13, 1993—Vietnam 2, Singapore 3
April 16, 1993—Qatar 4, Singapore 1
April 16, 1993—Vietnam 1, Indonesia 0
April 18, 1993—Indonesia 0, Singapore 2
April 18, 1993—Qatar 1, N. Korea 2

In Singapore
April 24, 1993—Indonesia 4, Qatar 1
April 24, 1993—Vietnam 0, N. Korea 1
April 26, 1993—Singapore 1, N. Korea 3
April 26, 1993—Vietnam 0, Qatar 4
April 28, 1993—Indonesia 1, N. Korea 2
April 28, 1993—Singapore 1, Vietnam 0
April 30, 1993—Indonesia 2, Vietnam 1
April 30, 1993—Singapore 1, Qatar 0
May 2, 1993—N. Korea 2, Qatar 2
May 2, 1993—Singapore 2, Indonesia 1

1. North Korea (7-0-1, 19-6, 15)   Standings
2. Qatar (5-2-1, 22-8, 11)
3. Singapore (5-3-0, 12-12, 10)
4. Indonesia (1-7-0, 6-19, 2)
5. Vietnam (1-7-0, 4-18, 2)

Group D
In Lebanon
May 7, 1993—Hong Kong 2, Bahrain 1
May 7, 1993—Lebanon 2, India 2
May 9, 1993—Bahrain 0, S. Korea 0
May 9, 1993—Lebanon 2, Hong Kong 2
May 11, 1993—India 1, Hong Kong 2
May 11, 1993—Lebanon 0, S. Korea 1
May 13, 1993—India 0, S. Korea 3
May 13, 1993—Lebanon 0, Bahrain 0

May 15, 1993—Bahrain 2, India 1
May 15, 1993—Hong Kong 0, S. Korea 3

In South Korea
June 5, 1993—Bahrain 0, Lebanon 0
June 5, 1993—S. Korea 4, Hong Kong 1
June 7, 1993—India 0, Bahrain 3
June 7, 1993—S. Korea 2, Lebanon 0
June 9, 1993—Hong Kong 1, Lebanon 2
June 9, 1993—S. Korea 7, India 1
June 11, 1993—Bahrain 3, Hong Kong 0
June 11, 1993—India 1, Lebanon 2
June 13, 1993—Hong Kong 1, India 3
June 13, 1993—S. Korea 3, Bahrain 0

Standings
1. S. Korea (7-0-1, 23-1, 15)
2. Bahrain (3-2-3, 9-6, 9)
3. Lebanon (2-2-4, 8-9, 8)
4. Hong Kong (2-5-1, 9-19, 5)
5. India (1-6-1, 8-22, 3)

Group E
In Malaysia
May 1, 1993—Macao 0, Saudi Arabia 6
May 1, 1993—Malaysia 1, Kuwait 1
May 3, 1993—Macao 1, Kuwait 10
May 3, 1993—Malaysia 1, Saudi Arabia 1
May 5, 1993—Kuwait 0, Saudi Arabia 0
May 5, 1993—Malaysia 9, Macao 0

In Saudi Arabia
May 14, 1993—Kuwait 2, Malaysia 0
May 14, 1993—Saudi Arabia 8, Macao 0
May 16, 1993—Kuwait 8, Macao 0
May 16, 1993—Saudi Arabia 3, Malaysia 0
May 18, 1993—Macao 0, Malaysia 5
May 18, 1993—Saudi Arabia 2, Kuwait 0

Standings
1. Saudi Arabia (4-0-2, 20-1, 10)
2. Kuwait (3-1-2, 21-4, 8)
3. Malaysia (2-2-2, 16-7, 6)
4. Macao (0-6-0, 1-46, 0)

Group F
In Japan
April 8, 1993—Japan 1, Thailand 0
April 8, 1993—Sri Lanka 0, United Arab Emirates 4
April 11, 1993—Japan 8, Bangladesh 0
April 11, 1993—Thailand 1, Sri Lanka 0
April 13, 1993—Sri Lanka 0, Bangladesh 1
April 13, 1993—United Arab Emirates 1, Thailand 0
April 15, 1993—Japan 5, Sri Lanka 0
April 15, 1993—United Arab Emirates 1, Bangladesh 0
April 18, 1993—Japan 2, United Arab Emirates 0
April 18, 1993—Thailand 4, Bangladesh 1

In United Arab Emirates
April 26, 1993—Thailand 1, Japan 0
April 26, 1993—United Arab Emirates 3, Sri Lanka 0
April 30, 1993—Bangladesh 1, Japan 4
April 30, 1993—Thailand 1, United Arab Emirates 2
May 3, 1993—Bangladesh 0, United Arab Emirates 7
May 3, 1993—Sri Lanka 0, Thailand 3
May 5, 1993—Bangladesh 1, Thailand 4
May 5, 1993—Sri Lanka 0, Japan 6
May 7, 1993—Bangladesh 3, Sri Lanka 0
May 7, 1993—United Arab Emirates 1, Japan 1

1. Japan (7-0-1, 28-2, 15)   Standings
2. United Arab Emirates (6-1-1, 19-4, 13)
3. Thailand (4-4-0, 13-7, 8)
4. Bangladesh (2-6-0, 7-28, 4)
5. Sri Lanka (0-8-0, 0-26, 0)

SECOND ROUND
In Doha, Qatar
Oct. 15, 1993—N. Korea 3, Iraq 2
Oct. 15, 1993—Saudi Arabia 0, Japan 0
Oct. 16, 1993—Iran 0, S. Korea 3
Oct. 18, 1993—N. Korea 1, Saudi Arabia 2
Oct. 18, 1993—Japan 1, Iran 2
Oct. 19, 1993—Iraq 2, S. Korea 2
Oct. 21, 1993—N. Korea 0, Japan 3
Oct. 22, 1993—Iran 1, Iraq 2

Oct. 22, 1993—S. Korea 1, Saudi Arabia 1
Oct. 24, 1993—Iraq 1, Saudi Arabia 1
Oct. 25, 1993—Japan 1, S. Korea 0
Oct. 25, 1993—Iran 2, N. Korea 1
Oct. 28, 1993—S. Korea 3, North Korea 0
Oct. 28, 1993—Saudi Arabia 4, Iran 3
Oct. 28, 1993—Iraq 2, Japan 2

Standings

1. **Saudi Arabia*** (2-0-3, 8-6, 7)
2. **South Korea*** (2-1-2, 9-4, 6)
3. Japan (2-1-2, 7-4, 6)
4. Iraq (1-1-3, 9-9, 5)
5. Iran (2-3-0, 8-11, 4)
6. North Korea (1-4-0, 5-12, 2)

Results of the 14 World Cups

1930 Uruguay

First round

Group 1

France 4, Mexico 1
Argentina 1, France 0
Chile 3, Mexico 0
Chile 1, France 0
Argentina 6, Mexico 3
Argentina 3, Chile 1

Group 2

Yugoslavia 2, Brazil 1
Yugoslavia 4, Bolivia 0
Brazil 4, Bolivia 0

Group 3

Romania 3, Peru 1
Uruguay 1, Peru 0
Uruguay 4, Romania 0

Group 4

U.S. 3, Belgium 0
U.S. 3, Paraguay 0
Paraguay 1, Belgium 0

Semifinals

Argentina 6, U.S. 1
Uruguay 6, Yugoslavia 1

Final

Uruguay 4, Argentina 2

1934 Italy

First round

(single elimination)
Italy 7, U.S. 1
Spain 3, Brazil 1
Hungary 4, Egypt 2
Austria 3, France 2
Germany 5, Belgium 2
Sweden 3, Argentina 2
Switzerland 3, Netherlands 2
Czechoslovakia 2, Romania 1

Second round

Italy 1, Spain 1
Italy 1, Spain 0 (replay)
Germany 2, Sweden 1
Czechoslovakia 3, Switzerland 2

Semifinals

Italy 1, Austria 0

Czechoslovakia 3, Germany 1

Final

Italy 2, Czechoslovakia 1 (extra time)

1938 France

First round

(single elimination)

Italy 2, Norway 1

France 3, Belgium 1

Czechoslovakia 3, Netherlands 0

Brazil 6, Poland 5

Cuba 3, Romania 3

Cuba 2, Romania 1 (replay)

Switzerland 1, Germany 1

Switzerland 4, Germany 2 (re-play)

Hungary 6, Dutch East Indies 0

(Sweden received a bye)

Second round

Italy 3, France 1

Brazil 1, Czechoslovakia 1

Brazil 2, Czechoslovakia 1 (re-play)

Sweden 8, Cuba 0

Hungary 2, Switzerland 0

Semifinals

Italy 2, Brazil 1

Hungary 5, Sweden 1

Final

Italy 4, Hungary 2

1950 Brazil

First round

group 1

Brazil 4, Mexico 0

Yugoslavia 3, Switzerland 0

Yugoslavia 4, Mexico 1

Brazil 2, Switzerland 2

Brazil 2, Yugoslavia 0

Switzerland 2, Mexico 1

Group 2

Spain 3, U.S. 1

England 2, Chile 0

U.S. 1, England 0

Spain 2, Chile 0

Spain 1, England 0

Chile 5, U.S. 2

Group 3

Sweden 3, Italy 2,

Sweden 2, Paraguay 2

Italy 2, Paraguay 0

Group 4

Uruguay 8, Bolivia 0

Final Pool

Uruguay 2, Spain 2

Brazil 7, Sweden 1

Uruguay 3, Sweden 2

Brazil 6, Spain 1

Sweden 3, Spain 1
Uruguay 2, Brazil 1

Final Pool Standings
1. Uruguay (2-0-1, 7-5, 5)
2. Brazil (2-1-0, 14-4, 4)

3. Sweden (1-2-0, 6-11, 2)
4. Spain (0-2-1, 4-11, 1)
Uruguay wins

1954 Switzerland

First round

Group 1
Yugoslavia 1, France 0
Brazil 5, Mexico 0
France 3, Mexico 2
Brazil 1, Yugoslavia 1

Group 2
Hungary 9, South Korea 0
West Germany 4, Turkey 1
Hungary 8, West Germany 3
Turkey 7, South Korea 0
Special playoff
West Germany 7, Turkey 2

Group 3
Austria 1, Scotland 0
Uruguay 2, Czechoslovakia 0
Austria 5, Czechoslovakia 0
Uruguay 7, Scotland 0

Group 4
England 4, Belgium 4
Switzerland 2, Italy 1
England 2, Switzerland 0
Italy 4, Belgium 1
Special playoff
Switzerland 4, Italy 1

Quarterfinals
West Germany 2, Yugoslavia 0
Hungary 4, Brazil 2
Austria 7, Switzerland 5
Uruguay 4, England 2

Semifinals
West Germany 6, Austria 1
Hungary 4, Uruguay 2
Third-place Match
Austria 3, Uruguay 1

Final
West Germany 3, Hungary 2

1958 Sweden

First round

Group 1
West Germany 3, Argentina 1

Northern Ireland 1, Czechoslovakia 0
West Germany 2, Czechoslovakia
2
Argentina 3, Northern Ireland 1

West Germany 2, Northern Ireland 2

Czechoslovakia 6, Argentina 1

Special playoff

Northern Ireland 2, Czechoslovakia 1

Group 2
France 7, Paraguay 3

Yugoslavia 1, Scotland 1

Yugoslavia 3, France 2

Paraguay 3, Scotland 2

France 2, Scotland 1

Yugoslavia 3, Paraguay 3

Group 3
Sweden 3, Mexico 0

Hungary 1, Wales 1

Wales 1, Mexico 1

Sweden 2, Hungary 1

Hungary 4, Mexico 0

Sweden 0, Wales 0

Special Playoff

Wales 2, Hungary 1

Group 4
England 2, Soviet Union 2

Brazil 3, Austria 0

England 0, Brazil 0

Soviet Union 2, Austria 0

Brazil 2, Soviet Union 0

England 2, Austria 2

Special Playoff

Soviet Union 1, England 0

Quarterfinals
France 4, Northern Ireland 0

West Germany 1, Yugoslavia 0

Sweden 2, Soviet Union 0

Brazil 1, Wales 0

Semifinals
Brazil 5, France 2

Sweden 3, West Germany 1

Third-Place Match

France 6, West Germany 3

Final
Brazil 5, Sweden 2

1962 Chile

First round

Group 1
Uruguay 2, Colombia 1

Soviet Union 2, Yugoslavia 0

Yugoslavia 3, Uruguay 1

Soviet Union 4, Colombia 4

Soviet Union 2, Uruguay 1

Yugoslavia 5, Colombia 0

Group 2

Chile 3, Switzerland 1

West Germany 0, Italy 0

Chile 2, Italy 0

West Germany 2, Switzerland 1

West Germany 2, Chile 0

Italy 3, Switzerland 0

Group 3
Brazil 2, Mexico 0

Czechoslovakia 1, Spain 0

Brazil 0, Czechoslovakia 0

Spain 1, Mexico 0
Brazil 2, Spain 1
Mexico 3, Czechoslovakia 1

Group 4

Argentina 1, Bulgaria 0
Hungary 2, England 1
England 3, Argentina 1
Hungary 6, Bulgaria 1
Argentina 0, Hungary 0
England 0, Bulgaria 0

Quarterfinals

Yugoslavia 1, West Germany 0
Brazil 3, England 1

Chile 2, Soviet Union 1
Czechoslovakia 1, Hungary 0

Semifinals

Brazil 4, Chile 2
Czechoslovakia 3, Yugoslavia 1
Third-Place Match
Chile 1, Yugoslavia 0

Final

Brazil 3, Czechoslovakia 1

1966 England

First round

Group 1

England 0, Uruguay 0
France 1, Mexico 1
Uruguay 2, France 1
England 2, Mexico 0
Uruguay 0, Mexico 0
England 2, France 0

Group 2

West Germany 5, Switzerland 0
Argentina 2, Spain 1
Spain 2, Switzerland 1
Argentina 0, West Germany 0
Argentina 2, Switzerland 0
West Germany 2, Spain 1

Group 3

Brazil 2, Bulgaria 0

Portugal 3, Hungary 1
Hungary 3, Brazil 1
Portugal 3, Bulgaria 0
Portugal 3, Brazil 1
Hungary 3, Bulgaria 1

Group 4

Soviet Union 3, North Korea 0
Italy 2, Chile 0
Chile 1, North Korea 1
Soviet Union 1, Italy 0
North Korea 1, Italy 0
Soviet Union 2, Chile 1

Quarterfinals

England 1, Argentina 0
West Germany 4, Uruguay 0
Portugal 5, North Korea 3
Soviet Union 2, Hungary 1

Semifinals

West Germany 2, Soviet Union 1

England 2, Portugal 1

Third-Place Match

Portugal 2, Soviet Union 1

Final

England 4, Germany 2 (extra time)

1970 Mexico

First round

Group 1

Mexico 0, Soviet Union 0

Belgium 3, El Salvador 0

Soviet Union 4, Belgium 1

Mexico 4, El Salvador 0

Soviet Union 2, El Salvador 0

Mexico 1, Belgium 0

Group 2

Uruguay 2, Israel 0

Italy 1, Sweden 0

Uruguay 0, Italy 0

Sweden 1, Israel 1

Sweden 1, Uruguay 0

Italy 0, Israel

Group 3

England 1, Romania 0

Brazil 4, Czechoslovakia 1

Romania 2, Czechoslovakia 1

Brazil 1, England 0

Brazil 3, Romania 2

England 1, Czechoslovakia 0

Group 4

Peru 3, Bulgaria 2

West Germany 2, Morocco 1

Peru 3, Morocco 0

West Germany 5, Bulgaria 2

West Germany 3, Peru 1

Bulgaria 1, Morocco 1

Quarterfinals

Uruguay 1, Soviet Union 0

Italy 4, Mexico 1

Brazil 4, Peru 2

West Germany 3, England 2

Semifinals

Italy 4, West Germany 3

Brazil 3, Uruguay 1

Third-Place Match

West Germany 1, Uruguay 0

Final

Brazil 4, Italy 1

1974 West Germany

First round

Group 1

West Germany 1, Chile 0
East Germany 2, Australia 0
West Germany 3, Australia 0
Chile 1, East Germany 1
Australia 0, Chile 0
East Germany 1, West Germany 0

Group 2

Brazil 0, Yugoslavia 0
Scotland 2, Zaire 0
Yugoslavia 9, Zaire 0
Scotland 0, Brazil 0
Brazil 3, Zaire 0
Scotland 1, Yugoslavia 1

Group 3

Sweden 0, Bulgaria 0
Netherlands 2, Uruguay 0
Netherlands 0, Sweden 0
Bulgaria 1, Uruguay 1
Sweden 3, Uruguay 0
Netherlands 4, Bulgaria 1

Group 4

Italy 3, Haiti 1
Poland 3, Argentina 2
Poland 7, Haiti 0
Argentina 1, Italy 1
Argentina 4, Haiti 1
Poland 2, Italy 1

Semifinal round

Group A

Netherlands 4, Argentina 0
Brazil 1, East Germany 0
Netherlands 2, East Germany 0
Brazil 2, Argentina 1
Netherlands 2, Brazil 0
Argentina 1, East Germany 1

Group B

West Germany 2, Yugoslavia 0
Poland 1, Sweden 0
Poland 2, Yugoslavia 1
West Germany 4, Sweden 2
West Germany 1, Poland 0
Sweden 2, Yugoslavia 1
Third-Place Match
Poland 1, Brazil 0

Final

West Germany 2, Netherlands 1

1978 Argentina

First round

Group 1
France 1, Italy 2
Argentina 2, Hungary 1
Italy 3, Hungary 1
Argentina 2, France 1
France 3, Hungary 1
Italy 1, Argentina 0

Group 2
West Germany 0, Poland 0
Tunisia 3, Mexico 1
West Germany 6, Mexico 0
Poland 1, Tunisia 0
Poland 3, Mexico 1
Tunisia 0, West Germany 0

Group 3
Austria 2, Spain 1
Sweden 1, Brazil 1
Brazil 0, Spain 0
Austria 1, Sweden 0
Spain 1, Sweden 0
Brazil 1, Austria 0

Group 4
Peru 3, Scotland 1
Netherlands 3, Iran 0
Scotland 1, Iran 1
Netherlands 0, Peru 0
Peru 4, Iran 1
Scotland 3, Netherlands 2

Semifinals

Group A
West Germany 0, Italy 0
Netherlands 5, Austria 1
Italy 1, Austria 0
Netherlands 2, West Germany 2
Netherlands 2, Italy 1
Austria 3, West Germany 2

Group B
Argentina 2, Poland 0
Brazil 3, Peru 3, Peru 0
Argentina 0, Brazil 0
Poland 1, Peru 0
Brazil 3, Poland 1
Argentina 6, Peru 0

1982 Spain

First round

Group 1
Italy 0, Poland 0
Cameroon 0, Peru 0
Italy 1, Peru 1
Cameroon 0, Poland 0

Poland 5, Peru 1
Cameroon 1, Italy 1

Group 2
Algeria 2, West Germany 1
Austria 1, Chile 0
West Germany 4, Chile 1

Austria 0, Algeria 0
Algeria 3, Chile 2
West Germany 1, Austria 0

Group 3
Belgium 1, Argentina 0
Hungary 10, El Salvador 1
Argentina 4, Hungary 1
Belgium 1, El Salvador 0
Belgium 1, Hungary 1
Argentina 2, El Salvador 0

Group 4
England 3, France 1
Czechoslovakia 1, Kuwait 1
England 2, Czechoslovakia 0
France 4, Kuwait 1
Czechoslovakia 1, France 1
England 1, Kuwait 0

Group 5
Honduras 1, Spain 1
Northern Ireland 0, Yugoslavia 0
Spain 2, Yugoslavia 1
Honduras 1, Northern Ireland 1
Yugoslavia 1, Honduras 0
Northern Ireland 1, Spain 0

Group 6
Brazil 2, Soviet Union 1
Scotland 5, New Zealand 2
Brazil 4, Scotland 1
Soviet Union 3, New Zealand 0
Scotland 2, Soviet Union 2
Brazil 4, New Zealand 0

Second round

Group A
Poland 3, Belgium 0
Soviet Union 1, Belgium 0
Poland 0, Soviet Union 0

Group B
England 0, West Germany 0
West Germany 2, Spain 1
England 0, Spain 0

Group C
Italy 2, Argentina 1
Brazil 3, Argentina 1
Italy 3, Brazil 2

Group D
France 1, Austria 0
Austria 2, Northern Ireland 2
France 4, Northern Ireland 1

Semifinals
Italy 2, Poland 0
West Germany 3, France 3
(West Germany advanced on penalty kicks, 5-4)
Third-Place Match
Poland 3, France 2

Final
Italy 3, West Germany 1

1986 Mexico

first round

Group A

Bulgaria 1, Italy 1
Argentina 3, South Korea 1
Italy 1, Argentina 1
South Korea 1, Bulgaria 1
Italy 3, South Korea 2
Argentina 2, Bulgaria 0

Group B

Mexico 2, Belgium 1
Paraguay 1, Iraq 0
Mexico 1, Paraguay 1
Belgium 2, Iraq 1
Mexico 1, Iraq 0
Paraguay 2, Belgium 2

Group C

France 1, Canada 0
Soviet Union 6, Hungary 0
France 1, Soviet Union 1
Hungary 2, Canada 0
France 3, Hungary 0
Soviet Union 2, Canada 0

Group D

Brazil 1, Spain 0
Algeria 1, Northern Ireland 1
Brazil 1, Algeria 0
Spain 2, Northern Ireland 1
Brazil 3, Northern Ireland 0
Spain 3, Algeria 0

Group E

Uruguay 1, West Germany 1
Denmark 1, Scotland 0
West Germany 2, Scotland 1
Denmark 6, Uruguay 1
Denmark 2, West Germany 0
Scotland 0, Uruguay 0

Group F

Morocco 0, Poland 0
Portugal 1, England 0
England 0, Morocco 0
Poland 1, Portugal 0
Morocco 3, Portugal 1
England 3, Poland 0

Second round

Argentina 1, Uruguay 0
England 3, Paraguay 0
Belgium 4, Soviet Union 3
Spain 5, Denmark 1
Brazil 4, Poland 0
France 2, Italy 0
West Germany 1, Morocco 0
Mexico 1, Bulgaria 0

Quarterfinals

Argentina 2, England 1
Belgium 1, Spain 1
(Belgium advanced on penalty kicks, 5-4)
France 1, Brazil 1
(France advanced on penalty kicks, 4-3)
West Germany 0, Mexico 0

(West Germany advanced on penalty kicks, 4-1)

Semifinals
Argentina 2, Belgium 0
West Germany 2, France 0

Third-Place Match
France 4, Belgium 2

Final
Argentina 3, West Germany 2

1990 Italy

first round

Group A
Italy 1, Austria 0
Czechoslovakia 5, U.S. 1
Italy 1, U.S. 0
Czechoslovakia 1, Austria 0
Italy 2, Czechoslovakia 0
Austria 2, U.S. 1

Group B
Cameroon 1, Argentina 0
Romania 2, Soviet Union 0
Argentina 2, Soviet Union 0
Cameroon 2, Romania 1
Argentina 1, Romania 1
Soviet Union 4, Cameroon 0

Group C
Brazil 2, Sweden 1
Costa Rica 1, Scotland 0
Brazil 1, Costa Rica 0
Scotland 2, Sweden 1
Brazil 1, Scotland 0
Costa Rica 2, Sweden 1

Group D
Colombia 2, United Arab Emirates 0

West Germany 4, Yugoslavia 1
Yugoslavia 1, Colombia 0
West Germany 5, United Arab Emirates 1
West Germany 1, Colombia 1
Yugoslavia 4, United Arab Emirates 1

Group E
Belgium 2, South Korea 0
Uruguay 0, Spain 0
Belgium 3, Uruguay 1
Spain 3, South Korea 1
Spain 2, Belgium 1
Uruguay 1, South Korea 0

Group F
England 1, Ireland Republic 1
Netherlands 1, Egypt 1
England 0, Netherlands 0
Ireland Republic 0, Egypt 0
England 1, Egypt 0
Ireland Republic 1, Netherlands 1

Second round
Cameroon 2, Colombia 1
Czechoslovakia 4, Costa Rica 1
Argentina 1, Brazil 0
Germany 2, Netherlands 1

Ireland Republic 0, Romania 0
(Ireland Republic advanced on penalty kicks, 5-4)
Italy 3, Uruguay 0
Yugoslavia 2, Spain 1
England 1, Belgium 0

Quarterfinals

Argentina 0, Yugoslavia 0
(Argentina advanced on penalty kicks, 3-2)
Italy 1, Ireland Republic 0
West Germany 1, Czechoslovakia 0
England 3, Cameroon 2

Semifinals

Argentina 1, Italy 1
(Argentina advanced on penalty kicks, 4-3)
West Germany 1, England 1
(West Germany advanced on penalty kicks, 4-3)
Third-Place Match
Italy 2, England 1

Final

West Germany 1, Argentina 0

World Cup Records

TEAM RECORDS
Career

Most appearances
14—Brazil
12—Italy, West Germany
10—Argentina
9—England, France, Hungary, Mexico, Uruguay

Most games
68—West Germany
66—Brazil
54—Italy
48—Argentina

Most victories
44—Brazil
39—West Germany
31—Italy
24—Argentina

Most ties
15—West Germany
12—Italy and England
11—Brazil

Most losses
17—Mexico
15—Argentina

14—West Germany, Uruguay, France, Sweden, Czechoslovakia, Hungary, Sweden, Belgium

Longest winning streak
7—Italy (1934-1938)
6—England (1966-1970), Brazil (1970), Brazil (1978-1982)

Longest unbeaten streak
13—Brazil (1958 to 1966; 11-0-2)
11—Uruguay (1930 to 1954; 10-0-1); Brazil (1970 to 1974; 9-0-2); Brazil (1978 to 1982; 8-0-3)

Longest losing streak
9—Mexico (1930 to 1958)
7—Switzerland (1954 to 1966)
6—El Salvador (1970 to 1982)

Longest winless streak
16—Bulgaria (1962 to 1986; 0-10-6)
13—Mexico (1930 to 1962; 0-12-1)

11—Uruguay (1970 to 1990;
  0-7-4)

6—Italy
4—Argentina, Uruguay

Most shutouts
24—Brazil
23—Germany

**Most appearances (champion-
  ship game)**
6—West Germany
4—Argentina, Brazil, Italy
2—Czechoslovakia, the Netherlands, Hungary, Uruguay
1—England, Sweden

Most appearances (semifinals)
9—West Germany
7—Brazil

Tournament Records
Most victories

6—Brazil, 6-0-0 (1970), West
  Germany, 6-1-0 (1974), Ar-

gentina, 6-0-1, (1986)

GAMES
Most goals, two teams

12—Austria vs. Switzerland
  (1954); Austria won, 7-5
11—Brazil vs. Poland (1938);
  Brazil won, 6-5; Hungary vs.
  West Germany (1954), Hungary won, 8-3; Hungary vs. El
  Salvador (1982); Hungary
  won, 10-1

9—Hungary vs. South Korea
  (1954); Hungary won, 9-0;
  Yugoslavia vs. Zaire (1974);
  Yugoslalvia won, 9-0

Highest goal differential
9—Hungary vs. El Savlador,
  10-1 (1982); Hungary vs.
  South Korea, 9-0, (1954), and
  Yugoslavia vs. Zaire, 9-0
  (1974)

Most goals by a team
10—Hungary vs. El Salvador
  (1982); Hungary won, 10-1

ATTENDANCE

Largest crowd
199,850—Brazil vs. Uruguay, at
  Maracana Stadium, Rio de Janeiro, Brazil on July 14, 1950

Largest aggregate attendance
2,510,686, Brazil (1950)

Largest average attendance
60,772, Brazil (1950)

Smallest crowd
300, Romania vs. Peru, in Montevideo, Uruguay on July 14,
  1930

Largest crowds

Tournament opener: 107,000, Mexico vs. Soviet Union, Azteca Stadium, Mexico City, May 31, 1970

First round (other than tournament opener): 142,409, Brazil vs. Yugoslavia, Maracana Stadium, Rio de Janeiro, July 1, 1950

Second round: 114,580, Mexico vs. Bulgaria, Azteca Stadium, Mexico City, June 15, 1986

Quarterfinals: 114,580, Argentina vs. England, Azteca Stadium, Mexico City, June 22, 1986

Semifinals: 110,420, Argentina vs. Belgium, Azteca Stadium, Mexico City, June 25, 1986

Third-place: 87,696, Portugal vs. Soviet Union, Wembley Stadium, Wembley, England, July 28, 1966

Championship: 199,854, Uruguay vs. Brazil, Maracana Stadium, Rio de Janeiro, Brazil, July 16, 1950

Smallest crowds

Tournament opener: 1,000, France vs. Mexico, Pocitos Stadium, Montevideo, Uruguay, July 13, 1930

First round (other than tournament opener): 300, Romania vs. Peru, Pocitos Stadium, Montevideo, Uruguay, July 14, 1930

Second round: 25,000, Brazil vs. Czechoslovakia, Parc de Lescure, Bordeaux, France, June 12, 1938

Quarterfinals: 11,690, Czechoslovakia vs. Hungary, Braden Stadium, Rancagua, Chile, June 10, 1962

Semifinals: 10,000, Czechoslovakia vs. West Germany, PNF Stadium, Rome, Italy, June 3, 1934

Third-place: 7,000, Germany vs. Austria, Asarelli Stadium, Naples, Italy, June 7, 1934

Championship: 49,737, Brazil vs. Sweden, Rasunda Stadium, Stockholm, Sweden, June 29, 1958

INDIVIDUAL RECORDS
GAMES

Most appearances in finals:

5—Antonio Carbajal, Mexico (1950, 1954, 1958, 1962, 1966).

4—Djalma Santos, Brazil (1954, 1958, 1962, 1966); Pele, Brazil (1958, 1962, 1966, 1970); Gianni Rivera, Italy (1962, 1966, 1970, 1974); Pedro Rocha, Uruguay (1962, 1966, 1970, 1974), Karl-Heinz Schnellinger, West Germany (1958, 1962, 1966, 1970), Uwe Seeler, West Germany (1958, 1962, 1966, 1970), Wladislaw Zmuda, Poland (1974, 1978, 1982, 1986).

Most appearances, games:
21—Uwe Seeler, West Germany (1958, 1962, 1966, 1970) and Wladislaw Zmuda, Poland (1974, 1978, 1982, 1986).

20—Grzegorz Lato, Poland (1974, 1978, 1982).

19—Wolfgang Overath, West Germany (1966, 1970, 1974), Berti Vogts, West Germany (1970, 1974, 1978), Karl-Heinz Rummenigge, West Germany (1978, 1982, 1986), Diego Maradona, Argentina (1982, 1986, 1990).

Most appearances, games
Active players

19—Diego Maradona, Argentina (1982, 1986, 1990).

15—Lothar Matthaeus, West Germany (1982, 1986, 1990).

Most appearances, goalkeeper

18—Sepp Maier, West Germany (1970, 1974, 1978)

Most appearances, championship teams
3—Pele, Brazil (1958, 1962, 1970)

Most goals
14—Gerd Mueller, West Germany (1970, 1974)

Most victories, goalkeeper
11—Sepp Maier, West Germany (1970, 1974, 1978); Gilmar, Brazil (1958, 1962, 1966).

Best winning percentage, goalkeeper
.885—Gilmar, Brazil, 11-1-1 (1962, 1966, 1970)

Best goals-against averages (at least five games):
0.20—Peter Shilton, England (1982, 1986)

Best goals-against average (at least 20 games)
0.79—Jan Jongbloed, Netherlands (1974, 1978)

Most shutouts, lifetime
8—Sepp Maier, West Germany (1970, 1974, 1978)

Most losses, lifetime
8—Antonio Carbajal, Mexico (1950, 1954, 1958, 1962, 1966)

TOURNAMENT

Most goals
13—Just Fontaine, France (1958)

Most multiple-goal games
4—Just Fontaine France (1958)

Most victories, goalkeeper
6—Felix, Brazil (1970), Sepp Maier, West Germany (1974), Nery Pumpido, Argentina (1986)

Best goals-against average (at least five games)
0.20—Peter Shilton, England (1982)
Longest scoreless streak

517 minutes—Walter Zenga, Italy (1986, 1990)
499 minutes—Peter Shilton, England (1982, 1986)

GAMES

Most goals scored
4—(by 9 players) Gustav Wetterstroem, Sweden, vs. Cuba (1938); Leondias da Silva, Brazil, vs. Poland, (1938); Ernest Willimowski, Poland vs. Brazil (1938); Ademir, Brazil vs. Sweden (1950); Juan Schiaffino, Uruguay vs. Bolivia (1950); Sandor Kocsis, Hungary vs. West Germany (1954); Just Fontaine, France vs. West Germany

(1958); Eusebio, Portugal vs. North Korea (1966), and Emilio Butragueno, Spain vs. Denmark (1986).

Fastest goal
27 seconds—Bryan Robson, England vs. France (June 16, 1982)

Most penalty kicks
2—Eusebio, Portugal vs. North Korea (July 23, 1966)

MISCELLANEOUS RECORDS

Longest scoring drought
335 minutes—El Salvador (1970, 1982)

Scoring Leaders
All-time

Gerd Mueller (West Germany)	14
Just Fontaine (France)	13
Pele (Brazil)	12
Sandor Kocsis (Hungary	11
Uwe Rahn (West Germany)	10
Nene Cubillas (Peru)	10
Grzegorz Lato (Poland)	10
Gary Lineker (England)	10
Karl-Heinz Rummenigge (West Germany)	9
Paolo Rossi (Italy)	9
Eusebio (Portugal)	9
Grzegorz Lato (Poland)	9
Vava (Brazil)	9

Jairzinho (Brazil)	9
Uwe Seeler (West Germany)	9
Ademir (Brazil)	9
Leondias da Silva (Brazil)	9

Tournament

Just Fontaine, France (1958)	13
Sandor Kocsis, Hungary (1954)	11
Gerd Mueller, West Germany (1958)	10
Eusebio, Portugal (1966)	9
Leonidas da Silva, Brazil (1938)	8
Guillermo Stabile, Argentina (1930)	8
Gyula Zsengeller, Hungary (1938)	7
Grzegorz Lato, Poland (1974)	7

All-Time World Cup Standings

All-Time World Cup Standings

Team	G	W	L	T	GF	GA	Pts.
Brazil	66	44	11	11	148	65	99
West Germany	68	39	14	15	145	90	93
Italy	54	31	11	12	89	54	74
Argentina	48	24	15	9	82	59	57
England	41	18	11	12	55	38	48
Uruguay	37	15	14	8	61	52	38
Soviet Union	31	15	10	6	53	34	36
France	34	15	14	5	71	56	35
Yugoslavia	33	15	13	5	55	42	35
Hungary	32	15	14	3	87	57	33
Spain	32	13	12	7	43	38	33
Poland	25	13	7	5	39	29	31
Sweden	31	11	14	6	51	52	28
Czechoslovakia	30	11	14	5	44	45	27
Austria	26	12	12	2	40	43	26
Netherlands	20	8	6	6	35	23	22
Belgium	25	7	14	4	33	49	18
Mexico	29	6	17	6	27	64	18
Chile	21	7	11	3	26	32	17
Scotland	20	4	10	6	23	35	14
Portugal	9	6	3	0	19	12	12
Switzerland	18	5	11	2	28	44	12
Northern Ireland	13	3	5	5	13	23	11
Peru	15	4	8	3	19	31	11
Paraguay	11	3	4	4	16	25	10
Romania	12	3	6	3	16	20	9
Cameroon	8	3	2	3	8	10	9

All-Time World Cup Standings (continued)

Team	G	W	L	T	GF	GA	Pts.
Denmark	4	3	1	0	10	6	6
East Germany	6	2	2	2	5	5	6
United States	10	3	7	0	14	29	6
Bulgaria	16	0	10	6	11	35	6
Wales	5	1	1	3	4	4	5
Algeria	6	2	3	1	6	10	5
Morocco	7	1	3	3	5	8	5
Ireland Republic	5	0	1	4	2	3	4
Costa Rica	4	2	2	0	4	6	4
Colombia	7	1	4	2	9	15	4
Tunisia	3	1	1	1	3	2	3
North Korea	4	1	2	1	5	9	3
Cuba	3	1	1	1	5	12	3
Turkey	3	1	2	0	10	11	2
Honduras	3	0	1	2	2	3	2
Israel	3	1	2	0	1	3	2
Egypt	4	0	2	2	3	6	2
Kuwait	3	0	2	1	2	6	1
Australia	3	0	2	1	0	5	1
Iran	3	0	2	1	2	8	1
South Korea	8	0	7	1	5	29	1
Norway	1	0	1	0	1	2	0
Dutch E. Indies	1	0	1	0	0	6	0
Iraq	3	0	3	0	1	4	0
Canada	3	0	3	0	0	5	0
UAE	3	0	3	0	2	11	0
New Zealand	3	0	3	0	2	12	0
Haiti	3	0	3	0	2	14	0
Zaire	3	0	3	0	0	14	0
Bolivia	3	0	3	0	0	16	0
El Salvador	6	0	6	0	1	22	0

CROWDS

Year	Country	Games	Total Attendance	Average
1930	Uruguay	18	434,500	24,139

CROWDS (continued)

Year	Country	Games	Total Attendance	Average
1934	Italy	17	395,000	23,235
1938	France	18	483,000	26,833
1950	Brazil	22	1,337,000	60,772
1954	Switzerland	26	943,000	36,270
1958	Sweden	35	868,000	24,800
1962	Chile	32	776,000	24,250
1966	England	32	1,614,677	50,458
1970	Mexico	32	1,673,975	52,312
1974	West Germany	38	1,774,022	46,685
1978	Argentina	38	1,610,215	42,374
1982	Spain	52	1,766,277	33,967
1986	Mexico	52	2,401,480	46,182
1990	Italy	52	2,510,686	48,282

Goals—By World Cup

Year	Games	Goals	Avg.
1930	18	70	3.88
1934	17	70	4.11
1938	18	84	4.66
1950	22	88	4.00
1954	26	140	5.38
1958	35	126	3.60
1962	32	89	2.78
1966	32	89	2.78
1970	32	95	2.96
1974	38	97	2.55
1978	38	102	2.68
1982	52	146	2.81
1986	52	132	2.53
1990	52	115	2.21

Goals—Individuals

Year	Player (Team)	Goals
1930	Guillermo Stabile (Argentina)	8
1934	Angelo Schiavio (Italy)	4
	Oldrich Nejedly (Czechoslovakia)	4
	Edmund Cohen (Germany)	4
1938	Leonidas da Silva (Brazil)	8
1950	Ademir (Brazil)	9
1954	Sandor Kocsis (Hungary)	11
1958	Just Fontaine (France)	13
1962	Drazen Jerkovic (Yugoslavia)	5
1966	Eusebio (Portugal)	9
1970	Gerd Mueller (West Germany)	10
1974	Grzegorz Lato (Poland)	7
1978	Mario Kempes (Argentina)	6
1982	Paolo Rossi (Italy)	6
1986	Gary Lineker (England)	6
1990	Salvatore Schillaci (Italy)	6

Winning Coaches

Year	Coach	Country
1930	Alberto Supicci	Uruguay
1934	Vittorio Pozzo	Italy
1938	Vittorio Pozzo	Italy
1950	Juan Lopez	Uruguay
1954	Sepp Herberger	West Germany
1958	Vicente Feola	Brazil
1962	Aymore Moreira	Brazil
1966	Alf Ramsey	England
1970	Mario Zagalo	Brazil
1974	Helmut Schoen	West Germany
1978	Cesar Luis Menotti	Argentina
1982	Enzo Bearzot	Italy
1986	Carlos Bilardo	Argentina
1990	Franz Beckenbauer	West Germany

Milestones

100th goal: By Sven Jonasson of Sweden in a 3-2 win over Argentina in 1934.

200th goal: By Gustav Wetterstroem of Sweden in an 8-0 win over Cuba in 1938.

300th goal: By Chico of Brazil in a 6-1 win over Spain in 1950.

400th: By Kucucandoniadis Lefter of Turkey in a 7-2 loss to West Germany in 1954.

500th goal: By Helmut Rahn of West Germany in a 2-2 tie with Czechoslovakia in 1958.

600th goal: By Drazan Jerkovic of Yugoslavia in a 3-1 win over Hungary in 1962.

700th goal: By Bobby Charlton of England in a 2-0 win over Mexico in 1966.

800th goal: By Jairzinho of Brazil in a 1-0 win over England in 1970.

900th goal: By Hector Casimiro Yazalde of Argentina in a 4-1 win over Haiti in 1974.

1,000th goal: By Robbie Rensenbrink of the Netherlands in a 3-2 loss to Scotland in 1978.

1,100th goal: By Oleg Blokhin of the Soviet Union in a 3-0 win over New Zealand in 1982.

1,200th goal: By Jean-Pierre Papin of France in a 1-0 win over Canada in 1986.

1,300th goal: By Gary Lineker of England in a 3-0 win over Paraguay in 1986.

Appendix F

The World Cup Has Already Been to the U.S.

Mexican striker Hugo Sanchez will enjoy the unique distinction of being the only player at the 1994 World Cup to have played professionally in the United States.

Sanchez, who now toils for Rayo Vallecano in the Spanish First Division, played parts of two seasons for the San Diego Sockers of the North American Soccer League in the 1979 and 1980, scoring six and seven goals in 10 and nine regular-season matches, respectively. He was only 21-years-old then, at the beginning of a fabulous career that would take him to Real Madrid, for whom he led the Spanish League in scoring five times.

The impressive list includes three World Cup championship captains—Bobby Moore (England, 1966), Carlos Alberto (Brazil, 1970) and Franz Beckenbauer (West Germany, 1974).

And that's not to forget Pele (Brazil), Johan Cruyff (Netherlands), the original Dutch master,, Gordon Banks (England), who made arguably the greatest save in World Cup history on Pele, Eusebio (Portugal), who connected for four goals in a match in 1966, Johan Neeskens (Netherlands), who converted a penalty kick in the opening minute of the 1974 championship game, Geoff Hurst (England), who scored a controversial game-winning goal in the 1966 final, Gerd Mueller (Germany), who is the all-time scoring leader (14 goals), and the great Ferenc Puskas (Hungary).

All totalled, 92 players/coaches with NASL playing and coaching experience have participated in the World Cup.

And that doesn't include several other players, including Paul Mariner (England, 1982), who played for the Albany Capitals (1991) and San Francisco Bay Blackhawks (1992) in the American Professional Soccer League, and 11 Canadians who participated in the 1986 World Cup in Mexico. That list includes Tino Lettieri (Minnesota, 1977-81, 1984, Vancouver, 1982-83), Bob Lenarduzzi (Vancouver,

1974-84), Bruce Wilson (Vancouver, 1974-77, Chicago, 1978-79, New York, 1980, Toronto, 1981-84), Randy Ragan (Toronto, 1980-84), Ian Bridge (Seattle, 1979-83 Vancouver 1984), Carl Valentine (Vancouver, 1979-84), Gerry Gray (Vancouver, 1980-82, Montreal, 1983, New York, 1984, Chicago, 1984), Branko Segota (Rochester, 1979-80, Fort Lauderdale, 1981-83, Golden Bay, 1984), , Igor Vrablic (Golden Bay, 1984), Michael Sweeney (Edmonton, 1980-82, Vancouver 1983-84, Golden Bay, 1984), Dale Mitchell (Vancouver, 1977-78, Portland, 1979-82, Montreal, 1983).

The NASL list (players' name, World Cup, clubs and years):
Javier Aguirre (Mexico, 1986)—Los Angeles Aztecs, 1980.
Carlos Alberto (Brazil, 1970)—New York 1977-80, 1982, California 1981.
Adrian Alston (Australia, 1974)—Tampa Bay 1977-78.
Arsene Auguste (Haiti, 1974)—Tampa Bay 1975-79, Fort Lauderdale 1980-81.
Alan Ball (England, 1966)—Philadelphia 1978-79, Vancouver 1979-80.
Gordon Banks (England, 1966, 1970)—Cleveland 1967, Fort Lauderdale 1977-78.
Julio (Chico) Baylon (Peru, 1970)—Rochester, 1979-80.
Peter Beardsley (England, 1986)—Vancouver, 1981-83.
Colin Bell (England, 1970)—Minnesota, 1980.
Jose Oscar Bernardi (Brazil, 1978, 1982)—New York, 1980.
Franz Beckenbauer (West Germany, 1966, 1970, 1974, coach in 1986 and 1990)—New York, 1977-80, 1983.
Vladislav Bogicevic (Yugoslavia, 1974)—New York, 1977-84.
Peter Bonetti (England, 1970)—St. Louis, 1975.
Bill Brown (Scotland, 1958)—Toronto, 1967.
Ivan Buljan (Yugoslavia, 1974)—New York, 1981-82.
Omar Caetano (Uruguay, 1966)—New York, 1975.
Roberto Cabanas (Paraguay, 1986)—New York, 1986.
Carmelo (Spain, 1962)—Baltimore, 1967-68.
Giorgio Chinaglia (Italy, 1974)—New York, 1976-83.
Jeung Young Cho (South Korea, 1986)—Portland 1981-82, Chicago, 1983.
Vic Crowe (Wales, 1958)—Atlanta, 1968-69, Portland,1975-76, 1980-82 (as coach).
Johan Cruyff (Netherlands, 1974)—Los Angeles, 1979, Washington, 1980-81.

Teofilo Cubillas (Peru, 1970, 1978, 1982)—Fort Lauderdale, 1979-83.

Leonardo Cuellar (Mexico, 1978)—San Diego 1979-81, San Jose 1982.

Iraj Danaifard (Iran, 19778)—Tulsa, 1979-82.

Kazimerz Deyna (Poland, 1974, 1978)—San Diego, 1981-84.

Willie Donachie (Scotland, 1974, 1978)—Portland (1980-82).

Andranik Eskandarian (Iran, 1978)—New York 1979-84.

Eusebio (Portugal, 1966)—Boston, 1975, Toronto, 1976, Las Vegas, 1977.

Elias Figueora (Chile 1966, 1974, 1982)—Fort Lauderdale, 1981.

Trevor Francis (England, 1982)—Detroit), 1978-79.

Robert Gadocha (Poland, 1974)—-Chicago, 1978.

Archie Gemmill (Scotland, 1978)—Jacksonville, 1982.

David Harvey (Scotland, 1974)—Vancouver, 1980-82.

Mark Hateley (England, 1986)—Detroit, 1980.

Jim Holton (Scotland, 1974)—Miami, 1976, Detroit, 1980.

Bernd Holzenbein (West Germany, 1974, 1978)—Fort Lauderdale, 1978.

Geoff Hurst (England, 1966)—Seattle, 1976.

Tommy Hutchison (Scotland, 1974)—Seattle, 1980.

Willie Johnston (Scotland, 1978)—Vancouver, 1979-80, 1982.

Wim Jansen (Netherlands, 1974, 1978)—Washington, 1980.

Ernst Jean-Joseph (Haiti, 1974)—Chicago, 1978.

Helmut Kremers (West Germany, 1974)—Calgary, 1981.

Ruud Krol (Netherlands, 1974, 1978)—Vancouver, 1980.

Peter Lorimer (Scotland, 1974)—Toronto, 1979-80, Vancouver 1981-83.

Peter McParland (Northern Ireland, 1958)—Atlanta, 1967-1968.

Raul Magana (El Salvador, 1970)—Toronto, 1968.

Francisco Marinho (Brazil, 1974)—New York, 1979, Fort Lauderdale, 1980.

Juan Masnik (Uruguay, 1974)—New York, 1975.

David McCreery (Northern Ireland, 1982, 1986)—Tulsa, 1981-82.

Cesar Luis Menotti (Argentina coach, 1978 and 1982)—New York, 1967-68.

Ramon Mifflin (Peru, 1970, assistant coach in 1982)—New York, 1976-77, Los Angeles, 1978.

Mirandinha (Brazil, 1974)—Tampa Bay, 1978-79, Memphis 1979.

Bobby Moore (England, 1962, 1966, 1970)—San Antonio, 1976, Seattle, 1978.

Willie Morgan (Scotland, 1974)—Chicago, 1977.
Gerd Mueller (West Germany, 1970, 1974)—Fort Lauderdale, 1979-81.
Johan Neeskens (Netherlands, 1974, 1978)—New York, 1979-84.
Jimmy Nicholl (Northern Ireland, 1982, 1986)—Toronto, 1982-84.
Bjorn Nordqvist (Sweden, 1974, 1978)—Minnesota, 1979-81.
Ruben Pagnanini (Argentina, 1978)—Minnesota, 1981.
Miro Pavlovic (Yugoslavia, 1974)—San Jose, 1976-77.
Pele (Brazil, 1958, 1962, 1966, 1970)—New York, 1975-77.
David Primo (Israel, 1970)—Baltimore, 1967, New York, 1975.
Rob Rensenbrink (Netherlands, 1974, 1978)—Portland, 1980-81.
Salvador Reyes (Mexico, 1959, 1962, 1966)—Los Angeles, 1967.
Wim Rijsbergen (Netherlands, 1974, 1978)—New York, 1979-83.
Rildo (Brazil, 1966, 1970)—New York, 1977.
Bruce Rioch (Scotland, 1978)—Seattle, 1980-81.
Julio Cesar Romero (Paraguay, 1986)—New York, 1980-82.
Guy St. Vil (Haiti, 1974)—Baltimore, 1967-68, 1975.
Hugo Sanchez (Mexico, 1978)—San Diego, 1979-80.
Manu Sanon (Haiti, 1974)—San Diego, 1980-82.
Dragoslav Sekularic (Yugoslavia, 1858, 1962)—St. Louis, 1967.
Moredchai Shpigler (Israel, 1970)—New York, 1975.
Antonio Simoes (Portugal, 1966)—Boston, 1975-76, San Jose, 1976-77, Dallas, 1979).
Thomas Sjoberg (Sweden, 1978))—Chicago, 1979.
Graeme Souness (Scotland, 1986)—Montreal, 1973.
Willem Suurbier (Netherlands, 1974, 1978)—Los Angeles, 1979-81, San Jose, 1982.
Horst Szymaniak (West Germany, 1958, 1962)—Chicago, 1967.
Jean-Pierre Tokoto (Cameroon, 1982)—New England, 1980, Jacksonville, 1981).
Novak Tomic (Yugoslavia, 1958)—Oakland, 1967-68.
Wim van Hanegem (Netherlands, 1974)—Chicago 1974.
Vava (Brazil, 1958, 1962)—San Diego, 1968.
Jose Velasquez (Peru, 1958, 1962)—Toronto, 1981.
Phillipe Vorbe (Haiti, 1974)—New York, 1967.
Giuseppe (Pino) Wilson (Italy, 1974)—New York, 1978.

NASL COACHES IN THE WORLD CUP

Claudio Continho (Brazil, 1978)—-Los Angeles, 1981.
Rinus Michels (Netherlands, 1974, 1978)—Los Angeles, 1979-80.

Ladislao Kubala (Spain, 1978)—Toronto, 1967-68.
Ferenc Puskas (Hungary, 1954*)—Vancouver, 1968.
Blagoje Vidinic (Zaire, 1974)—San Diego, 1968.

*as a player.

Appendix G

Bibliography

1992 Information Please Almanac, The
1993 Information Please Almanac, The
America's Soccer Heritage, by Sam Foulds
Associated Press
Complete Book of Soccer/Hockey, The New York Times
Complete Book of the Olympics, The by David Wallechinsky
Dizionario Del Calcio, a publication of La Gazzetta dello Sport
Encyclopedia of World Soccer, The by Richard Henshaw
Encyklopedia Pitkarskich Mistrzostw Swiata,
    by Andrzej Gowarzewski
European Football Yearbook, 1991-92, The edited
    by Mike Hammond
European Football Yearbook, 1992-93, The edited
    by Mike Hammond
FIFA Magazine
FIFA News
FIFA Technical Report of the 1984 Olympics
FIFA Technical Report of the 1992 Olympics
FIFA World Cup—Italia '90 (official report)
FIFA World Cup—Mexico '86 (official report)
FIFA World Cup—Spain '82 (official report)
France Football
Guinness Book of Olympic Facts and Feats, The by Stan Greenberg
History of the World Cup, The by Brian Glanville
International Herald Tribune
Italia '90 information service
Jack Rollin's Complete World Cup Guide (1982), by Jack Rollins
Mexico '86 information service
NASL, A Complete Record of the North American Soccer League,
    by Colin Jose

Newsday
New York Daily News
New York Post
New York Times
North American Soccer League press releases, 1982
Playfair World Cup, Mexico 1986, edited by Peter Dunk
Playing in Europe – 1993-94
Reuters
Rochester Democrat and Chronicle
Rothman Presents World Cup 1982,
    by John Morgan and David Emery
Simplest Game, The by Paul Gardner
Soccer America
Soccer Digest
Soccer International
Soccer Magazine
Soccer Tribe, The by Desmond Morris
Soccer Week
Spain '82, by Phil Soar and Richard Widdows
The Times (of London)
United Press International
USA TODAY
U.S. Soccer 1993 Media Guide
U.S. Soccer vs. The World, by Tony Cirino
The Washington Post
World Cup, 1930-90, The by John Robinson
World Cup, 1930-90, Sixty Glorious Years of Soccer's Premier Event,
    The by Jack Rollin
World Cup 1930-82, The by Jimmy Greaves
World Cup 86, by Philip Evans
World Cup, A Complete Record 1930-90, The by Ian Morrison
World Cup Espana '82, by Franz Beckenbauer
World Cup, The by Walt Chyzowych
World Cup USA '94 media guides of the competing countries
World Soccer